THE
PSYCHOLOGY
RESEARCH
HANDBOOK

To Sandra, Kate, and Sarah, the sources of my inspiration.

FTL

To my wife, Michele, and my daughter Jennifer Renée.

JTA

THE PSYCHOLOGY RESEARCH HANDBOOK

A Guide for Graduate Students and Research Assistants

Frederick T. L. Leong and James T. Austin

editors

SAGE Publications

International Educational and Professional Publisher

Thousand Oaks   London   New Delhi

For information address:

 SAGE Publications, Inc.
2455 Teller Road
Thousand Oaks, California 91320
E-mail: order@sagepub.com

SAGE Publications Ltd.
6 Bonhill Street
London EC2A 4PU
United Kingdom

SAGE Publications India Pvt. Ltd.
M-32 Market
Greater Kailash I
New Delhi 110 048 India

Printed in the United States of America

Library of Congress Cataloging-in-Publication Data

Main entry under title:
The psychology research handbook : a guide for graduate students and
    research assistants / editors, Frederick T. L. Leong, James T. Austin.
        p.   cm.
    Includes bibliographical references and index.
    ISBN 0-8039-7048-X (alk. Paper). — ISBN 0-8039-7049-8 (pbk. :
alk. paper)
    1. Psychology—Research—Methodology.   I. Leong, Frederick T. L.
II. Austin, James T.
BF76.5.P795 1996
150'.72—dc20   96-10017

This book is printed on acid-free paper.

    97 98 99 10 9 8 7 6 5 4 3

Production Editor: Vicki Baker
Typesetter: Christina Hill

Contents

PART I
Research Planning

PART II
Design, Instrument Selection, and Sampling

PART III
Data Collection

PART IV
Data Analyses

PART V
Research Writing

PART VI
Special Topics

Foreword

The Psychology Research Handbook: A Guide for Graduate Students and Research Assistants is destined to become a standard reference work for students seeking to master psychology research methods and procedures. The editors, Dr. Frederick Leong and Dr. James Austin, are to be congratulated for providing students with a comprehensive guide for conducting many types of psychology research on human participants.

It's all here in clear and lucid prose: from identifying a research topic to applying for research grants, the reader is treated to an intellectually stimulating and fun-filled journey into the world of psychology research. The volume contains 29 chapters, some of which are coauthored by advanced graduate students. All of the authors have considerable expertise and experience in their respective topics. The chapters all contain detailed "scripts" on the various research procedures. This touch of the real world adds to the clarity and practicality of many chapters.

An added advantage of this book is that it has been organized in a sequential model representing the research process from start to finish. This organization makes the *Handbook* an ideal text for psychology undergraduate students taking independent research courses with faculty. However, the design of the *Handbook* is also such that the reader can obtain useful information from any single chapter rather than reading the book in a linear fashion, because each chapter can be used as an independent lesson. Furthermore, the chapters are organized into six modules—those who need assistance with research design and instrument selection can focus on Part II of the *Handbook,* and others who need to learn about research writing will find much useful advice and guidance in Part V.

Unlike other research handbooks that are filled with arcane material that frighten the budding researcher, this volume will spark a lifelong love affair with the psychology research process. Of special value are the chapters on topics typically missing from other texts, including cross-cultural research, dealing with journal editors and reviewers, conducting meta-analyses, and using archival data sets.

In my opinion, this is the book of choice for introducing the psychology research process to students and research assistants.

Anthony J. Marsella

Acknowledgments

We began this project with the hope of helping psychology faculty help graduate and undergraduate students learn the research process. In completing this volume, we have come to the realization that a project like this could never have been completed in a timely manner without the contributions of numerous individuals, whom we wish to recognize here. First, Professor and Chair James C. Naylor provided support through the creation of an achievement-oriented departmental environment here at The Ohio State University. Our colleagues in the psychology department at The Ohio State University have been a constant source of stimulation and support for us, and many of these colleagues contributed to the present volume. Linda Hixon and Angela C. Bassett provided clerical support throughout the course of the undertaking, a period of some 2 years. We also wish to acknowledge all the graduate and undergraduate students at OSU with whom we have worked who served as a primary impetus for this handbook.

The staff at Sage Publications was instrumental in taking our manuscript and turning it into a reality. Among them are Jim Nageotte, Nancy Hale, Vicki Baker, and Giselle Anaya, as well as numerous others who worked behind the scenes. The contributors themselves, and especially those who worked heroically under time constraints, deserve the lion's share of the accolades. Without their willingness, responsiveness, and expertise, this project could not have been completed. Those leading scholars in the field who provided advance reviews of the document also deserve our special gratitude. Finally, we would like to thank our spouses for their patience and support as we labored on this project for the past 2 years.

As editors, we wish to thank all of these individuals and also the many others who helped in the process of turning our imagination into reality.

Introduction

Given the team-based nature of much psychological research, many academic faculty face the dilemma of delegation when it comes to allocating time for training undergraduate and graduate research assistants. On the one hand, it is important to work with this population because they are the source of future researchers, because valuable exchange relationships can benefit both faculty and student parties, and because research supervision is a component of the faculty role. On the other hand, the "agency costs" of instructing research assistants in the basic skills of research (e.g., data collection, data entry, literature searches, and writing) are prohibitive in the daily routine because of competition with other important tasks. Further, many undergraduate students do not remain long with one faculty member but instead move on to acquire a diversity of experiences. We have observed that difficulties arise when faculty try to complete basic research tasks themselves rather than delegating them to graduate research assistants. Conversely, delegating work to graduate research assistants who lack the requisite knowledge or skills to accomplish a task results in either wasted efforts or more supervision time than the time required to perform the task on one's own. A similar problem exists for psychology faculty who are faced with numerous talented yet inexperienced undergraduates seeking opportunities for independent studies or supervised research (e.g., honors theses).

Partial solutions to this dilemma include instructing research assistants in a group setting, utilizing advanced graduate students to supervise beginning graduate students and undergraduates, and requiring course work or research skills as part of selection to a research assistant position. Our solution is a handbook geared to the novice level, rather than the expert level to which such handbooks are usually directed. Although the idea of a handbook is often associated with specialized material presented to experts in a field, there is no reason that basic research skills cannot be presented similarly. Miller's *Handbook of Research Design and Social Measurement* (1991) accomplishes the same purpose, but at an advanced level.

Thus the present handbook is designed to provide one solution to the dilemma of delegation by arranging chapters written by a diverse group of researchers to address research as a skill that can be analyzed into components. This solution, treating research as a script, allows researchers to require their assistants to purchase the handbook before enrolling in a supervised research experience. This book could also be used as a required or supplementary textbook for a research methods sequence. The intended audience is graduate and undergraduate psychology students. Also, psychology faculty who work with large research teams may wish to have reference copies available. The need for the current handbook is further supported by a recent survey of graduate training in statistics, methodology, and measurement in psychology that found that the "statistical and methodological curriculum has advanced little in 20 years" (Aiken, West, Sechrest, & Reno, 1990, p. 721).

Unlike existing treatments, this handbook uses a more comprehensive framework to encompass the research process from research planning through design/instrument selection, data collection, data analyses, research writing, and working in a research group. Competing publications exist, but they concentrate on one or two aspects of the research process and are usually written by a small number of authors. For example, several books discuss scientific writing (e.g., Pyrczak & Bruce, 1992; Sternberg, 1993), the American Psychological Association (APA) publishes guidebooks for the library component of research (Reed & Baxter, 1992) and for mastering APA style (Gelfand & Walker, 1990), and other books address various design and statistical issues (e.g., Bruning & Kintz, 1987; Sommer & Sommer, 1991; Yaremko, Harari, Harrison, & Lynn, 1986). In contrast, one major contribution of the present handbook is its comprehensiveness in covering the sequence of research at a basic level, and another is the diverse perspectives on research provided by the chapter authors, who are all practicing researchers.

In this preface, we preview the chapters that make up the handbook within a framework that views the research process as a cognitive script. Cognitive scripts are knowledge structures, sometimes called *linear orders,* that organize proceduralized knowledge of how to do something in a temporal sequence (Smith, 1994). Our guiding assumption is that a major difference between experts and novices is the greater elaboration of an expert's scripts for doing research combined with greater domain-specific knowledge. Recent studies suggest that individuals at increasing levels of expertise (i.e., beginning undergraduates, graduate students, and junior and senior faculty) possess increasingly elaborated scripts for research (Hershey, Wilson, & Mitchell-Copeland, 1996). *The Psychology Research Handbook: A Guide for Graduate Students and Research Assistants* exposes undergraduate and graduate psychology research assistants to various specific research scripts in a detailed and pragmatic manner. In summary, the handbook is a resource for faculty to deal with the dilemma of delegation when it comes to supervising either research assistants or students completing research projects (honors or master's theses).

The higher-level sequence of research we used to organize the chapters consists of research planning, design and instrument selection, data collection, data analysis, research writing, and special-topic components. Each of these six sections contains multiple chapters written at a basic level by practicing researchers.

Overview of Specific Chapters

Research planning can be viewed as a sequence of activities ranging from finding a research topic to using the library effectively, conducting a literature search, and reviewing and evaluating a research article. In Part I, "Research Planning," Leong and Pfaltzgraff (Chapter 1) consider the subject of finding a research topic and provide a framework for using personal, interpersonal, and computer strategies as well as printed sources. Reed and Baxter (Chapter 2) illustrate issues involved in using the university library. Stockdale and Kenny (Chapter 3) show the intricacies of conducting a literature search as part of research planning. Finally, the literature gathered must be evaluated critically, which is the topic of the chapter by Oleson and Arkin (Chapter 4).

Part II, "Design, Instrument Selection, and Sampling," concerns ways of putting hypotheses to the test. The activities we have chosen are designing a research study (Wampold, Chapter 5), evaluating and selecting research instruments (Ponterotto, Chapter 6), designing questionnaires and surveys (Goddard & Villanova, Chapter 7), and applying sampling procedures (McCready, Chapter 8).

Part III focuses on data collection, a crucial step in testing hypotheses derived from theories. The activities comprise applying for human subjects committee approval (Schmidt & Meara, Chapter 9), conducting a mail survey (Vaux, Chapter 10), conducting a telephone survey (Chen, Chapter 11), and collecting data from groups (Zaccaro & Marks, Chapter 12).

The chapters in Part IV are on data analysis. Statistics give researchers tools for probing their data in exploratory and confirmatory studies. The activities involved range from cleaning data and running preliminary analyses (Dollinger & DiLalla, Chapter 13) to selecting statistical tests (Yaffee, Chapter 15), answering research questions with basic analyses (Dickter & Roznowski, Chapter 16), and answering research questions with more advanced analyses (Levy & Steelman, Chapter 17). Other activities include performing meta-analyses with the study rather than the individual as the unit of analysis (Cooper & Dorr, Chapter 18), constructing tests (Betz, Chapter 19), and using archival data (Zaitzow & Fields, Chapter 20). We also included a chapter on qualitative analysis (Highlen & Finley, Chapter 14).

Writing is a communicative act for scientists that ensures that research is disseminated to others for critique and compilation. In the present context, it is applied to a mass of research detail to provide a coherent account of a study. In Part V, "Research Writing," Austin and Calderon (Chapter 21) discuss the rationale and mechanics of APA style (according to the fourth edition of the APA *Publication Manual*; APA, 1994). Peterson (Chapter 22) talks about how to write an initial draft of a manuscript, and Nagata and Trierweiler (Chapter 23) discuss the process of revising a manuscript in accordance with feedback received from peers and reviewers. Last, Osipow (Chapter 24) presents advice for dealing with editors and reviewers.

Chapters in Part VI, "Special Topics," consider topics important for the conduct of research but not traditionally emphasized in similar texts. These include coordinating a research team (Molfese et al., Chapter 25) and understanding the diversity of work styles (Brenstein, Chapter 26). Three other important topics are applying for research funding

(Borkowski, Chapter 27), cross-cultural research methodology (Leung & Van de Vijver, Chapter 28), and applying theories to research (Gelso, Chapter 29).

We have provided one solution to the dilemma of delegation in this book. It is important to qualify this by noting that procedural knowledge requires behavior, broadly defined, by the individual. Thus it is imperative that the reader practice implementing the material presented in this text. To that end, we recommend that the reader try to generate examples while reading the chapters and try out specific scripts. For example, the script of evaluating articles critically is not acquired without obtaining several articles and practicing on them. As Peterson (Chapter 22 of this volume) suggests, do not be afraid to seek out feedback from others to supplement your own self-evaluation. Statistics especially requires repetition; therefore we advise the interested reader to attempt different analyses on the same data, perhaps a data set from a textbook. Writing is similar. In conclusion, active engagement with the material presented in this book will help in the transition from declarative to procedural knowledge.

References

American Psychological Association. (1994). *Publication manual of the American Psychological Association* (4th ed.). Washington, DC: Author.

Aiken, L. S., West, S. G., Sechrest, L., & Reno, R. R. (1990). Survey of graduate training in statistics, methodology, and measurement in psychology: A survey of Ph.D. programs in North America. *American Psychologist, 45,* 721-734.

Bruning, J. L., & Kintz, B. L. (1987). *Computational handbook of statistics* (3rd ed.). Glenview, IL: Scott, Foresman.

Gelfand, H., & Walker, C. J. (1990). *Mastering APA style: Student's workbook and training guide.* Washington, DC: American Psychological Association.

Hershey, D. A., Wilson, T. L., & Mitchell-Copeland, J. R. (1996). Conceptions of the psychological research process: Script variation as a function of training and experience. *Current Psychology, 14,* 293-312.

Miller, D. C. (Ed.). (1991). *Handbook of research design and social measurement* (5th ed.). Thousand Oaks, CA: Sage.

Pyrczak, F., & Bruce, R. R. (1992). *Writing empirical research reports: A basic guide for students of the social and behavioral sciences.* Los Angeles: Pyrczak.

Reed, J. G., & Baxter, P. M. (1992). *Library use: A handbook for psychology* (2nd ed.). Washington, DC: American Psychological Association.

Smith, E. (1994). Procedural knowledge and processing strategies in social cognition. In R. S. Wyer, Jr., & T. K. Srull (Eds.), *Handbook of social cognition* (Vol. 1, pp. 99-151). Hillsdale, NJ: Lawrence Erlbaum.

Sommer, B., & Sommer, R. (1991). *A practical guide to behavioral research: Tools and techniques* (3rd ed.). New York: Oxford University Press.

Sternberg, R. J. (1993). *The psychologist's companion* (3rd ed.). New York: Cambridge University Press.

Yaremko, R. M., Harari, H., Harrison, R. C., & Lynn, E. (1986). *Handbook of research and quantitative methods in psychology for students and professionals.* Hillsdale, NJ: Lawrence Erlbaum.

PART I

Research Planning

Chapter 1

Finding a Research Topic

FREDERICK T. L. LEONG
RHONDA E. PFALTZGRAFF

In the introduction of this book, the editors use the concept of cognitive scripts as a framework for conducting research. They argue that skill acquisition is dependent on the building of these scripts through practice. In a linear research project, finding a topic is the first basic script. Other scripts for subsequent stages in the research process include choosing a research design, selecting research instruments, applying sampling procedures, and conducting data analyses. The skill of finding a research topic is developed by experience, but learning about how others find topics is also helpful. The purpose of this chapter is to illuminate the components of the "finding a research topic" script for less experienced researchers by using examples of how other psychologists find topics for study.

What does and does not interest each of us is the result of a combination of different factors that vocational psychologists have been researching a long time (e.g., see Osipow & Fitzgerald, 1996). In some sense, finding a research topic is a matter of personal interest and preference in the same way that music and food preferences are personal matters. Given individual differences in what constitutes an interesting topic for research, the best approach to providing guidance on the process of finding a research topic would be the "menu approach." Using the food metaphor again, if there are significant individual differences in which type of foods are interesting and appealing, then a restaurant with a diverse menu of foods cooked in many different ways would be most likely to satisfy the most individuals. In the same way, different individuals will exhibit a wide variety of preferences in how they find research topics that are of interest to them. Such an approach also takes into account individuals' different learning and cognitive styles (e.g., see Pintrich & Johnson, 1990). The reader should also see Brenstein (Chapter 26 of this volume) on how individual differences can influence working in a research team. Therefore, we will offer in this chapter a series of different strategies for finding research topics. Despite individual differences in preferences for research strategies, we strongly recommend that the reader make use of multiple strategies rather than just relying on one preferred strategy. As Einstein once said, "Chance favors the prepared mind." The best way to find an interesting and important research topic is to be prepared to consider a wide range of options, at least at the beginning of the search process. The initial stage of finding a research topic is really a multifaceted process that requires openness to new ideas and problems rather than simply reprocessing well-developed research topics. Art Fry, the inventor of 3M's ubiquitous Post-it note, came on his brilliant idea when he linked (and was open to linking) the nonbinding glue discovered by a junior colleague with the bookmarks that kept falling out of his church hymnals. The rest, as they say, is history.

Another reason to use multiple strategies for finding a topic is time urgency. Time urgency is usually associated with many research projects. From the master's thesis to the first six publications as an assistant professor, people usually experience some urgency when attempting to find an exciting and doable research topic that would also make a significant contribution to their field. Often, using a problem-focused approach helps us identify certain problems that are of interest and relevance to us. For example, if one had a close friend or relative who suffered from depression, then one might be interested in researching depression as a major mental health problem. Yet having identified "depression" as a problem to be researched, one could take many different directions. A multiple-strategy approach would aid in deciding which direction to take. The rest of this chapter will present multiple strategies for finding a specific research topic.

Finding a research topic can be broken down into two stages: (a) search strategies and (b) narrowing and refining the topic. Some authors have referred to the first stage as "identifying the general area in which you want to do research" (Cone & Foster, 1993, p. 28). According to our current scheme, the first stage is finding a topic area. There are four general categories of search strategies: (a) personal, (b) interpersonal, (c) printed sources, and (d) computer resources (see Figure 1.1). We will discuss each of these categories of strategies in turn.

Search Strategies

PERSONAL STRATEGIES

Personal experience and observation are sources of general research topics that are readily accessible to everyone. Many psychologists study the forms of human behavior that have become meaningful to them through their personal experience. For example, an African American social psychologist may be more apt than a European American social psychologist to select research topics that clarify the processes of racial stereotyping. A clinical psychologist who has lived abroad may be more prone to examine the cross-cultural differences in manifestations of schizophrenia. Another psychologist who grew up as an only child may become curious about how personality develops when there is one child in a family versus multiple children in a family.

Personal observation can lead to new insights as well. A psychologist who has the opportunity to observe human behavior over long periods of time will have many chances to recognize possible research topics. For example, a counselor who notices that children of alcoholic parents have shorter attention spans may want to explore this relationship to determine if it is genetically or environmentally based. Obviously, you do not need to be a fully trained psychologist to take advantage of your personal observations as a source of ideas for research. By attending to your observations and writing them down, you too can

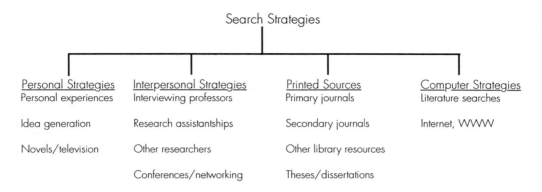

Figure 1.1. Search Strategies for Finding a Research Topic

generate research topics almost without effort. Research ideas can come from such personal experiences as noticing how your family members "cope" with illnesses to observing how sibling rivalry varies across the families of people you know. Or you might become intrigued with group dynamics after watching the classic Henry Fonda movie *Twelve Angry Men,* in which one person was able to sway the decision-making process of a jury.

"Brainstorming" is helpful for finding a research topic when an assignment is very broad or when other strategies are not working. This general process of idea generation starts by writing down all topics that come to mind, independent of an immediate judgment of each idea's worth. Only after a substantial list of ideas has been produced should you allow yourself to eliminate an idea. The process of elimination should edit all ideas that are implausible or cannot be adequately addressed within the confines of the research at hand. If you have an assignment to write about the development of children, write down all ideas you have about the processes by which children develop or the types of behaviors children display as they mature. When you are satisfied with your list, examine the feasibility of each idea for the assignment, the availability of research in the area, and your motivation to stick with each topic. By eliminating ideas in this way, you will choose a topic that is plausible and enjoyable.

Another creative strategy for idea generation is to use the "Martian perspective" as a cognitive device. By asking yourself to imagine how a Martian who had just landed on earth would view a particular problem or a particular situation, you may uncover interesting topics not considered by others. For example, if we adopted this Martian perspective, it would become quite evident that our fascination with automobiles in this country goes beyond an interest in cars merely as a form of transportation. Further, as Martians, we might notice that many earthlings prefer to solve conflicts by harming others physically or materially rather than attempting to deal with the underlying issues that generated the dispute. Using this type of exploration, we may be able to discover an area that greatly interests us and that has not yet been fully explored in psychology.

Reading novels, listening to the radio, or watching television can also lead to research topics. These sources of information reveal problems that may need research to aid in their resolution. For example, when the news tells us of the plight of servicemen and servicewomen as they adjust to civilian life after returning from an armed conflict, a person may realize that what is currently known in the area of post-traumatic stress disorder (PTSD) is not sufficient for providing a full explanation of their adjustment problems. After hearing a newscast, a student who is interested in clinical psychology may want to research in more detail the real and imagined barriers these people have when adjusting to civilian life. The key aim of the personal search strategy is to be aware of and analyze your personal experiences to identify unanswered questions.

INTERPERSONAL STRATEGIES

Other people are also good sources of ideas for research topics. One good source is a college professor. We suggest that you view your professors as resource persons and use a series of strategies to tap their knowledge and expertise. An interview with a professor who works in your general interest area regarding his or her current research can be very helpful. Most college professors are knowledgeable about discrepancies in research findings and gaps in the current literature that can be explored. Taking a course with a particular professor is another way to find out about possible research topics. Either during or after the course, you may ask the professor to recommend important articles to read for a comprehensive review of your potential research area. The type of course you choose could range from a commonly offered formal course to one directed specifically to your interests or needs. One type of directed study is the specialized reading course, which may be available to most advanced undergraduate and graduate students. Reading courses provide an opportunity to be personally supervised in a particular topic area in which a professor specializes. Another way to use a professor as a resource is to ask a professor to share some of his or her reprints with you so you can learn more about that professor's research (Cone & Foster, 1993).

After reading a professor's reprints or speaking with a professor, you might discuss the possibility of becoming a research assistant for that professor. Research assistantships are very good sources of research topics. As a research assistant, you may become aware of current research topics and be able to make useful contributions to the literature by extending the research of the professor with whom you are working. Through assistantships, you may become immersed in a particular literature, and this may help you find areas of research that are congruent with your interests and need further exploration. The research assistantship experience not only affords you the opportunity to become familiar with a professor's research project but may also provide a chance to develop your own research topic if you are able to extend creatively your professor's research to another level or problem. For example, you may be helping a professor with a project aimed at identifying the family dynamics associated with drug abuse. Having become familiar with that project, you might be able to explore potential racial/ethnic and gender differences in the relationships found by your professor.

Besides college and university professors, other active researchers can also serve as sources of research ideas. Applied researchers may be able to describe important problems that require research. For example, applied researchers may tell you their opinion regarding the public's current attitudes toward AIDS. You may decide to follow up this idea by studying how attitude change toward the HIV virus may reduce discriminatory actions taken against people with the HIV virus. Researchers can also be found in business settings.

For example, researchers for insurance companies may examine how people react to risk factors or attempt to determine the personality characteristics of individuals who would make good insurance salespeople. Federal and state governments also support a wide range of researchers. These researchers deal with topics such as public health and voting behavior. Telephone or personal interviews with researchers outside your university may provide you with additional research topics.

Two other useful strategies for finding research topics are attending conferences and networking. Presentations and poster sessions at conferences can expose you to the wide range of ideas currently being explored by a discipline. Listening to and reading about the ideas developed by others may lead you to a research topic. Combining others' research with your own ideas or extending their research into a new area is an effective strategy for developing ideas and finding a research topic. Networking at conferences or getting to know professors and students within your institution is also a helpful search strategy. Listening to others' ideas and current areas of interest is a way to broaden your views and scope of ideas. Networking is a way to become acquainted with others who have similar research interests and who may be helpful for suggesting possible areas of research.

PRINTED SOURCES

Printed sources are also beneficial for generating research ideas (see Reed & Baxter, 1992). The most immediately available and relevant sources of research topics are primary scientific journals. Browsing through recent issues of these journals may reveal topics of current concern. Briefly read the table of contents and abstracts of the articles found in three or four consecutive years of a relevant journal. To determine the most relevant scientific journal to examine, first decide the area that you are most interested in, then find a highly regarded journal in that area of psychology. For example, to find ideas about counseling, choose the *Journal of Counseling Psychology*; for industrial and organizational psychology, look at the *Journal of Applied Psychology*; for social psychology, scan the *Journal of Personality and Social Psychology*.

Those who cannot decide which area of psychology interests them may wish to consult *Journals in Psychology* (American Psychological Association [APA], 1993). This publication lists many of the leading journals in psychology (more than 360 in the fourth edition, 1993) and provides a brief summary of their editorial policies (i.e., what types of articles are appropriate and what topics are covered by the journal). This publication also provides a very useful classified index that allows readers to identify journals in different subject areas (e.g., consulting/clinical, criminal and legal issues, developmental) as well as subtopics (e.g., health psychology under "consulting/clinical" and aging under "developmental"). Browsing through this publication may help you select journals to review in more detail for research topics.

Another approach to reviewing primary scientific journals is to scan the specialized abstracting periodicals offered by the APA. As a service to busy researchers and clinicians, the APA has produced periodicals that reproduce the table of contents from a collection of journals that are clustered around a particular theme. For example, there is one on clinical psychology, one on applied psychology, and one on psychoanalysis. These periodicals are produced at regular intervals and provide a quick and convenient way to get a general view of the research being conducted in a particular area. Similar resources, such as *Current Contents,* are published by other organizations and may be available in your university library as well. The reader should consult Stockdale and Kenny (Chapter 3 of this volume) for further details on these library resources.

Primary journal sources come in two types. We have been discussing primary scientific journals as a source of research ideas. Another valuable source of ideas is primary clinical journals. Many journals publish clinical information such as case discussions and formulations that can be useful for generating research ideas. For example, an article in one of these journals described several cases in which male patients had rather unusual sexual phobias (Beit-Hallahmi, 1985). Specifically, these men had a fear that a woman's vagina had teeth (i.e., vagina dentata) and that they would be severely injured if they were to have a sexual relationship with women. According to psychoanalytic theory, vagina dentata (or the fantasy of a vagina with teeth) symbolizes men's castration anxiety (Eidelberg, 1968, p. 465). Whether or not one believes in Freud's concept of castration anxiety, this particular example serves as a good illustration of how clinically oriented journals contain many interesting human problems and can serve as a valuable resource for research ideas that should not be overlooked.

Secondary sources are materials that summarize primary source materials for dissemination to other readers. One example of a secondary source is textbooks. When conducting research, it is often best to consult primary sources for information about the finding of studies on your research topic and how these studies were conducted. Secondary sources such as introductory textbooks and specialized texts, however, are valuable sources of ideas for research topics as well. They are especially helpful if you know little about your topic area. For example, if you are given a broad topic area to choose from, such as "any topic in cognitive psychology," a good place to start to get a general idea of what topics are covered in cognitive psychology would be the table of contents of a cognitive psychology textbook. The summary sections within specialized textbooks are also useful for generating research topics because they give you a quick overview of the issues and challenges currently facing a particular research area.

After examining the chapters that are of interest to you in a textbook and eliminating those that are not, look at the studies and topic areas within each chapter to determine which ones you would like to explore in more detail. Finding the studies that have been cited by that chapter may quickly reveal whether that topic area will be interesting to look at in depth. Specialized texts, such as the *Annual Review of Psychology,* are also helpful because they review a topic area and point out areas that could benefit from further research. These texts also cite studies that are considered classics in the field and may provide necessary background information for your research. Other specialized texts that provide general yet useful overviews of topics are the various handbooks and encyclopedias that are available in libraries. These are excellent books to browse to find out quickly about all the different topics within a specific field (e.g., Eidelberg's *Encyclopedia of Psychoanalysis,* 1968).

Besides introductory textbooks and specialized/professional texts, other sets of materials can serve as valuable secondary sources of information. These include technical reports, white papers (called "consensus papers" at the National Institutes of Health), and conference proceedings. Many of these special reports, which can be found in the "Federal

Government Depositories" sections of university libraries, are underutilized sources of research ideas. These reports, like primary scientific journals, contain cutting-edge materials in many different areas of psychology. They give the reader an added advantage by being in a summary form that can be readily reviewed. For example, the publication entitled *Special Report: Schizophrenia 1993* (National Institute of Mental Health, 1993) summarized the cutting-edge research being conducted on schizophrenia. It summarized in 90 pages what might take an individual schizophrenia researcher years of reading and reviewing. A similar source of information and overview of behavioral medicine is provided by the report *New Research Frontiers in Behavioral Medicine: Proceedings From the National Conference* (National Institute of Mental Health, 1994).

Beyond primary and secondary sources of research, theses and dissertations are useful for finding ideas. Theses and dissertations are somewhat unusual because they are not published scientific studies yet are widely available. These sources are especially helpful to students who are in the process of determining a research topic for a thesis or dissertation or some other type of research. By examining theses and dissertations that have been written by other students, you may get an idea of the breadth and depth of the topics usually explored by these kinds of research. Also, many of these theses and dissertations contain a literature review chapter that contains useful ideas for future research. As detailed reviews of a particular area of psychology, these literature reviews often contain much more in-depth information about various studies than those found in the introductory sections of journal articles, which are necessarily brief. Most university libraries will serve as a depository for all the theses and dissertations that have been completed at that university. You could also search the *Dissertations Abstracts International*, which is a serial abstracting many of the dissertations completed in the United States annually.

COMPUTER STRATEGIES

The final category of search strategies consists of using computer resources. No matter how creative we are or how knowledgeable our consultants are, personal and interpersonal search strategies can never match the computer in terms of memory, comprehensiveness, and speed. We are referring to the computer databases that can be searched for various topics by entering particular key words (see Stockdale & Kenny, Chapter 3 of this volume). Within the field of psychology, the primary computer database would be the PsycLIT database produced by the APA.

Like other indexing systems, the PsycLIT database started out as a paper medium in which selected journals in psychology were abstracted, indexed, and published as a library periodical. It began in 1927 as the periodical *Psychological Abstracts*. With the increasing availability of personal computers and CD-ROM drives, the PsycLIT database was eventually developed as a more efficient computerized version of *Psychological Abstracts*. The PsycLIT database is available in most university libraries, either in the CD-ROM version or via a telephone dial-up connection (e.g., DIALOG).

When trying to identify a research topic in psychology, it is useful to begin with the PsycLIT database, but you should not limit your search to only one database because each database is limited to a selected set of journals. Articles on the particular topic in which you are most interested may be in a journal that is not indexed by a specific database. The other mainstream databases that are useful for psychological research include ERIC (educational journals), MedLine (medical and health sciences journals), and Sociological Abstracts (sociology journals). For example, if you were interested in exploring a topic in behavioral medicine, a search of both the PsycLIT and MedLine databases would give you a much more comprehensive set of studies than would be provided by just one database.

Besides the mainstream databases that are available in most university libraries, there are other specialized databases you should know about. It would not be possible for us to list all of these specialized databases because there are so many of them and because they are not widely available. But it is important for you to realize that other specialized databases are available and that you should check in your university library or computing center to determine if there are specialized databases related to your topic in addition to the mainstream databases.

At this point, we will illustrate how integrating and using the different strategies discussed in this chapter may prove worthwhile. Suppose that you are interested in abnormal psychology in general and post-traumatic stress disorder (PTSD) specifically. You conduct a computerized literature search using PsycLIT and MedLine and find quite a few articles produced by researchers affiliated with the National Center for PTSD, which is part of the Veterans Administration. On reviewing these articles, you find that Dr. Matthew Friedman is a frequent author of these articles and that he is the director of the National Center for PTSD headquartered at the White River Junction VA Medical Center in Vermont. You decide to use an interpersonal strategy as well, so you arrange a telephone interview with Dr. Friedman to discuss your research ideas. During the interview, he informs you that the National Center for PTSD also maintains its own computerized database on the worldwide literature on PTSD, and he arranges for you to search that database. Through this specialized database, you are able to find many more articles related to your topic than those generated by PsycLIT and MedLine. Other examples of specialized databases include one on alcoholism and drug abuse maintained by Dartmouth Medical School and one on the Myers-Briggs Type Indicator (a personality instrument based on Carl Jung's theory) maintained by the Center for Applications of Psychological Type in Gainesville, Florida.

Another helpful database is the Social Science Citation Index (SSCI). Although it is a widely available database, it is quite different from others and provides a separate advantage. Instead of indexing specific articles, the SSCI indexes the citations of specific articles. For example, if you were interested in Bandura's theory of self-efficacy, you could use the SSCI database to identify all the different studies that have cited Bandura's original presentation of his model in *Psychological Review*. Alternatively, if you were interested in what studies Bandura used to formulate his model, you could use the SSCI to find all the references cited in Bandura's *Psychology Review* article. The disadvantage of the SSCI is that the computerized version is quite expensive and available only in selected university libraries. The paper version of the SSCI in the form of a periodical is available in a larger number of libraries, but it does not have the advantages of a computerized database.

With any computerized database, it is usually best to begin with the thesaurus or manual that comes with the database. The thesaurus or manual will tell you which journals are abstracted in that particular database, as well as the terms used to index those journals. It is quite important to use correct terms when searching for a topic because the use of unacceptable terms may result in a lower than expected output from the search. For example, if you were interested in the topic of career goals and searched PsycLIT (1990-1995) using those terms, you might end up with very few articles and conclude that there had not been a great deal of research on that topic in the last 5 years. On the other hand, if you had consulted the *Thesaurus of Psychological Index Terms* (APA, 1994), you would have discovered that the acceptable term in PsycLIT is *occupational aspirations*. Using this acceptable terms, you would have found that there were 207 studies on the topic of occupational aspirations between 1990 and 1995 instead of the 38 studies found when you used the term *career goals*. Therefore it is highly advisable to spend some time with the thesaurus or manual of a particular database to plan your search and ensure use of the correct search terms.

The thesaurus or manual also serves another valuable function, namely that of a stimulus for new ideas. In reviewing the thesaurus, one could examine the various concepts and constructs within psychology and begin cross-classifying different variables to check out potential research questions. For example, in browsing through the thesaurus, having found that *occupational aspirations* is the correct term to use in the PsycLIT database, one may stumble on the interesting concept of psychological androgyny and wonder if there is a relationship between psychological androgyny and occupational aspirations: Do androgynous women have different occupational aspirations than feminine women? Armed with these different concepts and search terms, one can then begin searching for studies that have examined these questions.

In addition to these computerized databases, the computer can also be a useful strategy for finding research topics through another avenue—namely, the Internet. There is a series of guidebooks on the Internet (i.e., Wiggins, 1995). A large part of the Internet is its collection of news groups and electronic discussion groups. There are many of these groups that one can tap into as a source of research ideas. For example, if one were interested in ethnic identity among Asian Americans, one could log onto the Soc.Culture. Asian American newsgroup and find out about some of the issues facing Asian American youths and young adults (e.g., pros and cons of interracial dating and how much to Americanize and become a "Banana"—yellow on the outside and White on the inside). Alternatively, if one were interested in John Bowlby's theory of attachment, one could subscribe to a special discussion group that addresses the clinical and research implications of attachment theory. Another example is the HRNet (Human Resources), maintained by the Academy of Management. It is quite a common practice for persons belonging to these news and discussion groups to post messages asking for help with different problems or questions. For example, someone may post a message asking if anyone on the network knows of a particular scale to measure ethnic identity. Others may post messages asking for help in identifying articles related to specific topics.

Another recent development within the Internet is the World Wide Web (WWW), a collection of multimedia sites that are linked together via hypertext for easy access. Hypertext is based on a special computer language (hypertext markup language, HTML) that allows users to jump from one information source directly into another simply by clicking on specially designated text. One could use the WWW to access different psychology department home pages to check out what different faculty members were researching, or one could log onto the National Institute of Mental Health's home page to find out what types of research grants were available. Many of these sites have reports that can be downloaded and read or printed on your computer. For example, there is a Federal Glass Ceiling Commission maintained by Cornell University on the WWW with some very interesting reports on occupational discrimination against women and minorities. Most WWW browsers and Internet programs have "search engines" that allow you to search various databases for information on the topic in which you are interested. That is how we found that site on the Glass Ceiling Commission on the WWW. A useful way to learn about the WWW would be to browse through recent issues of the *Internet World* magazine, which is available in most public and university libraries.

Narrowing and Refining the Topic

In the first stage of finding a research topic, you are primarily interested in identifying a general topic area, such as masked depression or job satisfaction among women. Once you have found a general topic area that interests you by using the strategies outlined above, the next stage is to narrow and refine the topic. As suggested by Cone and Foster (1993), a useful way to narrow your topic is to develop a research question from your general topic. They pointed out that a research question has three characteristics. First, it should be a question: You need to phrase what you would like to study in the form of a question (e.g., "Do men and women react differently to violence in movies?"). Second, the research question should propose a relationship between variables that need to be examined (e.g., "Are adolescents with higher self-esteem less likely to become addicted to drugs than adolescents with lower self-esteem?"). Third, the research question should use terminology that allows it to be tested empirically (e.g., *self-esteem* versus a vague idea such as "adolescents who come from good homes").

Just as you were able to use and combine the initial search strategies to help you find a general research topic, you can use the same search strategies to help you narrow and refine your topic into a research question. For example, if your initial search led you to the topic of gifted children, you might be able to seek out professors in education (personal strategies) who could tell you more about that area of research. Professors who are actively involved in research in a particular area can usually guide you to some promising areas for additional research. Following up on some leads from the personal strategies, you could do a computer literature search using PsycLIT (computer strategies) to determine if any research had been conducted on the relationship between birth order and giftedness among children. Alternatively, you might wish to proceed directly to the printed sources and begin reading different textbooks on special education to get a sense of the major research questions in the topic of educating gifted children. Having familiarized yourself with the major theories and issues, you might then use computer strategies and start searching different topics related to gifted children on your own. Regardless of how you mix and match the different search strategies, your goal in this stage of finding a topic is to narrow your general topic down to a research question that is specific, empirically testable, doable within a certain time frame, and likely to make a significant contribution to the scientific knowledge base.

Once you have narrowed your general topic down to a research question, the next step is to formulate one or more hypotheses from your research question (Cone & Foster, 1993). Because the goals of science are to understand, explain, predict, and control phenomena, one of the major functions of psychological research is to be able to predict human behavior. A hypothesis is a prediction about the relationship between certain variables (e.g., adolescents with low self-esteem will be more likely to become addicted to various drugs). Testing and confirming hypotheses about human behavior is how psychological science progresses. In general, we use null and research hypotheses to test our research questions. Null hypotheses are necessary because they are the ones we can test directly. The research hypothesis is usually a converse of the null hypothesis in that the latter stipulates no relationship between the variables, whereas the former proposes that there is a relationship. For example, a null hypothesis might be as follows: "There is no relationship between adolescents' level of self-esteem and their drug use and addiction." Therefore the research hypothesis would be "There is a negative relationship between adolescents' level of self-esteem and their drug use and addiction." In addition to specifying the variables (e.g., self-esteem and drug addiction), hypotheses also specify the nature of the relationship (i.e., positive, negative, curvilinear).

Both your research questions and hypotheses can come from the four categories of search strategies we have outlined above. For example, you may be able to identify a general research topic from reading a textbook (printed resources), and the professor with whom you are working as a research assistant may help you find a specific research question (interpersonal strategies). Moreover, you may have identified some specific hypotheses to test from the articles you were able to locate using the PsycLIT computer database (computer strategies).

Finally, we would like to offer several conceptual frameworks or strategies that may be useful in helping you narrow and refine your research topics. Within the field of psychology, a common conceptual scheme for understanding human behavior is the ABC model. When using this model, psychologists first identify a specific behavior that is of particular interest to them for further research. The behavior of interest can range from bed-wetting among grade school children to the functioning of military personnel under highly stressful conditions. The ABC model places a target behavior within the three-part model: *a*ntecedents-*b*ehavior-*c*onsequences. Within this model, the target behavior is supposed to have identifiable antecedents, sometimes assumed to be causal, and also certain consequences. If bed-wetting is the target behavior, the antecedent might be familial stress, such as the parents' undergoing a divorce, and one of the consequences might be the redirection of the parents' attention from conflict with each other to the stress experienced by the child.

It is sometimes useful to apply the ABC model to a general topic that you have selected so as to identify some research questions for exploration. Using an earlier example, assuming that you have become very interested in the general topic of job satisfaction among women, you may apply the ABC model by asking what are the various antecedents of job satisfaction among women. As you use this model to search for more literature, you may discover that a common variable in the existing career literature is whether women are in traditional (overrepresentation of women) or nontraditional (underrepresentation of women) careers. You could then narrow your general topic to a research question on traditionality of career choice as a significant antecedent of women's job satisfaction level. You might then hypothesize that women in traditional careers will have higher levels of job satisfaction then women in nontraditional careers.

Another conceptual scheme or strategy that may be useful in narrowing your research topic is to look for potential moderators. According to Baron and Kenny (1986), a moderator is "a qualitative (e.g., sex, race, class) or quantitative (e.g., level of reward) variable that affects the direction and/or strength of the relation between an independent and a dependent or criterion variable" (p. 1174). In a correlational analysis framework, the moderator would be a third variable that affects the zero-order correlation between two other variables. In an analysis-of-variance framework, the moderator would be the variable represented by the interaction terms between the independent and dependent variables (see Chapter 16 by Dickter & Roznowski and Chapter 17 by Levy & Steelman in this volume for more details on data analyses).

The recent polls showing major differences in African Americans' and White Americans' perceptions of the O. J. Simpson verdict illustrated that race is a significant moderator of perceptions of the police and justice systems in this country. Other researchers have tried to identify different variables that represent culture as a major moderator variable in psychology. Returning to the women's job satisfaction example, using the concept of a moderator (i.e., not all women in traditional careers will be highly satisfied with their jobs), you might notice that sex-role orientation seems to be a significant variable in that research area. Could the relationship between the traditionality of women's career choice and their level of job satisfaction be moderated by their sex-role orientation? The sex-role literature would suggest that highly feminine women would be more likely to enter and enjoy traditional careers, whereas androgenous women would be less likely to be satisfied with such career positions. Applying the concept of a moderator, you might then propose a research study to test this moderated relationship between the traditionality of women's career choice and their job satisfaction level.

Another useful conceptual scheme that we have found helpful in narrowing down a research topic and identifying a research question is to look for possible cross-fertilization between specialties (e.g., social psychology and industrial/organizational psychology). Often there are natural and logical links between the research topics being examined by different specialties that require only a small amount of creativity and innovation to combine so as to develop a research question worth further pursuit. For example, let us assume that you are interested in industrial/organizational psychology and more specifically in gender bias in performance appraisals as a possible factor underlying the "glass ceiling effect" (see Morrison, White, & Van Velsor, 1987). Briefly, the glass ceiling effect is a hypothesized barrier for occupational advancement for women in corporations due to their gender. To use the strategy of cross-fertilization of specialties, you may decide to review the leading social psychology journals during the last few years. In your review, you discover that the area of social cognition is a new and exciting area of research in social psychology. Specifically, you are intrigued by the "out-group homogeneity effect" (e.g., see Mullen & Hu, 1989; Park, Judd, & Ryan, 1991). This robust effect, which has been discovered by social psychologists, consists of the tendency in human beings to perceive greater homogeneity in out-groups (e.g., to perceive most African Americans as having greater musical talent, or most women as terrible drivers) and greater heterogeneity in in-groups.

It is argued that this out-group homogeneity effect underlies the stereotyping process. You realize that the "out-group homogeneity effect" may be a factor underlying occupational stereotyping, and you decide to test the hypothesis that this effect is operative in performance appraisals and indeed accounts for the gender biases that contribute to the glass ceiling effect reported by others.

The final conceptual framework or strategy we would recommend to help you narrow and refine your research topic is to search for new constructs in other areas of psychology. When using the strategy of cross-fertilization of specialties, you may find concepts and constructs that are new to you but have been around for a while within the other specialty (e.g., social cognition). When trying to find new constructs in psychology, you are trying to locate constructs, and the measures associated with them, that have been recently developed. For example, in the area of counseling and clinical psychology, there has been a great deal of research on the help-seeking process or service utilization patterns among racial and ethnic minorities (see Leong, Wagner, & Tata, 1995, for a review). Many previous studies have examined variables such as accessibility of the mental health services and the theoretical orientation of the clinicians and counselors. In a recent study, Leong, Wagner, and Kim (1995) decided to test the role of a new construct in psychology—namely, the culturally based concept of "loss of face"—as a possible factor in the attitudes of Asian Americans toward seeking group counseling. Efficient ways to identify new constructs in psychology are to review recent issues of journals (printed sources) as well as to attend conferences where these new ideas and measures are presented (interpersonal strategies).

In our opinion, two essential components underlie the strategies described above for finding a research topic. These components are mastery of the subject and creativity. There is no getting around the fact that one must have a certain level of mastery of a subject to come up with important and significant new research studies. Mastery of a subject matter can come about only from investing the time and energy in learning about a research topic (identifying and studying the relevant sources of information on the topic).

Building on this mastery of the subject, the second component for finding and conducting an important study is creativity. Although it remains controversial whether creativity is a personality trait or a skill that can be learned, we believe that creativity is probably a combination of nature and nurture. Several books offer suggestions for raising one's current level of creativity (e.g., Adams, 1986; Sternberg, 1988; Weisberg, 1993). Several articles offer similar suggestions; the one by Wicker (1985) serves as an excellent example. It would be worthwhile, especially for those with an interest in a research career, to spend some time learning about the nature and process of creativity and how one might improve one's level of creative ability and thus one's ability to generate important research ideas.

In conclusion, we hope that the search strategies as well as the conceptual schemes for narrowing and refining your research topic that we have offered here will prove to be helpful in your search for a meaningful and important research study.

Recommended Readings

Readers interested in learning more about finding research topics may wish to consult the relevant chapters in Cone and Foster's (1993) book entitled *Dissertations and Theses From*

Start to Finish: Psychology and Related Fields. Useful information on finding a research topic can also be found in Chapter 2 of Long, Convey, and Chwalek's *Completing Dissertations in the Behavioral Sciences and Education* (1985). Another useful resource is the chapter "Selecting a Problem" in Dixon, Bouma, and Atkinson's *Handbook of Social Science Research* (1987). Finally, the book entitled *What to Study: Generating and Developing Research Questions*, by Campbell, Daft, and Hulin (1982), is also a very useful reference for finding a research topic (especially the last two chapters).

References

Adams, J. L. (1986). *The care and feeding of ideas: A guide to encouraging creativity.* Reading, MA: Addison-Wesley.

American Psychological Association. (1994). *Thesaurus of psychological index terms* (7th ed.). Washington, DC: Author.

Baron, R. M., & Kenny, D. A. (1986). The moderator-mediator variable distinction in social psychological research: Conceptual, strategic, and statistical considerations. *Journal of Personality and Social Psychology, 51,* 1173-1182.

Beit-Hallahmi, B. (1985). Dangers of the vagina. *British Journal of Medical Psychology, 58,* 351-356.

Campbell, J. P., Daft, R. L., & Hulin, C. L. (1982). *What to study: Generating and developing research questions.* Beverly Hills, CA: Sage.

Cone, J. D., & Foster, S. L. (1993). *Dissertations and theses from start to finish: Psychology and related fields.* Washington, DC: American Psychological Association.

Dixon, B. R., Bouma, G. D., & Atkinson, G. B. J. (Eds.). (1987). *Handbook of social science research.* New York: Oxford University Press.

Eidelberg, L. (1968). *Encyclopedia of psychoanalysis.* New York: Free Press.

Leong, F. T. L., Wagner, N. S., & Kim, H. (1995). Group counseling expectations among Asian Americans: The role of culture-specific factors. *Journal of Counseling Psychology, 42,* 217-222.

Leong, F. T. L., Wagner, N. S., & Tata, S. P. (1995). Racial and ethnic variations in help seeking attitudes. In J. Ponterotto, J. M. Casas, L. Suzuki, & C. Alexander (Eds.), *Handbook of multicultural counseling* (pp. 415-438). Thousand Oaks, CA: Sage.

Long, T. J., Convey, J. J., & Chwalek, A. R. (1985). *Completing dissertations in the behavioral sciences and education.* San Francisco: Jossey-Bass.

Morrison, A., White, R., & Van Velsor, E. (1987). *Breaking the glass ceiling: Can women reach the top in America's largest corporations?* Reading, MA: Addison-Wesley.

Mullen, B., & Hu, L. (1989). Perceptions of in-group and out-group variability: A meta-analytic integration. *Basic and Applied Social Psychology, 10,* 233-252.

National Institute of Mental Health. (1993). *Special report: Schizophrenia 1993* (NIH Publication No. 93-3499). Rockville, MD: Author.

National Institute of Mental Health. (1994). *New research frontiers in behavioral medicine: Proceedings from the National Conference* (NIH Publication No. 94-3772). Rockville, MD: Author.

Osipow, S. H., & Fitzgerald, L. F. (1996). *Theories of career development* (4th ed.). Boston: Allyn & Bacon.

Park, B., Judd, C. M., & Ryan, C. S. (1991). Social categorization and the representation of variability information. *European Review of Social Psychology, 2,* 211-245.

Pintrich, P. R., & Johnson, G. R. (1990). Assessing and improving students' learning strategies. In M. D. Svinicki (Ed.), *The changing face of college teaching* (pp. 83-92). San Francisco: Jossey-Bass.

Reed, J. G., & Baxter, P. M. (1992). *Library use: A handbook for psychology* (2nd ed.) Washington, DC: American Psychological Association.

Sternberg, R. J. (1988). *The nature of creativity: Contemporary psychological perspectives.* New York: Cambridge University Press.

Weisberg, R. W. (1993). *Creativity: Beyond the myth of genius.* New York: W. H. Freeman.

Wicker, A. W. (1985). Getting out of our conceptual ruts: Strategies for expanding our conceptual frameworks. *American Psychologist, 40,* 1094-1103.

Wiggins, R. W. (1995). *The Internet for everyone: A guide for users and providers.* New York: McGraw-Hill.

Chapter 2

Using a Library Effectively

JEFFREY G. REED
PAM M. BAXTER

Reference Versus Research

A researcher uses a library—any library—for a variety of reasons and to meet a number of needs. Use generally falls into one of two categories: reference or research. You may use a library to meet an immediate reference need: to find a fact or definition, to locate an individual or institution, to scan an overview of a concept or idea, or to verify a statistic. You may also approach a library in support of research activity, looking for information to support or refute a hypothesis. Unlike searching for a specific fact or piece of information, information seeking in support of research is more time consuming and requires you to use a variety of strategies, some of which will be successful and others of which will not. There is also no guarantee that the research you seek is available in a library or even that it has been published. Although a library can meet both reference and research needs, we focus in this chapter on how libraries meet the needs of researchers.

Location: Personal Library Versus
Local Institution Library Versus Virtual Library

Most researchers rely on several libraries. One is the personal library maintained in one's office or home. Another is the library serving one's academic institution. If located in an area where several libraries house collections of interest, a researcher may avail him- or herself of more than one collection. Researchers are also becoming aware of the "virtual library," an electronic library that does not exist in a physical place supported by a staff of professionals and filled with books and journals. Use of each type of library affords distinct advantages and disadvantages (see Figure 2.1).

LIBRARY TYPES

The Personal Library

Libraries have always been associated with a physical location. One of these locations, and one most often and immediately consulted by researchers, is the personal library. This

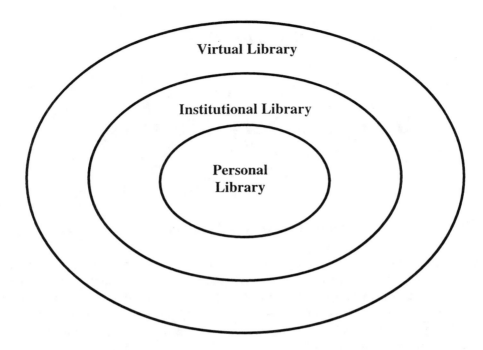

Figure 2.1. Types of Libraries in Terms of Proximity to the Psychologist User

is usually a collection of purchased books and journal subscriptions, generally in your area of specialization (see below for a description of the types and uses of these materials). The personal library may also contain files of article reprints, copies of conference papers, and other materials requested or received from colleagues who conduct research in your area of expertise.

There are several distinct advantages to using a personal library for reference needs. Because it is readily accessible in your office, you need not worry about inopportune library hours, whether items you need are being used by someone else, or other access inconveniences. Having acquired the materials yourself, you know what kinds of information they contain, and you know that they reflect your particular research interests and those of your colleagues.

There are also disadvantages to relying heavily—or solely—on a personal library for reference and research needs. The most obvious is cost: Maintaining journal subscriptions and an up-to-date core of texts and handbooks can be prohibitively expensive. It can also affect the quality of the information at hand. Cost and your diligence in acquiring the most current and authoritative sources affect the size and quality of your personal library.

The Local Library

Your institution's library offers many advantages over the office library at your disposal. The size and scope of the collection are larger, and access to reference tools in other disciplines is especially important when considering the interdisciplinary aspects of much research in psychology. You can rely on the library to purchase material that is too expensive or peripheral to your research areas to warrant purchasing it yourself. Depending on the selection criteria and procedures followed by the library staff, the collection may also be more up to date and authoritative than an office collection. Most academic libraries invite and encourage faculty members to suggest titles for purchase. The institution's library also provides an important "value-added" feature: staff who offer services that can expand your use of information sources.

Like your personal collection, however, an institutional library can provide rapid access only to those materials actually on its shelves. Although basic tools may be housed in a reference collection and therefore on the library's shelves much of the time, other factors can thwart access to information: A journal volume may be at the bindery just when you need a particular issue, books may be signed out by another individual, volumes may be mis-shelved, the library may be closed when you need it. Budget considerations can restrict how frequently libraries purchase texts and how broadly they acquire material. Most libraries do not acquire certain types of materials, such as standardized tests and unpublished conference papers. Finally, the organization of even modest-sized libraries can be daunting: Whereas you know where every book and journal you own is on your shelves, the collections of libraries are organized in a predetermined hierarchy that appears arbitrary and arcane to many.

The Virtual Library

The "virtual library" can best be defined as "all the stuff out there," beyond the physical locations of your personal and institutional libraries. It can consist of other libraries and their collections, whether or not you know what they contain. Fortunately, the on-line catalogs of many libraries are available for searching via dial-up or Internet so that you can find specific titles in their collections. If you need a particular book or article, interlibrary loan services at your local library can obtain it for you, whether the items are owned by libraries across the state or in a foreign country.

Increasingly, the virtual library is taking an electronic form, represented by on-line catalogs, electronic discussion groups that are read by researchers with similar interests, or research materials for which there are no printed equivalents (such as refereed electronic journals and data archives). The exploding size, scope, and content of the virtual library make it almost impossible to define and categorize. Although it is practically impossible to keep up to date, *The Whole Internet* (Krol, 1994) and *The Internet Directory* (Braun, 1994) list resources and, more important, provide information on how to keep yourself abreast of developments on the virtual library.

Because you can use many features of the virtual library from your home or office, it can, in a way, become part of your personal library. Aside from possible connect-time charges and purchase of requisite hardware and software, you can use it without incurring direct costs. Electronic sources can be updated frequently, access time can be quick, and the cost of electronic storage makes cost-effective and flexible access to information efficient even when used by a small number of researchers.

As with any computer network, there can be inconveniences such as downtime, hardware/software incompatibility, and access. In the case of research material, information quality and control/ownership are significant concerns associated with the virtual library. A number of refereed electronic journals and moderated discussion lists strive for responsible and authoritative content. The speed of communication and diversity of recipients/contributors, however, permit a variety of undesirable results: release of preliminary research reports; unsubstantiated research results; equal weight given to all contributions, regardless of methodological or ethical standards employed; and outright fraudulent or plagiarized communications.

TRADE-OFFS IN USE OF LIBRARY TYPES

As noted above, each type of library—personal, institutional, virtual—affords a number of advantages and disadvantages. In addition, there are several other considerations when researchers seek and use information sources.

Serendipity

When flipping through a journal issue, browsing a library's shelves, or scanning a current-awareness service, you may unexpectedly encounter an article that is related to your research or that discusses an aspect of a topic you had never considered when designing a study. Although not a reliable or predictable method on which to base a research program or study, serendipity plays a role by exposing you to the many unexpected twists and turns of your quest for information. Serendipitous access to information also points out one of the shortcomings of computer-based information retrieval systems, such as an on-line catalog or computerized index to journal articles. A well-tailored search results in information using only the words you enter; it excludes what may be related but does not use the exact terminology you expect.

The Invisible College

Much of the information that researchers convey to their peers makes its way into the published literature as an article, book, or chapter. On the other hand, many elements of a research project never appear in a readily distributed form. These include negative research findings, difficulties with using a specific type of research apparatus or method (which is subsequently abandoned in favor of another that is more appropriate), or information conveyed in a paper presented at a scholarly conference but never published. Often the best—and sometimes the only—way to find out about this information is through the "invisible college," that informal network of communication that takes place around the coffeepot at break, in informal encounters at a professional gathering, or at a paper presentation at a scholarly meeting. The products of some of these informal contacts may become part of your personal library (for example, when you request reprints of paper presentations) or may come to you via the virtual library (when you monitor communications of electronic discussion lists).

Nonlibrary Information Sources

Some information sources and formats are difficult to find in any library, whether personal, local, or virtual. These include departmental or research reports with limited distribution, data sets that are institution specific or not Internet accessible, and retrospective data compilations or special collections that are not well represented in standard bibliographic tools. Another significant—and frustrating—group of literature is that for which insufficient information exists to identify it. This includes incomplete or inaccurate information supplied by an author in his or her reference list.

It is in these situations that relying on an information professional is most important to the information-seeking process and that the value-added nature of the local library is apparent. A large number of queries fielded by reference librarians involve these types of problems. The nature of a librarian's job is to recognize how information is organized, to understand the structure and scope of available resources, and to match your research need with information to meet it. Because they often deal with literature from a variety of disciplines, they can bring a broader perspective to your search strategy.

Sources

This section describes types of sources that may be found in the personal, institutional, or virtual library. For each type of source, we describe the purpose and format (what it is), use in research, and typical location (personal vs. institutional vs. virtual library) and provide examples. For additional information, extensive listings of sources, and specific examples of how to use particular tools not included here, refer to Baxter (1993), McInnis (1982), Reed and Baxter (1992), or Sternberg (1993). In this chapter, we will focus on the field of industrial/organizational/engineering psychology to provide examples of sources.

TEXTBOOKS

Purpose and Format

Textbooks perform an instructional function and typically are organized to support an educational program. Introductory textbooks provide a broad overview of a field such as industrial/organizational psychology (e.g., Landy, 1985; Muchinsky, 1983). They summarize key principles, theories, research findings, and trends in the field. Intermediate and advanced textbooks provide more detailed treatment of a subfield such as work motivation (e.g., Steers & Porter, 1991).

Use in Research

Every good textbook should refer to key sources related to the topics it covers. Thus a textbook may provide an entry into the literature of a field. Recognize, however, that a textbook is a secondary source, summarizing and reporting the work of others. Despite the advantage of providing a summary and overview of a field, the risk is always that as a secondary source, a textbook may misinterpret, oversimplify, or ignore research findings.

Location

Most professionals keep introductory textbooks in their personal library pertaining to each area of significant interest, as well as advanced textbooks relating to their specialization. Although libraries tend not to acquire large numbers of textbooks, focusing instead on primary sources, most institutional libraries have one or several textbooks on major topics of interest. The reference department of your institutional library, or the virtual library, should be able to provide information about most textbooks.

KEY MONOGRAPHS

Purpose and Format

In every field, there are a few book-length sources that go beyond the textbook to furnish an original contribution, with some providing monograph-length research reporting. In time, some become "classic" works in the field, with which every practitioner in that field is expected to be familiar. Some of these classic works become the textbooks of graduate courses and have an impact on future generations of psychologists (e.g., Katz & Kahn, 1966).

Use in Research

To the extent that classic monographs provide critical new approaches to a field, they become primary sources and furnish a starting point for further investigation. For example, Campbell, Dunnette, Lawler, and Weick (1970) stimulated numerous studies on managers, and March and Simon's (1958) work is recognized as a point of departure for many subsequent works on organizational theory, structure, and conflict.

Location

As in the case of the advanced textbook, practitioners tend to have several key classic monographs in their personal library. Because some seminal works are out of print and difficult to obtain, they may be available only in the institutional library or in some cases must be accessed through the virtual library.

HANDBOOKS

Purpose and Format

At intervals, persons decide (and publishers agree) to prepare a comprehensive reference work that summarizes a field. At the time it is published, a handbook provides a comprehensive assessment of the "state of the art" in a particular field, including theory, research, methodology, and issues. This is typically offered as a multichapter handbook with numerous contributors, each a specialist/expert in his or her particular chapter topic.

Use in Research

Because a handbook chapter provides an overview of a topic, it usually supplies an extensive bibliography of important sources in that area. It can be an excellent starting point for further investigation. In addition, a handbook will point to key variables that have been investigated, and its absence may indicate areas lacking in extensive research.

Location

The *Handbook of Industrial and Organizational Psychology* (Dunnette, 1976) was considered a key statement of the state of the art at the time of its publication. Many professionals in the field acquired copies for their personal libraries. Many graduate students used it as a key source in work on advanced degrees. Some professors even viewed it as a textbook for graduate students. The subsequent four-volume second edition updated and expanded the original, making it even more valuable in the personal professional library (Dunnette & Hough, 1990-1994). Because we all have limits on our finances, related or more specialized handbooks (e.g., *Bass and Stogdill's Handbook of Leadership* [Bass, 1990]) can often be found in the institutional library. The virtual library provides information about and access to additional handbooks.

ANNUAL REVIEWS

Purpose and Format

Reviews present selective and evaluative review of status and recent progress in main areas of the field. Volumes such as the *Annual Review of Psychology,* published each year since 1950, follow a master plan for regular review of topics in the field.

Use in Research

Each *Annual Review of Psychology* volume of about 20 chapters is authored by an expert on the field covered. Each topic review includes an extensive reference list, providing a good starting point for many research projects. An advantage of a review is that such compendia may be issued annually and provide updates more frequently than handbooks. Some areas within psychology are supported by more specialized reviews.

Location

Some academic professionals receive each volume in an annual series to insure awareness of work such as that of O'Reilly (1991). Many institutional libraries include complete sets of volumes of annual reviews. However, you may have to rely on the virtual library for more specialized review monographs.

PROFESSIONAL DIRECTORIES

Purpose and Format

These sources provide brief biographical information, including current address, workplace, and educational background. There are numerous directories, and most associations maintain a directory of their members (e.g., the American Psychological Society *Directory*).

Use in Research

Directories can facilitate communication among researchers by providing location information and indicate a researcher's background by listing credentials of biographees.

Location

A benefit of membership in most associations is a membership directory. Many professional psychologists will have directories for associations of which they are members in their personal library. Institutional libraries may carry directories of major national organizations (e.g., the American Psychological Association [APA] *Membership Directory*) but will not carry all directories of all associations. Many institutional libraries tend to focus on nondisciplinary directories of distinguished individuals: for example, *Who's Who in America*. The virtual library expands the scope and reach of printed directories. Many academic institutions make their campus directories, telephone books, and electronic mail directories available electronically for remote searching on the Internet. As use of World Wide Web technology expands, a few academic institutions are providing more in-depth information about their faculty and researchers: for example, a list of current publications and descriptions of current research interests.

CURRENT-AWARENESS SERVICES

Purpose and Format

Current-awareness services provide information on recently published articles in a particular field or set of fields. This is important because few people have the money to subscribe to all potentially relevant journals, and most do not have sufficient time to browse all relevant publications in their fields.

Use in Research

Current-awareness services help to keep a researcher abreast of published research in the field. For example, *Current Contents: Social and Behavioral Sciences* is published weekly and reproduces the tables of contents from over 1,300 journals over the course of a year. Other services focus on specific subject areas. For example, researchers who are members of the APA's Division 21 receive the quarterly *PsycSCAN: Applied Experimental and Engi-*

neering Psychology as a benefit of membership. This service provides abstracts of articles from over 100 journals in areas such as computer applications, human factors, ergonomics, safety, and working conditions. Other area-specific PsycSCAN publications cover such areas as psychoanalysis, developmental psychology, and clinical psychology.

Location

An individual may have one such service in his or her personal library, and more are usually available in the institutional library. Some institutional libraries provide current-awareness services of their own. After compiling a profile of interests on participating members, they may provide copies of tables of contents to recently published journals of interest to the participants in hard copy or electronic form.

JOURNALS

Purpose and Format

Most published research in psychology appears as articles in journals. There are hundreds of journals of interest to psychologists. Even the field of industrial/organizational/engineering psychology has dozens of potentially relevant journals, depending on the interests of the practitioner.

Use in Research

The competent researcher does a thorough retrospective search of prior publications in his or her area of interest while defining the scope of a research project and before beginning the data collection phase of research investigation. This is done to learn from findings of prior research, to ensure that relevant variables are being addressed, to relate the current piece of research to relevant trends in the field, and to determine that the particular project has not been previously investigated and reported (unless the intent is to replicate a particular study).

Location

Most psychologists subscribe to a few key journals for their personal library that represent their primary interests (e.g., *Journal of Applied Psychology*). The institutional library will contain a larger collection of potentially relevant journals (e.g., *Organizational Behavior and Human Decision Processes*). However, institutional libraries, like individuals, have insufficient resources to acquire all relevant journals, especially those that are more specialized (e.g., *Organizational Dynamics*). Thus the researcher may need to tap the virtual library through methods such as interlibrary loan for full coverage of a topic. In addition, as of 1994, some refereed journals are beginning to appear in electronic form, available over the Internet.

ABSTRACTS AND INDEXES

Purpose and Format

Most indexing and abstracting tools provide author, title, and subject access to articles within journals. Some more specialized sources index published conference papers and proceedings, book chapters, dissertations and master's theses, federal and state publications, and technical reports. They can be printed or computer searchable. Some are available in just one format, whereas others are available in several publication formats.

Use in Research

One use is current awareness. Although they are updated less frequently than true "current-awareness" tools (such as *Current Contents*), they can cover thousands of journal titles and provide access to articles in many languages. The other function is the ability to search the journal literature retrospectively—in the case of the printed *Psychological Abstracts*, even into the 19th century.

Location

Until the 1980s, most psychologists relied on the printed *Psychological Abstracts* to conduct searches of the literature or the services of a librarian to perform a computer search of the PsycINFO database. Increasingly, availability of this information in electronic formats using relatively easy search software means that researchers can initiate their own computer searches and in some cases can do so from offices or homes. Some government-produced databases, such as ERIC, are mounted at publicly accessible sites and can be searched on the Internet.

DISSERTATIONS AND THESES

Purpose and Format

A requirement of almost all scholarly doctoral programs (e.g., Ph.D.) and of many research-oriented master's programs is the completion of a thesis or dissertation. The dissertation/thesis is expected to be an original piece of research in the discipline that demonstrates one's knowledge of the literature in an area, use of appropriate methods and tools in conducting research, and skill in communicating and defending the content and merits of the research contribution to the field.

Use in Research

Because dissertations/theses contain an extensive review of relevant literature, they can be useful in identifying prior research. Because most research raises as well as answers questions, a dissertation/thesis can provide ideas for future research. Reviewing a prior dissertation/thesis can provide guidance in completing one's own project.

Location

Academic programs typically require the degree candidate to file a copy of the dissertation/thesis in the college or university library. In the case of doctoral dissertations, most also require that a copy be submitted to University Microfilms International (UMI). UMI makes an archival microfilm copy of each dissertation received, announces its availability in the *Dissertation Abstracts International* (or the electronic Dissertation Abstracts Online), and sells copies of dissertations to individuals and institutions. Under certain circumstances, copies of dissertations and theses may be obtained on interlibrary loan.

In summary, sources such as textbooks, handbooks, and reviews can be useful in defining and narrowing your research topic (see Chapter 1 of this volume for details). Abstracts and indexes enable you to perform a thorough retrospective literature search (see Chapter 3 for details). Evaluating the quality of papers, articles, reports, and other materials you retrieve in your search is addressed in Chapter 4.

LIBRARIES OF THE FUTURE

What does the future hold for libraries? Scholarly research and communication are in the midst of significant trends that will shape how people acquire and use information in the future:

- The cost of print materials and information can be expected to continue to increase. At the same time, the volume of information available continues to expand. If current trends continue, this may result in increasing pressure on both personal and institutional library budgets and may force increased reliance on nonlocal information sources.
- Electronic publishing and the use of electronic media in publishing are occurring with increasing frequency. Increasing numbers of sources are available as electronic documents—encyclopedias, almanacs, atlases on CD-ROM. Some journal publishers are investigating the role of electronic journals in addition to—or instead of—their print products.
- Data sets from researchers and research institutions may become increasingly available in electronic form.
- Use of the Internet has exploded since the early 1990s. Graphical user interfaces such as Mosaic and Netscape allow rapid electronic written communication worldwide and afford increasing flexibility in the type and format of information shared among researchers.
- Scanning of hard copy documents for preservation and for demand reprinting may mean an increasing retrospective information base accessible in electronic form.

The availability of full-text sources on line will mean greater access to information. Electronic formats will also allow more rapid transfer of information over distances. However, users will face a number of obstacles in use of the virtual library: For example, the quantity of information will be imposing and difficult to negotiate effectively, and monetary charges will increasingly be levied for retrieval of information from remote sites.

Recommended Readings

Library Use: A Handbook for Psychology (Reed & Baxter, 1992) provides much additional information on how to conduct library research. It includes examples of most key sources and guides the reader through the library research process. Its purpose is to "teach" library use skills to college/graduate psychology students. *Psychology: A Guide to Reference and Information Sources* (Baxter, 1993) offers a bibliography of hundreds of sources, complete with annotations.

In addition to Krol (1994) and Braun (1994), King and Kovacs (1994) list and provide access instructions for thousands of scholarly electronic journals and discussion lists.

References

Bass, B. M. (1990). *Bass and Stogdill's handbook of leadership* (3rd ed.). New York: Free Press.

Baxter, P. M. (1993). *Psychology: A guide to reference and information sources.* Englewood, CO: Libraries Unlimited.

Braun, E. (1994). *The Internet directory.* New York: Fawcett Columbine.

Campbell, J. P., Dunnette, M. D., Lawler, E. E., & Weick, K. E. (1970). *Managerial behavior, performance, and effectiveness.* New York: McGraw-Hill.

Dunnette, M. D. (Ed.). (1976). *Handbook of industrial and organizational psychology.* Chicago: Rand McNally.

Dunnette, M. D., & Hough, L. M. (Eds.). (1990-1994). *Handbook of industrial and organizational psychology* (2nd ed., 4 vols.). Palo Alto, CA: Consulting Psychologists Press.

Katz, D., & Kahn, R. L. (1966). *Social psychology of organizations.* New York: John Wiley.

King, L. A., & Kovacs, D. (1994). *Directory of electronic journals, newsletters and academic discussion lists* (4th ed.). Washington, DC: Association of Research Libraries. [http://www.mid.net:80/KOVACS]

Krol, E. (1994). *The whole Internet: User's guide and catalog* (2nd ed.). Sebastopol, CA: O'Reilly & Associates.

Landy, F. J. (1985). *Psychology of work behavior.* Homewood, IL: Dorsey.

March, J. G., & Simon, H. A. (1958). *Organizations.* New York: John Wiley.

McInnis, R. G. (1982). *Research guide for psychology.* Westport, CT: Greenwood.

Muchinsky, P. M. (1983). *Psychology applied to work.* Homewood, IL: Dorsey.

O'Reilly, C. A. (1991). Organizational behavior: Where we've been, where we're going. *Annual Review of Psychology, 42,* 427-458.

Reed, J. G., & Baxter, P. M. (1992). *Library use: A handbook for psychology* (2nd ed.) Washington, DC: American Psychological Association.

Steers, R. M., & Porter, L. W. (1991). *Motivation and work behavior* (5th ed.). New York: McGraw-Hill.

Sternberg, R. J. (1993). *The psychologist's companion: A guide to scientific writing for students and researchers* (3rd ed.). New York: Cambridge University Press.

Chapter 3

Conducting a Literature Search

MARGARET S. STOCKDALE
THERESA KENNY

Probably the least pleasant and most anxiety-producing research task is conducting a literature search and writing the literature review. If you are intellectually curious, an avid reader, and a gifted writer, you are already a step or two ahead. This chapter is for those who still find the literature review a daunting task. In this chapter, we hope to reveal the mystery of literature searching and prove that by breaking down and organizing the literature search into a few manageable steps, it is not only achievable but highly rewarding as well.

In this chapter, we are going to provide a step-by-step guide to conducting a literature review, keeping in mind that there is no one best way to do this. We will also provide a nonexhaustive list of bibliographic, encyclopedic, and indexing sources that will help you get started. We will also give you some guidance in how to use these sources. However, we will say it now and repeat it many times again: Your librarian is your friend. His or her job is to help you figure out where to find and how to use the reference aids and resources that we will be discussing. Do not be afraid to ask!

Finally, this chapter will give you some suggestions for what to do with all of the literature once it has been located (and read). That is, we will provide some ideas for how to organize your literature review.

This chapter is not going to cover everything you need to know to conduct and write a competent literature review. For developing a research idea, we recommend that you read Chapter 1 of this volume, by Leong and Pfaltzgraff. For finding your way around the library, we refer you to Chapter 2, by Reed and Baxter. Chapter 21, by Austin and Calderon, will help you master American Psychological Association (APA) style. You should also read Oleson and Arkin's chapter (Chapter 4) on reviewing and evaluating research articles. For technical assistance for conducting meta-analyses (a specific type of literature review), you should also consult Cooper and Dorr (Chapter 18 of this volume).

Steps to Conducting a Literature Review

PRELIMINARY DECISIONS

Before you dash off to the library (or log on to the Internet), you need to determine three things: (a) what purpose this literature review will serve in your research, (b) the scope of your review, and (c) what exactly you are looking for. Questions (a) and (b) can be answered pretty easily. Question (c) may require you to do a preliminary literature review before you can adequately define your topic.

Types of Literature Reviews

Almost every scholarly report should contain a literature review, but different types of literature reviews serve different purposes. Often literature reviews serve as an intro-duction to a research study for which you should review literature that addresses the particular domain of the study. For example, if you plan to conduct a study on the role of commitment in goal-setting success, you should review literature on goal setting and on commitment processes, as well as some general research and theory on work motivation because this is the context in which goal setting is applied. Another type of literature review is one in which the research *is* the literature review. Thus you should attempt to get as much of the literature on your topic as you can, if not all of it, and try to glean some "truths" or develop criticisms from the extant literature. This type of literature review might be published in *Psychological Bulletin, Annual Review of Psychology,* or a book or book chapter. Although theses and dissertations typically include an empirical research project, the literature review chapter should be treated as a comprehensive, stand-alone review paper. So ask yourself, "Is this a specific, highly focused literature review that will be used to support a research study, or is this a comprehensive literature review that will be published by itself?"

Scopes of Literature Reviews

Your answer to the question above, in part, helps answer the next question: "How comprehensive should my literature review be?" If you are writing a stand-alone literature review, the scope of your review should be *exhaustive:* Find all the literature that bears on your topic. This requirement may be (and usually is) relaxed for term papers, but if you are working with a research team that wants to publish a stand-alone literature review, chances are you will need to conduct an exhaustive literature search.

Limited literature searches are nonexhaustive (obviously), which makes the decision about the scope of your search more important. In what way is your search limited? You may be interested only in literature published during a certain time period (e.g., the past 10 years) or only in certain types of documents (e.g., articles published in peer-reviewed psychology journals, government documents) or populations (e.g., Asian American women). You should determine the scope of your search so that you do not waste time and resources collecting material that will not be used.

Topic and Search Specificity

The more specific or narrow your topic, the less literature you will find on the topic. This may have advantages and disadvantages. If the topic is too narrow, you may not find anything that is relevant; if it is too wide, you will be overwhelmed. A narrowly defined topic, however, allows you to study and write about an issue in depth and thus is often preferred for scientific writing. Furthermore, if you define your topic narrowly and specifically, chances are that you will be able to conduct an exhaustive search without a great deal of difficulty. It is often difficult, however, to define a topic specifically before you head to the library. Most of us need to read about the topic generally before we can focus on the specific issue.

BEGINNING THE SEARCH: WHERE DO I START?

Conducting a thorough literature search involves several steps and requires looking at different types of sources. Both monographs (e.g., books) and journal articles should be consulted to gain a comprehensive picture of the topic. And because topics in psychology can often be approached from a variety of viewpoints—such as social, education, medical, and organizational, to name a few—a variety of resources should be consulted to ensure that your topic is adequately represented.

General Information

As suggested in Chapter 2, a good way to gain a general understanding of a topic is to review some textbook and handbook discussions of the topic. Such discussions will include bibliographies (a selected list is provided in the references), which can then be used to access additional information on your topic. Although most college and university libraries do not carry extensive textbook collections, they will generally include at least a few basic textbooks in support of the institution's curriculum.

For a more in-depth discussion of your topic, you may want to review some book-length treatments of the subject as well. Browsing in the appropriate call number area can lead you to books devoted entirely to a particular subject. However, keeping in mind that many psychology topics can be approached from alternate points of view, it is also important to do a subject search for books on your topic. For instance, books on educational psychology may be assigned to call numbers in the area of education; books on industrial and organizational psychology may be catalogued in the areas of business or management.

There are two steps to doing a subject search for a book. The first is to determine the appropriate term, or subject heading, to use for your search. Because books are catalogued by librarians to be accessible to any person, and because terms used to describe a subject often change over time, you will sometimes find that the term that you are most familiar with or that seems the most apparent is not the term libraries use to catalog books on that subject. The *Library of Congress Subject Headings (LCSH)* serves as your guide to choosing the best search term. This is a multivolume alphabetical listing of subject headings used by libraries when cataloguing books. If your initial search term is not an official subject heading, you will be directed to the appropriate term. *LCSH* may also provide you with broader terms (BT) and related terms (RT), which can be useful for expanding the scope of your search, as well as narrower terms (NT), which can help make your search more specific.

Once you have determined the best subject heading(s) to use, the second step is to consult your library's book catalog. This may be either a card catalog or, more and more frequently, an on-line (computerized) catalog. Any single library will not own books on all subjects found in *LCSH*, so you may need to search some broader or related terms. Also, your librarian can help you conduct a regional or national search and let you borrow a specific book through interlibrary loan.

Specific and Up-to-Date Information: Journals

Although books can provide you with in-depth background information on your topic, they are often not the most up-to-date sources of information due to the length of time it takes to produce and publish a book. To learn about relevant current research, it is vital to review journal articles on the topic as well. The tools used to find journal articles are indexes and abstracts. Both give you lists of articles written on a subject during a specified time period and provide you with the information (i.e., citation) necessary to access each article. Abstracts will also give you a brief summary of the articles. As with *LCSH*, no one library will own each journal covered in an index or abstract; these tools are meant to let you know what is available in the broader research community. But again, if you find an article you are interested in reading and your library does not own the journal, you may get a copy of it through the interlibrary loan system.

Like book catalogs, indexes and abstracts may be in either print or electronic formats, such as CD-ROM databases. The major advantage of an electronic index, in addition to speed, is its capacity to search your term over a span of years. Each volume of a print index is usually limited to a year or less. Although automated indexes can save time, it is important to remember that many of these tools do not go back as far as their print counterparts. Use both.

In addition to using indexes and abstracts to find journal articles, another very fruitful search technique is to browse the table of contents of several volumes of journals that tend to publish research on your subject matter. Also, your library may subscribe to *Current Contents in Social and Behavioral Sciences,* which prints the upcoming tables of contents for many psychology-related journals. You may send a reprint request to the author to get an advance copy of the article.

General Guidelines in Using Indexes

Before noting a few of the most useful sources for locating journal articles in the field of psychology, at this point we will outline the general search strategies used. When you are locating books on a subject, it is again important to use the appropriate terminology. But for books, there is no one resource like *LCSH* to give you the correct subject headings for all indexes and abstracts. You can begin searching index tools with some key words or phrases you have found to be associated with your topic. Most indexes and abstracts include alphabetical subject listings, including cross-references to direct you to alternate terms as needed. In addition, an indexing tool may come with a companion volume called a *thesaurus* that directs you to the proper terms to use when conducting a search in that particular resource. CD-ROM databases include the alphabetical subject listing or the thesaurus on line as part of the database itself.

RELEVANT PSYCHOLOGY INDEXES

Psychological Abstracts (PA) and the computerized PsycLIT index both book chapters and journal articles related to psychology. The companion tool is the *Thesaurus of Psychological Index Terms* (Walker, 1994). Although the card or on-line catalog will lead you to books as complete works on a topic, many books contain chapters by different people and on different aspects of a topic that are not indexed in the card or on-line catalog. *PA* and PsycLIT are the major indexing tools for psychology-related research.

As mentioned earlier, many psychology topics can be approached from many viewpoints. One major area of overlap with psychology is sociology. A major indexing tool in this area is *Sociological Abstracts* and its companion tool, the *Thesaurus of Sociological Indexing Terms* (Booth, 1992). The electronic version of *Sociological Abstracts* is called Sociofile. An additional multidisciplinary resource in both print and on-line form is the *Social Sciences Index*. This is a straightforward alphabetical list of subject headings, each followed by the citations for articles written on that topic during the time period specified. Although there is no companion thesaurus, per se, to the *Social Sciences Index*, the electronic version does have a "browse" function that may guide you to more appropriate subject headings for your topic.

Another related discipline is education, for which the most extensive electronic resource is ERIC (Educational Resources Information Center). The two print counterparts are *Current Index to Journals in Education (CIJE)* and *Resources in Education (RIE)*. *CIJE* contains citations for journal articles; *RIE* provides access to information presented in other arenas, such as research reports and conference proceedings, which can otherwise be difficult to find. This resource also comes with a companion tool, the *Thesaurus of ERIC Descriptors* (1980), which is useful in determining the "best" subject headings to use in your search. Another education indexing tool is the *Education Index*, which is produced under that title in both print and electronic formats.

The major medical indexing tool is called *Index Medicus*, a portion of which (mainly of interest to clinicians) is covered in the electronic database MedLine. These resources use a standard list of subject headings established by the National Library of Medicine. For industrial and organizational-related topics, a good tool is *Business Periodicals Index*—again the same title whether in print or electronic format.

Another way to build your search results is through the use of a citation index, such as the multidisciplinary resources *Social Sciences Citation Index (SSCI)* and *Science Citation Index (SCI)*. A citation index can be an excellent way to expand your search by providing lists of articles that share the same references. For example, if through your search in one of the indexes mentioned above you find an article that is particularly relevant to your research, you can check that article in the appropriate citation index. If it has been indexed, you will find a list of additional articles that have cited it. These additional articles, then, may contain information relevant to your topic. Both citation indexes mentioned above are available in print and electronic formats.

There are, of course, many additional indexing tools that may be useful in a literature search in the field of psychology, depending on the viewpoint you are taking. This brings us to one additional and very valuable resource: librarians. They will be able to tell which of the aforementioned indexing tools your library subscribes to (and in which formats), suggest alternative or additional resources for your search, and provide assistance in using the wide variety of sources available.

FUGITIVE LITERATURE AND GOVERNMENT DOCUMENTS

Systematic and thorough use of the search techniques described above will lead you to much if not all of the published literature on your subject. A good deal of research and literature, however, will not be uncovered with these processes because it is either unpublished, proprietary, or published in obscure sources. This is the "fugitive literature," and if you are conducting an exhaustive search, this literature is important to locate. Therefore, in addition to the steps described above, you should do the following if you wish to locate fugitive literature (Rosnow & Rosnow, 1995):

1. *Contact known authors in the field* and ask them for copies of any study they have written on your topic—published or not published. You may also ask them to suggest other sources on your topic. This request will be taken more seriously if you provide them with a list of your current bibliography so that they can merely add to it if possible (instead of creating an entire list).

2. *Consult the National Technical Information Service* (see your librarian). This is a database that contains summaries of completed research, including conference proceedings and theses.

3. *Use the Internet.* Although the procedures for "surfing the Internet" change daily, with a little tutoring, you can search on key words and access all sorts of information, including names of people who may be able to suggest additional resources. If you can find an electronic discussion group focused on your topic, you may be able to join the discussion and obtain archival resources posted on that network.

4. *Search for government documents* on your topic. Although government documents are typically published, they are sometimes difficult to find. Government publications provide a vast resource of information. The Government Printing Office (GPO) is the largest publisher in the world, issuing thousands of documents each year on every topic imaginable. The main indexing tool for government documents is the *Monthly Catalog of Government Documents* and, for periodicals, the *Index to United States Government Periodicals*. There is also an electronic resource, Government Documents Index. These tools can be especially helpful for researching topics on which you are having a hard time finding information.

Organizing Your Literature

We hope that you read through this entire chapter before you start your literature search because you should know a few tips about organizing your literature before you get started. We have known people who spent a small fortune photocopying every article that turned up in their search, only to read about a third of it. You can gather much of the information you will need right in the library and save yourself a lot of time and money. In this section, we will provide tips on taking notes, making an outline, and writing the review.

TAKING NOTES

If you are conducting a meta-analysis, you will need to record some very specific information about each study you read (see Cooper & Dorr, Chapter 18 of this volume). For most other types of literature reviews, however, the important and interesting points vary from source to source. In some cases, you may want a particular quote. In others, you want to jot down the reasoning that supported a hypothesis. If you are reviewing empirical studies, you probably want to record the general findings as well. We will go over some specifics shortly. Regardless, the tried-and-true "note card" method remains one of the most efficient and organized ways of recording study information.

Note Cards

Generally, there are two methods of recording information on note cards. As implied by the name, with the *single-point* method, one salient piece of information is recorded per note card. A single quote (remember to record the page number), a construct definition, a statistical finding, and a brief explanation of a theory or hypothesis are examples of the types of information you might record, each on a single card.

You may prefer to summarize the complete study on one note card using the *article-summary* method. You may not be able to record as much information as you would with a series of single-point cards, but you will have fewer note cards to deal with, and you can gain a gestalt (whole) impression of the study when you study your notes again. This is very similar to an abstract, but we find it helpful to summarize the article in your own words instead of merely copying the author's abstract.

Computerized Note Taking

Following similar conventions for taking notes on note cards, you can record your information on a computer, using a variety of software programs. The advantage of computerized note taking is that you can apply a variety of sorting and search techniques to organize your notes. For example, if you give some thought to how information will be recorded before you begin taking notes, you can create a database that will allow you to search on key words, authors, publication years and/or sources, and so forth. In other words, you can create a computerized bibliographic program much like PsycLIT or other such programs, but one tailored to you. Another advantage of computerized note taking is that you can often download bibliographic information from on-line or CD-ROM indexes and import the data into your own database program. Do not let this be a substitute for reading the full, original sources, however.

Key Information to Record

Whether you take notes on note cards or on a computer, at a minimum, you should record the following information: (a) full citation (follow APA conventions), (b) purpose of the study, (c) central hypotheses, (d) type of sample (size, demographic characteristics, sampling procedures), (e) type of analysis, (f) key findings (you may want to record effect sizes if provided), (g) brief conclusion statement, and (h) (optional) number of references (this may be helpful to remember if this is a good source to look for additional references).

WRITING AN OUTLINE

Students and professionals alike balk at writing outlines. Some feel that their thoughts are not well organized enough to create an outline or feel that the outline is a waste of time because they will change course as the paper develops. Typically, when you find the outline difficult to structure, it means that your thoughts are too vague and fuzzy. Read more literature, and an outline in your head will begin to emerge. Outlines help tremendously, and almost all good reports follow an outline. Fortunately, you can choose to do this up front or after the fact as long as the final product is structured (Parrott, 1994).

In the up-front or *planful* approach, your notes are organized into topic areas. If your notes are on note cards, then create piles of cards that address a specific topic. If your notes are on computer, then enter a code or key word that identifies the topic area, and sort accordingly. If possible, try to write your outline with a word-processing program. Most have outline features that help keep your outline organized. Major topics and subpoints should be *parallel*. That is, points at the same level in the outline (e.g., I, II, III) should be at the same level of specificity and should be written in the same grammatical form. Similarly, the subpoints under each of these major points (e.g., A, B, C, D) should be parallel. The more thought you put into the outline, the easier it will be to write the report.

In the *after-the-fact* approach, your thoughts develop freely and the structure "emerges" as you write. Some people find that a planful outline squelches their creativity, and they do not want to be tied to it. After you have finished the first draft, however, outline the paper as you have written it. With this after-the-fact outline, you can check to see if your ideas are clearly structured and if your topics are in parallel form. Adjust accordingly.

GENERAL WRITING TIPS

Writing well is not difficult, but it requires practice and knowledge of some rules, conventions, and a few tips. In this final section of the chapter, we provide a few tips for writing literature reviews. Keep in mind that these are not set in stone. You may find that a different style than the one advocated here is more suited to you. Also keep in mind, however, that scientific writing follows a more conventional, less flexible style than do other forms of creative writing.

Although the introduction of your literature review should not be flamboyant, it should be compelling. The reader should be enticed to continue. *Dramatic statistics* (but certainly not false or misleading, unless that is the point you want to make), an *interesting quote* or *anecdote,* or a *series of questions* may start you off well. However, more important, do not worry about writing that fascinating introductory paragraph when you first sit down. This can always be added later. Often a good place to start is to write a *road map* paragraph in which you outline how your paper will be organized and how your points will be developed. If readers have a cognitive map of your paper, they will follow and understand you much more easily.

Use *headings* to organize your paper. Again, this is very helpful to the reader and will help keep your thoughts organized as well. Often your headings come right from your outline. Remember to keep them parallel. In addition, use well-crafted *transition statements* between sections of your review. End major sections with a *summary paragraph* to remind readers of the salient points that you have made.

In general, your literature review should flow from *broad to specific* concepts or topics. Start with a statement of the problem. Discuss and critically analyze general theories that have been posited to account for the problem, then summarize the relevant research literature bearing on the topic. The novice scientific writer often makes the mistake of giving equal weight to each empirical study that is being reviewed. For example, a paragraph may be devoted to each study in the review. This will read like a list of abstracts—boring! One useful tip is *not to start a paragraph with the name of an author.* If you do so, you are bound to write that whole paragraph on that study. Critically important articles are an exception and may warrant more in-depth treatment. But as much as possible, try to integrate similar bodies of research and summarize the main points, key findings, or interesting contradictions.

Conclusion

Searching for literature and writing a review are skills that you can learn and master. We hope that we have provided you with enough tips and pointers for learning this task. Once you become familiar with the indexing or abstracting resources that we have described, the amount of time and energy needed to conduct a comprehensive search will be greatly reduced. There are two points we want you to remember if nothing else: (a) Approach your search from a variety of different angles—do not rely solely on one search method (e.g., PsycLIT), and (b) ask your librarian for help!

Recommended Readings

We found the following resources to be very helpful guides to conducting literature reviews and preparing papers in psychology.

Borchardt and Francis's *How to Find out in Psychology: A Guide to the Literature and Methods of Research* (1984) contains excellent bibliographic sources for finding literature related to psychology and provides well-constructed advice for developing a research or review question.

Although the focus of Hunter and Schmidt's *Methods of Meta-Analysis* (1990) is a technical presentation of the advanced tools for conducting state-of-the-art meta-analyses, Chapter 12 ("Locating, Selecting, and Evaluating Studies") provides a thorough, step-by-step guide to locating psychological literature. This is an especially useful guide for finding the fugitive literature but also provides good general advice for conducting competent reviews.

Parrott's *How to Write Psychology Papers* (1994) is a helpful book written for undergraduate students in psychology. It is easy to read and provides many pointers not only for conducting a literature review but also for selecting topics, using the library, creating references, writing an outline, and so forth. Parrott provides an excellent bibliography.

Rosnow and Rosnow's *Writing Papers in Psychology* (1995) is similar to Parrott (1994). It is easy to follow, has a thorough bibliography, and provides help in using various reference sources.

Useful encyclopedias are Corsini's *Encyclopedia of Psychology* (1994), Gregory's *Oxford Companion to the Mind* (1987), and Ramachandran's *Encyclopedia of Human Behavior* (1994).

The *Bibliographic Guide to Psychology* is an annual comprehensive list of publications catalogued during the past year by the Research Libraries of the New York Public Library, with additional entries from Library of Congress MARC tapes for complete subject coverage.

Some useful handbooks are *Stevens' Handbook of Experimental Psychology* (Atkinson, 1988), the *International Handbook of Behavior Modification and Therapy* (Bellack, Hersen, & Kazdin, 1990), the *Handbook of Neuropsychology* (Boller & Grafman, 1988-1991), the *Handbook of Industrial and Organizational Psychology* (Dunnette & Hough, 1990-1994), the *International Handbook of Psychology* (Gilgen & Gilgen, 1987), and the *Handbook of Cognitive Psychophysiology* (Jennings & Coles, 1991).

Some other reference sources that you might wish to consult are *Contemporary Psychology,* an APA journal devoted entirely to book reviews; *Current Contents in Social and Behavioral Sciences,* which lists tables of content for upcoming issues of psychology-related journals; the *Cumulative Book Index,* a comprehensive reporting service for monograph titles; Sheehy's *Guide to Reference Books* (1986); the *National Union Catalog: A Cumulative Author List,* which provides bibliographic data for an author approach; and Wang's *Author's Guide to Journals in the Behavioral Sciences* (1989).

Finally, other books offering guidance on how to conduct a literature review are Cooper (1984) and Stewart (1984).

References

Atkinson, R. C. (Ed.). (1988). *Stevens' handbook of experimental psychology* (2nd ed.). New York: John Wiley.
Bellack, A. S., Hersen, M., & Kazdin, A. E. (Eds.). (1990). *International handbook of behavior modification and therapy* (2nd ed.). New York: Plenum.

Boller, F., & Grafman, J. (Eds.). (1988-1991). *Handbook of neuropsychology* (5 vols). New York: Elsevier.

Booth, B. (1992). *Thesaurus of sociological indexing terms* (3rd ed.). San Diego: Sociological Abstracts, Inc.

Borchardt, D. H., & Francis, R. D. (1984). *How to find out in psychology: A guide to the literature and methods of research.* New York: Pergamon.

Cooper, H. (1984). *The integrative research review: A systematic approach.* Beverly Hills, CA: Sage.

Corsini, R. J. (Ed.). (1994). *Encyclopedia of psychology* (2nd ed., 4 vols.). New York: John Wiley.

Dunnette, M. D., & Hough, L. M. (Eds.). (1990-1994). *Handbook of industrial and organizational psychology* (2nd ed., 4 vols.). Palo Alto, CA: Consulting Psychologists Press.

Gilgen, A. R., & Gilgen, C. K. (Eds.). (1987). *International handbook of psychology.* New York: Greenwood.

Gregory, R. L. (Ed.). (1987). *The Oxford companion to the mind.* New York: Oxford University Press.

Hunter, J. E., & Schmidt, F. L. (1990). *Methods of meta-analysis.* Newbury Park, CA: Sage.

Jennings, J. R., & Coles, M. G. H. (Eds.). (1991). *Handbook of cognitive psychophysiology.* New York: John Wiley.

Parrott, L., III. (1994). *How to write psychology papers.* New York: HarperCollins.

Ramachandran, V. S. (1994). *Encyclopedia of human behavior* (4 vols.). San Diego: Academic Press.

Rosnow, R. L., & Rosnow, M. (1995). *Writing papers in psychology* (3rd ed.). Pacific Grove, CA: Brooks/Cole.

Sheehy, E. P. (1986). *Guide to reference books.* Chicago: American Library Association.

Stewart, D. W. (1984). *Secondary research.* Beverly Hills, CA: Sage.

Thesaurus of ERIC descriptors (8th ed.). (1980). Phoenix, AZ: Oryz.

Walker, A., Jr. (1994). *Thesaurus of psychological index terms* (7th ed.). Washington, DC: American Psychological Association.

Wang, A. Y. (1989). *Author's guide to journals in the behavioral sciences.* Hillsdale, NJ: Lawrence Erlbaum.

Chapter 4

Reviewing and Evaluating
a Research Article

KATHRYN C. OLESON
ROBERT M. ARKIN

Reading a research article is as much an art and science as writing one. In this chapter, we touch on aspects of the skill of critical reading. But we hasten to advocate that you also read and think about Chapters 21 through 24 in this handbook as you develop your approach to the reading of research. Learning to read about research is so intimately linked with learning to write about it that to us the two seem inseparable. Effective reading and writing are both reflections of comparable critical thinking skills (e.g., Squire, 1983). Both also involve communication, in one case of the "transmitter" variety and in the other of the "receiver" variety. The principles of effective transmission and effective receiving are mirror images of one another. To be a good transmitter of information, it is key to imagine yourself in the role of receiver; to be an effective receiver, it is key to imagine what the author is trying to transmit.

Our central mission in this chapter is to describe a set of tools to use in reading, reviewing, and evaluating research. Some of these tools are more like delicate instruments than like spades and drills. It takes a great deal of experience and a deep appreciation of research to use the "delicate instruments" well—for instance, the tools needed to dissect a research design and to consider the various statistical approaches a researcher might use. Other tools are more the garden-variety tools with which you are already familiar.

In our experience as teachers, it is almost as common for beginners to be as anxious and frustrated in reading research as it is for them to be paralyzed by the prospect of writing about it. Our metaphor about delicate instruments and garden tools is intended to help you put some of those concerns aside. There are many levels of critical reading, and one can do a good job at some of those levels even before completing "Delicate Instruments of Research Design and Statistical Analysis 101."

AUTHORS' NOTE: This research was supported in part by an NIMH postdoctoral fellowship to Kathryn C. Oleson (T32 MH 19728). We are indebted to a large number of teachers and colleagues who, over the years and while we were writing this chapter, talked with us about the various ways to think about, review, and evaluate empirical research.

Purpose and Audience

The crucial starting point is actually before you read one word of an article. You are headed for greater efficiency and greater effectiveness if you ask yourself (a) What is my purpose in reading the article? and (b) What is the audience for the assessment I will make? Sometimes people read psychology articles for the pure pleasure of it. More often, you will have some purpose in mind, and it will involve informing someone about the research or communicating your evaluation of it.

Your purpose will range from informal to formal and will also depend on whether you are reading just one study or surveying a literature (see Figure 4.1). For a class assignment, you may be asked merely to describe a study from beginning to end. You may also be expected to offer a brief evaluation of its strengths and weaknesses. Your task is to find your way around the research article, to gain a general sense of the story it tells, and to offer some critical analysis. On other occasions, your purpose is to read and synthesize a range of articles (the literature review). Toward that end, your first reading has a specific purpose, in addition to learning the lay of the land in a research literature, such as (a) finding studies that all use the same method, (b) locating studies that uncover the same general finding, or (c) identifying studies that stem from the same theory (see Chapters 1 through 3 of this book for helpful suggestions on ways to find a research topic, use the library effectively, and conduct a literature search).

Finally, the formal review of a manuscript for consideration for publication is generally undertaken at the request of the journal's editor (or associate editor). The purpose of the review is ordinarily (a) to make a recommendation to the editor about whether the paper should be published in the journal and (b) to provide some commentary about your assessment of the article, judging its merits—ranging from theoretical contribution to the specifics of research design and statistical analysis (see also Chapter 24 of this book).

The Light Survey

Once you have identified your purpose and audience, you are ready to read. But here, we suggest again that you avoid the temptation to "Just Do It!" Start with a light survey.

Those who specialize in the study of reading and writing recommend that you begin reading a book with the preface and foreword. From these pages, one can learn what the authors intend, who their mentors and colleagues were, and in what tradition or stream of knowledge they place their work. Next, a survey of the chapter headings throughout the book can reveal the main themes and show how the author will proceed to develop them (Rheingold, 1994). Only then do you read the first chapter—*followed by the last!* Together, these steps in your survey will convey a fairly complete sense of the book as a whole. If your appetite is whetted, the first and last paragraphs of the intervening chapters will be next, along with a survey of the index, a rereading of the table of contents, and a careful reading of the middle of the book coming last, if at all (Rheingold, 1994). In just a few hours, you will have uncovered the main idea of the book, become familiar with the author's style, and placed the book in context. Most important, you will have gauged the relevance of the book to your purposes and interests in a progressive way; at each step, you could abort

Number of Articles

	One or a Few	Many
Informal (i.e., educational purposes— your goal is to learn; audience of classmates, an advisor, or colleague; often oral presentation or conversation)	*class assignment (e.g., oral report) *background reading	*literature review *meta-analysis
Formal (i.e., professional purposes— your goal is to assess or decide; audience of author(s), editor, and other reviewers; written)	*journal review	*you've just been named editor of the *Journal of Good Ideas and Good Research*

Figure 4.1. Your Purpose and Audience in Reading Research

your survey and move to your next learning task. This strategy is both efficient and effective.

You can easily export the same survey techniques to the reading of empirical research articles. The effective light survey does not always rigidly adhere to the time-honored flow from Introduction through Method and Results to Discussion. You will surely develop your own style, but an excellent place to start is the abstract. It acts like an "executive summary" for those without time or inclination to go further. It provides you with context and landmarks and even foreshadows specifics. The first paragraph of the introduction then provides more detailed background, and the first paragraph or two of the Discussion section then summarizes the findings and reveals how well the study met its goals. The specifics of the hypotheses (at the end of the introduction, usually) may be next, followed by a general scanning of the Results section and then a scanning of the Method section. Whatever your preferred order, your approach is likely to change to fit your specific purpose (e.g., literature review or formal review). Regardless of your purpose, however, we think a good trick (following the abstract) for a quick and effective survey is to read the first (usually, topic) sentence of every paragraph in the article, in order. Generally, this highly manageable task requires only a few minutes and conveys a remarkable amount of information about the article and a pretty clear sense of whether a more detailed reading will be profitable.

We urge you to try these strategies, and we think you will be impressed and pleased. For a start, you might locate a journal that includes "brief articles" (e.g., *Personality and Social Psychology Bulletin, Journal of Consulting and Clinical Psychology,* or *Health Psychology*). Try the first-sentence strategy a few times to see how much you can get with this small expenditure of time and effort. Then see how quickly you can locate the essential theory involved, the specific independent variable, or the general finding for several empirical articles. Finding your way around a research article in psychology this way is a quick and sure way to boost a newcomer's confidence.

Reviewing a Research Article

Here we turn to specific suggestions that can guide your in-depth review of an article, whether it is for an informal class project or to assess a manuscript under consideration for publication.

Generally speaking, when evaluating a manuscript, you ask of the author's work the very same questions that would guide you in conducting research and writing your own manuscript to report it (see Chapters 21 to 23 of this book). In a formal review of research, you have two purposes: (a) assessing the quality of content and making a recommendation about whether the research merits publication and (b) providing commentary to the author and the editor about strengths and shortcomings you perceive in the manuscript and advice about how it might be improved. A classroom assignment version of this task might be briefer and might be presented orally, and of course the author and editor would not be the audience. The fourth edition of the *Publication Manual* of the American Psychological Association (APA, 1994) provides a nice abstract ("executive summary") of the questions that make up this task, for whatever audience:

- Is the research question significant, and is the work original and important?
- Have the instruments been demonstrated to have satisfactory reliability and validity?
- Are the outcome measures clearly related to the variables with which the investigation is concerned?
- Does the research design fully and unambiguously test the hypothesis?
- Are the participants representative of the population to which generalizations are made?
- Did the researcher observe ethical standards in the treatment of participants—for example, if deception was used for humans?
- Is the research at an advanced enough stage to make the publication of results meaningful? (pp. 3-4)

However, the list of potential criteria is quite long. Gottfredson (1978) identified 83 attributes that editors and reviewers use in evaluating manuscripts; Lindsey (1978) narrowed the evaluation task to 12 dimensions. Perhaps it is no surprise, then, that statistical analyses of reviewers' agreement with one another show only a modest relationship (e.g., Fiske & Fogg, 1990).

REVIEWER AGREEMENT?

But saying that two reviewers do not agree does not imply that they disagree. Instead, analyses of reviewers' commentaries and recommendations show that they tend to write about different topics, each making points that are appropriate and accurate (Fiske & Fogg, 1990). Fiske and Fogg's (1990) search for statements about weaknesses in submitted manuscripts showed that across the reviews, the number of points cited ranged from 0 to 37. The mean number cited was 8.6. For your purposes, the mean number (fewer than 10) may be the most informative as you search for a model review as a prototype against which to match your own effort (see Appendix 4.1 at the end of this chapter). The range (none to many) is also revealing, however. It is important to note that editors are familiar with nonoverlap in commentaries; indeed, they expect it. Editors pick reviewers of different types (older, younger; expert, wise generalist; sympathetic, dispassionate, unsympathetic; etc.) and expect that they will emphasize different kinds of points.

Whether two reviewers agree that a paper should be published or do not agree, they may weight their reasons differently. A ground-breaking study on a novel question may have the potential for high impact but be flawed from a design or analysis perspective (Perlman & Dean, 1987), and the weighting of these two factors is to a great extent a reflection of the reader's values. The editor in turn must weigh the recommendations and commentary and apply his or her own cognitive gymnastics to the equation and conclusion. The process requires expert and balanced judgment, and editors are selected on that basis. You might be relieved to know that there rarely is just one "right answer" in reviewing; in reviewing, your job is not to get it right but to do the best job you can, be balanced, and bring your own skills and perspectives to bear on the task.

A typical rating form used by a "reviewer" in making a recommendation to an editor is shown in Table 4.1.

On a separate page, the reviewer ordinarily includes a commentary about facets of the manuscript that seem notable, whether positive or negative. These commentaries vary dramatically, depending on the nature of the manuscript and the type of the journal. However, one clear dimension that emerges in these critiques is that they range from broad to narrow. The narrow type is focused on methodological matters and statistical procedure—the "delicate instruments" dissection. The broad type deals more with the ideas at hand, the importance of the theory under study, how persuasive or compelling the hypothesis is, the excitement the work might generate, and the work's novelty. These two types of reviews are exemplified in starkly contrasting reviewers' commentaries in Appendix 4.1. Importantly, most real reviews of articles are a mix of narrow matters of procedure and broader matters of the theoretical importance, interest value, and judgments of the paper's likely impact.

PITFALLS FOR THE NOVICE REVIEWER

Interestingly, novice reviewers show three tendencies. First, they tend to be picky at times, noting shortcomings or outright mistakes—but ones that are not very consequential (see Review B, Appendix 4.1). This is a bit ironic because the novice is attempting delicate dissection. However, the art of dissection is distinguishing the benign from the malignant, and that requires experience. Second, novices tend to be overly critical at times. The newcomer to reviewing is more likely than the seasoned reader to zero in on deficiencies like a laser and to weight them heavily. More experienced evaluators know that all research is flawed, and they are usually predisposed to forgive the minor, inconsequential flaws and dwell only on the crucial. Finally, novice reviewers tend to write much longer, more detailed commentaries than do seasoned reviewers. Naturally, the more lengthy the commentary, the more helpful it might be to the editor and author who read and try to learn from it. But lack of confidence often leads novices to take a shotgun approach, hoping

TABLE 4.1 A Typical Evaluation Form for a Journal Reviewer

Journal of Good Ideas and Good Research

1) Overall Appraisal of the Manuscript (place a check mark):

_____ Accept

_____ Accept, with revisions as indicated

_____ Reject, with invitation to resubmit in revised form

_____ Reject, for reasons indicated in the enclosed critique

2) Confidential Appraisal of the Manuscript:

    A) On a scale of 1-10, with 10 representing excellence, how would you rate this paper with respect to:

        adequacy of the literature review   _____

        theoretical importance   _____

        adequacy of quantitative analysis   _____

        sophistication of methodology   _____

        clarity of communication   _____

        likelihood of being cited in future   _____

    B) Additional comments for the editor:

---

that some criticism will hit the target. When extreme, this approach, coupled with a tendency to be harsh and narrow, can lead to a laundry list of shortcomings that is more likely to hurt the author's feelings than to provide constructive criticism or to inform the editor.

One important goal of reviews of research is to be supportive of the author. The author's hard work in bringing the research and manuscript to completion should be commended. The author's risk in exposing his or her work to evaluation should be rewarded, not punished. Civility is a very important quality of any review for an author's consumption.

No research article is perfect. You need to be able to identify flaws when reviewing research articles; however, the key matter is to rest your evaluation on whether the flaws are consequential. If you have a firm understanding of the paper's main purpose, the conceptual questions the paper sets out to address, the methods used, the clarity of the conclusions, and the extent to which the conclusions follow from the findings, you are equipped to understand whether the paper's shortcomings are fatal flaws or garden-variety problems of little import. Conceptual shortcomings are the most fatal; if the research questions or theoretical assumptions are illogical or flawed, then even brilliant empirical realizations of variables may not matter. Flaws in the empirical aspects of research are fatal only to the degree they influence the paper's conclusions. Further, as we said above, it is every bit as important to search for and mention strengths as to search for shortcomings.

MORE DETAIL ON HOW TO EVALUATE
THE SECTIONS OF A RESEARCH PAPER

We now expand on the *Publication Manual* abstract by discussing in more detail how to evaluate each of the sections of a research paper: Introduction, Method, Results, and Discussion/Conclusions. It is important to note that we are both social psychologists, so some issues that we consider key may be less relevant to other domains of psychology. Take this into account. For each section, we list some important issues that you should consider, but keep in mind that each section should be assessed within the overall framework of the paper and its objectives. As we will say a number of times, it is the "big picture" that matters.

The Abstract and Introduction

Your concerns here are

- Objectives of the paper
- Importance of the research questions
- Research idea at the conceptual level

What You Are Assessing/How to Assess It. Read the abstract and introduction with the goal of understanding why the research was conducted. You are trying to get a sense of the "big picture." Ask yourself, "What is the goal of this research, this paper?" "What is the hypothesis?" "Is the question clearly presented?"

Consider the importance of the question asked. Is it significant? If answered, would it change how we think about human behavior? Also consider how the question relates to previous research. Does the researcher accurately and usefully convey past research in this area? Is the researcher familiar with past work, and is the description complete? Does the current work change or add to our theoretical understanding of the problem? Does it add to our general knowledge, and will it lead others to do more research in this area? After reading the review of previous research, think about what predictions you would make. Examining these predictions carefully will both help you assess the author's hypothesis and cause you to think about possible alternative explanations for the findings.

Pop Quiz. When you have finished reading the paper, you should be able to describe it and assess its importance in no more than two or three sentences. You should have an understanding of the conceptual logic of the paper. You should also be able to convey to someone whether the paper convincingly addressed the questions posed. Try this pop quiz on yourself at every opportunity. It is a test of your growing ability to move easily from the "receiver" to the "transmitter" mode.

The Method Section

Your concerns here are

- Internal validity
- Construct validity
- External validity

What You Are Assessing. When reading the Method section, once again keep the "big picture" in mind. Think about what ideas the author is trying to test at the conceptual level and what steps would be required to realize those ideas operationally. Have the researchers successfully translated their conceptual variables into concrete operations? By evaluating the methods carefully, you want to determine whether the research is valid (Aronson, Brewer, & Carlsmith, 1985; Aronson, Ellsworth, Carlsmith, & Gonzales, 1990; Cook & Campbell, 1979). You are considering whether it accomplishes the goals that it set out to reach. In particular, you are assessing three types of validity: internal, construct, and external (see Cook & Campbell, 1979, for a more detailed discussion of these three types of validity).

In assessing *internal validity,* you examine whether factors *other than the independent variables* could have caused the effects on the dependent measures. Are there elements in the procedure that accompanied the independent variables and therefore could have caused, or at least influenced, the results? Two major factors to consider when assessing a study's internal validity are whether participants were randomly assigned to conditions and whether the proper control or comparison groups were included in the experimental design.

If you believe an experiment has *construct validity,* then you judge that the researchers are actually testing the conceptual level of the hypothesis they pose. Have the researchers operationalized their hypotheses in a way that captures the concepts they were trying to study? Finally, if the research has *external validity,* the findings may be generalized to the populations and settings to which the experimenters wish them to apply. With external validity, the results have application to other people and situations.

In evaluating the methods used, you should always consider whether the researchers treated their participants ethically.

How to Assess It. First, consider the overall research design of the studies presented. What experimental groups did the researchers include, and are these adequate to test the research question? Were subjects randomly assigned to conditions? Are there appropriate control or comparison groups? You are examining here, on the basis of common sense and what is known about research design, whether this experiment allows the researchers to test their hypotheses without artifact or ambiguity.

Next, think about the experimental situation created in the study. Try on for size the perspective of the participants in the study. How would it feel to participate in this study? Does the procedure seem to make sense? Are participants apt to guess the hypotheses? If so, were checks on suspicion taken? Also, look at the experimental situation from the viewpoint of the experimenter. Were steps taken to control for biases? Were the experimenters kept blind to condition and so forth? In thinking about the experimental situation, keep in mind that problems or biases are important to the extent that they affect the validity of the study, including internal, construct, and external validity. That is, could these problems or biases, instead of the independent variables, have caused the effects measured and observed on the dependent variables of interest? Also, do various problems seem to influence whether the conceptual variables are realized in a meaningful way or whether the results can be generalized to other populations?

Next, to assess construct validity directly, examine the way that the experimenters realized their conceptual variables. How did the researchers operationalize the variables of their hypotheses? Do these operationalizations seem appropriate? Do you have enough information from the paper to understand how the variables were manipulated? Is there independent evidence (e.g., manipulation checks) that the operationalizations were reasonable? Do you believe that the manipulated variables accurately capture the phenomena of interest? Why or why not?

If you think that the operationalization is not reasonable, consider whether there are better ways to manipulate the variable; have the researchers captured the variables in the best way possible given current research? Keep in mind that researchers who are conducting exploratory studies on exciting new topics may have less of a basis for operationalizing their variables. The standards for assessment should necessarily be more stringent when researchers are using well-established paradigms than when they are using novel, home-cooked strategies.

Next, consider the dependent measures used. As with the manipulations, do you believe that these measures accurately capture the phenomena of interest? Why or why not? Are the measures reliable and valid?

Take into account the sample of the subjects. How large was the sample size (*N*)? What were the demographics (gender, race) of the sample? Are these demographics appropriate to this research? In asking these questions, you are considering whether the research has external validity: Do the results generalize to other situations? If so, what situations?

Finally, assess whether the researchers treated their participants ethically. For instance, if deception was used, were the participants debriefed? Did the researchers seem to take the perspective of their participants and treat them in a sensitive and ethical way?

The Results Section

Your concerns here are

- Statistical conclusion validity

What You Are Assessing/How to Assess It. In the Results section, you are assessing the statistical conclusion validity, or the validity of the conclusions that are drawn from the data (see Cook & Campbell, 1979). First, you should consider again the sample size of the study. Keep in mind that the number of participants in the study affects how easy it is to find a result (see Chapter 17 for a fuller discussion). With small samples it is difficult to find an effect, whereas with extremely large samples, it is much easier. Was the sample size adequately large for finding a result? Was it so large that a result, although statistically significant, might have little practical significance? By examining the size of the sample, you are considering whether the study was sensitive enough to detect a relationship between the independent and dependent variables.

Next, consider the statistical tests that were run on the sample. Are the analyses valid and appropriate? If possible, assess whether they meet the necessary statistical assumptions, and whether they use the appropriate error terms. If the statistical tests are inappropriate, then you should consider how they seem to affect the conclusions drawn from the data.

Finally, consider the results reported. Are the data clearly presented? Do the researchers seem to be ignoring parts of the data? Did they drop some subjects? If so, why? Is their rationale appropriate? If the rationale seems appropriate, the paper should still report what the results look like with dropped subjects included. How strong are the results—by both p values and absolute values (see Chapters 15, 16, and 17)? Are the measures reliable?

Pop Quiz. The Results section of a research article is often the most difficult to assess, particularly for a beginner. Have you said something in your formal review or class presentation that you could not support in a pop quiz? We have identified many things to note while reviewing this section of the paper, but where the matter we identify outstrips your base of knowledge and experience, you should seek more information for your review rather than doing a feeble (or downright incorrect) job of dealing with it. In a formal review, when you lack expertise or feel unqualified to address a matter, say so! Your observation can be judged in that light. If you are not sure about something, either acknowledge it or skip over it. You may miss an obvious or subtle point to make, but it is often better to make an error of omission than to step outside the bounds of your knowledge and experience and make an error of commission. Similarly, in a classroom presentation, there is wisdom in acknowledging your limitations before others strive to point them out first.

The Discussion/Conclusions Section

Your concerns here are

- Validity of conclusions

What You Are Assessing/How to Assess It. In the Discussion section, you are evaluating whether the researchers found significant results and are stating their results fairly. As with each section of the paper, assess the conclusions in terms of the "big picture." Given the objectives of the paper, the questions it set out to address, and the methods that were used, do the findings follow? Have the authors put their findings back into the theoretical framework with which they began? Did the authors consider alternative explanations for their data? How do the data fit with their theory? How do the data fit with conflicting data from other research? It is obviously best if the data uniquely fit the authors' theory. Have they discussed the limitations of their data, such as possible artifacts and problems?

Conclusion

If your goal is to be a psychologist, we recommend that you take every opportunity to try out and improve your research assessment skills. By becoming a better consumer of others' research, you will be better equipped to develop your own research topics. Our goal in this chapter was to provide you with a set of tools to use in reading, reviewing, and evaluating research. We hope that you apply these tools, expand on them, and eventually develop your own style or approach. As your critical skills expand and are refined, we think you will also see growth in your efforts as a theorist, methodologist, and author. In sum, becoming immersed in evaluating existing research on a topic helps set the stage to think critically about important new questions, and the critical skills associated with reading, reviewing, and evaluating research provide the foundation for designing and implementing one's own research ideas effectively.

Recommended Readings

We have cited in our references a few guides to the task of article reviewing (see Maher, 1978; Schwab, 1985). In one of these, Maher (1978), then editor of an important journal, offered a "reader's, writer's, and reviewer's guide to assessing research"; the title of his offering reminds us of our opening observation about the intimate link between learning to read about research and learning to write about it. In that vein, we also commend you to the *Publication Manual* of the APA (1994). It is almost as much a handbook for reviewers as for authors; your growth as an author will lead to commensurate, collateral growth in your critical skills in reviewing. In our experience, the causal arrow also points in the opposite direction. We also recommend your reading various books on evaluating research, including Aronson et al. (1990), Cook and Campbell (1979), and Campbell and Stanley (1966).

References

American Psychological Association. (1994). *Publication manual of the American Psychological Association* (4th ed.). Washington, DC: Author.

Aronson, E., Brewer, M., & Carlsmith, J. M. (1985). Experimentation in social psychology. In G. Lindzey & E. Aronson (Eds.), *The handbook of social psychology* (3rd ed., pp. 441-486). New York: Random House.

Aronson, E., Ellsworth, P. C., Carlsmith, J. M., & Gonzales, M. H. (1990). *Methods of research in social psychology* (2nd ed.). New York: McGraw-Hill.

Campbell, D. T., & Stanley, J. C. (1966). *Experimental and quasi-experimental designs for research*. Chicago: Rand McNally.

Cook, T. D., & Campbell, D. T. (1979). *Quasi-experimentation: Design and analysis issues for field settings*. Boston: Houghton Mifflin.

Fiske, D. W., & Fogg, L. (1990). But the reviewers are making different criticisms of my paper! Diversity and uniqueness in reviewer comments. *American Psychologist, 45,* 591-598.

Gottfredson, S. D. (1978). Evaluating psychological research reports: Dimensions, reliability, and correlates of quality judgments. *American Psychologist, 33,* 920-934.

Lindsey, D. (1978). *The scientific publication system in social science: A study of the operation of leading professional journals in psychology, sociology, and social work.* San Francisco: Jossey-Bass.

Maher, B. A. (1978). A reader's, writer's, and reviewer's guide to assessing research reports in clinical psychology. *Journal of Consulting and Clinical Psychology, 46,* 835-838.

Perlman, D., & Dean, E. (1987). The wisdom of Solomon: Avoiding bias in the publication review process. In D. N. Jackson & J. P. Rushton (Eds.), *Scientific excellence* (pp. 204-221). Newbury Park, CA: Sage.

Rheingold, H. (1994). *The psychologist's guide to an academic career.* Washington, DC: American Psychological Association.

Schwab, D. P. (1985). Reviewing empirically based manuscripts: Perspectives on process. In L. L. Cummings & P. J. Frost (Eds.), *Publishing in the organizational sciences* (pp. 171-181). Homewood, IL: Richard D. Irwin.

Squire, J. R. (1983). Composing and comprehending: Two sides of the same basic process. *Language Arts, 60,* 581-589.

Appendix 4.1

Sample Review Commentaries

This appendix presents two abbreviated, illustrative reviewer commentaries. Both commentaries are reviews of the same hypothetical manuscript, written by the hypothetical authors K. C. Oleson and R. M. Arkin.

The first review was written to illustrate a fairly balanced, useful review—one typical of those an editor would be pleased to receive. The second was written to exemplify a number of the pitfalls of the novice reviewer, the unmotivated or careless reviewer, or the nasty reviewer. Editors cringe when they receive these sorts of reviews, and some editors have the strength of character to hold them back from the author. Sometimes editors will seek additional reviewers' commentaries as substitutes or to offset such a poor or unhelpful review. In any event, publishers (including the American Psychological Association) instruct editors to take a point of view, indicating which reviewers' observations they agree with and which they do not. Most editors write decision letters to authors (whether acceptances or letters of rejection) that spell out some of their own views alongside summaries of the reviewers' collective wisdom.

We know that these two prototype reviews do not exhaust the list of attributes of a quality article review—or the unhelpful, picky, or negative review. They merely serve as examples to get you started on the path toward doing strong article reviews that reflect your own skills and style. Do not read them for content; instead, they are most useful if you speed-read them for format and style.

The following are a few notable qualities you can find in these two reviews:

A

1. The review begins with a useful summary of the study. The summary shows that the reviewer understands the study, and it helps the reviewer, editor, and author grasp the essence of what they are communicating about.
2. Next, the review assesses the manuscript's handling of general conceptual issues, discussing both its strengths and weaknesses. It focuses on alternative explanations for the data but suggests how they might be addressed.
3. The review then lays out smaller concerns, such as methodological issues that may have influenced the findings.
4. Finally, the review ends with a general evaluation of the manuscript, one that places the work in context.
5. Throughout, the reviewer makes a variety of constructive comments, including ways to improve the research design and to improve and clarify the dependent measures, and notes future research avenues to explore.
6. The review is critical, yet constructive, and balanced throughout.

B

Reviewer B's commentary reflects both errors of omission (i.e., it is missing most of the positive qualities we noted in Reviewer A's commentary) and many errors of commission. Review B is pretty nasty, narrow, and picky. The review is more of a laundry list of complaints than a constructive, supportive review. There are unsupported allegations (some of which might have been supportable, others not), and the reviewer seems to have extended the criticism well beyond his or her base of expertise.

Journal of Good Ideas and Good Research

Reviewer's Commentary

"Is There a Self-Serving Bias in Self-Attribution for Outcomes?";
    Kathryn C. Oleson & Robert M. Arkin

Ms. #96-777

Date: January 1, 1996

Reviewer A

This interesting research was designed to investigate whether there is a tendency for individuals to assume greater personal responsibility for successful than for failing outcomes, a phenomenon the authors say would reflect a "self-serving bias." The work reported here seems to be a reasonable and potentially important first step in systematically demonstrating this phenomenon, one that seems to have both theoretical and practical implications. The study involves two conditions: Participants learned that they had either succeeded (85th percentile) or failed (15th percentile) on a supposed "social sensitivity test" (feedback was "false"). Participants in the success condition were much more likely to attribute the outcome to themselves (their ability and effort) than was the case for participants who failed. Failing participants were much more likely to cite task difficulty and bad luck in explaining the outcome than were successful participants.

This one study seems like a useful first demonstration of this "self-serving bias" phenomenon; however, the one study alone does little to pin down the precise process underlying this result. Consequently, although this intriguing demonstration of the difference in self-attribution for success and failure outcomes may be heuristic and novel enough to justify publication, it was disappointing that this initial finding was not taken further into the realm of examining the psychological processes involved. A couple of points stem from this concern.

First, the present finding does not clarify the directionality: Is the result due to heightened responsibility for success, lessened responsibility for failure, or both? Without a neutral or control group, the precise source of the phenomenon is unclear. The control group might reflect either "moderate success" (say, 60%) or no information about outcome at all—or both groups could be included.

The absence of this control condition is linked with a theoretical issue that bothered me as well. Although the authors' "motivational" (i.e., "self-serving") explanation of the attributional difference is plausible, there may be other explanations equally plausible. For instance, success typically covaries with one's effort—and with one's ability—and it could be that participants merely based their guesses about the causes of success on this typical covariation (or on actual covariation they perceived in this experimental setting); this would be more of an information-processing interpretation of this finding than a motivationally based interpretation. Kelley and others have written a good deal on this covariation idea, and there is good research by Cunningham on the point. Second, could it be that the subjects in this study—who were closely observed—were merely presenting themselves favorably (and did not, in their private perceptions, believe what they were portraying in their questionnaire responses)? There are other, related alternative interpretations too. I think this initial demonstration of the "self-serving bias" would be much, much stronger if this sort of "process" evidence was provided and if the interpretation of the findings was clearer and more compelling. The present study has more of a "preliminary investigation" feeling to it than is desirable.

In addition to these general concerns, I have three smallish concerns to raise:

1. It seems problematic that the attribution measure is anchored on one scale, ranging from self-attribution to task-attribution. This strategy clouds whether the result might be mostly or solely in the self-attribution domain or in the task-attribution domain (but not both). In the future, I'd separate these into two separate scales to find out.

2. The experimenter's delivery of the false feedback worried me for two reasons. First, the experimenter was not kept blind to the induction, and the description (requiring lots of good acting ability) presented plenty of opportunity for experimenter bias. Second, it was difficult to tell from the manuscript if subjects were fully, sensitively, and carefully debriefed; this raised ethical concerns for me.

3. The Discussion section could be trimmed a bit. It rambles in places, and several opportunities to foreshadow applications of this work and its implications were overlooked. These could be included, and in even less space. Some of the implications are as follows: (a) Could interpersonal conflict result from the self-serving bias, as when a small group of people might divide credit for a collective success (or blame for a collective failure)? (b) Is the effect qualified by any motive for "modesty" that prevails in our culture? Would participants still engage in a self-serving bias if modesty were at a premium? (c) Are there individual differences in self-serving bias tendencies, and could these help explain things like dysphoria, moodiness, unhappiness?

Conclusion

In general, I think the logic of the work is well thought out and presented. The research is truly groundbreaking in certain ways; there isn't anything published on this topic—at least so far as I am aware. I think the researchers captured the key conceptual elements in their paradigm. Overall, then, I am inclined to lean toward recommending publication of the paper. At the same time, I really wish the authors had conducted replication work to include the crucial sort of control conditions I described and the distinguishing of the dependent measures too. With those two additions, this work would constitute a fine contribution to the literature.

Journal of Good Ideas and Good Research

Reviewer's Commentary

"Is There a Self-Serving Bias in Self-Attribution for Outcomes?";
  Kathryn C. Oleson & Robert M. Arkin

Ms. #96-777

Date: January 1, 1996

Reviewer B

This research seems to be inherently flawed. The authors start out with a fairly obvious idea—one derived from little more than common sense—people take more responsibility for success than they do for failure—and then the authors fail to shed a whole lot of light on it.

As I read the manuscript, I had a number of specific problems I found in it and in the research it reports:

1. The number of subjects is too small. They need to have a larger sample size.
2. There are a number of typos, two on one page!
3. The statistics used (a *t* test to compare the two conditions) are inappropriate for the comparison. They should be more careful about their use of statistics.
4. They did not include all necessary control groups. I can't believe they didn't include a control condition in which no feedback was included or in which a moderate level of success was described. We learn nothing from this one finding without that.
5. The experimental protocol or paradigm seems flawed. Scoring at the 15% seems so low; did subjects even believe that? I wouldn't; I think that the failure should have been higher, and more plausible—maybe at 40% or something.
6. The authors did not consider alternate explanations for their findings. What is the precise mechanism behind the effect? Does it have to be a "self-serving bias"?
7. Manuscript needs to be much shorter in length.
8. The research does not seem to be that rigorous. I suppose two conditions in a study might be elegant in some ways, but this much simplicity seems more like "simple" than simplicity.
9. The authors did not seem to know about other studies that have already been conducted on this topic, and although I can't think of them just now, I know there are some.
10. The measures used seemed invalid.
11. The authors did not counterbalance the different ratings that they had subjects make, and I have this nagging feeling that they haven't reported all their findings.

I don't think there is a contribution of any scope or magnitude here. I don't think there is much merit in the whole area of motivation anyway. This paper really doesn't qualify as cognitive social psychology, and that is clearly where the field is going. So the research here seems more old-fashioned than anything. I can't see publishing the paper, and I don't think very many readers would be interested in reading it. There aren't even any applied questions raised, and the theoretical implications seem uninteresting.

PART II

Design, Instrument Selection, and Sampling

Chapter 5

Designing a Research Study

BRUCE E. WAMPOLD

As you approach the automobile dealer to buy the automobile of your dreams, the reality occurs that any car you purchase will not meet all of your criteria. These criteria might involve reliability, utility, comfort, price, resale value, and visual appeal—clearly there are trade-offs. You might want a Volvo but not be able to afford it. Moreover, you might want an automobile that you realize would not satisfy others (e.g., your partner). Even after deciding to purchase a certain make and model, you will probably modify it by choosing various options and then make further additions by purchasing floor mats, trash receptacles, and so forth. Even the most sophisticated buyer will occasionally be disappointed, perhaps because he or she weighted criteria suboptimally or because of chance factors (the particular automobile had an unknown defect). Moreover, during the period of ownership, events occur that frequently alter your satisfaction with the automobile: Newer models have features that were not obtainable with the present model, your needs and attitudes toward automobiles change, and the automobile deteriorates.

Designing a study and purchasing an automobile have many similarities. To select an appropriate design, one should have (a) the specific purpose that the design should accomplish, (b) criteria for deciding whether the design has a high probability of accomplishing that purpose, and (c) knowledge of the logic of the design so that the design can be modified to accomplish the goal optimally and to avoid problems. Just as there is no perfect automobile, there is no perfect study, and choice of a particular design involves trade-offs of known factors; moreover, unexpected events will occur that will demand modification of the design and perhaps termination of the study and design of a different study. Some studies will become classics; others will be forgotten—the Dodge Darts of psychological research.

This chapter will outline the general considerations involved in designing a psychological study. Knowing the rules of research and applying them to one's area of interest will not lead linearly to the optimal design; designing research is a creative process. Ingenuity often is needed to find a parsimonious way to discover truths about behavior.

Purpose of the Study

The overarching guiding principle in designing a research study is to ensure that the study addresses the purpose of the research. In generic terms, the purpose of research is to discover knowledge: that is, to know something that was previously unknown. Research cannot be adequately designed unless the purpose of the research is carefully thought out and well stated.

In the received view of science, research is conducted to refine or reject extant theories or to develop new theories. The relation between theory and empirical research is complex and deeply embedded in philosophy of science. Nevertheless, a synopsis of this relation will be useful to understand how the design of a research study should be tied to theoretical propositions. One conception of a theory is that it is a general statement specifying the relations among psychological constructs. To conduct research that provides information about this theory, it is necessary to examine various implications of the theory. That is, if theory adequately explains the true situation, then it can be predicted that some event or series of events should occur in a specified context. For example, if depression is caused by a lack of reinforcers in the environment, then increasing these reinforcers should decrease depression of depressed people. Research is focused when this implication is stated as a specific prediction, known as a *research hypothesis*. Research is then designed such that an experimental result will fall into one of two categories: (a) The experimental result is consistent with the prediction, or (b) the experimental result is inconsistent with the prediction.

If the experimental result is consistent with the prediction, our faith in the theory that germinated the prediction is increased. On the other hand, if the experimental result is inconsistent with the prediction, then the theory is suspect. However carefully the research is designed, there will be flaws, and conclusions about theory should be made conservatively. Theories should be revised, rejected, or developed only when the research evidence is strong.

Knowledge accumulates by repeated studies. Every study that has investigated the connection between smoking behavior of humans and health was flawed, although the conclusion that smoking causes physical disease is inescapable given the totality of the results. The problems with one study were corrected in other studies, although these latter studies also had problems. No study is perfect, but the consistent accumulation of conclusions tends to rule out competing points of view.

It should be clear that the faith one places in the conclusions made from a study is related to the quality of the study. Consequently, to design a good study, one must be cognizant of the problems that can occur. *Validity* is the general descriptor that is used to discuss the "goodness" of research. If the validity of the study is high, one places faith in the conclusions made from the study and will consider carefully the implications for theory. On the other hand, if the validity is low, then the conclusions are meaningless, and it would be foolish to adjust theory in any way. Validity is often discussed in terms of threats. Threats are possible explanations for a particular experimental result other than the one intended by the researcher. A valid study is one in which threats are few and minor.

Finding a research topic (Leong & Pfaltzgraff, Chapter 1), using the library effectively to understand the literature in an area (Reed & Baxter, Chapter 2), systematically conducting the literature search (Stockdale & Kenny, Chapter 3), reviewing individual research articles (Oleson & Arkin, Chapter 4), and applying theory to research (Gelso, Chapter 29) are discussed elsewhere in this volume.

The following sections will discuss (a) steps in designing a study and drawing inferences from the research, (b) types of research design, and (c) a taxonomy of validities and the threats to these validities.

Design and Inference Steps

There are many stages of research, and critical inferences are made in each. Consider the following process of hypothesis testing. The first step is to develop a research hypothesis that reflects an implication of theory. Suppose one has a theory that the stability of personality is caused, in part, by the selection of environments that are compatible with personality. One implication of this theory would be that extraverts choose activities that allow them to interact with others, whereas introverts choose solitary activities.

A research hypothesis is a specific prediction about how two or more constructs will be related. A hypothesis is of the general form: Under specific conditions, a phenomenon will be expected to occur. Development of the research hypothesis, in the minds of many, is the most creative and the most difficult step in research. Certainly, knowledge of the substance area is a prerequisite for developing a hypothesis. Some hypotheses will be developed to extend knowledge in a small and deliberate way; others will bring together disparate areas to influence the field profoundly by changing its direction (Platt, 1964). "Examining crucial hypotheses leads to the extension of knowledge, the winnowing of theories, the clarification of discrepancies, the identification of active ingredients of treatments, and so on, [whereas] inconsequential research hypotheses . . . do not produce resolution because they do not lead to a convergence of knowledge" (Wampold, Davis, & Good, 1990, p. 362).

In the second step, operations are chosen to represent the constructs referenced in the hypothesis. In the example of extraversion/introversion and choice of environments involving various degrees of social interaction, extraversion/introversion and the environmental choice must be operationalized to conduct the research. One might choose to use a paper-and-pencil test to measure extraversion/introversion (see Ponterotto, Chapter 6 of this volume, for a discussion of selecting instruments). Socialization in the environment could be designed into the experiment by having two activities that are similar in all respects other than degree of socialization and then giving the participants their choice of activities. For example, participants in the research might be led to believe that their problem-solving ability is being judged and then be given a choice of participating in a group that solves the problem or being able to solve the problem by themselves. The choice of solitary or group problem solving is then an operation intended to reflect choice of environments.

Third, the study is designed so that the covariation of the operations can be examined. That is, are the scores yielded by the operations of the constructs referenced in the hypothesis related in a systematic way? In the continuing example, one might test the extraversion/introversion of participants and then give them a choice of problem-solving situations; in that way, one could determine whether participants who scored high on extraversion would be more likely to choose group problem-solving situations than would participants who scored high on introversion. That is, the researcher designs the study so that the covariation of measured variables can be examined. In an experimental study, the independent variables are manipulated so that the effect on the dependent variable can be observed.

Fourth, it is determined whether or not the measured variables do indeed covary as expected. That is, one examines the results to determine whether the results reflect the predictions. This examination is usually accomplished by applying a statistical test. Figure 5.1 reflects the general procedure of designing a study.

Having designed and conducted the study, the investigator reverses the direction of the sequence described above, making inferences along the way. Figure 5.1 illustrates how inferences are made from the statistical tests back up to theory. The measured variables do indeed covary; the independent variable was the cause of the concomitant covariation in the dependent variable; the independent variable and the dependent variable accurately reflect the constructs of interest; the results apply to various persons, settings, and times; and the results have implications for theory and/or practice.

Before explicating validity of research, this chapter discusses various types of research designs. Although there are many variations on the theme of research designs, a useful way to conceptualize research designs is to classify them as passive, experimental, or quasi-experimental.

Types of Research Designs

PASSIVE DESIGNS

Passive designs are designs in which the researcher examines the covariation of variables without manipulating some aspect of the study. Generally, there are two types of passive designs: correlational and between-group designs. As shown in Figure 5.2, the correlational design involves selecting a random sample from a population, measuring two variables on each subject, calculating the correlation coefficient r_{AB}, and then testing whether the true (i.e., the population) correlation between these two variables is zero (H_0: $\rho_{AB} = 0$; see Yaffee and Dickter & Roznowski, Chapters 15 and 16 of this volume, for a discussion of the logic of statistical tests). For example, a researcher may wish to know whether depression and anxiety covary in the general population. A random sample of subjects is drawn from a population, the levels of depression and anxiety are measured (perhaps with depression and anxiety inventories), and the correlation of the measured levels of depression and anxiety is calculated and tested. If the sample correlation is sufficiently large, the null hypothesis of a zero population correlation is rejected, and it is concluded that anxiety and depression covary in the population. Because this is a passive design, it is not possible to make causal statements from the design: Depression might cause anxiety, anxiety might cause depression, or each might be caused by a third construct.

The between-groups passive design involves taking random samples from two populations, as shown in Figure 5.2. The goal is to determine whether the true (i.e.,

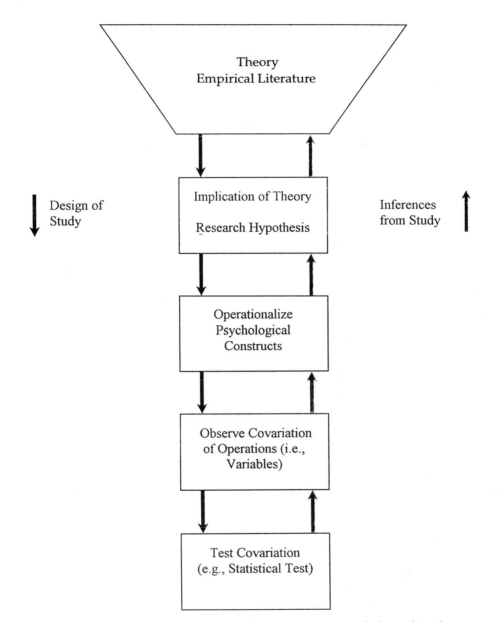

Figure 5.1. Steps to Designing and Making Inferences From a Psychological Study

population) means of two (or more) populations are the same. The sample means M_A and M_B are calculated, and if these sample means are sufficiently different, the null hypothesis that the population means are equal (i.e., H_0: $\mu_A = \mu_B$) is rejected (probably with the use of a t test for two groups or an analysis of variance for three or more groups). One can then make the conclusions that the populations means differ. For example, one might want to

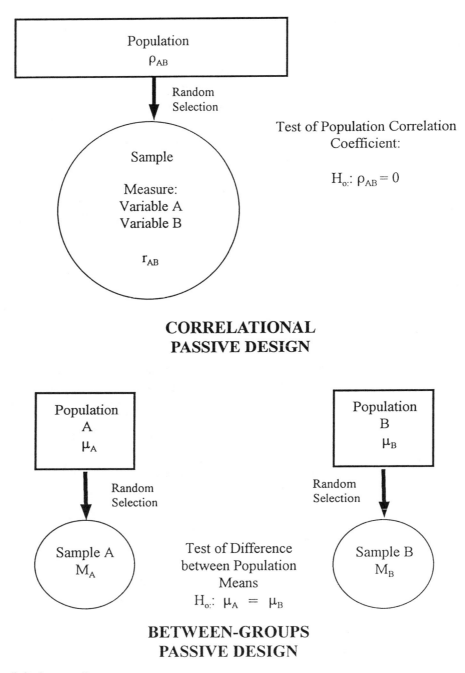

Figure 5.2. Passive Designs

test whether the ability of males and females to decode emotional expression differs. Again, because this is a passive design, no causal statements can be made; any differences found may be due to socialization, biological differences, or motivation.

EXPERIMENTAL DESIGN

In an experimental design, the researcher manipulates some variable so that the comparison between groups yields a causal statement about the manipulated variable. The goal of the experimental design is to create conditions (variously called *groups, treatments,* or *levels*) such that the conditions differ in only one aspect, the aspect intended by the researcher. This manipulated variable is called the *independent variable.* Figure 5.3 presents the simplest two-group experimental design. Subjects are randomly selected from a population and then randomly assigned to two conditions, A and B. In this way, any differences between the two conditions are due to chance. Then the researcher has the subjects in Condition A and Condition B do something that creates differences in these two conditions in the way planned by the researcher. Next, the subjects are assessed on the relevant variable, which is called the *dependent variable,* and sample means are calculated (M_A and M_B); if the sample means are sufficiently different, then the null hypothesis of no population differences (i.e., $H_0: \mu_A = \mu_B$) is rejected, and it is concluded that the manipulation was the cause of the differences. For example, to examine the effect of evaluation on performance, a study might be designed in which the subjects in Condition A are led to believe that their performance on some task will be evaluated by the research team, whereas the subjects in Condition B are led to believe that their performance will be aggregated by computer and that the research team will not be knowledgeable of individual performance. Ideally, the conditions differ only with respect to the belief by subjects that their performance is being evaluated by psychologists or not; in this way, differences in performance (the dependent variable) can be attributed to the effect of evaluation.

There are many variations on the experimental design theme. Of course, more than two conditions could be included (e.g., public evaluation, private evaluation, and no evaluation). The researcher might also want to include two independent variables, each with two or more levels. In the performance example, the researcher might want to make the difficulty of the task an independent variable (e.g., two groups, easy and difficult). Repeated designs, in which subjects are assessed on more than one condition of an independent variable, are often used. For example, the subjects in the performance experiment may complete both the easy and difficult task.

It is useful to emphasize the difference between passive and experimental designs. The key difference between the designs is that in the experimental design, the researcher determines the conditions, and the groups differ only in the intended way. Passive and experimental designs may involve testing exactly the same statistical hypothesis (e.g., $H_0: \mu_A = \mu_B$) and use the same statistical test (e.g., t test), but the logic is fundamentally different. To make matters more confusing, designs may have experimental as well as passive aspects: For example, the performance experiment might contain a nonexperimental variable, such as gender.

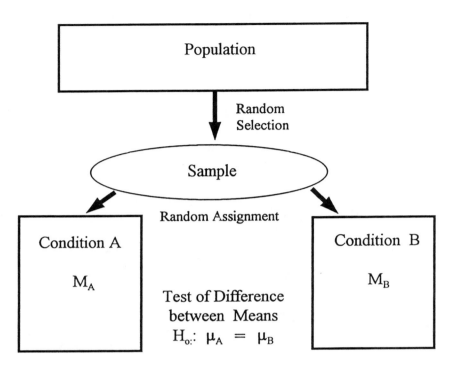

Figure 5.3. Experimental Designs

QUASI-EXPERIMENTAL DESIGNS

Often true experimental designs are difficult to conduct because of ethical or practical constraints or because one wants to conduct research in the field to get a better approximation of the "real world." Any design that approximates an experimental design is called a *quasi-experimental design*. Technically, any design that has one or more threats to validity (as described in the next section) is a quasi-experimental design. Sometimes when one attempts to design an experimental design, various threats to validity creep in, creating a quasi-experimental design. In other instances, one cannot design an experimental design, and one therefore deliberately designs a quasi-experimental design. In either case, the logic of the design is good enough so that one can have reasonably good faith in the conclusions. Campbell and Stanley (1966) were the first to discuss the concept of quasi-experimentation and to describe such designs; Cook and Campbell (1979) discussed these issues further in the context of conducting field research.

Validity of Research

In the research process, the inferences made at each step may or may not be proper. If the validity of the study is high, then there are few rival interpretations, and these are relatively implausible; if the validity is low, there are many alternative and veridical explanations for an obtained result. The overall conclusion of a study is whether the inferences lead to support for the hypothesis (i.e., the obtained pattern of results is consistent with the prediction of the research hypothesis) or whether the hypothesis is not supported (i.e., the obtained pattern of results is not consistent with the prediction of the hypothesis). If validity is high, one places faith in the inferences and the resulting conclusion about the hypothesis. Given high validity, the conclusion about the hypothesis can be used to revise, reject, or develop theoretical propositions.

The seminal work of Campbell and Stanley (1966) explicated two types of validity, internal and external. Bracht and Glass (1968) expanded on the external validity concept. Concerned about drawing inferences in field settings, Cook and Campbell later (1979) divided both internal validity and external validity, yielding four types: statistical conclusion validity, internal validity, construct validity of putative causes and effects, and external validity. Recently, Wampold et al. (1990) expanded the concept of validity by considering the theoretical context of research and proposed threats to hypothesis validity. A brief description of each type of validity follows.

STATISTICAL CONCLUSION VALIDITY

The first inference typically made in a study is whether the variables in a study truly covary. Typically, statistical tests are used to make this inference. When statistical tests are employed, the null hypothesis is that there is no relationship between (or among) variables in the population. When the null hypothesis is rejected, the decision is made that in the relevant population, the two variables covary. For example, in a randomized-treatment design, in which subjects are randomly assigned to a treatment condition and to a control group, a statistically significant t test indicates that scores on the dependent variable covaried with the manipulation to the extent that it was unlikely that the obtained result would have occurred by chance had there been no true population relationship. In a design in which conditions are not manipulated by the researcher, one might want to examine the relationship between two variables, such as the Graduate Record Examination (GRE) Quantitative subtest and grades in statistics classes. In this instance, a statistically significant Pearson correlation coefficient would indicate that the observed linear relationship between GRE scores and grades in statistics was sufficiently large for one to conclude that it did not occur by chance and thus that there was a true linear relation between these two variables.

Statistical inferences are based on probabilities, so one is never sure whether they are true. Type I error involves deciding that variables are related (i.e., rejecting the null hypothesis of no relationship) when in fact there is no true relationship. Type II error involves deciding that there is no relationship (i.e., variables do not covary) when in fact there is a relationship. Alpha, the probability of making a Type I error, and beta, the probability of making a Type II error, are indicators of statistical conclusion validity. If a study is designed so that alpha equals .05, then there are fewer than 5 chances out of 100 that the investigator has made an incorrect inference by concluding that the variables covary. Yaffee (Chapter 15 of this volume) discusses the logic of statistical testing in more detail.

Threats to statistical conclusion validities are conditions that inflate the error rates. For example, if the assumptions of a statistical test are violated, the chances of falsely concluding that variables covary may be much greater than the nominal alpha set by the investigator. Similarly, if power is low, the probability of falsely concluding that there is no covariation is high. Threats to statistical conclusion validity include low statistical power, violated assumptions of statistical tests, fishing and error-rate problems, unreliability of measures, unreliability of treatment implementation, random irrelevancies in the experimental setting, and random heterogeneity of respondents (Cook & Campbell, 1979).

Statistical conclusion validity applies to inferences about covariation whether or not inferential statistics per se are used. For example, single-subject designs often are used to establish the functional relation between an intervention and behavior (Barlow & Hersen, 1984). Essentially, *functional relation* means that the independent variable (baseline vs. intervention) covaries with the dependent variable (typically some behavior). In this context, Type I and Type II errors continue to exist: For example, one might falsely conclude that there is a true functional relation.

INTERNAL VALIDITY

After it has been determined that two variables covary (or do not covary), a causal attribution typically is made. For example, in an experimental design, when the manipulation of the independent variable results in a concomitant change in the dependent variable, the treatment is said to be the cause of the change. However, the causal inference may be incorrect. For example, the participants who were not benefiting from treatment may have dropped out of the treatment group, raising the mean for this group; mortality (i.e., participants dropping out of the study) is then an alternative explanation for the results. *Internal validity* refers to the degree to which an attribution of causality for a given relationship between variables is correct.

Internal validity is highest when subjects are randomly assigned to conditions, the conditions differ on only one dimension, and all treatments and assessments are given to the groups simultaneously. However, even under the best conditions (e.g., laboratory studies), threats to internal validity creep in. Nonrandomization presents special problems in that groups may not be comparable before the treatments are administered. Designs in which variables are not manipulated by the researcher (i.e., passive designs) present special challenges to causal inferences. For example, studies that have examined the causal link between smoking and health have been unable to assign participants randomly to a smoking and to a nonsmoking condition. Critics of the early smoking studies made the point that the poorer health of smokers may be due to factors other than smoking, such as general health behavior (e.g., smokers participate in riskier behavior), genetic predispositions (i.e., some people are predisposed to smoking and to poor health), diet, and so forth. Each of these alternative explanations presents threats to internal validity because the subjects were not randomly assigned to conditions and consequently selection of subjects may have resulted in systematic differences between the smoking and nonsmoking conditions other than smoking.

In any context in which causation is attributed, the trick is to rule out as many threats to internal validity as possible. An important aspect of internal validity is that it is related to the design of the study and not to the statistical procedure used (Cohen, 1968). For example, a regression analysis can be used just as well to analyze the data from a purely experimental design as to analyze the data from a passive design (Cohen, 1968; Cohen & Cohen, 1983; Kerlinger, 1985).

As discussed previously, studies in which subjects are not randomly assigned to conditions present special problems in causality. There is a saying that "correlation does not mean causation." A simple correlation coefficient indexes the degree of linear relationship between two variables but does not identify which is the cause of the other. Suppose it is found that scores on a depression inventory and scores of a test of social perception are related such that relatively depressed people tend to perceive falsely that people do not like them at a higher rate than nondepressed people. Does the depression cause the misperceptions, or do the misperceptions cause the depression, or does a third variable (e.g., a variable related to brain chemistry) cause both? In recent years, statistical methods have been developed to test various causal models from correlational data (e.g., structural equation modeling, Jöreskog & Sörbom, 1988; see Levy & Steelman, Chapter 17 of this volume, for a more complete discussion of using advanced statistical tests). Nevertheless, the most direct means to attribute causality is to manipulate a variable experimentally.

Threats to internal validity include history, maturation, testing, instrumentation, statistical regression, selection, mortality, interaction with selection, ambiguity about the direction of causal influence, diffusion or imitation of treatments, compensatory equalization of treatments, compensatory rivalry by subjects receiving less desirable treatments, and resentful demoralization of subjects receiving less desirable treatments (Cook & Campbell, 1979).

CONSTRUCT VALIDITY OF PUTATIVE CAUSES AND EFFECTS

Presumably, the measured variables in a study are reflective of psychological constructs. When Measured Variable X is thought to be the cause of Measured Variable Y, one wants to infer that the construct operationalized by X is the cause of the construct operationalized by Y. *Construct validity* means that all variables in a study, including the independent and dependent variables in an experimental study, reflect the theoretical constructs described in the theory and referenced in the hypotheses.

With regard to the independent variable, the experimental manipulation needs to indicate some construct. Suppose a social psychologist believes that people will be more likely to self-disclose to close friends than to strangers. The task for this researcher is to design conditions of the manipulated variable so that they differ on the object of the disclosure (friend vs. stranger) and on no other dimension. Clearly, it would be improper if the friends were female and the strangers were male because any differences between the conditions could be attributed to gender as easily as to closeness (friend vs. stranger). Other improper operationalizations may be more subtle. Suppose the researcher used pictures of persons who were either friends or strangers; it would then be vital to ensure that the pictures were matched on all attributes other than closeness, such as ethnicity, personal attractiveness, and age.

The dependent variable should also operationalize a construct. If a treatment is intended to affect depression, then any measures of the dependent variable used should reflect depression and not some other construct, such as social desirability. Betz (Chapter 19 of this volume) discusses how to construct tests to measure constructs, and Ponterotto (Chapter 6 of this volume) discusses how to evaluate and select the proper instruments to operationalize a construct.

When it is not clear whether the variable or variables in a study reflect one construct or another construct, a *confound* is said to exist. Explicitly, a confound is an alternative construct that cannot be logically or statistically differentiated from a hypothesized construct. In the self-disclosure study, if all friends were females and all strangers were male, then a complete confound would exist between gender and friend/stranger. If an instrument intended to measure depression actually measures, to some degree, social desirability, then depression and social desirability are confounded.

Often variables related to characteristics of people are naturally confounded. For example, in U.S. society, ethnicity is correlated with socioeconomic status (SES), and therefore attributions about ethnicity may more appropriately be made about SES. Sorting out naturally occurring confounds is problematic but can often be partially accomplished with statistical methods (see, e.g., Cohen & Cohen, 1983).

The threats to construct validity include inadequate preoperationalization of constructs, mono-operation bias, mono-method bias, hypothesis guessing within experimental conditions, evaluation apprehension, experimenter expectancies, confounding constructs and levels of constructs, interaction of different treatments, interaction of testing and treatment, and restricted generalization across constructs (Cook & Campbell, 1979).

EXTERNAL VALIDITY

Cook and Campbell (1979) focused their discussion on generalizability across types of persons, settings, and times. The central question in external validity is the degree to which the conclusions from a study apply equally to subsets of persons, settings, and times. Most often, it is generalizability across types of people that is most interesting. A recent study linking strenuous weekly exercise with reduced risk of cardiovascular disease was conducted on males only, leaving the important issue of whether this result generalized to females unanswered (and unanswerable). Inclusion of males and females in the study would have allowed the researchers to determine whether strenuous exercise was equally potent prophylactically for males and females. To determine whether a conclusion is equally applicable to subpopulations, the subpopulation must be a part of the design. Populations can be handled as a factor in a factorial design; interaction effects of the population factor with some other factor is evidence that the results vary as a function of the type of person. For example, the exercise study could be redesigned to include gender as a factor by comparing four groups: males undertaking strenuous exercise, males not undertaking strenuous exercise, females undertaking strenuous exercise, and females not undertaking strenuous exercise. An interaction between gender and exercise on the incidence of cardiovascular disease would indicate that exercise was not equally beneficial to males and females.

Possible choices for characteristics to examine vis-à-vis subpopulations are virtually unlimited. Important characteristics, from a policy or social perspective, include gender, ethnicity, SES, and age. Often there are theoretical or empirical reasons for examination of generalizability across various subpopulations. See McCready (Chapter 8 of this volume) for a more complete discussion of sampling issues and generalizability.

HYPOTHESIS VALIDITY

Wampold et al. (1990), concerned about the relation of method to theory, discussed hypothesis validity. *Hypothesis validity* refers to the extent to which results elucidate theoretically derived predictions about the relations between or among constructs. Hypothesis validity involves three criteria. First, the research hypotheses, which are statements about presumed relations among constructs, should be crucial to extending knowledge. This is the "who cares?" factor. Research may be beautifully designed and conducted, but unless it has important implications for psychology, few will be interested in the results.

Second, to have adequate hypothesis validity, the research hypothesis should be stated unambiguously and in a form that is falsifiable. If the hypothesis is ambiguous, it will be impossible to determine whether the obtained results are consistent with the hypothesis. Statements such as "The purpose of the present study is to explore the relation between . . ." lead to inferential problems because there are no predictions against which to compare the obtained results. Any study that examines the relationship among a set of two or more variables will inevitably "discover" a pattern of results, but this discovery cannot be used to support or reject a theoretical proposition because none was offered (Wampold et al., 1990).

Third, hypothesis validity involves a close association between research hypotheses and statistical hypotheses. Research hypotheses are stated in terms of relations among constructs, these constructs are then operationalized as observed variables, and the scores produced by these variables are statistically tested. Underlying each statistical test is a statistical hypothesis. Rejection of the statistical hypothesis should be informative relative to the research hypothesis. Problems occur when multiple statistical tests are used to verify a single research hypothesis because some of those statistical tests will probably be statistically significant and some will not. Is this evidence for or against the research hypothesis? Ideally, one statistical test will be focused on one research hypothesis (see Rosnow & Rosenthal, 1988).

Conclusions

In this chapter, the general considerations for designing a study were discussed. However carefully one designs a study, there will be threats to validity, just as there is no ideal automobile that can satisfy all one's dreams. Certainly, there are practical constraints, particularly in terms of researcher time, resources, availability of participants, and ethical considerations. We may all desire a Ferrari or a Rolls-Royce, but we need to settle for Toyota or Ford. The important question is, "Will the design get the job done?" If the design is adequate, the conclusion made will be believable (i.e., validity will be reasonably good), although there will be various threats that cannot be ruled out. Future research is always needed to continue the quest for the understanding of behavior.

Recommended Readings

There are many, many sources of information about research design and related topics, and the graduate student should seek advice from his or her advisor and methods instructors. Kerlinger (1985) presented a comprehensive overview of behavioral research that provides an excellent introduction to the many facets of research in the social sciences. Kirk (1982) presented well the variants of the experimental design theme as well as the statistical tests of each variation. For discussion of field research, Cook and Campbell (1979) discussed the many issues of conducting research outside of the laboratory. Keren and Lewis (1993) edited a volume that examined many of the current issues in behavioral research and quantitative methods inherent in such research. For qualitative research, which was not discussed in this chapter, see Highlen and Finley (Chapter 14 of this volume); Denzin and Lincoln (1994) have edited a collection of methods related to the qualitative paradigm. Methods applicable to specialized areas are discussed by metrologists in various subspecialties, such as counseling (Heppner, Kivlighan, & Wampold, 1992) and clinical psychology (Kazdin, 1992). Researchers are advised to acquire specific knowledge of designs most applicable to their area of interest.

References

Barlow, D. H., & Hersen, N. (1984). *Single case experimental designs: Strategies for studying behavior change.* New York: Pergamon.

Bracht, G. H., & Glass, G. V. (1968). The external validity of experiments. *American Educational Research Journal, 5,* 437-474.

Campbell, D. T., & Stanley, J. C. (1966). *Experimental and quasi-experimental designs for research.* Chicago: Rand McNally.

Cohen, J. (1968). Multiple regression as a general data-analytic strategy. *Psychological Bulletin, 70,* 426-443.

Cohen, J., & Cohen, P. (1983). *Applied multiple regression/correlation analysis for the behavior sciences* (2nd ed.). Hillsdale, NJ: Lawrence Erlbaum.

Cook, T. D., & Campbell, D. T. (1979). *Quasi-experimentation: Design and analysis issues for field settings.* Boston: Houghton Mifflin.

Denzin, N. K., & Lincoln, Y. S. (Eds.). (1994). *Handbook of qualitative research.* Thousand Oaks, CA: Sage.

Heppner, P. P., Kivlighan, D. M., Jr., & Wampold, B. E. (1992). *Research design in counseling.* Pacific Grove, CA: Brooks/Cole.

Jöreskog, K., & Sörbom, D. (1988). *LISREL 7: A guide to the program and applications.* Chicago: SPSS.

Kazdin, A. E. (1992). *Research design in clinical psychology* (2nd ed.). New York: Macmillan.

Keren, C., & Lewis, C. (Eds.). (1993). *A handbook for data analysis in the behavioral sciences: Methodological issues.* Hillsdale, NJ: Lawrence Erlbaum.

Kerlinger, F. N. (1985). *Foundations of behavioral research* (3rd ed.). New York: Holt, Rinehart & Winston.

Kirk, R. E. (1982). *Experimental design: Procedures for the behavioral sciences* (2nd ed.). Monterey, CA: Brooks/Cole.

Platt, J. R. (1964). Strong inference. *Science, 146,* 347-353.

Rosnow, R. L., & Rosenthal, R. (1988). Focused tests of significance and effect size estimation in counseling psychology. *Journal of Counseling Psychology, 35,* 203-208.

Wampold, B. E., Davis, B., & Good, R. H., III. (1990). Hypothesis validity of clinical research. *Journal of Consulting and Clinical Psychology, 58,* 360-367.

Chapter 6

Evaluating and
Selecting Research Instruments

JOSEPH G. PONTEROTTO

Selecting valid, reliable, and useful instruments is critical to the success of any empirical research study. Students in psychology can be overwhelmed by the myriad instruments cited in the literature. There are thousands of instruments (sometimes called *scales* or *measures*) available in the field of psychology, measuring virtually every construct put forth by the discipline. Some of these instruments are carefully designed, meticulously pilot-tested, carefully revised and validated over a number of studies, and including clear normative data and score interpretation guidelines. A majority of instruments, however, are not carefully thought out and pilot-tested. All too often, instruments are selected for research out of convenience rather than as the result of a systematic evaluation process.

The purpose of this chapter is to present a practical guide for researchers to follow as they select research instruments for their study. The focus of the chapter is on self-report measures common to the psychology discipline (see overviews in Miller, 1991). Particularly common in this vein are self-reported opinions, attitudes, and beliefs evaluated on Likert-type scales.

This chapter is concerned with only quantitative instruments (used primarily for research purposes); students interested in qualitative protocols (e.g., unstructured or semistructured interviews, participant-observation logs) should review the qualitative chapter in this text (Chapter 14, by Highlen & Finley). The present chapter guides the reader in the process of locating, reviewing, and evaluating the psychometric properties of instruments measuring psychological constructs.

Locating Instruments for Research

The instrument selection process begins with an informed understanding of the psychological constructs under study (see Gelso, Chapter 29 of this volume). Reviewing the literature on the construct will lead to a number of published studies on the topic, and within these studies reference will be made to instruments designed to measure the construct. For example, a student might be interested in the construct of "self-esteem." A

PsycLIT or ERIC computer search will yield many conceptual and empirical studies on this topic. By tracking down these studies, the psychology student will find that various self-esteem measures have been used in the research. The student will then focus on the Instruments or Measures section of the article that describes the instrument (hopefully in a comprehensive manner) and provides specific references to its original source as well as more detailed psychometric information on it.

Very often, particularly with more established psychological measures, one will find detailed critical reviews of the instrument published in books or journals. Appendix 6.1 at the end of this chapter presents resource books and journals that offer listings, descriptions, and/or psychometric reviews of a wide variety of instruments commonly used in psychological research. This appendix also lists a few major test publishers of psychological instruments and assessments. Further, Borg and Gall (1989) provided a valuable resource on locating information on a wide variety of tests and instruments.

Reviewing the Instruments Located

Once the researcher has identified a number of instruments measuring the construct of interest, the next step is to narrow down the list to a more manageable number. For example, let us say that the researcher located references to 10 self-esteem measures. Of the 10, which 2 or 3 appeared the most promising on the basis of the available descriptions? Once 2 or 3 instruments have been chosen, the researcher will want to conduct a thorough literature review on the instruments themselves, rather than the constructs they purport to measure. At this point, the researcher should seek the actual instruments, permission to use them, and the latest psychometric information on them.

OBTAINING INSTRUMENTS

It is very important to review the actual instrument during the evaluation process. Very often, research articles only describe the instrument or present a few sample items, and the reader does not get a sense of the format of the instrument or the specific item contents. Having the actual instrument before you, in the form that your research participants will complete it, is essential to establishing the instrument's face validity. I will discuss validity more extensively in the next section. To obtain an actual copy of the instrument, along with scoring guidelines, the researcher must write to the author or publisher of the instrument. The address of the copyright holder is often in the article where the instrument is first published. Also, various resources listed in Appendix 6.1 include the address of the instrument developer or publisher.

PERMISSION TO USE THE INSTRUMENTS

After reviewing the instruments and selecting one or more for use, the researcher must request, in writing, permission to reproduce and use the instrument. This written request should state, at a very minimum, the purpose of the study, the principal (and supervising) researchers for the project, the proposed sample and procedure for the study, and the expected completion date. Often, when requesting the measure itself, the copyright holder will send along a permission utilization form that must be completed and returned if the researcher decides to use the measure. Appendix 6.2 at the end of this chapter presents a sample of such a permission form developed by the author of this chapter for his Quick Discrimination Index.

COST FOR AND RESPONSIBILITY IN USING INSTRUMENTS

"For-profit" test publishers charge to use their copyrighted instruments. Many established personality, career assessment, and intelligence measures are available at a cost to the researcher. Prices for the assessments are listed in the respective advertising catalogs. However, a majority of commonly used self-report measures in psychology are not produced by major test publishers but are controlled by the author of the instrument. In many cases, the instrument author allows free use of the instrument by qualified researchers (or students under supervision). This is the case with the Quick Discrimination Index, for which the permission form is given in Appendix 6.2. Despite free use of many instruments, the researcher does have important responsibilities when incorporating instruments and sharing research results.

Naturally, any student selecting and using psychological instruments should have the prerequisite training (the minimum being a course in psychological measurement and testing) and supervision during the process. Different tests and instruments require different levels of competence in their use and interpretation. Important competencies for test user qualifications are provided in the *Standards for Educational and Psychological Testing* (American Educational Research Association [AERA], 1985) and, more recently, in Moreland, Eyde, Robertson, Primoff, and Most (1995).

In addition to minimum qualifications required for test use, the researcher has additional responsibilities to the profession of contributing to the evaluation of the instrument's validity, reliability, and utility. Given that all psychological instruments have limitations, it is the responsibility of the instrument developer (or publisher) to monitor continuously the instrument's use (and potential misuse). The validity, reliability, and practical utility of the instrument must be evaluated over time and across many samples, and the instrument must be modified, revised, or withdrawn (from future use) depending on the outcome of continued validation work. Therefore users of the instrument are often requested, as a condition for use, to make the results of their study (and sometimes the raw instrument data themselves) available to the instrument developer. In this way, the instrument author can assess the validity and reliability of the instrument with the researcher's sample and may add the data to work on national norm development.

Evaluating Psychometric Properties of Instruments

The validity and reliability of an instrument should be prime considerations in one's decision to incorporate a given measure. This section provides a brief review of the constructs of validity and reliability and concrete suggestions for assessing the psychometric strengths and limitations of a research instrument. Comprehensive reviews of validity and reliability are understandably beyond the scope of this chapter. Yet students of psychology must have a firm grasp of these constructs before beginning the instrument selection process.

Essential readings for the psychology researcher are *Standards for Educational and Psychological Testing* (AERA, 1985) and *Reliability and Validity Assessment* (Carmines & Zeller, 1979). A third helpful reference source is Sparks's (1990) "How to Read a Test Manual." Focusing on the selection of tests for business and industry, this source presents a concise overview of important issues to consider when reading a test manual and selecting instruments for practice. Naturally, it is recommended that psychology students complete one or more courses on psychological measurement and be very familiar with a comprehensive textbook on testing (e.g., Anastasi, 1982; Pedhazur & Schmelkin, 1991). Much of the validity and reliability discussion that follows stems from the sources referenced in this paragraph.

Validity

Validity is the most important consideration in selecting an instrument for research. Basically, an instrument is valid if it actually measures what it purports to measure. Strictly speaking, *validity* refers not to the instrument itself but to the appropriateness and usefulness of interpretations or inferences made from the instrument. There are various ways to assess the validity of a research instrument, and various procedures have led researchers to name different types of validity; however, it is important to remember that validity is a unitary concept (AERA, 1985). Traditionally, there are three means of establishing estimates of validity: content related, criterion related, and construct related. Finer validity distinctions could be made: For example, criterion-related validity can be assessed by both concurrent and predictive methods, and construct validity can be assessed by both convergent and discriminant procedures. Some researchers also discuss the concept of face validity, and this is where we will begin our validity overview.

FACE VALIDITY

Face validity refers to the researcher's subjective appraisal of what the content of the instrument is measuring. By reading the actual items of the instrument, the researcher can assess and conclude the following: "Yes, these items appear to be measuring the construct as I had envisioned it. The items make good sense to me." Conversely, the researcher may look at the instrument and think, "No, these items are not really asking of the research subjects what I had intended to investigate."

Another consideration related to face validity is the utility (or usefulness) of the instrument. Questions the researcher will want to ask him- or herself include the following: Is the length of the instrument appropriate for my intended use? (Some instruments are quite valid, but their length may be prohibitive in terms of time required to complete the instrument.) Is the wording and readability appropriate to my intended sample? Might the items be offensive to some segments of my sample? Is the format and layout of the instrument attractive?

CONTENT VALIDITY

Whereas face validity is a subjective evaluation of the instrument, content validity involves a systematic procedure for ensuring that the content inherent in the instrument items is measuring a defined domain. Content validity involves clearly defining the domain or construct under consideration, selecting a content sample of this domain for the instrument, and clearly operationalizing this content sample into instrument items. Often researchers establish evidence of content validity by having acknowledged experts in the topical area evaluate each instrument item on both clarity and domain appropriateness.

CRITERION-RELATED VALIDITY

If instrument scores can be shown to be related to one or more outcome criteria, than the instrument can be said to have evidence of criterion-related validity. There are two common designs for establishing evidence of criterion-related validity. First, scores on the instrument can be related to scores on a criterion when all data are collected concurrently (referred to as *concurrent validity*). Second, when criterion data are collected at some point after data on the instrument are collected, a relationship will yield evidence of predictive validity. A relationship between instrument scores and the criteria is calculated statistically through the use of a correlation coefficient, and the resultant index is termed a *validity coefficient*. Naturally, the higher the resultant coefficient, the more valid the instrument in serving as a criterion predictor.

CONSTRUCT VALIDITY

Construct validity is concerned with the degree to which a particular measure relates to other measures in a manner consistent with theoretically driven hypotheses. The construct of interest for a particular instrument should be embedded in a conceptual framework, even if the framework is imperfect or not fully developed. The conceptual or theoretical framework defines the construct, distinguishes it from other constructs, and hypothesizes how measures of the construct will relate to other measures. Common procedures employed to test construct validity include using theory to predict an instrument's relationship with a similar or unrelated construct and using factor analyses to explore the underlying hypothesized factor structure that best represents the scale items.

An established procedure for establishing construct validity is the multitrait-multimethod matrix (Campbell & Fiske, 1959), which examines, simultaneously, convergent and discriminant validity. This procedure requires the assessment of two or more traits (e.g., characteristics of people) by two or more different methods. To establish convergent and discriminant validity, the researcher would expect that the correlation between the same trait measured by different methods would be high (convergent validity) and that the correlation between different traits measured by the same or by different methods would be low (discriminant validity).

An example will clarify the procedure. Two traits of mental health dysfunction are depression and anxiety. Two methods to assess these constructs are self-report inventories and clinician ratings. In a multitrait-multimethod matrix, one would expect that the correlation between self-reported depression and clinician ratings of depression (same trait, different methods) would be higher than the correlation between depression and anxiety as measured by self-report or clinician ratings (different traits, same or different methods). Hypothesized findings from a multitrait-multimethod matrix can provide robust support for the construct validity of a measuring device. This procedure is becoming increasingly common in psychometric research, and the astute student will want to review the original (Campbell & Fiske, 1959) and more summative discussions of the procedure (e.g., Anastasi, 1982; Pedhazur & Schmelkin, 1991).

Establishing construct validity is critical to the validation process. In fact, some measurement specialists (e.g., Pedhazur & Schmelkin, 1991) are of the opinion that all "types" of validity revolve around construct validity, which serves as the central core of the validation process.

VALIDITY SUMMARY

The researcher should attempt to select instruments that have accumulated validity evidence over time. Of primary importance is to choose instruments that have validity evidence that matches your intended research purpose. Therefore, if you are using an instrument to measure a multidimensional construct—for example, state anxiety and trait anxiety—the instrument should have validity evidence supporting the separate use and interpretations of state and trait anxiety. As another example, if you intend to use an instrument as a predictor variable in a study, the instrument should have accumulated criterion-related validity evidence in previous research.

It is not necessary for an instrument to have received every possible "type" of validity support. It is important to remember that there are no separate validities: The concept is a unitary one. In fact, the "designated types" of validity (content, criterion-related, and construct) are very often interrelated. Thus, as one accrues criterion-related support for a measure (e.g., depression is related to and predictive of life dissatisfaction), one is also providing evidence of construct validity (e.g., that there is such a thing as depression and that it is operational in terms of the instrument items). In summary, then, the primary question a researcher must ask when choosing among instruments is, "Does this instrument have validity evidence for my intended use of the measure?"

Reliability

Reliability refers to the extent to which instrument scores are free from measurement error. A single administration of an instrument to an individual research participant reflects an "obtained score," not necessarily a "true" score. That is, if the participant completed the instrument a second time, she or he might receive a different score, perhaps due to changes in mood, energy level, or testing conditions. This variability in score from administration to administration reflects measurement error. A participant's true score is a combination of her or his "obtained" score and measurement error. When selecting instruments for a research study, one looks for measures with lower degrees of measurement error and therefore a greater approximation to true scores. Reliability coefficients allow the researcher to make an informed choice with regard to the degree of measurement error in a given instrument. The greater the reliability coefficient, the lower the measurement error, and therefore the more desirable the instrument.

There are a number of methods for estimating the reliability of an instrument: the retest method, the alternate-form method, the split-half method, and the internal consistency method. In this section, we will briefly review these basic reliability methods.

RETEST METHOD

The retest method of estimating reliability involves administering the same instrument to a given sample at two points in time. The correlation of scores across the two separate administrations produces a retest correlation coefficient. A concern with this method of reliability estimation is that true score change may be interpreted as measurement instability. For example, let us assume that at Point A one completes an "Attitude Toward the Elderly Scale" and that 2 weeks later, at Point B, the same group completes the measure a second time. Let us also assume that during the 2-week interval between administrations, much of the sample happens to watch the television show 60 Minutes, which presents a segment on the experiences and challenges of the elderly in America. The show may stimulate attitude change, and therefore at Point B, instrument scores may change. The resulting correlation coefficient will be lower, and if the researcher is not aware of the television show, the lower coefficient may be interpreted as evidence that the instrument has unsatisfactory retest stability.

Other concerns with the retest method are "reactivity," by which the very act of measuring some phenomena will cause change. In other words, completing the instrument causes you to consider or reconsider previously held thoughts and feelings, which then may change by the second administration. Finally, if the retest interval is short, there is the possibility of "overestimation" due to memory. The research participant may remember her or his responses to the items and respond similarly. Retest intervals vary widely depending on the nature and purpose of the assessment. Instruments purporting to measure relatively stable constructs (e.g., personality, intelligence) will require longer time periods between administrations, whereas instruments measuring less stable constructs (e.g., moods) will assess retest correlations over shorter periods of time. Two weeks is considered a minimum retest time period (Carmines & Zeller, 1979).

ALTERNATE-FORM METHOD

Similar to the retest method in that it requires two administrations with the same sample, the alternate-form method differs from the former in that two parallel versions of the instrument are developed and administered. Both forms, of course, are intended to measure the same construct. The two versions of the instrument look similar in terms of format, number of items, and so forth, as they are meant to be parallel. The typical procedure for establishing alternate-form reliability estimates involves administering one form of the instrument to a selected sample and then, about 2 weeks later (Nunnally, 1964), administering the alternate form. The correlation between the scores on the two versions is then interpreted as an estimate of alternate-form reliability.

This method is preferred to the retest method because the use of parallel forms controls for any practice effects. Yet given the time interval between completing the forms, true score change can still be masked as unreliability in measurement.

SPLIT-HALF METHOD

Unlike the retest and alternate-form methods, which require two administrations to the same sample, the split-half method requires only a single administration. In calculating the split-half estimate of reliability, the researcher divides the items into two equal halves (e.g., odd versus even items, or a random division of the items) and calculates the correlation between halves. Given, in this case, that one is calculating the reliability of only one half of the instrument, a statistical correction must be made to account for the full item pool. This mathematical correction is known as the Spearman-Brown prophecy formula. The formula is rather simple and can be found in any measurement or statistics textbook.

A limitation of the split-half method is that depending on the split used, slightly different reliability estimates will be calculated. For example, in a 10-item scale, there are 125 different ways to split the items into two halves (Carmines & Zeller, 1979). Each of the 125 resulting correlation coefficients may be slightly different. A more accurate estimate of the instrument reliability, then, would be the average of these 125 coefficients. This process forms the foundation of the more preferred internal consistency estimate of reliability, discussed next.

INTERNAL CONSISTENCY METHOD

Like the split-half method, the internal consistency coefficient is calculated after only a single administration of the instrument to a sample. The most popular coefficient of this type is Cronbach's alpha (Cronbach, 1951). Given that alpha can be considered the average of all possible split-half combinations, this method is preferred to the split-half method (Carmines & Zeller, 1979).

Alpha is considered a conservative estimate of an instrument's reliability. The magnitude of alpha depends on the average interitem correlation and the total number of items in the measure. As the average interitem correlations increase and as the scale increases in length (number of items), the alpha rises.

In a thorough review of the four reliability estimation methods, Carmines and Zeller (1979) indicated a strong preference for the alternate-form and internal consistency methods. In fact, these authors recommended that alpha should be computed for any multiple-item scale (see also Nunnally, 1978).

What Constitutes a Satisfactory Level of Reliability?

Psychology students, as well as experienced researchers, often ask what the minimum acceptable reliability coefficient should be when selecting instruments. There is no absolute answer to this question. Of prime consideration is the purpose the instrument is to serve. If instrument scores have significant life-altering implications (e.g., admissions and selection decisions) then one would demand the highest levels of reliability, usually .90 and above (Walsh & Betz, 1985). When choosing instruments for large-sample research purposes, a .80 (Carmines & Zeller, 1979; Sparks, 1990; Walsh & Betz, 1985), or even a .70 (Nunnally, 1978) may be acceptable.

It is important to remember that reliability is but one important criterion to use when selecting research instrumentation. Equally important is the proven validity of the instrument for your particular use, as well as the pragmatic utility of the instrument with your intended sample. When all evidence is weighed and the intended research purposes are clarified, an alpha coefficient of .70 may be satisfactory. It is suggested that whenever a research instrument is incorporated into a study, a new assessment of the instrument's reliability should be calculated as part of the study.

Conclusion

This chapter has highlighted that the selection of instruments for use in psychological research is a critical component of the research process. Instruments should not be selected on the basis of convenience, but rather should be carefully evaluated along a number of criteria. These criteria begin with a firm understanding of the psychological constructs under study, a knowledge of basic measurement concepts and considerations, and the careful scrutiny of an instrument on the basis of utility, reliability, and validity. If the instrument is not useful (e.g., if it is too long for your purpose), not reliable, or not valid, the results of your study are immediately called into question. Therefore I end this chapter with practical advice: Choose instruments wisely and carefully when designing your study.

Recommended Readings

The following selection of readings provides more in-depth discussions of the issues and recommendations put forth in this chapter: Anastasi's *Psychological Testing* (1982); Carmines and Zeller's *Reliability and Validity Assessment* (1979); Pedhazur and Schmelkin's *Measurement, Design, and Analysis: An Integrated Approach* (1991); AERA's *Standards for Educational and Psychological Testing* (1985); and Sparks's "How to Read a Test Manual" (1990).

References

Anastasi, A. (1982). *Psychological testing* (5th ed.). New York: Macmillan.

Borg, W. R., & Gall, D. G. (1989). *Educational research: An introduction* (5th ed.). New York: Longman.

Campbell, D. T., & Fiske, D. W. (1959). Convergent and discriminant validity by the multitrait-multimethod matrix. *Psychological Bulletin, 56*, 81-105.

Carmines E. G., & Zeller, R. A. (1979). *Reliability and validity assessment.* Beverly Hills, CA: Sage.

Cronbach, L. J. (1951). Coefficient alpha and the internal structure of tests. *Psychometrika, 16*, 297-334.

Miller, D. C. (Ed.). (1991). *Handbook of research design and social measurement* (5th ed.). Thousand Oaks, CA: Sage.

Moreland, K. L., Eyde, L. D., Robertson, G. J., Primoff, E. S., & Most, R. B. (1995). Assessment of test user qualifications: A research-based measurement procedure. *American Psychologist, 50,* 14-23.

Nunnally, J. C. (1964). *Educational measurement and evaluation.* New York: McGraw-Hill.

Nunnally, J. C. (1978). *Psychometric theory* (2nd ed.). New York: McGraw-Hill.

Pedhazur, E. J., & Schmelkin, L. P. (1991). *Measurement, design, and analysis: An integrated approach* (student ed.). Hillsdale, NJ: Lawrence Erlbaum.

Sparks, C. P. (1990). How to read a test manual. In J. Hogan & R. Hogan (Eds.), *Business and industry testing: Current practices and test reviews* (pp. 36-47). Austin, TX: Pro-Ed.

Walsh, W. B., & Betz, N. E. (1985). *Tests and assessment* (2nd ed.). Englewood Cliffs, NJ: Prentice Hall.

Appendix 6.1

Sources for Instruments and Tests: Books, Journals, and Test Publishers

Books and Monographs

Mental Measurements Yearbooks, updated periodically, published by the Buros Institute of Mental Measurements, University of Nebraska Press, Lincoln, NE.

Test Critiques, Vols. 1-7, 1984-1988, edited by D. J. Keyser & R. C. Sweetland, published by Test Corporation of America, Kansas City, MO.

Directory of Unpublished Experimental Measures, Vol. 1 (1974) and Vol. 2 (1978), edited by B. A. Goldman & J. C. Busch, published by Human Science Press, New York.

Dictionary of Behavioral Assessment Techniques (1988), edited by M. Hersen & A. S. Bellack, published by Pergamon Press, New York.

Measures for Psychological Assessment: A Guide to 3,000 Original Sources and Their Application (1974), edited by K. T. Chun, S. Cobb, & J. R. P. French, published by the Institute for Social Research, University of Michigan.

Measures of Personality and Social Psychological Attitudes (1991), edited by J. P. Robinson, P. R. Shaver, & L. S. Wrightsman, published by Academic Press, San Diego.

Measures for Clinical Practice: A Sourcebook (1987), by K. Corcoran & J. Fischer, published by the Free Press, New York.

ETS Test Collection Catalogue (1986), published by the Educational Testing Service, Princeton, NJ.

Handbook of Research Design and Social Measurement (1991) (5th ed.), edited by D. C. Miller, published by Sage Publications, Thousand Oaks, CA.

A Sourcebook for Mental Health Measures (1973), edited by A. L. Comrey, T. E. Backer, & E. M. Glaser, published by the Human Interaction Research Institute, Los Angeles.

Test: A Comprehensive Reference for Assessments in Psychology, Education, and Business (1986), edited by R. C. Sweetland & D. J. Keyser, published by Test Corporation of America, Kansas City, MO.

Journals

Applied Psychological Measurement
Educational and Psychological Measurement
Journal of Educational Measurement

Test Publishers

Consulting Psychologists Press, Inc., 3803 East Bayshore Road, P.O. Box 10096, Palo Alto, CA 94303 (1-800-624-1765).

Multi-Health Systems, Inc., 908 Niagara Falls Boulevard, North Tonawanda, NY 14120-2060 (416-424-1700).

Psychological Assessment Resources, Inc., P.O. Box 998, Odessa, FL 33556 (1-800-331-TEST).

The Psychological Corporation, Harcourt Brace and Co., 555 Academic Court, San Antonio, TX 78204-2498 (1-800-228-0752).

For a listing of 37 test publishers, see Appendix A in Moreland et al. (1995), *American Psychologist, 50,* 14-23.

Appendix 6.2

Sample Utilization Request Form

QUICK DISCRIMINATION INDEX (QDI)
(AKA Social Attitude Survey)
Utilization Request Form

In using the Quick Discrimination Index (QDI) I agree to the following terms/conditions:

1. I understand that the QDI is copyrighted by Joseph G. Ponterotto (Ph.D.) and colleagues at the Division of Psychological and Educational Services, Fordham University at Lincoln Center, 113 West 60th Street, New York 10023-7478 (212-636-6480).
2. I am a trained professional in psychology or a related field, having completed course work (or training) in multicultural issues, psychometrics, and research ethics, or I am working under the supervision of such an individual.
3. In using the QDI, all ethical standards of the American Psychological Association and/or related professional organizations will be adhered to. Furthermore, I will follow the "Research With Human Subjects" guidelines put forth by my university, institution, or professional setting. Ethical considerations include but are not limited to subject informed consent, confidentiality of records, adequate pre- and debriefing of subjects, and subject opportunity to review a concise written summary of the study's purpose, method, results, and implications.
4. Consistent with accepted professional practice, I will save and protect my raw data for a minimum of five years; and if requested I will make the raw data available to Dr. Ponterotto (who is ethically responsible to monitor developments on the scale in terms of utility, reliability, and validity) and to other students/scholars researching the discrimination/racism/sexism constructs.
5. I will send a copy of my research results (for any study incorporating the QDI) in manuscript form to Dr. Ponterotto, regardless of whether the study is published, presented, or fully completed.

Signature: _____ Date: _____

Name: _____

Address: _____

_____

_____

_____

Phone Number: _____

E-Mail Address: _____

If student, supervisor/mentor's name, affiliation, and signature:

Name: _____

Affiliation: _____

Signature: _____ Date: _____

Chapter 7

Designing Surveys and Questionnaires for Research

ROBERT D. GODDARD III
PETER VILLANOVA

Surveys and questionnaires are among the most frequently used research methods of the social sciences (Isaac & Michael, 1983). This popularity is really no surprise given that much of contemporary research, particularly in psychology, involves the study of individuals' perceptions of and beliefs about themselves and their immediate situation and the relationship of these perceptions and beliefs to behavior. In this chapter, we provide a design primer to assist students in the development of survey/questionnaire instruments for research purposes. We have organized the chapter to facilitate your development of a cognitive script to understand survey/questionnaire design and administration. The chapter begins with an overview of survey methods and a description of the survey/ questionnaire development process. This first section serves to orient you to survey/ questionnaire methods and provides a context in which to understand better the more specific issues and choices that follow. A second section takes up survey/questionnaire design issues in greater detail and is meant to reflect the variety of technical issues you might face once you have committed your project to the use of these methods. The final section reviews some alternatives to questionnaire methods of data collection.

Orientation to Survey/Questionnaire Design and Administration

WHAT IS A SURVEY?

A survey is a method of collecting information from people for descriptive or predictive purposes. A survey can be used to gather information about the nation's population as a whole (the decennial census of the United States) or to assess the reactions of a sample of consumers to a new soft drink. Surveys can take the form of questionnaires filled out by individuals, one-on-one interviews between subjects and the surveyor, or telephone interviews. Once the data have been collected, they may be archived so that other researchers may analyze them for their own purposes (see Zaitzow and Fields, Chapter 20 of this volume).

REASONS FOR SURVEYS

There are many reasons for conducting a survey, including facilitating decisions, evaluating the effectiveness of current policies or programs, or satisfying a need for information about a research topic.

Of course, there are many ways of obtaining information from people. For example, one could simply observe people to obtain the needed information. But what if the information needed is not behavioral? That is, one can observe behavior fairly simply, but what if the needed information is attitudinal in nature? We cannot observe attitudes, opinions or beliefs, but we can ask people about their attitudes, opinions, or beliefs by using a survey.

TYPES OF SURVEYS

The most commonly used forms of surveys are questionnaires, interviews, and telephone surveys. Questionnaires are written surveys containing items that address the goals of the project. Questionnaires can be self-administered or administered to groups of people by a trained administrator who explains the purpose of the survey, answers questions about the survey items and administrative procedures, and ensures that proper survey procedures are followed. A limitation of questionnaires is that the items are preset and respondents cannot fully express their opinions.

Interviews share many of the features of questionnaires in that there may be a set of items the researcher uses to gather information. With interviews, however, it is possible to ask for explanations and to provide information on the reactions of the respondents that cannot be obtained from a questionnaire.

Telephone surveys are interviews conducted by telephone. The researcher prepares a set of items to be asked and may have the flexibility to probe respondents' answers for elaboration.

ETHICS

The choice between anonymity and confidentiality is often an issue when conducting a survey. Respondents may not wish to have their identities known when responding to a survey, and protecting their identities may result in more valid responses to survey questions. A self-administered questionnaire mailed in to the researcher can preserve anonymity, as no one knows just who the respondent is if there is no identifying information on the envelope or questionnaire. Interviews and telephone surveys, by their nature, do not offer respondents anonymity.

Confidentiality is the more frequent level of protection given to survey respondents, whether they are responding to a questionnaire or to an interview. In the case of confidentiality, the specific individual's responses are identifiable to the researcher but are not disclosed to other parties. Frequently researchers provide respondents with a pledge of confidentiality, and this is usually honored by securing all survey responses and reporting only aggregate (i.e., grouped) data so that individual responses to questions cannot be identified. Researchers more frequently assure confidentiality rather than anonymity to respondents because this allows researchers to establish that the responses were provided by individuals whom the researchers intended to represent in their study. In any case, whatever promise is made to respondents regarding disclosure of their responses, it is imperative that the researcher maintain procedures to satisfy this pledge.

SURVEY DEVELOPMENT PROCESS

The process of developing a suitable survey involves several steps, with the success of each step dependent on how well the previous step was performed.

The first step in developing a survey requires the researcher to have clearly stated study goals and hypotheses that identify the information needed to conduct the study. One point of departure is to identify whether the study requires information about respondents' attributes (e.g., age, employment, education), attitudes, beliefs, intentions, and/or behaviors. Subsequently, the aim is to identify more precisely what set of attributes are relevant to the research question. A table of specifications is one way to detail better what items correspond to the attributes that the survey is designed to measure.

A table of specifications (Hopkins & Antes, 1978) is a two-dimensional matrix in which one dimension represents the domain of interest (e.g., job satisfaction, attitudes toward prison overcrowding, biographical data) and a second dimension represents the items or behaviors representative of these domains. A table of specifications' brief and accurate summary of the entire survey can facilitate decisions about the appropriateness of the items, what items should appear together or apart, and the best order in which to arrange the groups of items.

The second step involves identifying the characteristics of respondents that may serve as the sample for the study. This includes the respondents' ability to comprehend the terms appearing on the survey and their accessibility to the researcher. Is the population you wish to sample easily accessible? What arrangements need to be made to ensure representation? At what level of reading skill should questionnaire items be written to be understandable to the target population? McCready, in Chapter 8 of this volume, discusses a variety of sampling procedures to increase representativeness of your sample.

The third step involves the form that specific items should take to ensure that the desired information is obtained. This step involves writing questionnaire items and response formats that yield information most compatible with the aims of the study. For example, is a simple ranking of respondent preferences for program alternatives all you need, or do you wish to quantify their preference for alternatives using a continuous scale? Or is a simple "yes" or "no" response as to whether each program characteristic is desirable sufficient for the purpose of your study?

The fourth step considers the structure of the survey. This includes such matters as the instructions for respondents, how items should be ordered, which items should be grouped together, and whether and how many discrete sections should appear on the survey. As a general rule, it is often advisable to proceed from more general information to more specific information. What is most important here is that the survey be ordered in the manner most user-friendly to the respondent. Sometimes the most logical ordering of questions or sections of the questionnaire may not provide the best psychological sequence from the respondents' perspective. For example, some authors have recommended that demographic questions appear at the end of the survey because of the suspicion they may arouse (Frey, 1989; Miller, 1991).

Related to the physical design and appearance of the survey are the set of procedures to be followed during administration. It is essential to establish an administration protocol for any systematic research endeavor, including laboratory experiments or surveys. In the case of the survey, the protocol would include required materials for supporting data collection during a session, information that may need to be conveyed to respondents (such as what identifying code to include on their questionnaire or other factual data), instructions to be read to respondents, allowable answers to respondent questions about the items, and an appropriate event script to be communicated to respondents so that they can anticipate what follows with a minimum of confusion.

As a final step before going to the field with your survey, consider evaluating your effort as a package in a pretest prior to administration to the actual research sample. If pretesting suggests that additional problems need to be worked out, the entire process should be repeated until the survey meets the standards acceptable for research use. Pretesting is one of the most useful exercises you can engage in to identify potential problems and to produce a quality survey.

The different forms of pretesting basically invite different levels of respondent participation in the development of the survey. A participating pretest asks respondents to approach the survey as collaborators in the research project in that they are fully briefed about the intentions of the study and the aims of different questions. As they complete the survey, respondents may encounter "prompts" about different questions that ask them to evaluate them in terms of clarity, meaning, and prejudice. An undeclared pretest differs in that the respondents experience the same administration protocol as the "for keeps" sample. Finally, a focus group discussion can follow the survey administration. A focus group discussion involves having the respondents form small groups of six to eight people led by a member of the research team. The respondents are interviewed as a group about their reactions to and questions about the survey and the administration protocol. The focus group discussion can be structured according to an interview protocol that is prepared in advance, and it may also include opportunities for respondent-initiated inquiry.

Survey Design Issues

FORMAT

How long should your survey be? The answer to this question depends on two things: the purpose of your survey and the method you choose for administration. Your purpose—what you are trying to accomplish with it—will determine the number of questions needed to ensure the credibility of the data.

The type of survey you choose—questionnaire, interview, or telephone survey—also affects the length of your survey. Because of time and attention considerations, telephone surveys are generally limited to 30 minutes or less. Interviews are also limited by time considerations but can last longer and contain more items than telephone surveys. Questionnaires administered by a trained researcher can also be longer than telephone surveys but should take no longer than 1 hour. Self-administered questionnaires that are completed at the respondent's leisure can be even longer but should not take more than 1 to 2 hours to complete. Of course, the time and the amount of contemplation required of respondents to answer each question on the survey needs to be considered. Wordy questions or those that require considerable thought to generate an answer will take more time than those that require respondents to indicate how strongly they agree or disagree with a statement. Heberlein and Baumgartner's (1978) quantitative review of mail questionnaires involving 98 studies found that the average mail questionnaire consisted of 72 questions appearing on seven pages and required about one-half hour to complete.

DESIGN AND LAYOUT

Your survey should begin with an introduction describing its purpose and who you are. The introduction should not be long, probably no more than a paragraph. You might include an estimate of time to complete the survey, a statement as to why the respondent was chosen to participate in your survey, and an assurance of confidentiality or anonymity.

Item Ordering

The first survey item should be directly related to your purpose. After that, item order depends on your respondents. Some subjects may be more at ease when responding to objective items until they get used to the survey and its purpose. Your respondents may feel more comfortable if you order your survey items from most familiar to least familiar. Likewise, some thought should be given to the effect one survey item will have on the responses to succeeding items. People generally wish to be consistent in their behavior, and this tendency may artificially increase relationships among responses to different items. For this reason, it is sometimes wise to consider counterbalancing sections of the survey so that the questions appear in a different order for different respondents. This allows you to conduct analyses that will clue you to whether there are order effects as a result of placing items in different orders of appearance on the survey.

SCALES

Establishing response scales that are appropriate for the goals of the survey and the type of items used is an important consideration for researchers. It is important to distinguish among the various types of response scales so as to code responses properly and to facilitate the application of statistical analyses. Yaffee discusses what statistical analyses are appropriate for different data in Chapter 15 of this volume, and Betz describes test construction principles that generalize to survey and questionnaire design in Chapter 19.

Nominal Scales

Nominal scales are categorical in nature. That is, the values associated with the variable of interest have no real numerical meaning but describe categories. The values cannot be added, subtracted, multiplied, or divided but are more like labels used to describe the variable of interest (Kerlinger, 1985). Nominal scales are often used to gather factual information such as demographic information; there are usually better response scales available to a researcher for the measurement of attitudes (ordinal, interval). An example of a nominal scale would be:

My race is (check one):

(1) ___ African American

(2) ___ Asian American

(3) ___ Caucasian

(4) ___ Hispanic

(5) ___ Native American

(6) ___ Other

Ordinal

Ordinal scales indicate a rank ordering on a survey item. An ordinal scale indicates that there are differences among the responses but does not indicate the magnitude of those differences, nor does it suggest that the differences are the same across responses (Kerlinger, 1985). An example of an ordinal response scale is:

The service on this airline flight is (check one):

(1) ___ Better than the service on my last flight.

(2) ___ About the same as the service on my last flight.

(3) ___ Worse than the service on my last flight.

Interval

The most common interval scale used in surveys is the Likert or summated rating scale. Likert scaling is often used in attitude or opinion surveys that ask respondents to state their level of agreement or disagreement with an item. Responses are generally composed of five or more categories, as in the following example:

This company is a better place to work this year than it was last year.

(1) ___ Strongly Disagree

(2) ___ Disagree

(3) ___ Undecided or No Opinion

(4) ___ Agree

(5) ___ Strongly Agree

Respondents are asked to select one and only one response from the choices given. The response choices are mutually exclusive and collectively exhaustive, meaning that the respondent cannot select more than one category and that the choices cover all of the possible responses.

There is some controversy as to whether the continuum reflected in Likert scales is ordinal or interval, and considerable research has been conducted to ascertain which scale anchors provide the best approximation to interval data (e.g., Spector, 1992).

ITEM CHARACTERISTICS AND RESPONSE FORMATS

Several characteristics distinguish between good and bad items. Much of the distinction is determined by the kind of information one needs to obtain and the sample of respondents. Specific item characteristics can strongly influence response errors and biases (Bradburn, 1982).

Defining Terms

An interviewer should be provided with definitions for any word(s) and/or phrase(s) in the survey instrument that might be ambiguous or unclear. This is accomplished with an additional description—for example, "I am in favor of the death penalty (that is, I think death is an appropriate punishment for those who commit certain major crimes)." Do not assume that all members of the target sample share the same vernacular. When in doubt, provide the interviewer with definitions for any problematic words and phrases.

Questionnaires pose a greater challenge of equating item meaning across respondents. For example, without the advantage of an interviewer to define the term *fit*, the item "To what extent do you believe each employee below fits the job he or she currently performs?" leaves the meaning of the word *fit* to the individual respondent. One respondent might consider it to involve how well someone gets along with others in the workplace, someone else might take it to mean the extent to which one has the appropriate education and skills to qualify for the job, and yet another might believe the question asks if the employee is meeting work standards. Morrow, Eastman, and McElroy (1991) found that respondents' unfamiliarity with work attitude concepts resulted in considerable redundancy in responses to five different work attitude scales.

Item clarity can also be improved by providing verbal anchors along the response continuum that are specific and distinguishable. Bass, Cascio, and O'Connor (1974) and Spector (1976) provided helpful information about how different adjectival anchors (e.g., *occasionally, seldom, often, rarely*) are perceived to differ in absolute magnitude by respondents. The characteristics of anchors become increasingly important when the response involves some judgment of behavior observed by the respondent and when one is wanting to treat these responses as interval data.

OPEN- VERSUS CLOSED-ENDED QUESTIONS

Generally, the more specific a survey question is, the more probable that the same interpretation of that question will be made by respondents, and the more easily comparable and accurate the answers will be. On the other hand, open-ended questions allow respondents to give their own opinions about survey items. However, to set limits on just how subjects can respond, you can ask respondents to "list no more than three things" about the topic. Closed-ended questions consist of a stem in the form of a statement or question, such as "Which issue is of greatest significance to you?" or "Rank these issues from lowest (1) to highest (4) importance to you," followed by several alternative choices, such as

____ budget deficit

____ economic growth

____ health care

____ social justice

Open-ended questions are particularly useful in the early stages of research on some phenomenon that is poorly understood and for which you are seeking primarily descriptive information. Subsequent research might employ a closed-question format when the characteristics of the phenomenon (e.g., dimensions or the range of values along any dimension) are better understood.

Open-ended questions can also allow one to probe answers to closed-ended questions to gauge respondent familiarity with an issue. In the 1983 Detroit Area Study of attitudes toward welfare, for example, a significant majority of respondents agreed with the statement that "government is trying to do too many things that should be left to individuals and private businesses." However, when these respondents were asked the follow-up question "What things do you feel should be left to individuals or private businesses?" over 25% could not answer or give an example (Converse & Presser, 1986).

Generally, closed questions require less administrative skill and facilitate data analysis. They also enhance the comparability of responses. However, use of closed questions assumes that the response choices accurately represent the breadth of people's opinions. It really comes down to whether respondents should be more or less constrained in their response alternatives. Imagine, for example, a continuum ranging from absolutely free to absolutely constrained responses to questions. At the "free" end of the continuum are open-ended questions or questions that instruct a respondent to "list those things you believe the government does well." At the other end, representing completely constrained alternatives, are the yes or no answers that lawyers often favor from witness testimony, and of course the question sounds something like "Does the government do anything right?" Somewhere between these extremes are questions that frame responses but allow the respondent some freedom of expression: "List no more than three things . . . ," "Rank this list in order of . . . ," and "Choose one from this list. . . ."

Filtering Questions and Middle-Alternative Responses

Do not assume that respondents are equally well informed or have an opinion about everything you might ask them. If you force an opinion by not offering a "no-opinion" option, then you may reduce the accuracy of your survey results. Aside from offering a no-opinion option, you could use a filtering question that asks respondents whether they have an opinion about an issue and if so, to indicate what it is:

> Not everyone has an opinion about every world event. If you have no opinion, just say so. The statement is: "The United Nations is doing all it can to relieve suffering in Bosnia." Do you have an opinion about this? If yes, do you agree or disagree with the statement?

Some researchers prefer that the "undecided" or "no-opinion" category be eliminated, forcing the respondent to indicate an opinion one way or the other. Other researchers use the so-called "neutral" category to determine the relative importance of the survey item. If many respondents indicate that they are "neutral," it may indicate that the item is not of major concern to them or that they do not have enough information to take a position (Orlich, 1978). For instance, employees who have been with the company less than 1 year may indicate "undecided" or "no opinion" on the earlier example. Be careful in using the no-opinion option, as research has found that between 10% and 30% of respondents elect it as a response (Schuman & Presser, 1981).

Likewise, if your aim is measure the intensity of beliefs about an issue, you might want to consider omitting the middle alternative as a response option. For example, you might ask, "Should abortion in this state be easier to obtain, be harder to obtain, or stay as it is now?" By doing so, you invite many respondents who do not feel strongly about the issue to indicate that it should stay the same. However, if you limited responses to "easier" or "harder" and then followed up with a measure of "how strongly" respondents believed in their response, you would be better able to discriminate among respondents who held less extreme beliefs.

Yet another alternative is to force a choice between alternatives that seem equally desirable but are in fact at odds. For example, one could ask respondents to agree or disagree with the following statements:

(a) Government should guarantee health care for all individuals.

(b) It is the responsibility of individuals to provide for their medical care.

An agree response seems plausible for both Question (a) and Question (b), thus failing to distinguish between respondent preferences for one position or the other. A better alternative would be to combine the questions into one, as in (c):

(c) Should the government be required to guarantee medical care for everyone, or should individuals be responsible for their own medical care?

Single Object, One Meaning

Avoid instances in which more than one object is asked to be evaluated: For example, the question "Do you agree or disagree with the statement: Professors and students should determine the policies that affect their work?" obviously begs for clearer definition of *policies* and *work* but also confuses the reader because two objects (professors and students) are mixed together. A better strategy would be to separate them into two items.

Edit items so that they have one meaning that can be directly interpreted by respondents. For example, asking for an agree/disagree response to the statement "Professors should not be required to take class attendance" invites confusion. A disagree response may mean "I do not agree that professors should not be required to take attendance." Try to word these kinds of statements in a positive direction: "Professors should be required to take attendance."

Invitation of Response Acquiescence or Artificial Compliance

If your aim is to describe other people's opinions and beliefs, do not set them up to agree with a statement because it seems appropriate to do so. Avoid leading questions. For example, "Do you support President Clinton's progressive health care proposal?" assumes that President Clinton's health care proposal is "progressive"; moreover, does the respondent "support" the proposal or the president? Also, note that such a question is begging for filter questions such as the following: "Are you familiar with President Clinton's health care proposal? Do you now have an opinion about it? If so, would you say that you support it or oppose it?" Similarly, avoid beginning a question with an obvious request for compliance, as in "Don't you agree that . . . ?"; you risk tilting the results toward agreement with a particular position.

Alternatives to Questionnaires

INTERVIEWS

Probably the most time-consuming and most costly survey form to administer is the interview. Interviews have many advantages, however, including (a) allowing the respondent to reveal otherwise concealed attitudes; (b) revealing problems and their potential solutions through discussion; (c) encouraging free expression; (d) allowing for observation and recording of nonverbal communication; (e) discovery of personal information, attitudes, beliefs, and perceptions that a paper-and-pencil survey might not uncover; (f) ensuring a high rate of participation; (g) allowing interviewers to probe or follow up on survey items; and (h) facilitating the participation of individuals who are visually handicapped or who cannot read or write (Orlich, 1978, p. 8).

On the other hand, a trained staff of interviewers and extensive training may be required. This is so for several reasons. First, the interviewers can affect survey results by directly influencing respondents' attitudes toward the survey itself; interviewers can "turn off" potential respondents in the way they present the survey to the subject. Second, interviewers must teach subjects how to respond to their survey. Finally, interviewers must conduct the interview in a standardized way to avoid possible bias in responses (Fowler, 1993).

If you are conducting the interview, you need to gain the cooperation of your subject. Good interviewers gain cooperation by being businesslike, confident, and assertive. Good interviewers also have the ability to tailor their presentations to focus on and become personally involved with the respondent.

Training can help interviewers present their study to the respondent, ask their questions in a standardized way, and probe subjects when responses are incomplete. Training can also aid interviewers in recording responses correctly and consistently. Training is particularly important in instances requiring the interpretation and classification of responses to open-ended questions.

TELEPHONE INTERVIEWS

Perhaps you have watched a nightly news show in which the anchor casually asserts that "53% of those surveyed indicated that they believe the president of the United States is doing a fine job." In this high-tech world we live in, a means by which to collect information from large populations rests at our fingertips. Now, we can "reach out and touch someone" (if they have a phone, are home, and are willing to talk) and affect national policy by sharing the results with the television audience.

Telephone surveys use carefully constructed questions to obtain a variety of facts about people's attitudes and behavior—what they say they have done or would do in a variety of situations.

As noted by Fowler (1993), the decision to use telephone surveys has several advantages as compared to other methodologies. These include (a) potentially lower costs, (b) random-digit-dialing sampling of general populations, (c) access to certain populations, (d) potential for a short data collection period, (e) interviewer administration advantages, (f) ease of interviewer staffing and management considerations, and (g) better response rate from a list sample (p. 65).

Telephone surveys can be less costly than other methodologies in terms of financial and personnel-related needs if the sample is in the local calling area and if the survey does not require much training. Selection of the sample that will be contacted for the telephone interview is easily facilitated through random-digit dialing. This procedure ensures representativeness of the sample selected for inclusion. Of course, households without a telephone would be excluded, but as the estimate for this occurrence is small, researchers do not spend sleepless nights worrying about such omissions. Again, one must confront the issue of the usefulness of telephone surveys to the question being investigated. If you are hoping to find out what homeless people think about America's current domestic state (e.g., housing and job availability), you will not find a list of names and/or phone numbers of such persons from which to obtain a representative sample. Here an alternative data collection strategy would have to be devised. However, the use of telephone surveys to study community attitudes toward neighborhood development would surely be appropriate. You would have to obtain a telephone book from which potential respondents would be selected as part of the sample. Then you might want to consult the appropriate chapters in this text to help develop a sampling strategy (see Chapter 8 by McCready) and conduct telephone surveys (see Chapter 11 by Chen).

Summary

This chapter has presented a considerable amount of information about survey and questionnaire design for you to consider. But despite our best efforts to include many important issues and describe their implications for survey design, some issues cannot be discussed adequately because of page limitations. We encourage you to consider additional sources (such as those that appear in the references and are discussed in the Recommended Readings section) to assist you with the development of your survey. We hope that this chapter has prepared you for presentations of this material you may encounter in other sources.

Recommended Readings

For those readers who are interested in further information about this topic, please refer to the following sources in the reference list: Fink and Kosecoff, *How to Conduct Surveys* (1985); Guenzel, Berkmans, and Cannell, *General Interviewing Techniques* (1983); Payne, *The Art of Asking Questions* (1951); Rosenfeld, Edwards, and Thomas, *Improving Organizational Surveys: New Directions, Methods, and Applications* (1993); and Sudman and Bradburn, *Asking Questions* (1982). Useful information is also available in the following articles: Gibson and Hawkins (1968); Hunt, Sparkman, and Wilcox (1982); Wiseman and Billington (1984); and Yu and Cooper (1983).

References

Bass, B. M., Cascio, W. F., & O'Connor, E. J. (1974). Magnitude estimations of expressions of frequency and amount. *Journal of Applied Psychology, 59,* 313-320.

Bradburn, N. M. (1982). Question-wording effects in surveys. In R. Hogarth (Ed.), *New directions for methodology of the social and behavioral sciences: Question framing and response consistency* (pp. 65-76). San Francisco: Jossey-Bass.

Converse, J. M., & Presser, S. (1986). *Survey questions: Handcrafting the standardized questionnaire.* Newbury Park, CA: Sage.

Fink, A., & Kosecoff, J. (1985). *How to conduct surveys.* Newbury Park, CA: Sage.

Fowler, F. J. (1993). *Survey research methods* (2nd ed.). Newbury Park, CA: Sage.

Frey, J. H. (1989). *Survey research by telephone* (2nd ed.). Newbury Park, CA: Sage.

Gibson, F., & Hawkins, B. (1968). Interviews versus questionnaires. *American Behavioral Scientist, 12,* NS-9-NS-11.

Guenzel, P., Berkmans, R., & Cannell, C. (1983). *General interviewing techniques.* Ann Arbor, MI: Institute for Social Research.

Heberlein, T. A., & Baumgartner, R. (1978). Factors affecting response rates to mailed questionnaires: A quantitative analysis of the published literature. *American Sociological Review, 43,* 447-462.

Hopkins, C. D., & Antes, R. L. (1978). *Classroom measurement and evaluation.* Itasca, IL: Peacock.

Hunt, S. D., Sparkman, R. D., Jr., & Wilcox, J. B. (1982). The pretest in survey research: Issues and preliminary findings. *Journal of Marketing Research, 19,* 269-273.

Isaac, S., & Michael, W. B. (1983). *Handbook in research and evaluation* (2nd ed.). San Diego: EDITS.

Kerlinger, F. N. (1985). *Foundations of behavioral research* (3rd ed.). New York: Holt, Rinehart & Winston.

Miller, D. C. (1991). *Handbook of research design and social measurement* (5th ed.). Newbury Park, CA: Sage.

Morrow, P. C., Eastman, K., & McElroy, J. C. (1991). Concept redundancy and rater naivete in organizational research. *Journal of Applied Psychology, 21,* 219-232.

Orlich, D. (1978). *Designing sensible surveys.* Pleasantville, NY: Redgrave.

Payne, S. (1951). *The art of asking questions.* Princeton, NJ: Princeton University Press.

Rosenfeld, P., Edwards, J. E., & Thomas, M. D. (1993). *Improving organizational surveys: New directions, methods, and applications.* Newbury Park, CA: Sage.

Schuman, H., & Presser, S. (1981). *Questions and answers in attitude surveys.* New York: Academic Press.

Spector, P. E. (1992). *Summated rating scale construction.* Newbury Park, CA: Sage.

Sudman, S., & Bradburn, N. M. (1982). *Asking questions: A practical guide to questionnaire design.* San Francisco: Jossey-Bass.

Wiseman, F., & Billington, M. (1984). Comment on a standard definition of response rates. *Journal of Marketing Research, 21,* 336-338.

Yu, J., & Cooper, H. (1983). A quantitative review of research design effects on response rates to questionnaires. *Journal of Marketing Research, 20,* 36-44.

Chapter 8

Applying Sampling Procedures

WILLIAM C. McCREADY

Sampling is a tool for solving specific problems in research. Because we cannot see all of reality in a single glance, we are restricted to viewing events one at a time. The purpose of sampling is to provide systematic rules and methods for allowing us to estimate how well our sample represents the reality we are studying.

For example, think of the people who first tried to study humans beings from the inside. They had no idea what to expect. There was no map for them. The very earliest students of anatomy studied cadavers, the bodies of people who had died. By carefully describing what our circulatory systems and organ placements looked like, these early scientists eventually provided a map of the human body that became extremely useful in the development of Western medical science. The earliest practitioners of surgery followed this map and soon found that all human beings looked pretty much the same anatomically. Surgeons could generalize from this map created from a very small sample of the entire population to the entire population of humans because there is very little variation between humans when it comes to anatomical structures such as the circulatory system and the placement of our organs.

On the other hand, think of asking one person 10 questions about his or her goals in life. Does it seem reasonable to take that person's answers and assume that everyone else in the world will answer those questions the same way? Why does it make sense to use a very small sample to answer some types of questions when other questions require very large samples? Can you tell, other than by common sense, when you should use which method? Why do some scientists use sampling and others actually not? Remember that sampling is one of many research tools and is used only for specific purposes. That tool is the subject of this chapter.

Sampling and the Scientific Method

REPRESENTATIVENESS

The whole purpose of drawing a sample is to have a small group of "things" that will accurately represent the properties and characteristics of the larger group of the same "things." The small group is the *sample* and the larger group is the *population.* How you select the sample is a key to how representative it will be of the population. Whether you are conducting an experiment with a control group and a treatment group or whether you are doing a community survey, you will want your sample to represent the populations you are studying. Sampling provides methods for measuring how representative the small group is of the larger group.

It is important to remember that you cannot reach perfect representation. The sample will never perfectly replicate the population. Representativeness in science is about estimates and approximations, not duplication. We are trying to make a sample that is the best estimate of the population under the conditions we face. The rules and methods of sampling are aimed at producing reliable and accurate estimates. For example, suppose we want to know how many people will decide to provide support for a disaster victim under each of two circumstances: the first, when the victim had no warning of the disaster, and the second, when the victim had a warning but failed to take any appropriate action. We can construct an experiment to test for this difference, but our experiment can never perfectly replicate the total reality. The rules and methods of sampling can provide a guideline so that our sample will come close to the reality by a known amount. That is the most we can expect from a sample.

REPLICATION

One of the most essential aspects of science is conducting an investigation that can be repeated by another scientist who will obtain the same results you did—this is called *replication.* Different disciplines do this in different ways, but whether you are a biologist working in a laboratory investigating DNA or a social psychologist studying the connections between family life and community violence, you will want to conduct your study in such a way that its findings can be replicated.

Social scientists, such as psychologists and sociologists, tend to deal with research questions that contain more variation than the problems our early anatomists solved. Human behaviors are incredibly complex and contain many variations. Therefore you might think it was a simple matter of using very large samples so we could make sure to capture all the varieties of the behavior we are studying. You would be wrong.

EXPERIMENTAL METHOD

One of the most powerful tools researchers have is the experiment. For some types of experiments you need large samples, but for other types you do not. As a matter of fact, sometimes the experiment with the smaller sample is actually the more powerful of the two. The key to a powerful experiment is manipulating the conditions one at a time and observing the changes that occur. Many insights have been produced by this method. The famous American psychologist B. F. Skinner (1966) said, "Study one rat for a thousand hours rather than a thousand rats for one hour each or one hundred rats for ten hours each" (p. 21). Sigmund Freud, from the other end of the psychological spectrum, also studied a few subjects in great depth rather than many subjects superficially. The experiment is particularly useful when testing strong theories, and detailed observation of a single subject is particularly useful when you have a reason to think that all possible subjects are pretty much the same when it comes to what you are studying—as in the case of the human circulation system.

Experimental research frequently involves the random assignment of subjects to control and treatment groups. Members of the control group do not receive the experimental manipulation, and those in the treatment group do receive it. Subjects in the two groups are frequently matched on a number of variables such as gender, age, and physique so that the only thing being studied is the result of the experimental manipulation.

POPULATION ESTIMATION

On the other hand, there are research questions that do not lend themselves to being studied by conducting an experiment. For example, you may have no strong theory to test, or you may suspect that there is a great deal of variation among the subjects in your sample. Sometimes the research question involves trying to ascertain what conditions are like in the larger population: for example, "How are people in a community predisposed toward environmental issues?" In such an instance, a sample of the community is required.

CHAPTER OVERVIEW

Sampling provides different tools for different jobs, and the type of sample depends on the job you want it to do. There is sampling for experiments and sampling for community surveys. There is sampling to produce a feasible number of subjects and sampling to project to population estimates. In the next section, we will discuss the types and tools of sampling and offer some guidelines as to when to use which.

There are two general types of sampling, nonprobability sampling and probability sampling, and each has its uses. We will discuss nonprobability sampling first because psychologists frequently use this method to select subjects for experiments.

Nonprobability Sampling Techniques

THE POWER OF RELATIONSHIPS

C. James Goodwin (1995) wrote, "Of course, the hope is that the results of these studies will extend beyond the subjects participating in it, but the researcher assumes that if the relationship studied is a powerful one, it will occur for most subjects within a particular population, regardless of how they are chosen" (p. 109). This statement is an excellent description of the power attributed to the relationship between the variables being studied in many psychological experiments. Powerful relationships, such as that between obedience and the perceived legitimation of authority, will occur in the population regardless of how the participants in the experiments are chosen. In this type of research, various types of nonprobability samples are effective. There are several names for these samples, including judgmental, ad hoc, convenience, purposive, and matching samples.

THE PARTICIPANT POOL

There are those who would say that nonprobability sampling is not really sampling at all but rather involves systematic subject selection. For example, it is common practice for the subjects who volunteer for experiments at many university departments of psychology to be students in first-year psychology courses. These students form the "participant pool" from which participants in various experiments are drawn. Although student subjects may be randomly drawn from the pool, the pool itself may or may not be representative of any larger population. However, for the purpose of the experiment, the selected subjects are indeed a sample of all the possible subjects available for that experiment.

SELECTING AND ASSIGNING PARTICIPANTS

To ensure that ethical principles are maintained, participants in the pool should indeed be volunteers and should not be coerced in any way. Participants should not be allowed to choose which experiment or condition (e.g., control vs. treatment group) they will be in but should be randomly assigned. These randomization procedures prevent bias from occurring due to previous experience or knowledge of the experiment or other potential causes by distributing it across the groups. Bias is one source of error in a sample, and if it is due to such causes as prior knowledge or disposition, it can usually be prevented during the selection process. The researcher frequently uses his or her judgment about the characteristics of the members of the sample to assist in the selection. For example, if you were studying people for the presence of chronic fatigue syndrome, you would not be interested in people who at the outset of the interview said they had never felt tired a day in their life. Your professional judgment would exclude these people from your sample.

MATCHING SAMPLES

The ideal matched sample consists of identical twins, and twin registries in various countries have been used for research purposes. Putting one twin in a control group and the other twin in the experimental group goes about as far as possible in eliminating all the sources of experimental variation except the one we are studying, the one due to our experimental manipulation.

In most experiments, there are efforts to simulate the twinning process by matching members of the experimental and control group on as many salient characteristics as possible. Matching is usually done at the outset of the study when the sample is selected. Subject characteristics are tallied during the intake process, and matches are created; then random assignment to either the experimental or control group takes place. The result is that the control group and experimental group are as alike as can be, except for the administration of the experimental treatment or condition. Therefore, when we discover differences between the two groups on the experimental outcome, we can consider the difference to be the result of the experiment and not due to some other differences between the members of the groups.

SAMPLING "ERROR" IN NONPROBABILITY SAMPLES: A MISNOMER

Sampling error is a frequently misunderstood concept in the social sciences. The more appropriate term is *sample variance,* and it has to do with the replicability of the measurements one would obtain if one repeated the same sampling procedure many, many times. The use of the term *error* is unfortunate because sample variance is actually the smallest component of total error in a sample. (The other two components of total error, sample bias and response effects, are usually much larger. Sample bias has to do with making mistakes in the execution of the sample plan, and response effects are the result of the differences between the behaviors and attitudes that respondents report and respondents' true behaviors and attitudes.)

The issue here—and we will revisit it in the material on probability sampling as well—is whether you will get the same measurements or statistics from repeated samples of the type you are using. We estimate sampling variation by accumulating the variances in the measures derived from the repeated samples and taking the square root of that term. In other words, what some refer to as *sampling error* is usually better described as the *standard deviation of the variances between the measurements from repeated samples.*

We can compute this statistic for nonprobability samples, but interpretation is made difficult by the fact that the participant's probability of being selected is unknown. We will discuss this more in the following section, but because it is difficult to define the "population" for a nonprobability sample, it is also difficult to define the selection process in probabilistic terms. For these reasons, the subject of sampling error is not usually discussed in those sampling contexts in which participants are recruited from pools for experiments.

SAMPLE SIZE

The size of samples is a good bridge topic between nonprobability sampling and probability sampling because the issue of sample size is almost as frequently misunderstood as the concept of "error." How large should a sample be for an experiment? In experimental methods, this has everything to do with how many trials and conditions and manipulations you plan to make and virtually nothing to do with the need to estimate values in a larger population. The situation is virtually reversed when it comes to doing probability sampling for a project such as a community survey. That is, the precision of estimates of population parameters becomes paramount.

For nonprobability sampling, N (the sample size) should be sufficient to allow reliable detection of expected changes in the experimental variable(s). A pragmatic rule of thumb for the beginning researcher is to adopt the sample sizes observed during the review of the research literature that invariably precedes an experimental project. In other words, when you review the literature in your area, prior to designing your particular experiment, note the sample sizes being reported by others, and use the mean of those as your guide. As a rough guideline, include projects conducted within the past 3 years or so. Typical experimental samples range between 50 and 200 participants. Additional detail on the sample size issue is provided by Yaffee (Chapter 15 of this volume).

Clearly, the cost of running participants in experiments also figures into the choice of sample size. How many assistants do you have? How long does it take for a participant to complete an experiment? How many participants can the experiment accommodate at one time? Whether you are retrospectively trying to fit the design to a grant budget or prospectively trying to prepare a budget application, these are essential questions to consider. It is frequently possible to obtain useful information simply by querying colleagues who have conducted similar experiments. If that is not possible, a careful reading of the research literature will provide contacts for you to call.

Probability Sampling

The other major sampling procedure is probability sampling, in which members of a sample have known probabilities of membership. The probabilities may not be equal, but they are known.

SAMPLES, POPULATIONS, AND THE UNIT OF ANALYSIS

A sample is a portion of a population selected by some method that the researcher hopes will produce a smaller group representing the larger population. A population may consist of any elements. It may be people, families, schools, cities, crimes, graduations, financial transactions, events, decisions, tasks, or any other similar elements. An important part of the task in designing a survey is to define the population to be studied, and an important aspect of that process is to match the population to the unit of analysis for the project.

A typical unit-of-analysis problem occurs when one is trying to estimate how many persons were treated by medical facilities within a community during the past year. The governing agencies may keep counts of the number of times people were treated at the facilities, but unless there is a personal identifier attached to each element of the count, we cannot be sure how many persons are actually represented in the statistic. In this case, the researcher would have to decide whether to make the unit of analysis the "fact of being treated at a facility" or "the person being treated." There are data for the first unit of analysis (the event of being treated), but new data would have to be collected to study the second unit of analysis (the person being treated). In fact, need for these new data would necessitate a modification of the intake procedures to create a unique personal identifier for each participant.

PROBABILITY THEORY

The key contribution of probability theory to sampling is that it enables the researcher to know the odds, chances, or probabilities of a single respondent's being selected in the sample. Why is this information useful? Because if you know the odds or probabilities of selection you can also estimate the probabilities of nonselection and have a more precise estimate of the variation between repeated samples of the same design. By doing this, you can assign a numeric or quantitative value to the concept of representation. For example, suppose we draw a sample of a community. After finding that 25% of our respondents agree that the community needs a new school and that 75% disagree, we would like to have some assurances that this sample accurately represents the attitudes of the population in the community. What if we drew another sample? To what extent would we get the same results? Sample variance, the extent of the difference between samples, is an answer to this question in the form of numerical results that can be compared, analyzed, and replicated. You can compute sample variances only for probability samples, which is one reason they are chosen over nonprobability samples for some research projects, such as those that require a population estimate.

It may simplify things for beginning researchers to remember that virtually all social science statistics have either one of two purposes. We are trying to estimate either how close together things are or how far apart they are. The first goes under the heading of "centrality" and the second under the heading of "variance." Another way of thinking of this is that most social science research looks simply at how much alike or how different subjects are, according to sets of properties or characteristics that we call *variables*. Whether the similarities or differences are relevant or important is usually determined by our theoretical statements. The task of the sample design is to provide a framework or a map that makes sure that another researcher could replicate the way we selected participants for our study and that our findings are true for more than just one sample.

Probability theory is a specific field within mathematics, statistics, and philosophy and can be very complex. Probabilities are estimated for all sorts of events and happenings all the time. The reason that the news media provide point spreads for various athletic events is to facilitate gambling on those events, not just for fan information. Huge corporate marketing campaigns are based on the probabilistic estimates of groups of people with specific characteristics doing certain things. Your insurance rates are computed using probability methods. Probabilities frequently determine whether or not your tax return will be audited. Probabilities are all around us every day. We tend to accept statements such as "It is more likely that you will die from being struck by lightning than in an airplane crash" without knowing very much at all about how those estimates are derived.

The key thing to remember about probability theory and sampling is that the theory provides a way of assigning known values to the event of respondent or participant selection. The advantage of having a specific value assigned to selection, such as a 1-in-258,765 chance, is that the value can be manipulated and compared to other values using the principles of mathematical statistics. Without such specific values, it is not possible to know with precision what would happen during repeated trials of the same sampling method. Without this knowledge there is no precision to the replication, and without replication there is no scientific method.

The most common use of probability sampling is within survey research methodology because surveys are usually designed to use a sample of respondents to estimate the properties, characteristics, and parameters of a larger population. In a sense, whereas small samples for experiments can be selected nonprobabilistically without sacrificing precision, large samples are best selected using probability methods so that we can estimate their variation. A good expression of this phenomenon was provided by Kalton (1983). He observed that if you compare a small probability sample with a small judgmental or nonprobability sample, the sample variation for the probability sample will be so large as to make the sample virtually useless. Increasing the size of the probability sample reduces the sample variance and makes the sample useful.

On the other hand, because a sample variance for the nonprobability sample cannot be computed, the concern about bias grows as the sample gets larger because the larger sample size will magnify any bias due to errors of judgment in selecting the sample. Therefore the small size of the nonprobability sample is not a liability but rather actually a convenience. In a sense, it is like the relationship between a navigational inaccuracy and the distance being traveled. Over a short distance, an inaccuracy might result in a small error of a few hundred yards. Over a longer distance, the same inaccuracy will produce a much larger error, and you will miss your destination by many miles instead of a few yards. Using probability methods to select participants in larger samples ensures that we take advantage of the fact that the sample variance decreases as the sample size grows larger.

SAMPLING FRAME

The listing of probabilities for each member in the population to be selected into the sample is the *sampling frame*. The frame is not simply all the members of the population; rather, it is the array or listing of all the individual members' probabilities of being chosen for the sample. In a simple random sample, each member of the population has the same probability of being selected, but how that number is computed may be different for different members of the population, and that is what is meant by *sampling frame.*

SIMPLE RANDOM SAMPLING

A *simple random sample* is a selection from a population in which each element of the population has the same probability of being chosen for the sample and in which the selection is done all in one step or stage. For example, if we wanted to take a sample of a community that totaled 7,500 people we would make it so that each person had a 1-in-7,500 chance of being selected—correct? It *would* be correct if we intended to include all the babies and children in our sample, but we probably would not wish to do this. If we had census information as to the number of people in the community in each age group, we could replace the 7,500 with the number of adults (however we agreed to define *adult*) and make our sample so that each adult had a 1-in-"the total number of adults" chance of being chosen. If, as is often the case, we did not have census information because the community was too small or the census was too old, we would have to develop another strategy. That would probably involve doing one sampling to see what the distribution of ages was in the community and then doing another to select the adults for our study. The point here is that even simple random sampling gets complicated pretty quickly when we take it into the real world of project operations.

LIST OR SYSTEMATIC SAMPLING

A variation of a simple random sample is to sample randomly from a list of elements. In most instances, this is a true simple random sample, unless there are unusual periodicities, clusterings, groupings, or fragmentations of the list. To sample randomly from a list, first compute the sampling fraction (*n*th) by dividing the size of the sample you desire into the total number of elements in the list; then randomly choose a starting point and select every nth element, and you will produce a simple random sample of the members of the list. For example, suppose you have a class roster of Psych 100 with 300 students on it and you want a sample of 30 for your experiment. Create the sampling fraction (nth) by dividing 30 into 300, with the result being 10. Choose a random starting point and select every 10th student. (If you had wanted a sample of 25, you would have chosen every 12th student.) A random starting point can be generated by numbering the students from 001 to 300 and using a table of random numbers or by using the random-number-generator function found on many scientific calculators and selecting the first number between 001 and 300 to appear. If the list is available in a format you can use on your computer, it is also a good idea simply to scramble the names alphabetically before making the random selection. Sometimes the elements of the list will come with their own ID numbers that can be perused by the random number generator and used to select a starting point as well.

BLOCK QUOTA SAMPLING

Strictly speaking, quota sampling is a nonprobability method of judgmental sampling. In the early days of survey research, it was commonly used. Interviewers would be told to select a specific number of respondents with certain characteristics. For example, the instruction might be that out of a cluster of 30 respondents, they were to get 15 men and 15 women and that 7 of the men should be under 40 years of age and 8 should be older, whereas 8 of the women should be under 40 years of age and 7 should be older.

As probability sampling came to be used, researchers would combine certain aspects of probability selection with the older quota selection methods as a way of creating a cost-effective compromise. Residential blocks would be selected using probability methods, and once on a selected block, interviewers would use the quota method to select individual respondents from households. Some researchers still use this method on occasion for personal interviewing when costs have to be kept to a minimum.

FULL-PROBABILITY SAMPLING

The usual difference between a block quota sample and a full-probability sample in personal interviewing is that the probabilistic selection of the respondent continues right down to the selection of the individual respondent. Once an interviewer reaches the household, he or she asks the person who answers the door how many people live in the household. The respondent for the survey is selected from among that list by a probability method. Some variation of a Kish table is then used to tell the interviewer which person in the household to interview. A Kish table, named for the sampling pioneer Leslie Kish of the University of Michigan, is simply a table of numbers that are randomly generated that tell the interviewer, "If there are two people in the household, select the oldest," "If there are three people, select the youngest," "If there are four, select the second oldest," and so on. The secret to the success of this method is that these tables are randomly generated so they are different for each household the interviewer visits. For example, the next time the interviewer called on the table, instead of what we saw above, we might see "If there are two people in the household, select the youngest," "If there are three people, select the middle one," "If there are four, select the second youngest," and so on. In this way, we guarantee that each person in the household has the same chance of being chosen for an interview, thereby fulfilling the goal of the full-probability sampling method. Samples in which each individual in the population has an equal chance of being selected are frequently referred to as *epsem* samples, for "*equal probability of selection of each member.*"

Another way of selecting respondents within a selected household is to ask for the "respondent who has had the last birthday." Birthdays are randomly distributed in the population, and this method provides a reasonable method of randomly selecting a respondent in a household.

RANDOM-DIGIT-DIALING SAMPLING

Surveys are now being conducted over the telephone, and this is being done more and more as computer programs for the administration of surveys (computer-assisted telephone interviewing [CATI]) have been developed. In a country such as the United States, in which telephone coverage averages near 95%, telephone surveys represent a considerable cost savings over personal interviewing. Sampling for telephone surveys is usually done using some form of random-digit dialing (RDD). Typically this consists of developing estimates for how many listed household numbers exist for each three-digit exchange in an area code and selecting a sample proportionate to that distribution.

Today, with the rapid changes in telecommunications technologies, such as cell phones, beepers, faxes, and new area codes, it is more and more difficult for the researcher who works on one project at a time to keep up with the technology. Therefore many researchers who use CATI purchase the numbers they call from vendors such as Survey Sampling, Inc., or Genesys, Inc. These companies do all the statistical work of selecting the samples according to your specifications. Chen provides additional details on this topic in Chapter 11 of this volume.

SAMPLE SIZE

One of the first questions a student usually asks about sampling is, "How do you know how large or small a sample to create?" The answer to this question is complex and requires understanding some of the points we have already covered. But it seems intuitively simple because it seems that there should be a direct, positive relationship between sample size and sample quality—after all, isn't bigger better? Not always! It is absolutely crucial to remember that in sampling the salient question is not "How big is the sample?" but rather "How are the elements of the sample selected?"

Although it does not seem to make intuitive sense, it takes the same number of respondents to provide identical estimates of precision and accuracy, whether our populations are the entire country, a specific state, a city, or a smaller community. In other words, if it takes 1,500 respondents in a national sample of the adult population of the United States to provide a ±3% range of accuracy to survey questions with a 95% confidence interval, it will also take 1,500 respondents to depict the population of Cleveland, keeping to the same statistical specifications.

The Law of Large Numbers (Mosteller, Rourke, & Thomas, 1961) describes the reason for this state of affairs. The law states that as the size of a sample increases, any estimated proportion rapidly approaches the true proportion that the estimate represents. For example, increasing the sample size from 500 to 1,000 will decrease the range of accuracy around a percentage from approximately ±7% to ±4%, and increasing the sample to 1,500 will reduce the range to about ±3%. But after that, the decreases in the range are slight and are not usually worth the added cost of obtaining the extra cases. For example, doubling the sample to 3,000 respondents reduces the range only another 1.5% to ±1.5%. This illustrates diminishing returns in action.

A more intuitive way to think about the Law of Large Numbers is to imagine the following experiment. For the Fourth of July gala, I have emptied the swimming pool at the local park and filled it with Ping-Pong balls; some are red, some are white, and the rest are blue. I will award a prize of $500 to the person who give the best estimate of the proportions of red, white, and blue balls. If you select 50 balls and you see that 11 (22%) are red, 19 (38%) are white, and 20 (40%) are blue, are you very confident that you will win the prize? You shouldn't be. If another person does the same experiment, he or she may well come up with a different set of percentages.

If you select 500 balls, however, you are likely to be more convinced that the percentages you have will win you the prize, and you are even more sure after you have picked 1,000 or 1,500 balls. However, if you spend a lot more time and select a sample of 3,000 or 6,000 balls, you will find that your estimate has not changed very much and that it is hardly worth the extra effort. You are pretty well sure that the estimate you derive after 1,000 to 1,500 selections is as accurate as you are going to get: The Law of Large Numbers has been at work.

CLUSTER SAMPLING

Some populations have members that are in close proximity to one another, such as students, and these can be sampled by drawing clusters and then sampling individual members within the clusters. For example, if we want to sample students, we can first randomly select schools because that is where students can be easily found. Then we can randomly sample students within the selected schools, and we will still have a known probability for each of the students in our sample. The advantage is that we can do this with considerably less expense and effort than if we tried to find students by randomly sampling households.

STRATIFIED SAMPLING

Populations can also be divided into subgroups according to characteristics that are not geographically linked like clusters. For example, we may decide to separate our population into four groups; males under age 40, males 40 and over, females under 40, and females 40 and over. We may decide to do this because we are most interested in some aspect of the lives of females who are 40 and over and we want to concentrate our sampling efforts on maximizing that information.

Stratified sampling is not always appropriate and should be used carefully. Sudman (1976) has an excellent discussion of the possible negatives in stratifying your sample. There are generally three reasons why you might stratify. First, the strata themselves are interesting topics within your research design. This can be true especially in survey work in which demographic characteristics are important. Second, you may have good prior information about the differences between strata in terms of variances or other characteristics. Third, stratifying can generate cost savings, but one should take precautions so that stratifying for cost reasons does not actually produce a less efficient and accurate sample.

MULTISTAGE SAMPLING

Most national survey samples are multistage samples, whether data are collected by personal interviewing or CATI interviewing. This simply means that sampling is done in several stages, starting with natural clusters and ending with selection of the individual respondent. Probabilities are assigned to the selection of each unit at each stage and can be combined to provide a known unique probability for the selection of every member of the final sample. Natural geographic clusters, such as census tracts and area codes, are used to sort the population, and sampling proportionate to size is used within each to select individuals.

For example, if you live in a small town, your town will have a small chance of being in a national sample. (For many good national survey samples of 1,500 respondents or so, between 14 and 16 states are routinely left out because none of the towns in them make it to the final selection.) However, if your town does get selected at the early stages, you will personally have a much better chance of being selected in the national sample than someone who lives in a larger town.

Most beginning researchers will not need to know about multistage sampling. However, if you have the opportunity to work on a project using this technique, you will learn a good deal about the practical techniques of applied sampling, and they are worth learning. Applied sampling is best learned by being an apprentice to others who have been doing it for a long time. It is a skill that has been modified, refined, and handed down from one generation of samplers to the next—and that is the way to learn it best.

Other special-purpose sampling designs include sampling for longitudinal studies, cohort samples, cumulative sampling, aggregating across samples, and Bayesian sampling. Conceptual and operational treatments of such complex designs can be found in advanced treatments of sampling (Frankel, 1983; Sudman, 1983).

Summary

This chapter contains a basic overview of sampling theory and procedures for the beginning researcher. The importance of sampling for scientific research and for producing confidence in research findings served as an introduction. The distinction between non-probability and probability sampling was used to organize a review of the major designs for experiments and surveys. Now it is appropriate to conclude with a reminder of the ethical obligations of researchers and in particular sample designers. It is ethically sensitive to strive toward a goal of ensuring that all members of a defined population have a chance to appear in the sample of participants or respondents and share their views with researchers and policy makers. It is also ethically sensitive to ensure that the participation or response is provided voluntarily and without coercion or deception.

Recommended Readings

The following readings are merely a sample of the domain of the literature for those interested in further self-study and improvement. There is no substitute for asking questions of others, designing sampling frames yourself, and seeking constructive criticism from peers, supervisors, and yourself. A good source for the mathematical foundations of sampling is Cochran (1977). For other basic treatments of sampling, see Kalton (1983), Kish (1965), and Sudman (1976). A chapter by Sudman (1983) on the issues in applied sampling lists helpful bibliographies prepared by very experienced research organizations, including the National Opinion Research Center at the University of Chicago (NORC), the U.S. Bureau of the Census, and the Survey Research Center (SRC) of the Institute for Social Research (ISR) of the University of Michigan. A useful little pamphlet listing the definitions of sampling terms is also readily available (Survey Sampling, Inc., 1995). On-line searches can be made using standard Internet search engines. Survey Sampling, Inc., can be reached at info@ssisamples.com. Genesys Inc. can be reached at (215) 653-7100.

References

Cochran, W. G. (1977). *Sampling techniques* (3rd ed.). New York: John Wiley.

Frankel, M. (1983). Sampling theory. In P. Rossi, J. Wright, & A. Anderson (Eds.), *Handbook of survey research* (pp. 21-67). New York: Academic Press.

Goodwin, C. J. (1995). *Research in psychology: Methods and design.* New York: John Wiley.

Groves, R. M., & Kahn, R. L. (1979). *Surveys by telephone: A national comparison with personal interviews.* New York: Academic Press.

Kalton, G. (1983). *Introduction to survey sampling.* Beverly Hills, CA: Sage.

Kish, L. (1965). *Survey sampling.* New York: John Wiley.

Mosteller, F., Rourke, R. E. K., & Thomas, G. B., Jr. (1961). *Probability with statistical applications.* Reading, MA: Addison-Wesley.

Murray, J. (1978). *Continuous national sample: Project reports.* Chicago: National Opinion Research Center.

Piekarski, L. (1994). *Random digit telephone sampling methodology.* Fairfield, CT: SSI.

Skinner, B. F. (1966). Operant behavior. In W. K. Honig (Ed.), *Operant behavior: Areas of research and application* (p. 21). New York: Appleton-Century-Crofts.

Sudman, S. (1976). *Applied sampling.* New York: Academic Press.

Sudman, S. (1983). Applied sampling. In P. Rossi, J. Wright, & A. Anderson (Eds.), *Handbook of survey research* (pp. 145-194). New York: Academic Press.

Survey Sampling, Inc. (1995). *Glossary handbook: A survey researcher's handbook of industry terminology and definitions.* Fairfield, CT: Author.

PART III

Data Collection

Chapter 9

Applying for Approval to Conduct Research With Human Participants

LYLE D. SCHMIDT
NAOMI M. MEARA

A task that is absolutely necessary for conducting research with human participants is having the research approved by an Institutional Review Board (IRB). To keep one's research program running smoothly and to meet deadlines for required work such as theses and dissertations, one needs to know how to accomplish this task. To accomplish it effectively and efficiently, it is helpful to know not only the specific procedures and forms used at your university but also the rationale behind the formation of IRBs and the ethical and deliberative aspects of their responsibilities.

Development of Institutional Review Boards

Any institution in the United States in which research involving human participants is conducted, supported, or otherwise subject to regulation by almost any federal department or agency must have a procedure for protecting the research participants. The federal policy that regulates the procedure is presented in the Code of Federal Regulations, Title 45 CFR Part 46, as revised in 1991. Each institution formulates its own guidelines for complying with the federal policy and negotiates an assurance of their compliance with the Office for Protection From Research Risks (OPRR), a unit within the Department of Health and Human Services (DHHS) that implements the regulations for the protection of human subjects. If your institution has negotiated an assurance with OPRR, you should find an office in the institution's directory that is listed under "Human Subjects (Participants) Review Committee," "Institutional Review Board for the Protection of Human Subjects," or some combination of these terms. This office should be able to provide you the guidelines and materials necessary to apply for human subjects committee approval at your institution. In addition, your departmental colleagues or academic advisor may have not only this information but an understanding of the process based on their experiences in securing approval from the IRB.

The term used in almost all regulatory policy statements concerning human participants in research is *Institutional Review Board (IRB)*. This is an administrative body established to protect the rights and welfare of persons recruited to participate in research activities conducted within the institution. It may have one or more sections, which may be designated, for example, Social and Behavioral Sciences Review Committee, or Biomedical Sciences Review Committee, depending on the area of research to be reviewed. The committees review research protocols that you, the researcher, prepare. These protocols are descriptions of a research program or individual investigation, presented in sufficient detail for the committee (a) to assess the nature of the requirements of the human participants or subjects in the research and (b) to determine whether provisions have been made for adequate protection of the participants' rights and welfare.

Why have IRBs been established? Although regard for the welfare of human recipients of professional services, as in physicians' Hippocratic Oath, is of long standing, the history of human subjects' protection in the United States began in 1947. Abuses of prisoners in Nazi concentration camps by physicians and scientists conducting biomedical experiments were made public after the defeat of Nazi Germany in 1945. During the Nuremberg War Crimes Trials, the Nuremberg Code was drafted as a set of standards for judging those who had committed such offenses (OPRR, 1993, p. A6-9). The code became a model for later codes in the principles it set forth for the ethical treatment of human subjects who participate in research. First among these principles was that "the voluntary consent of the human subject is absolutely essential" (OPRR, 1993, p. A6-1). Other principles include a favorable risk/benefit ratio, the avoidance of harm and suffering, protection of subjects from injury, the necessity that investigators be qualified scientists, and freedom for subjects to withdraw at any time. An elaboration of these principles was made by the World Medical Association's Declaration of Helsinki in 1964 and revised in 1975, 1983, and 1989 (OPRR, 1993, p. A6-3). Both the Nuremberg Code and Declaration of Helsinki were concerned with medical research.

Government regulations protecting human subjects in the United States first appeared in 1966 as National Institutes of Health policies for the protection of human subjects. Passage of the National Research Act in 1974 created the National Commission for the Protection of Human Subjects of Biomedical and Behavioral Research. The commission's final report was submitted in 1978 under the title of *The Belmont Report: Ethical Principles and Guidelines for the Protection of Human Subjects of Research*. The name came from the meeting place of the commission in the Belmont Conference Center of the Smithsonian Institution. The report is reprinted in Appendix 6 of the OPRR's 1993 publication *Protecting Human Research Subjects*.

The Belmont Report distinguished between research and practice and identified three basic ethical principles in research with human subjects. Research was considered "an activity designed to test an hypothesis, permit conclusions to be drawn, and thereby to develop or contribute to generalizable knowledge" (National Commission, 1979, p. 3). The report considered practice to refer to "interventions that are designed solely to enhance the well-being of an individual patient or client and that have a reasonable expectation of success" (National Commission, 1979, p. 3). The three basic ethical principles discussed by the Commission were respect for persons, beneficence, and justice. *Respect* involved two convictions: that persons should be treated as autonomous individuals and that persons with diminished autonomy should be protected. *Beneficence* was understood as an obligation to protect subjects by maximizing possible benefits and minimizing possible harms. *Justice* was concerned with the fair distribution of the burdens and benefits of research.

In response to the Belmont Report, the U.S. Department of Health and Human Services in 1981 revised its human subjects regulations. They were codified in 1981 as Title 45, Part 46, of the Code of Federal Regulations, "Protection of Human Subjects" (45 CFR 46). Revisions became effective in 1983 and 1991, the latter involving the adoption of the federal policy for the protection of human subjects by 16 agencies of the federal government that support, conduct, or regulate human subjects research. The regulations apply "to all research involving human subjects conducted, supported or otherwise subject to regulation" by these agencies (45 CFR 46, 1991, p. 4).

What, then, are the research requirements that derive from the three basic ethical principles described in the Belmont Report? The first of these, *respect for persons,* underlies the requirement of informed consent. Subjects, to the extent they are capable, must be allowed to decide what shall or shall not happen to them. This process is said to contain the elements of information, comprehension, and voluntariness. *Information* ordinarily includes the research procedures; their purposes, risks, and possible benefits; alternative procedures if treatment is involved; the opportunity for subjects to ask questions; and a statement that subjects may withdraw from the research at any time. Although it is impossible to know all related information, the standard refers to communicating the information to subjects that would seem important enough to influence a decision to participate. Such information would include what they will do, how their data will be used, and, if the data are not anonymous, what measures are in place to ensure confidentiality. *Comprehension* means that the information is conveyed in manner and context so that each subject understands what is presented to him or her. Limited capacity to comprehend may require some persons (e.g., children) to be represented by third parties, and even then, such persons must be allowed to choose whether to participate unless the research involves a therapy that has some probability of success and is not otherwise available. *Voluntariness* requires that the consent to participate be given without coercion or undue influence—the latter occurring, for example, when excessive or unwarranted reward is offered for participation.

The second basic ethical principle, *beneficence,* underlies the requirement of a risk/benefit analysis to minimize the probability and severity of possible harm to subjects and to balance them against the probability and magnitude of anticipated benefits to health or welfare of the individual and possibly others. The analysis involves a consideration of the nature and scope of risks and benefits and their systematic assessment. This offers researchers an opportunity to evaluate the research design and assist prospective subjects in their decision to participate. Several considerations are necessary, among them the following:

1. Brutal or inhumane treatment of human subjects is never morally justified.
2. Risks should be only at the level necessary to the research objective, and lower-risk alternatives should be a major goal in research design.
3. The appropriateness of involving vulnerable populations must be demonstrated.
4. Risks and benefits must be made obvious in the consent process.

The third basic ethical principle, *justice*, underlies the requirement that there be fairness in the selection of subjects to distribute equitably the burdens and benefits of research. At the individual level, this means not offering potentially beneficial research only to favored subjects and risky research to less favored ones. At the social level, justice may be served by a preferential order, such as adults before children, and by avoiding, when possible, some populations already burdened by their conditions or circumstances, such as institutionalized persons. Injustice may occur when subjects are selected largely for convenience, as in the case of ethnic minorities, very ill persons, or students, who happen to be in settings where research is conducted or whose conditions may make them more vulnerable to manipulation or likely to consent. In general, justice would suggest that those groups who may benefit from research also should be the ones approached to participate in it. Some would argue, however, that particularly when no risk is present, individuals have a moral duty to their community to participate in research that could benefit others.

The best known early code for conduct of social and behavioral research was *Ethical Principles in the Conduct of Research With Human Participants,* first published by the American Psychological Association (APA) in 1973 and revised in 1982 (APA, 1973, 1982). The impetus for the development of these standards was professional and public criticism of social science research following Milgram's work (1965, 1974) and other studies in which there were questions about the appropriateness of the deception used, informed consent, and harmful effects for participants. (For a critique of such work, see Bok, 1989.) These criticisms prompted the APA to conduct a comprehensive review of research ethics. Similar to the procedures employed for the development of the original APA ethics code (Hobbs, 1948), an empirical approach was implemented. APA members were surveyed and asked to describe research involving ethical questions. Approximately 5,000 such descriptions were received. Ethical principles derived from these samples and other sources were circulated for APA membership review, then revised and circulated again. The principles developed from this process formed the basis for the publication and its revision.

It should be noted, however, that the first publication of the APA ethics code, *Ethical Standards of Psychologists* (APA, 1953), contained standards for research.

> These concerned the psychologists' responsibility for adequately planning and conducting research, reporting research results, and managing relations with research subjects. Specific principles included protecting subjects' welfare by not exposing them to unnecessary emotional stress and by removing harmful after-effects should any occur; fully informing subjects when a danger of serious after-effects exists, and giving them an opportunity to decline participation; withholding information or giving misinformation only when clearly required by the research problem and when the above principles are observed; not revealing the identity of research subjects without explicit permission; and fulfilling obligations to subjects which were offered in return for their coopera- tion in the research. (Schmidt & Meara, 1984, p. 66)

Subsequent revisions of the APA ethics code maintain sections devoted to research and contain these same general principles. The current code, *Ethical Principles of Psycholo-*

gists and Code of Conduct (APA, 1992), contains 14 specific standards related to research with human participants. These standards cover many of the same topics as the 1953 code (APA, 1953), such as informed consent, deception, and honoring commitments. These sections, as well, are concerned with the same general principles as set forth in the Belmont Report (respect for persons, beneficence, and justice) and relate to the focal issues (discussed below) of an IRB review of research proposals. In addition to these standards, the current APA code (APA, 1992) contains several related to the integrity of researchers, including the topics of plagiarism, publication credit, and responsibilities of professionals who review the research of others for publication. It seems worth noting as well that there is in the 1992 code a specific standard (Standard 6.09) dealing directly with institutional approval: "Psychologists obtain from host institutions or organizations appropriate approval prior to conducting research, and they provide accurate information about their research proposals. They conduct the research in accordance with the approved research protocol" (p. 1608).

Focal Points of an IRB Review

What are likely to be focal points of an IRB review of your protocol? They follow from the research requirements and the underlying ethical principles described above and are discussed in detail in the IRB guidebook, *Protecting Human Research Subjects* (OPRR, 1993).

INFORMED CONSENT

One focal point will be informed consent. The elements of information, comprehension, and voluntariness are important considerations for reviewers of protocols. Is the research described in sufficient detail so that prospective subjects can know what will occur to them and in a manner that will allow them to understand what the description means? Are the circumstances of the invitation to participate such that the consent is freely given?

The federal requirements as to the information to be provided prospective subjects are reported in the Code of Federal Regulations (45 CFR 46), in the IRB guidebook (OPRR, 1993), and in the policy and procedures materials of your institutional IRB. The reviewers will examine your protocol to determine if you have satisfied these requirements according to your institution's and the reviewers' interpretations of them. They may be especially concerned about the following: Is there adequate content in the consent process, and is it expressed in language and format understandable to the subject? Have you provided for the appropriate documentation of the consent? If you are requesting a waiver of the requirement of written consent, have you provided sufficient justification, consistent with federal and your IRB's policies? If your research involves existing data records or proposes to videotape or film subjects without their knowledge, have you satisfied the special consent requirements of these situations? And if you propose to deceive subjects or only partially disclose what will occur to them, have you provided full justification of the necessity for this, consistent with IRB requirements?

RISK/BENEFIT ANALYSIS

A second focal point will be risk/benefit analysis. If subjects of a research study are exposed to risk, their participation should be justified by anticipated benefits to them or to society. Risk is the probability that physical, psychological, social, or economic harm will occur from participating in the research. *Minimal risk* is a probability of harm not greater than that ordinarily present in daily life or in routine physical or psychological examinations or tests.

The members of IRBs are typically very concerned about any risks that accrue to the subjects and what, if any, benefits the research can provide for the individual participants or society in general. As Beauchamp and Childress (1994) noted, "In submitting a research protocol involving human subjects to an institutional research board (IRB) for approval, an investigator is expected to array the risks to subjects and probable benefits to both subjects and society, and then to explain why the probable benefits outweigh the risks" (p. 291). The members of an IRB usually make a reasoned rather than a numerical or statistical assessment of the balance between risks and benefits. A risk/benefit analysis involves the principles of beneficence, respect for persons, and justice. For example, if the research appears to have no potential benefit, it is unlikely to be approved. Sometimes IRBs will note that a design is below acceptable scientific standards. Although such a study may not contain any significant risks, the interpretability of the results obtained can be so ambiguous that there are no apparent benefits either. Badly designed research also can waste subject time and subject pool resources and thus is not fair to either participants or other researchers who need subjects for more beneficial research. If consent forms do not show proper respect for subjects (for example, by containing misinformation or not clearly stating potential risks and benefits), the IRB will most likely ask you to revise the forms to meet this important criterion. In preparing your protocol, you will be asked not only to state the risks and benefits for the IRB members but also to demonstrate how the informed consent and other information you provide for subjects make this information clear so they can make informed decisions with respect to participating.

PRIVACY/CONFIDENTIALITY

A third focal point of an IRB review will be privacy/confidentiality. *Privacy* has to do with one's control over the extent, timing, or circumstances of sharing physical, behavioral, or intellectual aspects of oneself with others. *Confidentiality* relates to what is done with information a person has disclosed in the expectation that it will not be revealed to others in a manner inconsistent with the original understanding about disclosure, without permission.

A research procedure that may seem routine and noninvasive to an investigator can require individuals to disclose information that is very personal, if not interpersonally threatening to some subjects. Often subjects are asked for information that they have revealed to no one else or perhaps only to one or two intimates whom they trust. Therefore issues of privacy and confidentiality are critical to sound research and the approval of your proposal.

Researchers have implicit contracts with subjects to do what they say and to treat the information obtained in a manner to which they agreed in advance. It seems important to remember as well that although a subject may have agreed to a certain use of the information, he or she has a right to remove identifiable information from a data set at any time. In general, it is better not to have any kind of identification in data files (electronic or hard copy) that could point to a specific subject. When such identification is necessary, extra precautions must be taken so that the data do not become available to anyone except those who have been specified in the original research agreement. When such breaches occur, subjects must be notified. The current APA code (APA, 1992) Standard 6.16 states, "Psychologists inform research participants of their anticipated sharing or further use of personally identifiable research data and of the possibility of unanticipated future uses" (p. 1609).

The APA code (APA, 1992) provides guidance with respect to invading subjects' privacy. Standard 6.13 raises special cautions in filming or recording subjects and Standard 6.17 enjoins investigators to minimize invasiveness. In addition to minimum invasiveness, another good general rule to follow is that potential subjects have the right to be left alone and not be repeatedly asked to participate in research. Some will argue that however important the project or potential benefit, researchers should not pursue a prospective subject beyond a simple refusal. If the person says "no," the researcher does not have warrant to mount a sales campaign about the virtues of the project or the obligation of the individual. If individuals have a moral duty to help society, it is not up to researchers to "badger" them into it or make individual decisions about who "ought" to participate in a given project. The best attitude for a researcher to adopt would seem to be that if persons agree to be research subjects, they are going beyond duty. Their motive may be to help the researcher, to contribute to some larger good, or to secure some minor benefit for themselves such as extra credit in a course. Whatever the motive, potential subjects are free to refuse, and when they agree to participate, what they tell us should be used only for science. Information obtained through research should not be trivialized or used to demean subjects or to betray their trust in the research enterprise.

SELECTION OF PARTICIPANTS

A fourth focal point will be the selection of participants. IRBs attempt to determine that the selection is equitable with respect to fairness in the distribution of burdens and benefits of the research. A few of the questions may be: Will the burdens of participating fall on those groups most likely to benefit from it? Will repeated demands on any participating group be avoided when possible? Does the research justify a particular subject group? If vulnerable subjects are proposed, could the research be conducted on other, less vulnerable persons?

Human research is time consuming and often hard to organize. Physics laboratories and chemistry experiments have a more or less captive audience at their disposal. Humans are more difficult to organize, and we have many more considerations in psychological science about rights and welfare in investigations of inanimate matter. The temptation is to look for captive audiences: college students, school children, prisoners, and others who are institutionalized by the state or federal government. These, the poor, the uneducated, the dying (in the case of medical research), and others may bear an undue burden in psychological research and may realize an insufficient share of the benefits. We are coming to realize as well that those who are culturally different may be put upon more than others to be research participants. Clarity about what is just and about one's own "taken-for-granted" scientific and everyday assumptions is critical for accurate science. Respect and sensitivity to these issues are essential for ethical science. Psychologists need to guard against the possibility that in using these ready subjects we may violate the principle of justice. As we discuss below, this issue can be more complicated when there are incentives for research. They need to be equally distributed but must not be coercive, particularly with more vulnerable populations.

INCENTIVES FOR PARTICIPATION

A fifth focal point may be the incentives offered for participation. To ensure that subjects' decisions to participate in research are voluntary, IRBs will try to determine whether consent has been solicited without coercion or undue influence. Are subtle or obvious threats present in the solicitation, or will participants be compensated so excessively that their refusal is rendered unlikely?

A fine line exists between respecting and appreciating the time and effort of research participants (and thus offering some reward or incentive) and making the incentives so large that the result is undue influence. For example, offering extra credit in a psychology class seems appropriate if students can earn the same credit in other ways with approximately the same investment of time and energy. Requiring students to participate in research to earn a significant portion of their course grade (say 10% to 30%) may be coercive. It would be difficult to argue in such circumstances that subjects' agreement to participate was in fact voluntary; it would seem more reasonable to argue that this important condition for informed consent was absent. The current APA code (APA, 1992) offers guidance on these issues. For example, Standard 6.14b states, "Psychologists do not offer excessive or inappropriate financial or other inducements to obtain research participants, particularly when it might tend to coerce participants" (p. 1609).

Researchers have to be cautious, as well, when they have a special relationship with potential subjects. For example, teachers and counselors have more power than students or clients and must be sensitive to that fact if they are recruiting subjects from among their classes or client load. Such a power differential can make potential subjects believe that they have no real choice except to participate. The more powerful one is, the more careful one has to be to respect potential subjects' right to refuse. There is a balance to be achieved between possibly changing the nature of a client-counselor relationship for some anticipated research benefit and being faithful to the implied contract that the therapeutic relationship represents (Meara & Schmidt, 1991). Again, the APA code (APA, 1992) might offer some assistance here. Standard 1.18 raises cautions and suggests guidelines with respect to the use of barter in exchange for psychological services, and Standard 6.14a speaks specifically to the issue of the psychologist's responsibilities when offering psycho-logical services as incentives for research participation. For most graduate students, barter may be a less significant issue because they are not usually in a position to offer excessive amounts of course credit or extended psychological services. Standard 6.11c (APA, 1992), however, seems worth noting because graduate students are often teaching assistants and need to be sensitive to how students may interpret requests or suggestions from their teachers. The standard reads, "When psychologists conduct research with individuals such as students or subordinates, psychologists take special care to protect the prospective participants from adverse consequences of declining or withdrawing from participation" (p. 1608). Members of an IRB will want to be certain that potential participants are protected in this regard. In short, they will look closely at research protocols to assure themselves that the procedures and precautions outlined do not treat subjects in a manner that is explicitly or implicitly exploitative or coercive.

Preparation for an IRB Review

One of the first things one can do in preparing an IRB proposal is to plan ahead. Without such planning, individuals often find that subjects may be available and the project may be ready for data collection but that approval has not yet been granted. IRBs usually have regular meetings about once a month. You need to know when yours meets and how far in advance of the meeting they need your protocol. Knowing these facts is an important consideration in scheduling your own work. Also, it is helpful, if you are a student, to know the policies of your advisor. University IRBs require that a faculty member be listed as one of the investigators on student research. You need to know, therefore, how much time your sponsor will require to read your proposal and how long it might take you to revise it.

You have to know where your IRB office is located so you can obtain the approval forms. Examples of such forms are reproduced in Appendix 9.1 at the end of this chapter. After you complete the forms, you need to ask your sponsor or supervisor to review them. Be sure to allow time for possible revisions. If you are completing one for the first time, it is helpful if you can have access to a protocol in a similar area of research that has already been approved. Studying one that has been successful alerts you to how other individuals have addressed some of the focal issues we have discussed above and gives you informa-tion with respect to such things as different ways of expressing important issues in an informed-consent document or describing your research instruments. Usually your advisor, other faculty members, or students may be willing to share examples of their protocols that have already been approved.

When you submit the protocol, you might ask if it is permissible for you to attend the meeting at which your proposal is being reviewed. Failing that, it is helpful, if possible, to attend an IRB meeting before you complete your protocol but after you are familiar with what the form requires.

The attitude with which one enters the process of completing a research protocol is important. Often students, and some faculty as well, think that the IRB is an adversary or at best just one more time-consuming hurdle they have to surmount. It can be helpful to remember that for the most part, members of the IRB want what you want: ethical, competent research. You try to achieve this through knowledge of your discipline and your research problem, methods, and design and by careful planning as well as by studying the ethical principles that the government, your institution, and the APA think important. To this list, the IRB members add their experience of dealing with many proposals and the deliberative process, in which viewpoints can be exchanged about the strengths and potential problems of proposals. Planning, attention to detail, modeling the work of others, watching the deliberations of an IRB, and understanding the communality of your goals with those of an IRB can facilitate the process of having your protocol approved. Such steps can make the process efficient, educational, and even enjoyable.

Recommended Reading

Although the APA's *Ethical Principles in the Conduct of Research With Human Participants* (1982) was originally written to parallel Principle 9 of the 1981 APA Ethics Code, this useful book remains timely. It elaborates on several issues with respect to conducting human research, such as freedom from exploitation in the research relationship, obligations for obtaining informed consent, and ensuring participant freedom from coercion. The APA may publish a revision soon. Although the principles embodied in such a revision will not change, they probably will be directly related to Standards 6.06 to 6.19 in the current APA code (APA, 1992).

In the chapter "Deceptive Social Science Research" in *Lying: Moral Choice in Public and Private Life*, the philosopher Sissela Bok (1989) critically examines the use of deception in social and behavioral science research. In particular, she focuses on how "disguises" and "cover stories" can interfere with a prospective research participant's right to an informed choice, harm both researchers and participants, and erode public trust in research.

The special section "Ethics in Research" in *Psychological Science* (1994, Vol. 5) consists of a general article by Robert Rosenthal (1994) and four commentaries by Pomerantz, Parkinson, Gurman, and Mann. Rosenthal argues that science and ethics are closely related and that studies of poorer scientific quality are not as ethically defensible as studies of higher scientific merit. Pomerantz is in general agreement with Rosenthal but believes that the cost-utility analysis Rosenthal brings to determining the ethicality of research might be too stringent. Such an analysis could leave one who is inefficient or who makes an honest mistake vulnerable to ethical challenge. Parkinson takes issue with the scientific/ethical relationship explicated by Rosenthal and explains that he judges "the scientific quality of a study independent of the ethical quality of a study" (p. 137). Gurman raises a concern with respect to the absence of debriefing for subjects who are excluded from a study on the basis of preliminary questionnaire responses or other prescreening procedures. Finally, Mann presents a study with college undergraduates assessing their comprehension of informed-consent documents. Results indicate that after reading and signing the forms, subjects were not knowledgeable about critical aspects of the experiment (contained in the form) or some of the rights they retain when agreeing to participate. Mann argues for shorter, less legalistic forms, if not oral consent procedures.

References

American Psychological Association. (1953). *Ethical standards of psychologists.* Washington, DC: Author.

American Psychological Association. (1973). *Ethical principles in the conduct of research with human participants.* Washington, DC: Author.

American Psychological Association. (1982). *Ethical principles in the conduct of research with human participants* (Rev. ed.). Washington, DC: Author.

American Psychological Association. (1992). Ethical principles of psychologists and code of conduct. *American Psychologist, 47,* 1597-1611.

Beauchamp, T. L., & Childress, J. F. (1994). *Principles of biomedical ethics* (3rd ed.). New York: Oxford University Press.

Bok, S. (1989). *Lying: Moral choice in public and private life* (2nd. ed.). New York: Vintage.

Code of Federal Regulations, Title 45 CFR Part 46. (1981, 1983, 1991). Washington, DC: Department of Health and Human Services, National Institutes of Health, Office for Protection from Research Risks.

Gurman, E. B. (1994). Debriefing for all concerned: Ethical treatment of human subjects. *Psychological Science, 5,* 139.

Hobbs, N. (1948). The development of a code of ethical standards for psychology. *American Psychologist, 3,* 80-84.

Mann, T. (1994). Informed consent for psychological research: Do subjects comprehend consent forms and understand their legal rights? *Psychological Science, 5,* 140-143.

Meara, N. M., & Schmidt, L. D. (1991). The ethics of researching counseling/psychotherapy processes. In C. E. Watkins & L. J. Schneider (Eds.), *Research in counseling* (pp. 237-259). Hillsdale, NJ: Lawrence Erlbaum.

Milgram, S. (1965). Some conditions of obedience and disobedience to authority. *Human Relations, 18,* 57-75.

Milgram, S. (1974). *Obedience to authority.* New York: Harper & Row.

National Commission for the Protection of Human Subjects of Biomedical and Behavioral Research. (1979). *The Belmont Report: Ethical principles and guidelines for the protection of human subjects of research.* (Reprinted in Office for Protection from Research Risks, 1993, *Protecting human research subjects,* Appendix 6, pp. A6-7 to A6-14)

Office for Protection From Research Risks, U.S. Department of Health and Human Services. (1993). *Protecting human research subjects: Institutional review board guidebook* (2nd ed.). Washington, DC: Author.

Parkinson, S. (1994). Scientific or ethical quality. *Psychological Science, 5,* 137-138.

Pomerantz, J. R. (1994). On criteria for ethics in science. *Psychological Science, 5,* 135-136.

Rosenthal, R. (1994). Science and ethics in conducting, analyzing, and reporting psychological research. *Psychological Science, 5,* 127-134.

Schmidt, L. D., & Meara, N. M. (1984). Ethical, legal and professional issues in counseling psychology. In S. D. Brown & R. W. Lent (Eds.), *Handbook of counseling psychology* (pp. 56-96). New York: John Wiley.

Appendix 9.1

Summary Sheets and Investigator's Checklist for the Behavioral and Social Sciences Human Subjects Review Committee of The Ohio State University

Protocols received in the Office of Research Risks after the deadline date (NOON, Friday preceding meeting date) will be scheduled for the following meeting. If all time slots are filled and a protocol is received on or before the deadline date, the protocol will be scheduled for the following meeting. Only protocols that are complete will be scheduled for review. Incomplete protocols will be returned.

Principal Investigator(s):
(If student, list advisor's name first)

Typed Name	Signature
Typed Name	Signature
Typed Name	Signature

Academic Title: _____   Phone No. _____

College: _____   Department _____

Campus Address: _____
(Faculty Member's Campus Address)

PROTOCOL TITLE: (Include proposal title in parentheses if different from the protocol.)

_____

_____

_____

SOURCE OF FUNDING FOR PROPOSED RESEARCH: (Check A or B):

A. OSURF: Sponsor   _____   RF Proposal/Project No. _____

B. Other   (Identify)   _____

Information about the funding/sponsorship of human subjects research activities is required for administrative purposes. Such information is generally not required as part of the human subjects review process.

NOTE: This and related information will become available on the World Wide Web in 1996.

SUMMARY SHEETS

The following summary must accompany your proposal. Be specific about exactly what subjects will experience when they participate in your research, and about the protections that have been included to safeguard them. Careful attention to the following may help facilitate the review process.

1. In a sentence or two, describe the background and purpose of the research.

2. Briefly describe each condition or manipulation to be included within the study.

3. What measures or observations will be taken in the study? If any questionnaires, tests, or other instruments are used, provide a brief description *and* either include a copy or indicate when a copy will be submitted for review.

4. Will the subjects encounter the possibility of psychological, social, physical, or legal risk? Yes _____ No _____ If so, please describe.

5. Will any stress to subjects be involved?   Yes _____ No _____ If so, describe.

6. Will the subjects be deceived or misled in any way?   Yes _____ No _____ If so, please describe and include an outline or script of the debriefing.

7. Will there be a request for information that subjects might consider to be personal or sensitive? Yes _____ No _____ If so, please describe.

8. Will the subjects be presented with materials that they might consider to be offensive, threatening, or degrading?   Yes _____ No _____ If so, please describe.

9. Approximately how much time will be demanded of each subject?

10. Who will be the subjects in this study? How will they be solicited or contacted. Subjects must be informed about the nature of what is involved as a participant, including particularly a description of anything they might consider to be unpleasant or a risk. Please provide an outline or script of the information that will be provided to subjects prior to their volunteering to participate. Include a copy of the written solicitation and an outline of the oral solicitation.

11. What steps will be taken to insure that each subject's participation is voluntary? What, if any, inducements will be offered to the subjects for their participation?

12. How will you insure that the subjects give their consent prior to participating? Will a written consent form be used?   Yes _____ No _____ If so, please include the form, and if not, please indicate why not.

13. Will any aspect of the data be made a part of any permanent record that can be identified with the subject?   Yes _____ No _____

14. Will the fact that a subject did or did not participate in a specific experiment or study be made a part of any permanent record available to a supervisor, teacher, or employer? Yes _____ No _____

15. What steps will be taken to insure the confidentiality of the data?

16. If there are any risks involved in the study, are there any offsetting benefits that might accrue to either the subject or society?

17. Will any data from files or archival data be used?   Yes _____ No _____

THE OHIO STATE UNIVERSITY
BEHAVIORAL AND SOCIAL SCIENCES
HUMAN SUBJECTS REVIEW COMMITTEE

CHECKLIST*   FOR PRINCIPAL INVESTIGATOR'S USE—DO NOT RETURN

_____ 1. Has a copy of the research proposal been included, and is it written in sufficient detail to allow the committee to make an informed decision?

_____ 2. Have copies of inventories/questionnaires been included?

_____ 3. If subjects are to be recruited from outside agencies (e.g., schools, penal institutions*, etc.), has a letter of agreement from these agencies been included?

_____ 4. Where subjects are recruited from groups, has the principal investigator done everything possible to insure that subjects will not be induced to participate through any kind of peer pressure?

_____ 5. Has a script been included of what will be told to subjects prior to gaining consent or assent from them? Is it written at a level appropriate to the subject's ability to understand?

_____ 6. Does the principal investigator recognize that the Psychology 100 sign-up procedure may satisfy the requirement of written consent?

_____ 7. If letters are to be sent to parents of children who will participate in the research, are these letters included?

　　　_____ Do these letters clearly indicate that the research is being done at OSU?

　　　_____ Is the principal investigator's name clearly indicated in the letter?

　　　_____ Is the letter written in language that the parent will clearly understand?

_____ 8. Has the principal investigator provided a justification for waiver of written consent if it is being requested?

_____ 9. Has the principal investigator used the appropriate consent form (HS-027 or HS-028A), or has he/she made an adaptation suitable to the comprehension level of the subject?

　　　_____ Has the form been properly completed with name of the principal investigator, title of study, and *signature* of the principal investigator?

　　　_____ Has the form provided for assent when children are involved?

_____ 10. Has the principal investigator made the distinction between anonymity and confidentiality of the subject?

_____ 11. If audio- or videotaping is to be done, has the subject or parent been informed?

_____ 12. Is a statement of the debriefing for subjects included? This is usually necessary for research involving deception.

_____ 13. Are any permanent records to be used in the study?

　　　_____ Does the principal investigator have evidence to indicate appropriate access to this information?

　　　_____ Have subjects been informed that records may be accessed?

_____ 14. Will any part of the data become a permanent part of the subjects' records?

_____ 15. Has the subject been informed of an accurate time estimate for completion of the data collection?

_____ 16. If in the course of the data collection it is found that the subject needs immediate psychological or medical help, what procedures have been included for this?

_____ 17. If there are any medical risks involved, has the principal investigator discussed the study with a qualified physician?

_____ 18. Where appropriate, has the subject's family physician been informed that the subject will be participating?

_____ 19. If subjects are to be transported, has the principal investigator made provisions for liability due to accidents?

---

*Guidelines for using children in research and guidelines for using prisoners in research may be obtained by calling the Office of Research Risks.

Chapter 10

Conducting Mail Surveys

ALAN VAUX

The mail survey is a widely used and extremely adaptable method in the social sciences. Most research psychologists will need to conduct a survey of some kind during their careers, and, for a substantial number, this will be a principal method of data collection. Further, with the advent of personal computers, high-quality printers, and sophisticated software, the production of high-quality surveys is easier than ever. Yet formal training in survey methodology is very rarely part of the research curriculum of psychology graduate programs.

This chapter is intended to provide a primer on the conduct of mail surveys. I will identify some key issues that need to be addressed by researchers using this method (or considering its use), and I will provide some suggestions on how to conduct surveys competently. A research assistant—or indeed an experienced researcher who is new to survey methodology—should find sufficient information here to avoid making serious errors and to conduct a survey that meets general scientific standards. As with all research methods, however, exceptional performance requires experience, creativity, talent, and further study. Valuable sources include Dillman (1978), Sudman and Bradburn (1982), Fowler (1993), Fink and Kosecoff (1985), and Goddard and Villanova (Chapter 7 of this volume).

Advantages and Disadvantages of the Survey Method

As with all research methods, an impeccably conducted survey is no guarantee of an important contribution to knowledge, but otherwise exceptional research can be undermined by a poorly implemented survey. Survey methods can be examined most usefully in terms of internal validity, construct validity, statistical conclusion validity, and external validity (Cook & Campbell, 1979).

INTERNAL VALIDITY

With respect to internal validity, mail surveys can be valuable as part of true experimental studies in which participants have been randomly assigned to different treatments. They are particularly valuable in large-scale field experiments, in which large samples are exposed to complex, ongoing interventions. True experiments also can be implemented through surveys, yet the scope for manipulating variables and randomly assigning participants to conditions (e.g., to different information, vignettes) is limited, and thus the opportunities for making strong inferences regarding causality are also limited. In both cases, differential response rates may yield threats of selection (i.e., groups may not be equivalent or may not remain so), undermining internal validity and reducing the study to a quasi-experiment. In sum, survey research is most useful for descriptive research, passive-observational research, or other situations in which internal validity is irrelevant, secondary, or otherwise unattainable. True experiments usually require more certain data collection than is possible with mail surveys.

STATISTICAL CONCLUSION VALIDITY

The likelihood of detecting an empirical relationship statistically depends on the many factors that influence power (N, test, etc.), but most relevant here is the reliability of measures. Mail surveys per se are no less reliable than any other method.

Care should be taken in the selection of instruments and in the subsequent assessment of their reliability. Constraints on survey length may require shorter instruments and thus threaten reliability. More often, researchers new to surveys forget elementary principles of reliability and rely on a single item when multiple items are not only better but quite feasible (cf. the carpenter's maxim, "measure twice, cut once"). In short, standardized procedures (careful and clear wording), repeated measurement (multiple semiredundant items), and other procedures that enhance measurement reliability are neither less critical nor inherently less achievable in mail surveys than in other methodologies.

CONSTRUCT VALIDITY

With respect to construct validity, surveys share the strengths and weaknesses of other self-report and other-report methods. There are many constructs of relevance to psychologists—beliefs, personality, attitudes, values, interests, activities—for which self-reports are an important measurement strategy. Also valuable are other-reports, such as teacher ratings of students, supervisor ratings of workers, or clinician ratings of clients. Obviously, other relevant constructs, such as blood pressure or evoked potentials, cannot be measured through self- or other-report. Reliability and validity of survey measures can be examined as with any other measure, and research findings support survey measurement of even "sensitive" constructs such as clinical problems (Fournier & Kovess, 1993). The key questions the researcher must ask are these: Is it reasonable to expect someone to provide the information of interest? Do relevant, reliable, and valid survey measures exist? Can an existing self-report measure be adapted to a mail survey method?

EXTERNAL VALIDITY

A key aspect of external validity has to do with participants: To whom can we generalize findings? Closely linked to mail survey methods are sampling procedures that formally address issues of generalizability and representativeness—issues that are very commonly overlooked in psychological research. A casual examination of journal articles will reveal that although participant samples are generally described in terms of number and demographic composition, they are usually volunteer convenience samples. Often we know little about recruitment procedures, refusal rates, and so forth.

MAIL VERSUS OTHER METHODS

Another relevant issue is choosing between mail survey, telephone survey, personal interview, and new options such as E-mail. Each of these methods has advantages and disadvantages that may recommend use in a particular situation. Several conditions argue against conducting a mail survey, including urgency of data collection, numerous open-ended questions, and an elaborate system of contingent questions (i.e., next question determined by a previous answer). These circumstances might suggest a telephone survey, perhaps computer assisted, or in-person interviews. On the other hand, when time allows for the careful selection or development of a set of closed-ended questions, data may be collected on a very large sample in a short period of time, and mail surveys may compare favorably in cost and data quality with telephone surveys (Fournier & Kovess, 1993; McHorney, Kosinski, & Ware, 1994).

Sampling and Return Rates

SAMPLING

Shoddy sampling can ruin the external validity of survey research, and relevant issues are often overlooked or misunderstood. As with other methods, mail surveys can be conducted on convenience samples. Yet representativeness is often important, and formal sampling can easily be incorporated into mail surveys. To supplement the brief treatment here, see McCready (Chapter 8 of this volume), Cook and Campbell (1979), or Henry (1990). For many research purposes, sampling frames are available that represent populations of interest well. These sampling frames may be organizational mailing lists, professional directories, community phone books, or lists generated from a synthesis of esoteric data-bases. Formal sampling may be random, systematic, or more elaborate, such as stratified random sampling or cluster sampling. Random sampling involves the assignment of numbers to persons or sampling elements and their subsequent random selection (i.e., each person or element in the sampling frame has an equal probability of inclusion). Systematic sampling involves the selection of every nth person or element (where n is the ratio of sampling frame to desired sample size) and may be as convenient as selecting every 10th person in every fifth column of names. (Periodic random starts are useful to make sure that every nth person does not coincide with a specific type, such as organizational officers or residents with a corner apartment.) Stratified random sampling involves selection within specified strata: for example, randomly selecting psychologists from groups defined by sex, American Psychological Association (APA) division, and region of the country. Cluster sampling involves layers of selection: for example, randomly selecting states, then universities, then departments, and then professors. Each method has advantages and disadvantages, relevant to a given context. Regardless, the advantages of formal sampling depend on adequate return rates.

RETURN RATES

A number of procedures can be used to enhance return rates. It is worth noting here that in proposing a mail survey (e.g., in a grant or a doctoral prospectus), the focus should be on procedures, not outcome: That is, be very cautious about "guaranteeing" a given obtained sample size. Most important, the research literature on survey return rates is growing and should be consulted to weigh the costs and benefits of particular procedures in a given research context. At a minimum, a carefully designed survey with a good cover letter may be sent out bulk mail with a postage-paid return envelope, followed 2 weeks later by a postcard (sent to entire sample) thanking those who participated and requesting those who have not to do so. Beyond this minimal procedure, Dillman (1978) and others strongly recommend first-class postage rather than bulk mail and a variety of other specific procedures, such as signing each cover letter. Other procedures to be considered include certified mail (Gitelson & Drogin, 1992), multiple follow-up reminders (by postcard or phone; Nederhof, 1988), repeat mailings of surveys to those who have not responded, prenotification (by letter or phone; Schlegelmilch & Diamantopoulos, 1991), and monetary incentives (Brennan, 1992). The feasibility and cost of these procedures may vary dramatically with sample size, but research findings indicate that they may substantially improve return rates, at least under some circumstances. Altschuld and his colleagues have attained return rates of 96% (Altschuld et al., 1992).

The Cover Letter

A common error made by novices is to pay too little attention to the cover letter, often a mere afterthought. The importance of this communication—and a hint at appropriate content—comes from Dillman's (1978) reminder to survey researchers that they are asking a stranger to do them a favor, expending time and effort to complete the instrument and perhaps to share personal feelings, thoughts, or beliefs. Consequently, apart from being polite and professional, the letter must serve several key functions.

IMPORTANCE OF THE RESEARCH

First, readers are probably asking themselves, "What is this, and why should I bother with it?" So the first paragraph of the letter must introduce the research and characterize it as important, noting possible benefits and its relevance to the potential respondent. Depending on the topic, this may be done quite generally: for example, "Violence is a serious social problem in many American communities. This research is being conducted to help us understand the problem and to provide guidance to schools and police departments about how violence can be controlled in towns like yours." Or the topic may be of more immediate interest: for example, "Managed care is changing how psychotherapy is paid for and practiced. As a clinical psychologist in private practice, you may be concerned about these changes. This research is being conducted so that we can help your state professional association to represent your interests and influence upcoming legislation." These and other examples are necessarily brief. See Dillman (1978) and other referenced sources for more complete examples.

IMPORTANCE OF THE RESPONDENT

Second, the reader may be asking, "Why me?" The letter must answer in two ways: to explain how the potential respondent was selected and to persuade the respondent of the importance of his or her participation. This can be tricky if participants are in the sample by chance! For example:

> You were randomly selected as part of a relatively small group of residents in Yourtown to participate in the study. To get a complete picture of the issue, it is extremely important that we get your opinions on this topic. So we would really appreciate it if you could take 15 minutes to complete the enclosed survey.

PRIVACY

Potential participants are likely to ask themselves, "Who will know how I answered these questions?" This is especially salient for surveys of sensitive information. The letter must tell potential respondents what degree of privacy they can expect and exactly how this will be achieved. Anonymity is easiest to communicate: "This survey is anonymous. Return the completed survey in the enclosed envelope, and do not write your name on the survey or envelope. There is no way that we can identify any person's answers or even who has or has not responded." Confidentiality is more difficult to communicate because the researcher is seeking the respondent's trust:

> Your survey data will be kept completely confidential. Your name will never appear directly on your survey or with your survey data. You will note an identification number on your survey. This will be used only to link up the four surveys that we will be sending you over the next year. The list of names and corresponding numbers will be kept in a locked file drawer and destroyed when the project is complete.

Researchers must be aware of, and give careful consideration to, relevant ethical issues. Betraying trust by covert identification of surveys or breaking confidentiality is a serious ethical breach. Omitting tricky confidentiality information in the hope of boosting return rates is ethically questionable and likely to backfire in any case (see APA, 1992).

To summarize, the cover letter is critically important. It may be the first contact between the researcher and a potential participant, creating a crucial first impression. In separate paragraphs, the letter should communicate the importance of the project, communicate the importance of this person's participation, and explain privacy procedures. A final paragraph may reiterate these points and encourage a phone call regarding any concerns. Researchers may find that a research ethics committee favors standard paragraphs or a format that runs counter to the recommendations here. These may include standard statements regarding risks, voluntary participation, and committee approval, identification of researchers as students, and so forth. At times, such statements may mar a good cover letter or even seriously undermine the credibility of a good survey without in any way enhancing the ethical treatment of participants. The researcher must weigh issues and negotiate with the ethics committee.

General Format

Survey design should reflect Dillman's (1978) point that the researcher is asking a favor of a stranger: It should facilitate rather than hinder participation. This is a statement of the obvious, yet novices often produce surveys that look untidy and disorganized, that seek information cryptically or impolitely, and that make it difficult for respondents to answer questions even when they want to. In short, the survey should look professional, interesting, and easy to complete. Powerful personal computers, sophisticated software, and high-quality printers have dramatically altered the ease with which professional-looking surveys can be produced, although they also may have raised the standards for acceptable correspondence! My recommendations here are adapted from Dillman's (1978) Total Design Method. They should be viewed as illustrative, though they appear to work very well. The main point is that the survey should follow some coherent design style and one that facilitates participation by a respondent.

LAYOUT

Overall, the survey, layout, fonts, and so forth should look professional, legible, and easy to complete. If the potential respondent gets the impression either that the researcher has not taken much care in constructing the survey or that it will be onerous to complete, then participation is unlikely. Several tactics may be used to make a survey look good and easy to complete. Producing the survey in pamphlet form may make it look more professional and shorter, while reducing paper and possibly postal costs. Using current word processors with flexible control of fonts, one can produce a pamphlet quite easily and without photocopy reductions. Thus one folded sheet of paper, printed front and back, yields four pages of questionnaire; two folded pages yield eight survey pages; and so on. Once the layout is correct, any copy shop can handle copying, stapling, and folding. Experienced researchers recommend that the face page contain only a project title or logo and that the last page be blank or be used for a final open-ended question and a statement of appreciation.

Every effort should be made to establish a consistent, legible style for the survey, one that gives it a simple appearance with lots of white space, that clearly distinguishes questions and answers, and that establishes a response set for how to answer questions. A section should begin with a transition paragraph that orients the reader to the topic (e.g., "Below are a series of statements regarding . . . "), asks the question ("To what extent do you agree or disagree with each of these statements?"), and provides instructions on how to respond (e.g., "Refer to the scale in the box below and, for each statement, circle one number that corresponds to your answer"). Items and response options should be clearly distinguished: This can be done spatially, by distinct fonts, by shading, by boxing, or other means. A consistent procedure for answering questions should be established: This might be checking a box, circling a number, or some other procedure. Circling numbers has the advantage of simplifying coding to a data set. When many questions have a common set of response options (e.g., a 4-point scale of agreement), a reference scale might be followed by items on the left with a corresponding scale to the right. When questions have different response options, Dillman (1978) recommended that each question have options listed vertically. This may seem to waste space, but usually "space-saving" formats are confusing and look cluttered. Although control of fonts can be invaluable in fitting question sets on pages, the common error of font chaos—using many different font sizes and types—should be carefully avoided.

ORGANIZATION OF QUESTIONS

The survey should be organized into sections reflecting different topics, with brief transition statements to facilitate movement from section to section. The survey should begin with an engaging question that follows the cover letter. Questions about a particular topic, with a similar format, or with a similar response format generally should be placed together. This will be, and will seem to be, easier for a participant to complete. Questions about demographics typically should come at the end rather than the start of a survey.

CONTEXT

In organizing survey components, one should keep in mind the possibility that context, especially prior questions, may influence a participant's answer to a question. Tourangeau and Rasinski (1988) proposed a cognitive model of how survey questions are answered, involving four steps: identifying the attitude a question is about, retrieving relevant beliefs and feelings, using these to make a judgment, and using the judgment to select a response. They argue that contextual material such as prior questions may prime a topical cluster of beliefs, set a norm or standard for making later judgments, or create a demand to be consistent or to be moderate. Tourangeau and others have demonstrated how context items relevant to a particular belief can increase access to related beliefs (Tourangeau, Rasinski, & D'Andrade, 1991) and alter survey responses (Rasinski & Tourangeau, 1991), especially when participants hold well-developed but conflicted views on a topic (Tourangeau, Rasinski, Bradburn, & D'Andrade, 1989). In short, context effects may simply facilitate answering of questions (by priming relevant beliefs), but they may also alter responses. Limiting such effects is relatively easy in personal or phone surveys by using multiple survey forms with different question order or, when computer assisted, through random presentation of questions. It is more difficult to deal with context effects in mail surveys.

Question Design

Psychologists often will use or adapt established instruments for a mail survey. Yet, for a variety of reasons, surveys often will involve new questions, and these must be carefully designed. The treatment here is necessarily brief, and readers are encouraged to read further (Dillman, 1978; Fowler, 1993). Note that many of these suggestions apply to question design in methods other than mail survey; similarly, knowledge from other methods often is pertinent to mail surveys. Large-scale ongoing surveys such as the General Social Survey (Davis & Smith, 1992) often involve studies of wording effects that yield useful information. Also, survey design increasingly involves consideration of the cognitive processes involved in survey participation: understanding questions, recalling information, making judgments, formulating answers, and so forth (Fienberg & Tanur, 1989). At present, knowledge generated by this approach has not yielded a set of simple guidelines for question design. In general, questions should be polite, clear, specific, and unbiased and should match specific research goals.

POLITENESS

Nothing will undermine a survey more quickly than asking questions in ways that are demanding, rude, disrespectful, or patronizing. Very common errors are the nonquestion question (e.g., "Age ____?"), the unnecessarily intrusive question (e.g., "Exactly what is your annual income? $_____"), the overly demanding question (e.g., "Rank these 25 topics in order of importance"), the impossibly precise question (e.g., "How many times in the past year did you read a magazine?"), the presumptuous question (e.g., "When you travel overseas, . . . ?"), and the patronizing question (e.g., to a group of experienced scientists, "Publishing is a complex process. Manuscripts must be submitted for review and often revised before publication. How . . . ?"). In sum, inquiries should always be in question form, be relatively easy to answer, not presume experience or knowledge, and seek personal information graciously and only to the degree necessary.

CLARITY AND PRECISION

Questions should be short, simple, and straightforward, brief but not cryptic. Ideally, all respondents will understand a question in the same way. Complex questions usually can be broken up. Common errors include unnecessarily elaborate structure (e.g., "Some people think that . . . , others that . . . ; what do you think?"), double questions (e.g., "Do you think that the U.S. deficit is too big and that spending should be cut?"), and double negatives (e.g., "Current graduate training does not adequately teach students how not to make basic research errors").

Language should be appropriate to the audience. Generally, this means using simple, short words, rather than long, more sophisticated words. Care must be taken to avoid abbreviations, acronyms, technical terms, and unconventional phrases with which a sample may be unfamiliar. On the other hand, an audience sophisticated in a given arena may experience the absence or misuse of technical terms and common abbreviations as patronizing or as a sign of incompetence. In general, terms and phrases that may be unfamiliar to respondents should be clarified in a preamble, and an acronym should appear first in parentheses after the phrase for which it stands.

Precision requires clarity about the research questions at hand. Questions may easily be too vague to be useful (e.g., "Is psychotherapy of high quality?"). Often precision involves a compromise between what a researcher would like to know and what a person is capable of reporting, as when questions elicit fake precision (e.g., "Exactly how many movies did you attend last year?"). Care also should be taken to avoid asking questions that presume knowledge that respondents may not have.

AVOIDING BIAS

Care should be taken to avoid wording questions in a leading way (e.g., "Do you agree that the numerous and intrusive APA requirements make graduate training more difficult than necessary?"). Response options too should be balanced and not skewed (e.g., "To enhance graduate psychology training, should APA requirements be increased slightly, decreased slightly, decreased substantially, or eliminated?").

SEEKING SENSITIVE INFORMATION

Psychological research often involves sensitive information, and material may seem more personal or private to others than to us. Questions may be made less intrusive by the use of broad response categories (e.g., a broad income range) or by approaching the topic gradually through a series of questions (e.g., asking about general views on drugs in society, others' use of drugs, then the respondent's use of soft drugs). Thought should be given to balance the desire for detailed sensitive information with the possibility of nonparticipation!

Conclusion

To sum up, the mail survey is a flexible, valuable, and widely used method. When used properly, it may provide a relatively inexpensive way to collect data on large samples of geographically, organizationally, or socially remote persons. Mail surveys may be used to collect sensitive information and in some contexts may provide better data at lower cost than telephone or personal interviews. Formal sampling, a rarity in psychological research, can easily be incorporated into mail surveys. Return rates may be enhanced by a variety of procedures based on a growing research literature. High return rates and quality data depend on thoughtful cover letters, well-designed layouts, and carefully crafted questions. The basics of survey methodology can readily be mastered by a conscientious researcher.

Appendix 10.1 at the end of this chapter presents a checklist of issues to address and tasks to complete in conducting a survey.

Recommended Readings

We recommend that the reader consult the following sources for more in-depth information about the topic covered in this chapter: Dillman (1978), Fink and Kosecoff (1985), Fowler (1993), Henry (1990), and Sudman and Bradburn (1982). Useful information is also available in Fienberg and Tanur (1989).

References

Altschuld, J. W., Thomas, P. M., McCloskey, W. H., Smith, D. W., Wiesmann, W. W., & Lower, M. A. (1992). Mailed evaluation questionnaires: Replication of a 96% return rate procedure. *Evaluation and Program Planning, 15,* 239-246.

American Psychological Association. (1992). Ethical principles of psychologists and code of conduct. *American Psychologist, 47,* 1597-1611

Brennan, M. (1992). The effect of monetary incentive on mail survey response rates: New data. *Journal of the Market Research Society, 34,* 173-177.

Cook, T. D., & Campbell, D. T. (1979). *Quasi-experimentation: Design and analysis issues for field settings.* Boston: Houghton Mifflin.

Davis, J. A., & Smith, T. W. (1992). *The NORC General Social Survey: A user's guide.* Newbury Park, CA: Sage.

Dillman, D. A. (1978). *Mail and telephone surveys.* New York: John Wiley.

Fink, A., & Kosecoff, J. (1985). *How to conduct surveys.* Newbury Park, CA: Sage.

Fournier, L., & Kovess, V. (1993). A comparison of mail and telephone interview strategies for mental health surveys. *Canadian Journal of Psychiatry, 38,* 525-533.

Fowler, F. J., Jr. (1993). *Survey research methods.* Beverly Hills, CA: Sage.

Gitelson, R., & Drogin, E. B. (1992). An experiment on the efficacy of certified final mailing. *Journal of Leisure Research, 24,* 72-78.

Henry, G. T. (1990). *Practical sampling.* Newbury Park, CA: Sage.

McHorney, C., Kosinski, M., & Ware, J. E. (1994). Comparison of the costs and quality of norms for the SF-36 Health Survey collected by mail versus telephone interview: Results from a national survey. *Medical Care, 32,* 551-567.

Nederhof, A. J. (1988). Effects of a final telephone reminder and questionnaire cover design in mail surveys. *Social Science Research, 17,* 353-361.

Rasinski, K. A., & Tourangeau, R. (1991). Psychological aspects of judgments about the economy. *Political Psychology, 12,* 27-40.

Schlegelmilch, B. D., & Diamantopoulos, A. (1991). Prenotification and mail survey response rates: A quantitative integration of the literature. *Journal of the Market Research Society, 33,* 243-255.

Sudman, S., & Bradburn, N. M. (1982). *Asking questions: A practical guide to questionnaire design.* San Francisco: Jossey-Bass.

Tourangeau, R., & Rasinski, K. A. (1988). Cognitive processes underlying context effects in attitude measurement. *Psychological Bulletin, 103,* 299-314.

Tourangeau, R., Rasinski, K. A., Bradburn, N., & D'Andrade, R. (1989). Carryover effects in attitude surveys. *Public Opinion Quarterly, 53,* 495-524.

Tourangeau, R., Rasinski, K. A., & D'Andrade, R. (1991). Attitude structure and belief accessibility. *Journal of Experimental Social Psychology, 27,* 46-75.

Appendix 10.1

A Mail Survey Checklist

RESEARCH GOALS

_____ What are the principal research questions to be addressed?

_____ Does a mail survey fit the research design (e.g., manipulations, time frame)?

_____ Can principal variables be measured reliably and validly by self- or other-report?

MAIL SURVEY OR OTHER METHOD

_____ Does the research involve a large sample? (The larger the sample, the more valuable a mail survey as compared to phone or in-person interviews.)

_____ Is sufficient time available to design a survey? (Mail surveys require careful preparation, though duplication is simple.)

_____ Are questions generally closed-ended?

_____ Does the survey involve few contingent questions and have easily followed skips?

SAMPLING

_____ What size sample do you need, given the research questions, design, power, etc.?

_____ Are suitable sampling frames available?

_____ What sampling strategy will you use? (e.g., random, systematic)

RETURN RATES

_____ What procedures will you use to enhance return rates? (e.g., prenotification, incentives, follow-up reminders, repeat surveys)

_____ Would a 30% return rate be fatal for your design?

COVER LETTER

_____ Have you carefully written your cover letter, providing information on the importance of the research, how the participant was selected, and privacy?

ORGANIZATION

_____ Have you selected reliable and valid measures of key variables that have been used previously in mail surveys or that can be suitably adapted?

_____ Have you placed high-interest questions at the start of the survey and demographic questions at the back?

_____ Have you considered alternative options for the organization of material in the survey?

_____ Are order or context effects likely to be a problem?

_____ If the survey seems too long, can you substitute shorter yet acceptable instruments?

LAYOUT

_____ Have you considered format options (pamphlet, etc.)?

_____ Have you established a coherent design style (margins, font type and size, etc.)?

_____ Are questions spatially or graphically distinct from answer options?

_____ Have you established a simple and consistent procedure for indicating answers?

QUESTION DESIGN

_____   Have you carefully adapted measures usually presented in some other fashion?

_____   Have you carefully written any new questions needed?

_____   Have you reviewed questions for politeness?

_____   Are questions clear and appropriately precise?

_____   Are any questions or response options biased?

_____   Have you reviewed sensitive questions and considered alternatives?

_____   Have you had expert and novice respondents complete the survey and provide feedback?

BEFORE YOU DUPLICATE!

I have very rarely seen a survey that was completely error-free! Errors range from a minor typographical error to disasters such as response-option scales reading from "Strongly Agree" to "Strongly Agree."

_____ Have you, colleagues, and a proofreader or two carefully checked the survey? Again?

Chapter 11

Conducting Telephone Surveys

PETER Y. CHEN

The telephone survey has become a widely used tactic in areas such as attitude survey and consumer behavior. Before the 1970s, this method was criticized for its methodological weaknesses, particularly sampling bias due to high noncoverage rate in the United States (about 20% in 1963; Thornberry & Massey, 1988). Over the years, this notorious record has been dramatically improved. For example, the coverage rate in some states exceeded 95% by 1986 (Frey, 1989), and the most recent average coverage rate has been estimated to be between 95% and 97% (Lavrakas, 1993). In this chapter, I will describe the process of conducting the telephone survey (see outline presented in Table 11.1), with emphases on criteria for choosing the telephone survey, sampling procedures, selection criteria, training, and supervision.

The first section is designed to provide you with a frame of reference for selecting the telephone survey method. Because the sampling procedures employed in the telephone survey are quite different from those used in other survey methods, a portion of the chapter is devoted to its unique techniques for sampling among households and within households. The emphases of selection criteria, training, and supervision reflect my belief that interviewers play an extremely important role during the process of a telephone survey.

In the end, I will briefly discuss the use of computers in the telephone survey, as well as new challenges (or threats) emerging from the development of telecommunication technology. Other important topics, such as questionnaire development and item analysis, are presented in Chapters 7 and 10 of this volume (by Goddard and Villanova, and by Vaux, respectively). The principles presented in these two chapters also apply to the telephone survey. However, the format of telephone questionnaires is somewhat different from that of the mail questionnaire. To aid you in the details of designing a telephone survey, you can consult sample questionnaires described by Lucas and Adams (1977), Cannell (1985a), and Thornberry (1987).

AUTHOR'S NOTE: I thank Jack Arbuthnot, Jim Austin, Paula Popovich, and Paul Spector for their valuable comments on earlier versions of this chapter.

TABLE 11.1 An Outline for Conducting a Telephone Survey

Define the goals and objectives of the survey.

Choose the telephone survey over other modes of data collection:

- Evaluate four aspects: administrative, sampling, measurement, and data quality.

- Assess whether the telephone survey is an appropriate choice.

Generate sampling pools.

Design the questionnaire and survey procedures.

Recruitment, initial hiring, training, and final selection:

- Recruit and select prospective interviewers who meet the initial standards.

- Proceed with orientation training, skill building, interviewer error training, and feedback and evaluation.

- On the basis of behavior criteria, select final candidates. If possible, assign other tasks to the remaining trainees who wish to stay in the project.

Conduct pilot test and item analysis, and revise the questionnaire and survey procedures.

Print the questionnaire and other forms.

Conduct the survey in a centralized setting:

- Continue on-the-job training and daily briefing.

- Carry out on-site taped monitoring or supervision.

- Assess performance according to behavior criteria, and give feedback promptly.

Assemble results.

Report findings.

Evaluate results and costs, determine next steps, and so forth.

Criteria for Choosing the Telephone Survey

In the past, it was not a very difficult task for survey users to select among the different modes of data collection because sophisticated methodologies were not very well developed. Facing abundant empirical evidence and techniques, as well as rapid change of telecommunication modules for either a single survey method (e.g., telephone survey) or combined survey methods (e.g., a combination of telephone and mail surveys), you may be perplexed and bothered by the many choices of survey tactics available today. Practically, the choice of method will depend on your goals, resources, characteristics of the sample, sample frame, and the strengths of the various methods. Although several studies (e.g., Groves & Kahn, 1979; Mangione, Hingson, & Barrett, 1982; Siemiatycki, 1979) have simultaneously compared two or more survey methods (mainly telephone survey, personal interview, and mail survey), only a few criteria were examined under research contexts. Most important, some extraneous variables were difficult to control in these studies (e.g., sampling frame, training procedures, wording in questionnaires that cannot be used identically across different methods). These confounding factors, and the problems of internal validity (e.g., different criteria used) as well as external validity (e.g., topics and contexts to be generalized) of these studies, seriously limit the conclusion about "pure mode effect" (Biemer, 1988). In the remainder of this section, I will summarize prior research pertaining to *relative* advantages and disadvantages of the telephone survey, along with a list of important criteria. A decision aid is also presented to facilitate decision making in weighing the potential benefits of choosing the telephone survey method.

CRITIQUES OF THE TELEPHONE SURVEY

The unique characteristics of the telephone survey cannot be fully recognized without comparing it with other survey methods across multiple criteria. Two alternative methods, personal interview and mail survey, will be compared to the telephone survey because of their popularity as survey methods and the availability of empirical findings on the techniques. The criteria will be scrutinized on the basis of four aspects: administrative (e.g., cost, personnel, training), sampling (e.g., noncoverage, nonresponse), measurement process (e.g., length of data collection and questionnaire, type of questions), and data quality (e.g., response validity, social desirability).

The Administrative Aspect

Cost. Although a budget for the telephone survey is usually required in a research or grant proposal, little information pertaining to overhead, indirect cost, and unexpected expense (e.g., three to six callbacks may be necessary) has been reported in the literature (Frey, 1989). Generally, the cost of the telephone survey rises when a large sample size or high response rate is planned. To achieve these goals, researchers must hire more personnel, make more callbacks (i.e., redial a telephone number at a different time or on a different day to reach a selected respondent), spend more time in preparing the database, and so on. If an initial screening (e.g., 40- to 55-year-old women who work) or a long questionnaire is part of a telephone survey, more time and money will also be spent in identifying eligible respondents or completing the interviews. The cost of reaching respondents living in different geographical areas will also be greater. However, the use of a leased line (e.g., a WATS line) can significantly reduce telephone charges because the line offers users low rates in calling anywhere in the country. If calls are to be made in one or more specific cities or locations, you might consider hiring on-site assistants to eliminate long-distance charges (although this may increase training and supervision costs).

Compared to the personal interview, the telephone survey can be less costly to implement due to reduced labor costs per interview. Generally, the cost of telephone surveys is about one third to two thirds less than that of personal interviews (Lucas & Adams, 1977; Siemiatycki, 1979). Frey (1989) cited evidence that the cost of the telephone survey is about one sixth to one half more than that of the mail survey. Regarding the mail survey, cost generally does not rise considerably, even if a diverse sample or a lengthy questionnaire is planned. However, these factors would add to the administrative costs in the telephone survey.

Personnel and Training. Compared to personal interviews, telephone surveys require a smaller staff for a given sample size. As a rule of thumb, approximately 10 interviewers would be adequate for a typical telephone survey, plus two to three supervisors. In practice, twice as many prospective interviewers may need to be recruited in the beginning because of attrition of interviewers due to inadequate skills or loss of interest. Fowler and Mangione (1990) estimated that it may take 20 to 30 hours to train an interviewer to perform at acceptable levels. In contrast, little personnel, training, or supervision is required in the mail survey.

The Sampling Aspect

Noncoverage. A major limitation of the telephone survey is that noncovered house-holds have zero chance to be chosen, rendering the results invalid. Reasons for noncoverage include unlisted, new, or just-changed telephone numbers and lack of telephone service. With the advanced random-digit-dialing sampling technique (described later), unlisted, new, or just-changed numbers could still possibly be accessible to researchers. However, it is impossible to interview people by telephone if they do not have telephones at home. A 1990 official report cited by Lavrakas (1993) revealed that there are 10 states (e.g., Alabama, Texas, and West Virginia) having household coverage of only 85% to 90%. In general, noncoverage is higher for people who live in rural areas and inner cities, have low income or are unemployed, are young (i.e., under 24), or are African Americans or Hispanics (Cannell, 1985b; Trewin & Lee, 1988). Hagan (1993) reported that coverage of Hispanics in the southwestern areas is as low as 65%. In addition, noncoverage is higher for very large (e.g., six or above) and single-person households. Thornberry and Massey (1988) reported that race, marital status, geographical region, family size, and employment status do not explain significant variance of telephone coverage while family income, age, and education are held constant. If researchers wish to survey variables of interest (e.g., health) that are related to the above noncoverage characteristics, they will very likely run into an under- or overestimation problem.

Nonresponse. Unlike noncovered households, nonresponse households are selected for a sample, but their responses are not assessed for either part or all of the survey questions. Failure to obtain measurement from the selected households may result from incapacity (e.g., selected respondents have physical, mental, or language disability and are not able to provide answers), noncontact (e.g., selected respondents cannot be reached by telephone more than six times), or refusal (Groves & Lyberg, 1988). Generally nonrespondents tend to be older and less educated (Weaver, Holmes, & Glenn, 1975). Non-response rate may also be affected by interviewer attributes, which will be discussed later in the training section.

The nonresponse rate is relatively higher in the mail survey than in the telephone survey. The "cold" telephone survey (i.e., no advance notice sent before calling) has a slightly higher nonresponse rate (about 3% to 5%) than does the personal interview (Cannell, 1985b). However, this latter difference disappears if the warm-call procedure (i.e., advance notice sent before calling) is used (Fowler, 1984).

High nonresponse rates may create potential difficulties in administration (e.g., multiple dialing, time used for persuasion, or monetary expenses) and threats to the validity of survey results (e.g., statistical conclusion validity, construct validity, or external validity). If nonrespondents are systematically different from the respondents on some individual characteristics, the survey results and conclusions could be distorted. Because all surveys are voluntary (or at least should be), it is very difficult for researchers to handle the aforementioned problems.

It should be noted that *nonresponse rate* is not a synonym of *nonresponse error*. The magnitude of nonresponse error varies as a function of both nonresponse rate and the size of the true difference between respondents and nonrespondents (Groves & Lyberg, 1988). High nonresponse rates, therefore, do not necessarily indicate the existence of nonresponse error if there is no difference between respondents and nonrespondents. Similarly, extremely low nonresponse rate (say 5%) may, theoretically, be associated with a great amount of nonresponse error, given that the nonrespondents are very different from the respondents.

Another confusion observed in the telephone survey is how to calculate response rate. Unfortunately, there is no universal guideline. As suggested by Groves and Lyberg (1988), researchers should use different measures of response rate, rather a single preferred calculation, to serve different purposes. An extensive list of response-rate formulas is given by Groves and Lyberg, including cooperation rate, contact rate, and refusal conversion rate. For example, the cooperation rate is calculated as a ratio of numbers of completed interview over the sum of numbers of interview (either completed or partial) and numbers of refusal.

The Measurement Aspect

Length of Data Collection and Interview. A strength of telephone surveys lies in the relatively short duration of the total interview period. Telephone surveys can generally be completed within a short period of time (a few days to a few weeks). However, they have been criticized for the inability to conduct lengthy individual interviews longer than 30 minutes (Lucas & Adams, 1977). Providing evidence for this characteristic, Collins, Sykes, Wilson, and Blackshaw (1988) found long interview length to be associated with high refusal rate. Their finding, however, was contradictory to that of Frankel and Sharp (1981), who reported that the length of the interview was not related to the refusal rate. Frey (1989) also cited several successful examples of lengthy (an average of 50 minutes) telephone surveys. I suspect that the time limitation of the telephone survey would be contingent on the interest level of the topic, types of interviewees (e.g., older people), experience of interviewers, the nature of the survey, and interview procedures.

Interviewing Process. In interview-related surveys, interviewers ask questions, probe short or incomplete answers, and record information provided by respondents. They have to read questions correctly with adequate tone of wording, probe incomplete answers without giving the respondents too much or too little feedback or instruction, and record information without subjective interpretation being involved. Because the process is dynamic and situation specific, it is not unusual to have many errors during the interviewing process. Even a well-trained interviewer who follows a standardized interview procedure will perform differently from interview to interview. The variation in interviewer performance (i.e., reliability) may be caused by interaction with interviewees, supervisors, and coworkers; physical or emotional conditions of interviewers; and attributes of interviewers. Although it is virtually impossible to eliminate completely the problems occurring in the process, they may be reduced by close monitoring, immediate feedback, daily debriefing, and/or on-the-job training.

Anonymity/Confidentiality and Type of Questions. In most cases, interviewees' names, telephone numbers, or even addresses are known in both the telephone survey and the personal interview. Hence it is virtually impossible to maintain anonymity in these types of methods. However, this would not be a problem in most mail survey studies. Because the respondents' identification is known, distorted responses to sensitive, threatening, or embarrassing questions could very possibly happen in interview-related surveys (Lucas & Adams, 1977). Even when confidentiality is assured to respondents in these surveys, data quality might suffer from their apprehensiveness (Frey, 1989).

Concerning the type of questions, the personal interview is appropriate in comparison with the telephone survey for more complex questions. It is not advisable to ask very complex questions in the mail survey. Cannell (1985a) suggested that researchers should make questions simple because respondents generally have difficulty understanding questions on the telephone. The use of less complex questions could also limit some interviewer errors resulting from inadequate probes. As will be discussed later, it usually takes a great deal of time to train interviewers to probe open-ended questions satisfactorily because (a) interviewers need to be able to detect inadequate responses and (b) many probes may be required for the frequently shortened answers given in interview surveys (Frey, 1989). The use and merit of open-ended questions, however, should not be dismissed or discounted. Responses to open-ended questions often shed new light on research questions or generate research ideas.

The Data Quality Aspect

Criteria used to assess data quality include accuracy (or response validity), absence of social desirability, item nonresponse, amount of information given in an open-ended question, and similarity of response distribution obtained by different methods. De Leeuw and van der Zouwen (1988) meta-analyzed previous studies and concluded that the differences between the personal interview and the telephone survey on the above criteria are small but in favor of the personal interview. However, the authors speculated that the difference in data quality between these two modes has become minimal over time. This trend could possibly be attributed to increased experience with the telephone survey.

Other data quality indexes include response styles (e.g., acquiescence, evasiveness, extremeness) and psychometric properties (e.g., test-retest or internal consistency reliability estimates). For example, Jordan, Marcus, and Reeder (1980) found that more agreement, extremeness, and evasiveness were found in telephone surveys than in personal interviews. However, no differences on psychometric properties were found between the two modes (Aneshensel, Frerichs, Clark, & Yokopenic, 1982; Herman, 1977).

A DECISION AID FOR CHOOSING THE TELEPHONE SURVEY

If only one survey method is permissible in a research project, one needs to evaluate the strength and weakness of each method. In most cases, there is no absolutely correct choice. It should be emphasized that the decision aid described below only serves as a guide and hence should not dictate the choice. While considering methods, first assess whether mail survey or interview-related methods (e.g., telephone survey, personal interview, or intercept survey) have fewer constraints in achieving the goals of research. This decision may be reached by asking the following questions:

1. Do many questions to be asked depend on respondents' previous answers?
2. Must the survey be conducted at a specific time?
3. Are survey questions very complex?
4. Are accurate mailing lists of eligible and representative subjects available?
5. Are survey questions very sensitive, threatening, embarrassing, or personal?
6. Are numbers of the sample widely dispersed over a broad geographical area?

If a series of questions to be asked will be different contingent on prior responses, interview-related methods may be considered. Likewise, interview-related surveys are appropriate when survey questions are complex, accurate mailing lists are not available, or a specific time of day to collect data is required (e.g., in the morning). Except for some cases (e.g., when experience sampling methodology is applied to prompt the respondent by a pager or a timer), it would be very difficult to administer a mail survey at a specific time because researchers cannot control when survey questions are answered.

However, interview-related methods are not the best choice if the survey questions are very sensitive or respondents are difficult to reach (e.g., residing in California, Florida, Canada, Hawaii, Alaska, or Guam). Because complete anonymity is almost impossible in interviews, interviewees have tendencies to terminate interviews early or to omit responses to sensitive questions. Reassurance of confidentiality may alleviate the refusal problem, although data quality may be affected. With regard to the widely diverse sample, the cost of long-distance telephone charges (even with the use of the WATS line) or visits increases drastically.

If interview-related surveys are considered to be the better choice over the mail survey, next determine which type of interview mode is desirable. The following questions may be helpful in making this decision:

1. Must data be collected at a special location, such as a workplace, supermarket, or post office?
2. Do interviewers need to show something to respondents?
3. Must eligible respondents be selected on the basis of their behaviors or physical characteristics?
4. Are many questions employed in the interview?
5. Are certain types of people to be excluded?
6. Must data be collected within a very short period of time?
7. Do respondents reside in a broad geographical area?
8. Is it likely that respondents' companions will influence their responses during the interviews?

The telephone survey is not the right choice if prospective respondents must be interviewed at a special location or must be shown something (e.g., product packages or colors of a car). Neither is it appropriate if eligibility of respondents is determined on the basis of their physical characteristics (e.g., blond hair) or behaviors (e.g., chewing tobacco) or if the questionnaire is lengthy (e.g., taking more than 60 minutes to complete). Telephones may not be available for certain geographical areas (e.g., Hispanics in the southwestern areas) or types of people (e.g., homeless people). If these people represent an important part of the sample, the telephone survey should at least not be the sole mode of data collection.

The telephone interview is often the quickest. For example, suppose that you received an urgent request from the president's office of your organization to find out employees' opinions about a new parking permit system within 10 days. You could probably spend 3 to 4 days to complete 300 interviews by telephone. However, it would not be easy to complete the same task by using other interview methods. The telephone survey would also be the preferred choice if respondents live in a diverse area or if their companions might affect the respondents' answers because others present would not hear the questions being asked, thereby alleviating to some extent the respondent's needs for face saving or self-presentation.

Generating Sampling Pools

Before conducting a survey, the researcher needs to decide how many and what kind of people are to be sampled. The interest should not be primarily in the sample to be surveyed but in attempting to specify the population (from which the sample is extracted). In other words, the goal is to understand the population through the selected sample. How well one can generalize from the sample to the population mainly depends on the sampling plan (i.e., sampling frame and sample size). Available information and readings about general sampling procedures can be found elsewhere in this text (Chapter 8 by McCready).

There are two distinctive but inseparable sampling plans employed in the telephone survey: sampling among households and sampling within households. The former is to sample representative households (i.e., telephone numbers) on the basis of directories or other procedures, and the latter is to sample respondents within the selected households.

SAMPLING AMONG HOUSEHOLDS

Sampling among households is a procedure whereby researchers randomly generate telephone numbers by means of directories, random-digit dialing (RDD), or Waksberg two-stage RDD sampling. The numbers in directories are usually obtained from telephone companies (e.g., GTE), organizations (e.g., employee directories), associations (e.g., American Psychological Association [APA] membership directories), or commercial list vendors (e.g., Dun's Market Identifiers). Spending less than $50, you can now purchase a CD-ROM database that includes 70 million households. However, directories other than telephone books are not easily accessible to the public. In addition to this obstacle, such directories generally contain duplicate or incorrect telephone numbers, cover ineligibles, and fail to cover eligible respondents (either new, unlisted, recently changed, or those without a telephone). Failure to cover eligible respondents presents a serious threat to statistical conclusions, as well as to external validities.

To generate sampling pools from one or more directories, randomly select numbers with the help of a computer or random-numbers table. The size of the sampling pool depends on your resources and the sampling errors you could tolerate. For stratified or area probability sampling, the telephone numbers could also be selected on the basis of geographical areas, prefix, or other characteristics of interest (e.g., size of companies, gender, job titles). Sampling pools can also be generated by the Add-a-Digit sampling method, which is a directory-assisted technique. This procedure requires researchers to add either one (or two or three) constant (or randomly assigned) digits to the last four digits of a selected telephone number. If the number 593-0822 is drawn, the actual number called is 593-0831 when number 9 is randomly assigned. In general, directory sampling will lead to biased samples because of incomplete records in directories, and even the Add-a-Digit sampling technique cannot eliminate the problem.

To reduce the bias resulting from noncoverage, RDD and several modified versions were developed (Cooper, 1964; Waksberg, 1978). RDD also eliminates the need to list household units prior to drawing a sample (Frey, 1989). Any given telephone number, such as 614-593-0822, is construed as three parts: area code (i.e., AC, 614), prefix or central-office codes (i.e., COC, 593), and suffix (0822). There are 640 3-digit COCs allotted to each AC, and there are 10,000 suffixes (from 0000 to 9999) assigned to each COC. However, no COC is completely filled with all possible suffixes. Suffixes are generally assigned in bundles of 1,000 or 100. For instance, a block of 1,000 suffixes may be assigned to a university, or a block of 100 suffixes may be assigned to a hotel. This information may be revealed from telephone directories or local telephone companies.

To conduct RDD sampling, first determine the ACs from which part of (or all) the sample is to be extracted. Then COCs are randomly selected. Certain numbers of suffixes within each COC are also randomly selected. This random generation could be done by random-numbers tables or computers. Lavrakas (1993, pp. 44-46) provided computer programs (written in BASIC language) that can generate suffixes randomly. Other important information pertaining to the RDD sampling, such as identifying nonworking blocks of suffixes and determining numbers of residential access line for each prefix, can also be found in Lavrakas.

Waksberg (1978) proposed a two-stage RDD sampling procedure that has been frequently used in large surveys. In Stage 1, researchers randomly select small combinations (about 50 to 100) of AC and COC (AC-COC). Then two random digits are added to each AC-COC combination. A series of the eight-digit combinations is compiled as the primary sampling units (PSUs), which serve as seeds to generate the final sampling pools. Each PSU provides a cluster of 100 numbers. For example, the possible 100 telephone numbers derived from the PSU of 614-593-08 start at 614-593-08-00 and go to 614-593-08-99. After two ending random numbers (e.g., 22) are added to the PSU, the final number called becomes 614-593-08-22. If this number is a residential number, the PSU will be retained for additional generation in Stage 2. Conversely, the PSU is discarded at this stage. In Stage 2, additional pairs of ending random digits are generated within each PSU until a certain number of respondents are reached. Overall, this sampling technique is efficient and cost-effective, with such trade-offs as an initial increase in clerical work and a small loss of precision on sampling (Frey, 1989; Groves, 1989).

SAMPLING WITHIN HOUSEHOLDS

When an interviewer dials the generated telephone number, he or she may immediately face a dilemma: who shall be interviewed within the household? The decision about choosing respondents can be made by one of the following procedures. The simplest way is to interview the first eligible person who picks up the telephone and also meets prior criteria (e.g., "male over 21 years of age"). However, this method creates underrepresentation of males because females tend to answer telephones first (Frey, 1989). Originally developed for personal interviews, Kish's (1949) procedure requires the person who answers the telephone first to name all members of the household and then to list them by gender and age. Each member is then assigned a number by the interviewer according to the order of age and gender. According to the Kish tables, the candidate is then selected and interviewed. Examples of Kish's procedure and its modified versions are available in Lavrakas (1993) and Frey (1989) as well as Kish. Kish's procedure is considered to be a probability sampling method that attempts to eliminate the noncoverage error within households. Because all eligible respondents may not be enumerated in some households (e.g., refused or misreported by respondents, interviewers' clerical error), a small amount of noncoverage error still occurs (e.g., underrepresentation of the youngest). Though minimizing noncoverage error, this procedure tends to suffer from a high nonresponse rate resulting from the laborious and demanding sampling process. Frey concluded that Kish's procedure would be more suited to the personal interview than to the telephone survey.

Another technique of sampling respondents within households is called the last (or next) birthday method. This is also considered to be a probability sampling technique because the assignment of birth date is assumed to be random. Furthermore, because each household always has a person with a next or last birthday, the gender and age bias is eliminated. Less intrusive or demanding, and easy to use, this method has gained popularity in telephone surveying since the mid-1980s.

Personnel

Telephone surveys cannot be implemented successfully without adequate interviewer training and on-the-job supervision. Before discussing interviewer training and supervision, two critical but often ignored topics need to be addressed first: the recruitment and initial selection of interviewers.

RECRUITMENT AND INITIAL SELECTION OF INTERVIEWERS

Ten interviewers are generally needed for 1,000 interviews, although the ratio may fluctuate depending on budget, sample size, time frame, available work space, and length of survey. Because of potential attrition, twice as many prospective interviewers as the number needed should be recruited. It is also advisable to provide the applicants with a realistic preview of their tasks. The content of the preview should consist of outcomes or rewards (e.g., pay, credit, grade, letter of recommendation, authorship), work hours and workload (e.g., 2 hours every night from 8 p.m. to 10 p.m., and numbers of subjects to be interviewed), selection criteria (e.g., prior experience, speech clarity, or training evaluation), responsibility (e.g., survey procedures or ethical principles), scope of the surveys, and other requirements (e.g., policies related to grooming, lateness, absence, smoking, food, drink, and so forth). Both positive and negative features of the job preview may prompt the applicants to reevaluate their own commitment. In addition, they may allow adjustment of unrealistic expectations before joining the training sessions. Any resulting self-selection will also make your task of selection easier.

If prospective interviewers decide to apply for the job, it is appropriate to evaluate the applicants' reading and writing abilities by means of sample tasks or role plays. Demographic characteristics (e.g., ethnicity, gender, age, religion) should not be used as selection criteria unless there is evidence that these characteristics might influence interview results (Lavrakas, 1993). Fowler and Mangione (1990) suggested that selected interviewers should possess good reading and writing skills and have a reasonably pleasant personality. They further concluded that there appeared to be no other "credible selection criteria for distinguishing among potential interviewers" (p. 140). However, other factors may become relevant criteria. For instance, Groves and Fultz (1985) found that prior experience is an important factor in decreasing the refusal rate. Given that little job analytical and validation evidence has been reported regarding what specific skills (e.g., persuasive skill, communication skill), abilities (e.g., speech clarity, pitch), or personal characteristics (e.g., friendliness, tolerance for rejection) are essential to the interviewing job, Fowler and Mangione's conclusion about selection criteria should be applied with caution.

TRAINING AND FINAL SELECTION

Following the initial selection, a series of training sessions (about 20 to 30 hours) is required, whatever prospective interviewers' prior experiences, to standardize presentation. Contents of the training should cover how to contact interviewees and enlist their cooperation, build good rapport with the interviewees, interview the respondents in a structured manner, and record the answers without personal opinions being involved. The training might include use of an interviewer manual, lectures/discussion, modeling, interactive computer-assisted programs, role playing, simulation, and supervised practice. Sample interviewer training guidelines are available in Frey (1989).

The training has a fourfold purpose: It orients the trainees about the scope of the survey, questionnaires, and survey procedures; it allows the trainees to sharpen their interview skills, to practice appropriate speech patterns, and to learn probing skills and feedback-seeking strategies; it reduces potential interviewer-related errors; and it evaluates the trainees' performance on which the final hiring decision will be based. The following sections describe how these purposes can be accomplished through the training.

ORIENTATION TRAINING

During the orientation, the trainees should learn the purpose of the survey, types of respondents they will interview, characteristics a good interviewer should have, ethical principles they are obliged to uphold, how telephone numbers are generated and processed, and other administrative policies. In addition, they should study and practice when and how to use properly the survey's call sheet, introduction statements, fallback statements, and refusal report form (sample forms are found in Lavrakas, 1993). The trainees should be given plenty of time to discuss and interpret questions in the questionnaire. It is not uncommon for interviewers not to understand some of the questions that they must ask, which can lead to confusion and errors.

SKILL-BUILDING TRAINING

Interviewers will receive quite a few rejections per day while conducting the telephone survey. The trainees should learn how to enlist respondents' cooperation and establish a good rapport with the respondents throughout the interview session. Furthermore, they need to understand the nature of refusal, how to persuade the subjects without being pushy, and how to deal with their own fear of rejection. Information about persuasion skills is available in Groves (1989).

Besides the skills described earlier, trainees should practice improving their voice quality. The interviewers sometimes become sloppy with respect to speaking properly such that they do not move their lips fully (Strafford & Grant, 1993). Oksenberg and Cannell (1988) found that refusal rate tends to decrease when interviewers are confident and competent in the interview or speak with a standard American accent, low pitch, loud voice, and relatively fast speaking rate. Strafford and Grant further suggested that interviewers should keep a *smile* in their voices (even though interviewees cannot see them) to lubricate communication.

Without visual cues during telephone surveys, interviewers usually attempt to seek out feedback to assure themselves that the communication is effective. The desire to seek feedback can be observed when the interviewers start to say more things than usual or say things they should not (Cannell, 1985b). During the training session, the trainees should learn that simple sentences such as "I understand" or "I see" are sufficient to maintain the communication. To avoid this problem, sentences such as "I see" could be printed next to each question on the questionnaire and read by the interviewers immediately after respondents answer each question.

INTERVIEWER ERROR TRAINING

Results of the telephone survey are obtained through the process in which interviewers read questions to respondents, probe ambiguous or incomplete answers, and record the final answers. Distorted results can easily appear, even when the questionnaire is perfectly designed, because of one or more interviewer errors. For example, interviewers may fail to read questions exactly as worded or to use probe questions when necessary. Errors can also occur when the interviewers probe answers in a directive way (which may influence respondents' clarification or elaboration) or record answers with their own discretion. Other errors include inappropriate interpersonal behavior (e.g., aggression), evaluative feedback to respondents (e.g., "That is great" or "You are lucky"). These potential errors can be reduced in the telephone survey by interviewer error training. However, there is evidence that trainees without prior experience may need a great deal of time to master the probing skills, particularly for open-ended questions. Fowler and Mangione (1990) reported that only 47% of their trainees demonstrated excellent or satisfactory skills for probing open-ended questions after a 10-day training.

FEEDBACK AND EVALUATION

Throughout the training session, the trainees should have plenty of opportunities to practice the aforementioned skills by means of case studies, behavior modeling, role playing, discussion/critique, and so forth. After the training, the trainees should be instructed to make three to five interviews. Without their knowledge, they should interview the same interviewees. Each "confederate" interviewee should answer questions on the basis of planned scripts. The trainees' performance should then be evaluated along a list of critical behaviors. These behavioral criteria include, but are not limited to, speech clarity (timing between items, mispronunciation, poor inflection or inadequate emphasis), number of questions read incorrectly, number of questions repeated unnecessarily or incorrectly, number of directive probes, frequency of skipping questions incorrectly, number of times the interviewer failed to probe incomplete answers, number of inaccurate recordings of answers, number of questions unnecessarily clarified, number of instances seeking or giving inappropriate feedback, number of instances of inappropriate interpersonal behavior, number of instances of laughing, and number of failures to follow instructions in the call sheet form or other forms (Cannell, 1985a; Fowler & Mangione, 1990). It should be emphasized that these criteria should be reliably measured. By using these criteria, not only are qualified interviewers selected with much less subjective judgment, but also overall training quality (e.g., reliability of interviewer performance) is evaluated. Furthermore, these criteria in conjunction with others (e.g., nonresponse rate within interviewers; speed of processing records) can be used to monitor and evaluate interviewer performance after the formal survey starts. In an academic setting, the unsuitable trainees could still be assigned to do other tasks (e.g., printing, data entry) as long as they wish to stay in the project.

Conclusions

With the development of advanced telecommunication and computer technologies, new challenges in the telephone survey are continuously appearing. For example, telephone survey users are facing the challenge of answering machines, caller ID devices, touch-tone data entry (TDE) or voice recognition (VRE) devices, call forwarding, car phones, cellular phones, and videophones. These new products are very likely to create problems such as an increase of nonresponse rate and sampling bias. However, the potential impact of these products is still not clear at the present time.

Another challenge arises from the evolution of computer-assisted telephone interview (CATI) programs over the past 25 years. Nicholls (1988) summarized three major functions of the CATI: facilitating telephone surveys (e.g., cost-effectiveness), enhancing and controlling survey data quality (e.g., error reduction), and allowing flexible survey designs (e.g., randomization of questions). In a typical CATI program, interviewers ask questions that are flashed on a monitor. All information is keyed into the computer by the interviewers immediately after respondents answer the questions. Some CATI programs are able to randomize question sequences and question wording or to choose the next questions to be asked (based on prior input), which would eliminate some interviewer errors.

Some programs are also capable of tracking inconsistencies in responses, generating telephone numbers randomly, scheduling calls and callbacks, or recording interviewer performance. There is no doubt that CATI programs offer researchers great flexibility and convenience, given that users are trained adequately and programs are bug-free. However, empirical findings about many advantages of the CATI are still inconclusive (Porst, Schneid, & van Brouwershaven, 1994). More research in data quality, nonresponse errors, interviewer errors, software evaluation, and training is needed. It should be emphasized that the CATI is not a panacea for problems caused by computer anxiety, poor questionnaire design, inadequate choice of sampling procedure, unstandardized interview process, biased selection, sloppy interview training and monitoring, or poor rapport with respondents.

Recommended Readings

Finally, it should be noted that there is no single mode of data collection that can address all the issues of concern in the social science. Each method has its limitations. However, by employing more than one approach (i.e., triangulation), researchers will be able to examine questions from different perspectives.

Four books are recommended to readers for further study of interviewing in general (Fowler & Mangione, *Standardized Survey Interviewing*, 1990, and Groves, *Survey Errors and Survey Costs*, 1989) and the telephone survey in particular (Frey, *Survey Research by Telephone*, 1989, and Lavrakas, *Telephone Survey Methods*, 1993). Important topics such as sampling, standardization, questionnaire development, persuasion skills, training, and use of the CATI are discussed in these books.

References

Aneshensel, C. S., Frerichs, R. R., Clark, V. A., & Yokopenic, P. A. (1982). Measuring depression in the community: A comparison of telephone and personal interviews. *Public Opinion Quarterly, 46,* 110-121.

Biemer, P. P. (1988). Measuring data quality. In R. M. Groves P. P. Biemer, L. E. Lyberg, J. T. Massey, W. L. Nicholls II, & J. Waksberg (Eds.), *Telephone survey methodology* (pp. 273-282). New York: John Wiley.

Cannell, C. F. (1985a). Experiments in the improvement of response accuracy. In T. W. Beed & R. J. Stimson (Eds.), *Survey interviewing: Theory and techniques* (pp. 24-62). Boston: George Allen & Unwin.

Cannell, C. F. (1985b). Interviewing in telephone surveys. In T. W. Beed & R. J. Stimson (Eds.), *Survey interviewing: Theory and techniques* (pp. 63-84). Boston: George Allen & Unwin.

Collins, M., Sykes, W., Wilson, P., & Blackshaw, N. (1988). Nonresponse: The UK experience. In R. M. Groves, P. P. Biemer, L. E. Lyberg, J. T. Massey, W. L. Nicholls II, & J. Waksberg (Eds.), *Telephone survey methodology* (pp. 213-231). New York: John Wiley.

Cooper, S. L. (1964). Random sampling by telephone: An improved method. *Journal of Marketing Research, 1,* 45-48.

de Leeuw, E. D., & van der Zouwen, J. (1988). Data quality in telephone and face to face surveys: A comparative meta-analysis. In R. M. Groves, P. P. Biemer, L. E. Lyberg, J. T. Massey, W. L. Nicholls II, & J. Waksberg (Eds.), *Telephone survey methodology* (pp. 283-299). New York: John Wiley.

Fowler, F. J., Jr. (1984). *Survey research methods.* Beverly Hills, CA: Sage.

Fowler, F. J., Jr., & Mangione, T. W. (1990). *Standardized survey interviewing: Minimizing interviewer-related error.* Newbury Park, CA: Sage.

Frankel, J., & Sharp, L. (1981, January). Measurement of respondent burden. *Statistical Reporter,* pp. 105-111.

Frey, J. H. (1989). *Survey research by telephone* (2nd ed.). Newbury Park, CA: Sage.

Groves, R. M. (1989). *Survey errors and survey costs.* New York: John Wiley.

Groves, R. M., & Fultz, N. H. (1985). Gender effects among telephone interviewers in a survey of economic attitudes. *Sociological Methods and Research, 14,* 31-52.

Groves, R. M., & Kahn, R. L. (1979). *Surveys by telephone: A national comparison with personal interviews.* New York: Academic Press.

Groves, R. M., & Lyberg, L. E. (1988). An overview of nonresponse issues in telephone surveys. In R. M. Groves, P. P. Biemer, L. E. Lyberg, J. T. Massey, W. L. Nicholls II, & J. Waksberg (Eds.), *Telephone survey methodology* (pp. 191-211). New York: John Wiley.

Hagan, F. E. (1993). *Research methods in criminal justice and criminology* (3rd ed.). New York: Macmillan.

Herman, J. B. (1977). Mixed mode data collection: Telephone and personal interviewing. *Journal of Applied Psychology, 62,* 399-404.

Jordan, W. H., Marcus, A. C., & Reeder, L. G. (1980). Response styles in telephone and household interviewing: A field experiment. *Public Opinion Quarterly, 44,* 210-222.

Kish, L. (1949). A procedure for objective respondent selection within the household. *American Statistical Association Journal, 44,* 380-387.

Lavrakas, P. J. (1993). *Telephone survey methods: Sampling, selection, and supervision* (2nd ed.). Newbury Park, CA: Sage.

Lucas, W. A., & Adams, W. C. (1977). *An assessment of telephone survey methods.* Santa Monica, CA: The Rand Corporation.

Mangione, T. W., Hingson, R., & Barrett, J. (1982). Collecting sensitive data: A comparison of three survey strategies. *Sociological Methods and Research, 10,* 337-346.

Nicholls, W. L., II (1988). Computer-assisted telephone interviewing: A general introduction. In R. M. Groves, P. P. Biemer, L. E. Lyberg, J. T. Massey, W. L. Nicholls II, & J. Waksberg (Eds.), *Telephone survey methodology* (pp. 377-385). New York: John Wiley.

Oksenberg, L., & Cannell, C. (1988). Effects of interviewer vocal characteristics on nonresponse. In R. M. Groves, P. P. Biemer, L. E. Lyberg, J. T. Massey, W. L. Nicholls II, & J. Waksberg (Eds.), *Telephone survey methodology* (pp. 257-269). New York: John Wiley.

Porst, R., Schneid, M., & van Brouwershaven, J. W. (1994). Computer-assisted interviewing in social and market research. In I. Borg & P. Mohler (Eds.), *New trends in empirical social research* (pp. 79-98). Berlin: de Gruyter.

Siemiatycki, J. (1979). A comparison of mail, telephone and home interview strategies for household health surveys. *American Journal of Public Health, 69,* 238-245.

Strafford, J., & Grant, C. (1993). *Effective sales management* (2nd ed.). London: Butterworth-Heinemann.

Thornberry, O. T., Jr. (1987). *An experimental comparison of telephone and personal health interview surveys.* Washington, DC: Government Printing Office.

Thornberry, O. T., Jr., & Massey, J. T. (1988). Trends in United States telephone coverage across time and subgroups. In R. M. Groves, P. P. Biemer, L. E. Lyberg, J. T. Massey, W. L. Nicholls II, & J. Waksberg (Eds.), *Telephone survey methodology* (pp. 25-49). New York: John Wiley.

Trewin, D., & Lee, G. (1988). International comparisons of telephone coverage. In R. M. Groves, P. P. Biemer, L. E. Lyberg, J. T. Massey, W. L. Nicholls II, & J. Waksberg (Eds.), *Telephone survey methodology* (pp. 9-24). New York: John Wiley.

Waksberg, J. (1978). Sampling methods for random digit dialing. *Journal of the American Statistical Association, 73,* 40-46.

Weaver, C. N., Holmes, S. L., & Glenn, N. D. (1975). Some characteristics of inaccessible respondents in a telephone survey. *Journal of Applied Psychology, 60,* 260-262.

Chapter 12

Collecting Data From Groups

STEPHEN J. ZACCARO
MICHELLE MARKS

Much human behavior occurs within a social context. People's actions are often influenced in some degree by the presence of other individuals. Such influence may be quite passive, in which case the mere presence of others affects the frequency, intensity, or appropriateness of behavioral responses (Zajonc, 1965). Alternatively, social influence may be integral to action, such that a person's response is entirely interdependent with the responses of other individuals (Orasanu & Salas, 1993). In either instance, or in any other that reflects social dynamics, behavior cannot be fully understood without considering the role of such dynamics. This is the elemental raison d'etre of most group research.

The differences between individual and group research are grounded primarily in the presence of interpersonal dynamics that characterize the latter. Conducting careful group research therefore requires a consideration of these dynamics, not only in the conceptualization of group phenomena but also in the design of studies, the collection of data from the group as a whole as well as from individual members, and the analysis of such data. In this chapter, we will offer prescriptions for conducting group research that proceed from this consideration. The major points that will be covered concern the selection of a research setting and relevant design issues; data collection procedures, including the selection/acquisition of groups and the measurement and coding of group process; and the analysis of data from group research.

What are some fundamental differences between individual and group research? One is that because the latter often examines aggregations of individuals working in coaction or interaction, collective and interpersonal processes are likely to mediate subsequent individual and collective responses. This distinction is illustrated, for example, in individual versus group decision-making research. Individual decision making involves the use of cognitive processes to assess decision scenarios, organize information, define decision alternatives, and select the "best-fitting" alternative (Lipshitz, 1993; Montgomery & Svenson, 1989; Pennington & Hastie, 1986). The selection process may reflect the application of various decision heuristics that in turn may result in multiple biases (Cohen, 1993; Tversky & Kahneman, 1972, 1974). The primary emphasis is on the cognitive dynamics applied by the individual when making decisions.

Group decision making also includes these cognitive dynamics as critical antecedents (Duffy, 1993). However, research on such decision making typically examines the group members' application of cognitive processes within the context of interpersonal dynamics (e.g., Gualtieri, Parker, & Zaccaro, 1995). For example, research on "groupthink" has demonstrated how collective norms that emphasize the paramount importance of group unanimity can create defective decision making by group members (Janis, 1982). Likewise, group polarization research has demonstrated that groups will make more polarizing decisions (i.e., more risky or more cautious) than individual members making decisions alone (Myers & Lamm, 1976; Wallach, Kogan, & Bem, 1962). Theorists explain groupthink and group polarization by focusing on the influences of interpersonal processes that cause individuals to act differently when in groups. As illustrated in several points in this chapter, the interpersonal quality of group research that distinguishes it from individual research affects how group studies are designed, the nature of variables chosen for study, and the statistical analyses required by such data.

The presence of interpersonal or collective processes leads to another characteristic of group research that becomes particularly critical when analyzing group data. When group members interact (even if such interaction is limited to nonverbal modes), their subsequent individual responses may be substantially influenced by the nature and content of these interactions. Kenny and La Voie (1985) called this "nonindependence" in that data from each individual cannot be considered as independent from the data of other individuals within the group. Because many statistical procedures require data independence (e.g., analysis of variance), this influence creates the need for different statistical treatments of the data (Anderson & Ager, 1978; Kenny & La Voie, 1985).

Individual-level research allows a single unit of analysis: that of the individual providing the data. Alternatively, when group research includes the collection of data from individuals within groups (i.e., when such research uses a "hierarchically nested design"; Kenny & La Voie, 1985), then two levels of analysis, the individual level and the group level, are possible. A common mistake in group research is to ignore one level or the other when conceptualizing about groups or when analyzing data from nested designs. Many collective phenomena are perhaps best understood by focusing on both the differences between aggregations (using group means, reflecting a group-level analysis) and the differences within aggregations (using member scores, reflecting an individual-level analysis). This means that when one is framing hypotheses, one ought to consider sources of variance at both levels. Also, when the data are collected from individuals nested within groups, statistical analyses need to account for multiple levels of influence.

This suggests another difference between individual and group research. Studies of individual behavior will often focus on the characteristics of the individual as sources of variance. In group research, sources of variance include not only the characteristics of individual group members but also qualities that emerge from the interaction of group members (e.g., group cohesion, normative pressures, role definition). Other group sources of variance include structural qualities of the group (group size, degree of hierarchical organization, communication structure). The design of group studies needs to account for these sources of variance, even if they are not the focal point of a study's hypotheses. For example, group size can influence the degree of cohesion in a group (Cartwright, 1968), the intensity of group conformity and obedience pressures (Asch, 1951, 1955; Milgram, 1963,

1965), and the amount of effort exerted by individual members on behalf of the group (Latane, Williams, & Harkins, 1979). Thus, when designing group research, researchers need to give considerable thought to the size of their sample groups, even if group size is not the focus of the study.

Selecting a Group Research Setting and Design

The setting for group research has been a source of significant debate in the literature. Much of group research has been completed in laboratory settings with experimental methodologies. Such approaches provide control over proposed predictors of group actions and allow plausible inferences of causality. Further, an experimental methodology allows the researcher to create a number of situations and scenarios in the group that may occur infrequently in natural groups (e.g., stressors, crises). This tactic permits the investigation of rare but critical events that often determine subsequent group norms, culture, and long-term group action. However, the frequent use by researchers of ad hoc groups in experimental settings has earned such research the criticism of artificiality and lack of external validity (Forsyth, 1990). Indeed, several group phenomena emerge only after group members have developed a significant set of shared experiences (e.g., group norms, cohesiveness). Because most laboratory groups meet for a short period of time and have no expectation of continued existence, an experimental investigation of these phenomena in such groups can become suspect.

Studying intact groups in their natural settings is an alternate and popular group research strategy. The most frequently used methodology in such studies is either correlational, in which surveys are given to group members, or observational, in which groups are observed for a period of time and their processes coded for significant events. Studies of "real" groups have the advantage of greater generalizability and applicability than studies of laboratory or ad hoc groups. However, such research can suffer from a number of other flaws. Correlational methodologies rarely provide the basis for causal inference regarding the key variables under study. This flaw significantly limits the ability of such approaches to assess hypotheses drawn from theories of group action. Further, if a survey is administered at a single point in the group's existence, key developmental issues such as the emergence of group norms or group cohesiveness cannot be investigated. Also, if the data consist solely of survey data collected from group members, then the results of correlational analyses may often be attributed to common method variance or other response biases. This situation is improved if (a) multiple surveys are administered over the history of the group, from its initial founding through a number of significant events, and (b) survey data from group members are combined with data from other sources (e.g., group observers, archival records).

Observational methods provide an ongoing assessment of group processes. However, such methods can be criticized on two important grounds. First, the time of observation may not provide enough instances of critical group events or actions to assess fully the hypothesized relationships among targeted variables. For example, if a researcher is interested in team responses to different kinds of stressors, an unrealistically long period may be required to observe the full range of relevant stressors and the group's subsequent reactions so as to understand this phenomenon fully. Also, such methods may result in the "Hawthorne" effect (Roethlisberger & Dickson, 1939), in which group members' knowledge that they are being observed changes the quality and frequency of their behavior. Although one answer to this effect is covert observational strategies, this approach raises significant ethical concerns.

We (and other group researchers) suggest several responses to this dilemma of laboratory/experimental versus natural/correlational group research. One is that the methodological approach should be dictated by the primary purpose of the researcher. Driskell and Salas (1992) noted that laboratory settings allow researchers to test under controlled and strenuous conditions particular theories and hypotheses about "real-world" group phenomena. They argued that "it is theory that is applied to the real world" (p. 106), not the findings or setting of any particular experiment. Thus, if the purpose of the group research is to assess theories of group action, then controlled experimentation is the preferred approach. If the purpose is to understand specific real-world group settings or apply theory to such settings, then research with natural groups is more appropriate (Driskell & Salas, 1992).

Ad hoc groups do not necessarily have to be limited to artificial settings, nor are real groups excluded from experimental manipulations. Investigators can create groups for research purposes that operate in natural settings. Likewise, experimenters can manipulate conditions confronted by existing and ongoing groups. Examples of such research include establishing project groups in classroom settings, having existing teams complete training simulations, and applying different work conditions to different organizational groups. Each of these strategies mitigates some (but not all) of the problems connected with exclusive laboratory/experimental or natural/correlational group research.

It is likely that a program of research on group phenomena will have multiple purposes. Accordingly, researchers are urged to consider a series of studies, some experimental with the intention of testing theories, others correlational with natural groups to examine the generalizability and applicability of experimental findings. Such a multi-strategy approach will compensate for the flaws of separate methodologies (McGrath, 1984) and provide a basis for both the evaluation of theories of group behavior and their extension to real-world groups (Driskell & Salas, 1992).

Two basic approaches to data collection characterize group research. The first involves the collection of data entirely at the group level. Such a design would be used, for example, by a researcher who was interested in the relationship between group size or group structure and group coordination. The dependent variable in such a study would be the product that emerged from the interaction of group members. Many decision-making studies in which the group is required to solve a problem collectively are examples of group-level studies. The unit of statistical analysis in such studies would be the group as a whole. A second design is the collection of data from individuals within the group. Such a design is called a *nested design* (Kenny & La Voie, 1985). As illustrated by Kenny and La Voie (1985), the unit of analysis in these studies can be both the individual and the group. Group researchers often mistakenly analyze the data from such studies only at the individual level when multiple levels of analysis are more appropriate. As will be discussed later in this chapter, even if (a) the data are collected from individual group members and

(b) hypotheses postulate individual-level relationships, the statistical analyses must still be used to evaluate the presence of group-level effects.

Data Collection Procedures

Other chapters in this book describe several aspects regarding the procedures used to collect data from individuals. However, some unique issues arise when one is collecting data from groups. These are related to subject acquisition and variable specification.

SUBJECT ACQUISITION

The issues regarding subject acquisition in group research vary according to whether the setting is laboratory/experimental or natural/correlational. When conducting laboratory experiments, researchers will begin by soliciting volunteers. In many universities, subject pools from introductory psychology courses are often the source of such volunteers. A critical point for group researchers, however, is that the number of individuals required for each group of a given size sign up to participate for a particular time period. If an insufficient number of people show up, the experiment session cannot be completed, and the researcher may lose the volunteers that did appear. One suggestion is that researchers sign up more subjects than needed for a particular experimental session. If more individuals appear than are needed, the actual participants ought to be randomly selected, and the others can be asked either to return to a later session or to participate in a concurrent unrelated research study.

Some experimental treatments may be confounded if individual members are friends or acquaintances before they meet in the experimental session. In such instances, investigators need to screen for such pairings either when soliciting volunteers or when assigning individuals to groups. For example, in a study of task-based and social-based group cohesion, Zaccaro and McCoy (1988) stipulated on a volunteer sign-up sheet that friends should not volunteer for the same experimental session. If friends did appear during the same session, they were assigned to different groups. In this way, the investigators minimized the chance that prior relationships would confound their manipulations of task and social cohesion.

A critical question for group researchers is the requisite size of their groups. If group size is to be manipulated, then this question is generally not applicable. However, most studies are likely to hold group size constant. What, then, should that size be? The larger the group, the more individual subjects must be solicited as volunteers. This can be quite problematic for large research designs. For example, a $2 \times 2 \times 2$ factorial design that uses five-person groups may require from 600 to 800 individual participants (i.e., eight experimental cells with 15 to 20 groups per cell)! One might be tempted to use the smallest aggregation possible, that is "groups" of two persons. However, some researchers have argued for qualitative differences between dyads and groups of three or more individuals (Simmel, 1902/1950). Therefore, unless it is required by the study's purpose (e.g., Zaccaro, 1984), researchers should establish groups of no fewer than three individuals.

Another critical question is the number of groups that should be collected for each level of experimental treatments. Convention in individual research is that 20 subjects per treatment level is sufficient to stabilize sampling error (although the number required for sufficient power may be more or less, depending on anticipated effect sizes; Cohen, 1977). However, in group research, when groups are the unit of analysis, means are more stable than in individual-level research having the same number of data points. Although such a convention has not emerged for group research, it is likely that fewer than 20 groups per treatment level are necessary for relative stability. Indeed, Hanges, Nelson, and Schneider (1990) completed a Monte Carlo simulation to compare the statistical power of the same number of individual- and group-level data points. They found, when assessing the significance of regression coefficients, that a group level of analysis had more power than an individual level of analysis. Thus fewer groups are likely to be necessary to provide the same level of statistical power as a particular number of individual subjects.

Natural Settings

When collecting data from natural or existing groups, researchers need to consider issues of group composition and the likelihood of restriction of range in the nature of groups being studied. Unlike laboratory groups, in which members are randomly assigned to groups, natural groups typically contain members who have chosen to belong to them or to the organizations within which the groups are embedded. Such groups are likely to be more homogeneous and reflect characteristics that may need to be assessed as covariates for subsequent statistical control. Also, the acquisition of a sample of natural groups typically requires permission from group leaders or from a superordinate governing organization. Leaders of successful and effective groups are more likely to grant permission to outside researchers than leaders of poor or ineffective groups. Thus researchers need to be sensitive to restriction-of-range issues when soliciting natural groups.

Preexisting groups will rarely be identical in terms of group size or group tenure. Yet these and other related variables are likely to be critical determinants of most group phenomena. Accordingly, researchers need to identify the qualities and characteristics that vary from group to group in their sample and are likely to explain significant variance in their focal criteria. Measures of such characteristics can then be treated as covariates in subsequent statistical analyses.

THE MEASUREMENT OF GROUP PROCESSES

The specification of key predictor and criterion variables to examine in a group research study obviously proceeds from the conceptual basis of the research. However, because a key mediator of most relationships between independent (or input) variables and dependent (or output) variables is the process (throughput) or interpersonal dynamics in the group, most researchers will need to consider measures of such processes and the procedures to gather such data. Group processes can be assessed either through self-report measures completed by group members or through observational methods. In some circumstances, self-report measures can be notoriously unreliable and influenced significantly by the outcomes of group processes (e.g., group performance). Further, if measures of group inputs and outputs are also gathered from group members (e.g., measures of group cohesion, group norms), then any significant findings among input, process, and output variables can be attributed to common method biases. Thus observational methods are generally more appropriate means of collecting group process data.

Some studies use coders who observe and record the ongoing processes of the group. A significant problem with such an approach is that unless the coder is highly trained and the coding scheme fairly simple, a significant amount of the group interaction is likely to be lost. This is because group interaction is often complex, can occur rapidly, and may feature multiple behaviors occurring simultaneously. Thus observational studies ought to utilize audio and visual recordings of group processes. This provides a more permanent record of the group's entire process and allows a more careful analysis of such processes from multiple raters. Three examples of observational systems that coders can use to analyze group interaction processes are Bales IPA (Bales, 1950a, 1950b), SYMLOG (Bales & Cohen, 1979), and TEMPO (Futoran, Kelly, & McGrath, 1989). Though differing in significant ways, these observational systems all provide a set of coding categories appropriate for a wide range of group performance situations. All three systems present categories that allow task-related group interactions to be differentiated from social-related interactions. For example, TEMPO (Futoran et al., 1989) provides a categorical structure that includes production functions (task-related statements) and nonproduction functions (socially oriented statements). Within the production functions, categories depict content- and process-related statements and idea-proposing and idea-evaluating statements.

Observational data can be collected through either covert or overt means. In laboratory settings, covert means may involve the use of one-way mirrors or hidden cameras. Although one-way mirrors are common, they rarely, if ever, fool group members who are the target of observation. Such members may focus on the mirror to determine the presence of observers and confound measures of group process. Hidden cameras obviate this problem but raise a number of ethical concerns. We have found in several studies that video cameras can be placed within the setting of the group without strong Hawthorne effects. Group members have indicated in debriefing sessions that after a relatively short time they did not attend to the camera, thus habituating to its presence. Thus we suggest that researchers place cameras within sight of the group; such placement avoids significant ethical issues and provides a usable record of group process without necessarily constraining such processes. We should note that more than one camera is likely to be necessary to capture the interactions and reactions of *all* members of the group.

Analysis of Data From Group Research

Particular issues that must be attended to when analyzing data collected from groups depend on the basic design of the study. If the criteria or dependent variables are collected entirely at the group level (i.e., only group-level scores compose the data set), then the statistical procedures and assumptions are the same as those that apply to the analysis of individual-level data. For example, in a study of group performance in which the dependent variable is a solution generated by the entire group, the independent variables are task and social cohesion, and high and low levels of each type of cohesion are manipulated, then a conventional 2×2 analysis of variance is used to analyze the data (Zaccaro & McCoy, 1988). Note that a group-level analysis is still required when the predictor or independent variable is measured at the individual level but the dependent variable is still a group-level score. Thus, if in the previous study the predictor was perceived cohesiveness as reported by each group member instead of manipulated levels of cohesion types, the analysis would be correlational, using group means of perceived cohesion and group performance scores as the data points.

When the data are collected from individual group members (i.e., in a hierarchical design, with individuals nested within groups), the appropriate unit of analysis needs to be determined before statistical tests of proposed effects are completed. That is, the researcher needs to determine if a "group effect" is present in the data. Such an effect means that an individual's membership in a particular group was a source of influence on that person's responses. When individuals interact in a group, their subsequent responses are not likely to be independent from one another. Generally (although not always), these responses tend to become more homogeneous.

There are several statistical procedures for determining whether a group effect exists in the data. If the data are collected as part of an experiment in which subjects are randomly assigned to groups and other independent variables are manipulated, then the group to which an individual belongs is entered as a random source of variance in a groups-nested-within-treatments analysis of variance (Anderson & Ager, 1978; Myers, 1979). If the group effect is significant, then its means square is used as the error term to test treatment effects; if it is not, then a pooled error term can be used to test these effects. See Anderson and Ager (1978), George (1990), Myers (1979), and Yammarino and Markham (1992) for additional information on these procedures.

Kenny and La Voie (1985) suggested that the presence of group effects in correlational data be assessed using the intraclass correlation. This statistic provides an index of how much variance in a measure exists at the group level by comparing within-group and between-group variance. Group effects are presumed to be present when within-group variance is significantly smaller than between-group variance. In such cases, Kenny and La Voie suggested that correlations be computed at both the group and the individual level, with individual-level correlations being adjusted for group effects and group-level correlations adjusted for individual effects (see Kenny, 1985, and Kenny & La Voie, 1985, for additional information on these procedures; also see James, Demaree, & Wolf, 1984, for an alternate procedure to assess group effects).

When data are collected from individual group members, it is absolutely necessary to assess for the presence of group effects before proceeding to other statistical analyses. This assessment is required even if the study's hypotheses specify individual effects. In these instances, group membership may still be a significant source of variance that needs to be accounted for. Alternatively, if a researcher is interested in group phenomena but does not uncover a group effect in this initial assessment, careful consideration must be given to the meaning of the data. If the individual's own group is a meaningless influence on his or her behavior, the investigator has to wonder if the data have any relevance regarding *group* or collective behavior. We have noted instances in which group researchers tested for the presence of group effects and, finding none, proceeded to analyze the data at the individual level. However, their findings were then interpreted in terms of group influences! If group effects are not discerned in preliminary tests to determine appropriate levels of statistical analysis, then such interpretations are unwarranted. Thus group researchers need to attend carefully to the presence or absence of group effects in their data and the meaning of such effects (or the lack thereof) for subsequent data analysis and interpretation.

Summary

We began this chapter by pointing out several differences between individual and group research. These differences are grounded in the interactions among individuals that characterize most group studies. A group researcher's interest is typically in the products of these interactions. Indeed, Lewin (1951) described groups as "dynamic wholes" and noted that the "structural properties of a dynamic whole are different from the structural properties of subparts" (p. 192). Further, he noted that "structural properties are characterized by *relations* between parts rather than by the parts or elements themselves" (p. 192). These properties that emerge from the relations or interactions among individuals require some special attention from researchers. This chapter describes procedures that are unique to data collection and analysis in groups. We believe that adherence to such procedures can promote better group research and accordingly stronger theories of group phenomena.

Recommended Readings

We recommend that the reader consult the following sources for more in-depth information about the topic covered in this chapter: Anderson and Ager, "Analysis of Variance in Small Group Research" (1978); Driskell and Salas, "Can You Study Real Teams in Contrived Settings? The Value of Small Group Research to Understanding Teams" (1992); Forsyth's *Group Dynamics* (1990, chap. 2); Kenny and La Voie, "Separating Individual and Group Effects" (1985); and McGrath's *Groups: Interaction and Performance* (1984, chaps. 3, 4).

References

Anderson, L. R., & Ager, J. W. (1978). Analysis of variance in small group research. *Personality and Social Psychology Bulletin, 4,* 341-345.

Asch, S. E. (1951). Effects of group pressure upon the modification and distortion of judgement. In H. Guetzkow (Ed.), *Groups, leadership, and men.* Pittsburgh: Carnegie.

Asch, S. E. (1955). Opinions and social pressures. *Scientific American, 193*(5), 31-35.

Bales, R. F. (1950a). *Interaction process analysis; A method for the study of small groups.* Cambridge, MA: Addison-Wesley.

Bales, R. F. (1950b). A set of categories for the analysis of small group interaction. *American Sociological Review, 15,* 257-263.

Bales, R. F., & Cohen, J. S. P. (1979). *SYMLOG: A system for the multilevel observation of groups.* New York: Free Press.

Cartwright, D. (1968). The nature of group cohesiveness. In D. Cartwright & A. Zander (Eds.), *Group dynamics: Research and theory* (pp. 91-109). New York: Harper & Row.

Cohen, J. (1977). *Statistical power analysis for the behavioral sciences.* New York: Academic Press.

Cohen, M. (1993). The naturalistic basis of decision biases. In G. Klein, J. Orasanu, R. Calderwood, & C. E. Zsambok (Eds.), *Decision making in action: Models and methods* (pp. 51-99). Norwood, NJ: Ablex.

Driskell, J. E., & Salas, E. (1992). Can you study real teams in contrived settings? The value of small group research to understanding teams. In R. W. Swezey & E. Salas (Eds.), *Teams: Their training and performance* (pp. 101-124). Norwood, NJ: Ablex.

Duffy, L. (1993). Team decision-making biases: An information processing perspective. In G. Klein, J. Orasanu, R. Calderwood, & C. E. Zsambok (Eds.), *Decision making in action: Models and methods* (pp. 346-359). Norwood, NJ: Ablex.

Forsyth, D. R. (1990). *Group dynamics* (2nd ed.). Pacific Grove, CA: Brooks/Cole.

Futoran, G. C., Kelly, J. R., & McGrath, J. E. (1989). TEMPO: A time-based system for analysis of group interaction process. *Basic and Applied Social Psychology, 10,* 211-232.

George, J. M. (1990). Personality, affect, and behavior in groups. *Journal of Applied Psychology, 75,* 107-116.

Gualtieri, J., Parker, C., & Zaccaro, S. J. (1995). *Group decision making: An examination of decision processes and performance.* Manuscript submitted for publication.

Hanges, P. J., Nelson, G. L., & Schneider, B. (1990). *Levels of analysis and statistical power.* Paper presented at the annual meeting of the American Psychological Association, Boston.

James, L. R., Demaree, R. G., & Wolf, G. (1984). Estimating within-group interrater reliability with and without response bias. *Journal of Applied Psychology, 69,* 85-98.

Janis, I. L. (1982). *Victims of groupthink* (2nd ed.). Boston: Houghton Mifflin.

Kenny, D. A. (1985). The generalized group effect model. In J. Nesselroade & A. von Eye (Eds.), *Individual development and social change* (pp. 343-351). New York: Academic Press.

Kenny, D., & La Voie, L. (1985). Separating individual and group effects. *Journal of Personality and Social Psychology, 4,* 339-348.

Latane, B., Williams, K., & Harkins, S. (1979). Many hands make light the work: The causes and consequences of social loafing. *Journal of Personality and Social Psychology, 37,* 823-832.

Lewin, K. (1951). *Field theory in social science.* New York: Harper & Bros.

Lipshitz, R. (1993). Converging themes in the study of decision making in realistic settings. In G. Klein, J. Orasanu, R. Calderwood, & C. E. Zsambok (Eds.), *Decision making in action: Models and methods* (pp. 103-137). Norwood, NJ: Ablex.

McGrath, J. (1984). *Groups: Interaction and performance.* Englewood Cliffs, NJ: Prentice Hall.

Milgram, S. (1963). Behavioral study of obedience. *Journal of Abnormal and Social Psychology, 69,* 137-143.

Milgram, S. (1965). Some conditions of obedience and disobedience to authority. *Human Relations, 18,* 57-75.

Montgomery, H., & Svenson, O. (1989). *Process and structure in human decision making.* New York: John Wiley.

Myers, D. G., & Lamm, H. (1976). The polarizing effect of group discussion. *American Scientist, 63,* 297-303.

Myers, J. L. (1979). *Fundamentals in experimental design* (3rd ed.). Boston: Allyn & Bacon.

Orasanu, J., & Salas, E. (1993). Team decision making in complex environments. In G. A. Klein, J. Orasanu, R. Calderwood, & C. E. Zsambok (Eds.), *Decision making in action: Models and methods* (pp. 327-345). Norwood, NJ: Ablex.

Pennington, N., & Hastie, R. (1986). Evidence evaluation in complex decision making. *Journal of Personality and Social Psychology, 51,* 242-258.

Roethlisberger, F. J., & Dickson, W. J. (1939). *Management and the worker.* Cambridge, MA: Harvard University Press.

Simmel, G. (1950). The significance of numbers for social life [excerpts]. In K. H. Wolff (Ed.), *The sociology of Georg Simmel.* Glencoe, IL: Free Press.

Tversky, A., & Kahneman, D. (1972). Availability: A heuristic for judging frequency and probability. *Cognitive Psychology, 4,* 207-232.

Tversky, A., & Kahneman, D. (1974). Judgement under uncertainty: Heuristics and biases. *Science, 211,* 453-458.

Wallach, M. A., Kogan, N., & Bem, D. J. (1962). Group influence on individual risk taking. *Journal of Abnormal and Social Psychology, 65,* 75-86.

Yammarino, F. J., & Markham, S. E. (1992). On the application of within and between analysis: Are absence and affect really group-based phenomena? *Journal of Applied Psychology, 77,* 168-176.

Zaccaro, S. J. (1984). Social loafing: The role of task attractiveness. *Personality and Social Psychology Bulletin, 10,* 99-106.

Zaccaro, S. J., & McCoy, M. C. (1988). The effects of task and interpersonal cohesiveness on performance of a disjunctive group task. *Journal of Applied Social Psychology, 18,* 837-851.

Zajonc, R. B. (1965). Social facilitation. *Science, 149,* 269-274.

PART IV

Data Analyses

Chapter 13

Cleaning up Data and Running Preliminary Analyses

STEPHEN J. DOLLINGER
DAVID L. DiLALLA

Cleaning up Data

The ideal of truth seeking in psychology and indeed all sciences goes hand in hand with the need to avoid error. This effort to avoid error can be seen in many activities of the psychologist-researcher, from double-checking his or her data entry to significance testing to avoid Type I error, and from designing studies with sufficient power to avoid Type II error to the critical thinking that goes into interpretation of one's own (and others') data. Because much of the data of psychology is collected by research assistants, a concern for error-free or "clean" data is an important quality that all psychologists value in their current or prospective assistants, whether in the lab or the clinic. The integrity of a single scientific investigation, of a clinical case study, and of the entire field depends on data sets that are as internally valid and free of error as we can make them. Preliminary analyses serve this end by helping identify several sources of error. They also help researchers best "tell the story" of their data.

GUIDES FOR CLEAN DATA

A particularly useful source of information on clean data was an article by Smith, Budzeika, Edwards, Johnson, and Bearse (1986) aptly titled "Guidelines for Clean Data." Smith et al. suggested a number of rules for ensuring clean data, particularly regarding use of large data sets that are combined or are to be used in secondary analyses (see Zaitzow & Fields, Chapter 20 of this volume). The Smith et al. suggestions apply to most data management contexts. To summarize the common theme in their recommendations: Pay attention to detail!

Before and During Data Collection

Smith et al. (1986) suggested that standard scales should never be altered or embellished without clear statements of how changes were made. So too, researchers should design their response measures with a method of analysis in mind; often, not doing so leads to complications that could have been prevented. Smith et al. noted that in the rush to meet deadlines, some researchers have introduced questionnaire items that they later did not know how to code, perhaps due to inappropriate response alternatives.

Although it is common for dissertation data to be reanalyzed (in new ways) before submission to a journal, it is always wise to plan a study's analyses before the data are collected (see Yaffee, Chapter 15 of this volume). Doing so will afford a more careful consideration of the possible outcomes of the study. (In one recent case in which this was not done sufficiently, the student realized that one of his hypotheses was untestable due to poor choice of measures—a problem not foreseen until the data were in hand and ready for analysis.) The message here is that once the data are collected, one has the "wisdom of hindsight" in how the study ought to have been designed. A priori planning for the analyses will help the researcher possess a bit of that wisdom. Better yet, if time and resources permit, do a pilot study!

Smith et al. (1986) also recommended that investigators actively participate in data collection—not just leave it entirely up to research assistants—and that they check instruments for omissions.

After Data Collection

Smith et al. (1986) advised researchers to be thoroughly familiar with their survey instruments, the scoring keys, and the scoring procedures for the survey instruments. These matters should be attended to before procedures are finalized. After the data are collected, one should ensure that the obtained item and scale values are consistent with scoring keys. Thus, if responses are recorded in a 1-2-3-4-5 format but some items are reverse-scored, these should be reflected (e.g., by recoding each response category of the item or by subtracting the item—in this instance, from 6). Failure to recode reversed items properly will transform potentially good data into garbage. To allow for spot checks later, it is useful to maintain the original (unreflected) variables and create new variables that correspond to reversed items. In knowing the range of possible values, be alert to instances that fall outside the appropriate range. Frequency distributions and graphs are useful tools for identifying out-of-range values.

Smith et al. (1986) offered another suggestion that is extremely useful for novice researchers: "Recode so that all items purporting to measure the same characteristic are scored in the same direction." For example, if test items were designed to measure anxiety and depression, interpretation would be easier and errors avoided if *high* scores meant *greater* negative affect for both items or scales. We would go one step further by suggesting that researchers routinely use higher numbers to signify more of the quantity in question (and to label the scale by its high end). Thus, if the researcher is measuring the trait of introversion-extraversion, the researcher's task, as well as that of his or her reader, is eased by consistent reference to the high-score endpoint. Similarly, the subject's task may be easier when *higher* scores are used to indicate *more* agreement or endorsement. (When using letters such as A, B, C, the letter A is sufficiently associated with higher performance in school that it should be used to indicate something more desirable or optimal rather than less so.)

Missing data can be coded differently in different statistical packages. In some, a unique number not otherwise used (e.g., 9) is taken to signify missing data. In others, a decimal point or a blank space signifies missing data. Keep this fact in mind when preparing analyses. If it is forgotten, two variables sharing "9"s that signify missing data will significantly correlate as an artifact of this neglect (as happened with considerable embarrassment to one of the author's assistants). Choosing an otherwise impossible value (e.g., −999) is another useful strategy for ensuring that missing data are not mistaken for valid data and vice versa. In addition, it is crucial to tell the statistical analysis software what values represent missing data lest one's means and other statistics be corrupted by a missing value masquerading as a valid data point. A key point here is to know your statistical software! (If you use decimal points to signify missing data, be sure to use a single decimal point even if two or more columns are allotted to that variable.)

Smith et al. offered two suggestions for the merging of several data sets, a situation that can be produced by a variety of circumstances in primary as well as secondary data analysis. The order of data input is critical; if more than one logical record is planned per subject and if lines are omitted for some subjects, the results will be uninterpretable. Worse, they will be interpretable but misleading. Similar problems occur when the input statement and data record are not in synchrony. Again, look for out-of-range scores in tables of descriptive statistics, or print a listing of selected subjects' data for comparison with raw responses. When the data sets are combined into a larger sample, make certain that they are compatible and are sorted on the same variable (e.g., subject number). Also be certain that subject numbers are not used for more than one subject!

Alternatively, one can maintain separate raw data files (each with some common identification number) and create "working" analysis files (*system files* in SPSS terminology), then merge these files into a main analysis file. This obviates the need for literally merging all data records. For example, in a large data set that one of us has used extensively, there are separate system files for diagnostic data, MMPI data, alcohol use data, personality trait data, and so on, each file with a common ID variable. To create a working data set, one simply chooses the variables of interest from the component files (matching by ID) and builds a new aggregate system file.

Smith et al. (1986) concluded with the recommendation to *label compulsively*. This includes retention of duplicate copies of the instruments, scoring keys, and coding of variables (e.g., "Were control subjects signified by 1 and experimental subjects 2, or did we use 1 and 0 in this study?") Label as if you will hand the data over to a stranger. If you set the project aside for 1 month to complete other tasks, many aspects of the data set will have been forgotten. In addition to labeling of computer files, keeping an analysis log that documents what has been done to the data will refresh the researcher's memory if he or she is away from the data for a while and will provide a sense of order when more than one person is working on data analysis.

FINDING "BAD" SUBJECTS

In a classic discussion of the human subject, Schultz (1969) noted that many participants in psychological studies attempt to be good or faithful subjects who provide meaningful data or perhaps help out the experimenter. Our concern here is with mistrustful and bad subjects—those who passively or actively sabotage a project with invalid data, who are motivated by testing conditions to fake good test profiles or to respond carelessly (e.g., "to get out of this boring project quickly" by not reading instructions or items). Such subjects may respond with strings of the same response (e.g., too many consecutive "5"s) or response patterns (e.g., 1-2-3-4-5-4-3-2-1) or may respond to test items in a quasi-random manner.

It may be useful to note *during data collection* the length of time that subjects take to complete the study, with a possible exclusion rule for those who finish too quickly. If you are testing in a large group setting (see Zaccaro & Marks, Chapter 12 of this volume), another method is to assign an identification number in order of completion and then determine whether this variable relates to the measures of interest. Just as time of participation in a semester can reflect personality and subject investment (Roman, Moskowitz, Stein, & Eisenberg, 1995), so completion time can be a sign of something meaningful that can affect a study's internal validity.

Obviously with questionnaires, especially those answered on optical scanning forms, visual inspection will identify some suspiciously bad subjects. If data are keypunched by the research assistant, some patterns may be noticed—and outliers of a different sort can be introduced by keypunching error!

Outliers who score out of range on individual variables should be easily detected. For example if one is coding for gender (e.g., male = 1 and female = 2), a frequency distribution will immediately identify subjects who, for whatever reason, erred by inserting any other option. If these outliers were not identified prior to correlating gender with other variables, consider how misleading the correlations would be if a few respondents had entered their gender with the response of 3, 4, or 5 on their optical scanning form.

Another method that may be useful is possible once all data are in the computer. This involves creating artificial variables that indicate a subject's overall response across all items in the data set (irrespective of the scales included). Thus the first step is to create the new variables, say GRANDMEAN and GRANDSD. We will use these names to represent the subjects' overall *M* and *SD* across all items. Next, identify those subjects whose scores on GRANDMEAN and GRANDSD fall 3, 4, or more standard deviations above or below the GRANDMEAN and GRANDSD means. In analyzing several different data sets, we have found that lists of such subjects will commonly identify individuals who too frequently use a string of consecutive high ratings, resulting in suspiciously high scores on GRANDMEAN and low scores on GRANDSD. Subjects who employ the 1-2-3-4-5-4-3-2-1 pattern, even occasionally, will obtain suspiciously high scores on GRANDSD.

Also useful is the strategy of building several "validity" items into the data set. For example, if endorsed with the response TRUE, several infrequency scale items such as "I make my own clothes and shoes" (Jackson, 1984) could identify random respondents. However, it is conceivable that the use of many outlandish items might have iatrogenic effects, prompting subjects to take their participation as a matter of frivolity rather than seriousness. Various versions of the Big-Five NEO Inventories (Costa & McCrae, 1992) include the simple item "I have tried to answer all of these questions honestly and accurately." If a subject endorses this item with a neutral or disagree response, it is likely that he or she either is not reading the item or has reversed the 5-point scale by giving higher ratings to the strongly disagree endpoint. Following this strategy, the senior author includes another item in long questionnaire sets but with the intent of identifying responses in the opposite direction; this involves an item such as "I have had a hard time under-standing many of the words in this questionnaire." An affirmative answer to this question, particularly a strong endorsement, may indicate that the subject is not reading the items or that in fact he or she has not understood much of what has been asked. Some combina-tion of this rational a priori method of identifying "bad" data along with the post hoc GRANDMEAN and GRANDSD formulas may help identify participants whose data should be discarded before the main analyses are conducted.

What has been said thus far pertains to univariate outliers. With multivariate outliers, a variety of methods are needed, and several procedures may do a better job of jointly identifying problem cases (Comrey, 1985; see also Barnett & Lewis, 1978; Hawkins, 1980). Comrey's method (1985) is based on the average squared deviation of a given subject's cross-product of standard score from the average overall correlations. Comrey noted that subjects should not automatically be excluded as outliers just because a formula identifies them as such. Rather, these methods help identify cases that need scrutiny. On the basis of our use of the GRANDMEAN/GRANDSD approach, we would agree. In this regard, a very useful step is to devise a series of preliminary graphs of the data that can also help identify outliers (see Anscombe, 1973).

"BAD" EXPERIMENTERS

From bad subjects we turn to bad experimenters, who can also dirty the data. Rosenthal's (1966, 1994) prodigious body of work has been particularly important in understanding the social psychology of the psychological experiment and in turning attention to experimenter effects. Commenting on and summarizing this literature, Barber (1976) identified 10 pitfalls of human research. One of these will concern us here, but first we comment briefly about the Experimenter-Failure-to-Follow-Procedures Effect and Experimenter-Fudging-the-Data Effect. If you are reading this chapter, we assume that you are a conscientious and honest person who knows that following procedures and not creating data are ethical imperatives of being a research assistant. Moreover, the falsifica-tion or creation of data is an absolute wrong that undermines the entire enterprise of science and can end a scholar's career as well as that of a scholar-in-training. (Note, however, that the discarding of data of outliers is not an ethical issue and, in some research areas such as that involving reaction time, is routine if done in accord with accepted norms for the research topic.)

Having said this, we turn to the less ethically serious but more pragmatic concern of the Experimenter-Misrecording Effect. A number of studies (see Barber, 1976) have shown that without evil intent, experimenters do misrecord data. People do make "honest" mistakes. A study by Laszlo (in Rosenthal, 1966, p. 13) in which three experimenters tested a total of 64 subjects found that these experimenters had error rates of 6%, 22%, and 26% in the recording of their data! Less troubling was a study by Rosenthal et al. (1964) in which 30 experimenters were involved in data transcription. Of 3,000 data points, 20 transcription errors occurred, giving an overall error rate of just .67%. What is the message to take from these studies? People err, and errors can be caught by double-checking. Taking a lesson from the methodology of applied behavior analysis, human data handlers (like behavioral observers) are likely to be more accurate if they know that their reliability will be checked periodically throughout the study.

When the experimenter's task involves something more than dealing with secretarial tasks, we also should be alert to the possibility of Experimenter-Expectancy Effects—the classic Pygmalion Effect in the classroom. Bringing this matter closer to what graduate students in the clinical areas might experience, consider the biasing effects of one's expectancies while administering psychological tests, one area in which this effect is moderately large (Badad, Mann, & Mar-Hayim, 1975; Sattler, Hillix, & Neher, 1970).

Preliminary Analyses

Once the data have been collected and "cleaned" for errors and outliers, it will still be useful to conduct preliminary analyses. In fact, we generally recommend that the Results sections of theses and dissertations follow the simple outline of Preliminary Results, Main Results, and Supplementary Results. Preliminary analyses will help the researcher decide how best to proceed with telling the story of the data. The first matter for preliminary analyses is to consider whether the sample "behaved"—that is, whether the descriptive statistics (M, SD) and reliability (e.g., alpha coefficient) for the measures were comparable to those reported by other researchers. Obviously, the concern here is with standard or control conditions of test administration rather than with treatment effects. If your basic descriptive statistics are "off" in some manner (e.g., your average IQ for a college student sample is 85), your subjects may be atypical, they may have misunderstood your instructions, or you may have erred in your reduction of the data into numerical form.

There may be several variables you wish to ignore beyond the preliminary stage, and your goal here is to show that the main results are not limited by age, gender, year in school, or whatever. Thus you may wish to test for differences by gender, interactions of other variables with gender, or a differential correlational pattern by gender. If using a true experiment rather than correlational design, you also may have built in several manipulation-check questionnaire items to document the internal validity of the treatment manipulation. Aside from these occasions of preliminary analyses, when you are using a large number of items or scales, there is the issue of data reduction via factor analysis.

USING FACTOR ANALYSIS

A number of specific preliminary analyses relate to the special case of factor analysis. Prior to the proliferation of high-speed computers and easy-to-use statistical packages, researchers undertook factor analysis of their data only after substantial forethought and planning. Currently, it is too often the case that researchers are tempted to "throw in" factor analyses of their data as part of a broad exploratory approach to data analysis. To the degree that factor analysis programs will happily attempt to extract factors from almost any unsuspecting data, it is important to recognize some limitations of data that could lead to erroneous interpretations if not detected.

The first step in appropriately using factor analysis, of course, is visual inspection of the correlation matrix. If correlations among variables are generally quite small, it is unlikely that the matrix will give rise to sensible common factors. Following this initial check, it is useful to evaluate two basic diagnostic statistics that are provided by most factor analysis programs. These give information about whether it is appropriate to subject data to factor analysis.

Bartlett's test of sphericity provides a statistical evaluation of the visual inspection recommended above. Specifically, it tests whether the correlation matrix of the variables to be factor-analyzed is actually an identity matrix (value of 1 for all diagonal elements of the matrix, with all off-diagonal elements equal to 0). The test statistic is distributed as a chi-square. When the value of the test statistic is sufficiently high, the probability level reaches statistical significance, and the researcher can comfortably reject the null hypothesis that the correlation matrix is an identity matrix. Generally, this appears to be a rather liberal test, and a significant value for the sphericity statistic is necessary but not sufficient for continuing with further factor analysis.

In addition to Bartlett's test, one should also evaluate the Kaiser-Meyer-Olkin Measure of Sampling Adequacy (KMO; Kaiser, 1974). This statistic reflects the degree to which it is likely that common factors explain the observed correlations among the variables and is calculated as the sum of the squared simple correlations between pairs of variables divided by the sum of squared simple correlations plus the sum of squared partial correlations.

To the degree that partial correlations approach zero as common factors account for increasing amounts of variance among the variables, the KMO statistic will be higher when a common-factor model is appropriate for the data. Small values for the KMO statistic indicate that correlations between pairs of variables cannot be accounted for by common factors. The KMO statistic can range from 0 to 1. Kaiser (1974) described KMOs in the .90s as "marvelous," in the .80s as "meritorious," in the .70s as "middling," in the .60s as "mediocre," in the .50s as "miserable," and below .50 as "unacceptable." If the value of the statistic is below .50, the researcher should seriously reconsider the appropriateness of a factor model given the observed correlations. It should be noted that even in cases in which the KMO statistic indicates inappropriateness of a factor model, the factor analysis program will doggedly extract and rotate what it believes to be the best factor solution.

DECISIONS, DECISIONS

After determining that one's data are well suited for factor analysis, a researcher is faced with a myriad of choices regarding type of factor extraction, number of factors to extract, whether to rotate the factors, and if so, what type of rotation strategy to use. All of these decisions should be guided by the goals of the research project.

Factor Extraction

Although a detailed discussion of factor extraction strategies is beyond our scope here (see Harman, 1967, and Kim & Mueller, 1978, for additional information), a few general points can be made. When the goal of analysis is reduction of a large number of variables to a more manageable (and analyzable) number, principal components analysis (PCA) is likely to be the extraction of choice. Formally, PCA is not factor analysis but a close statistical cousin that is often the default option for statistical packages such as SPSS. PCA extracts principal components that are linear combinations of observed variables to account for shared variance among the variables being analyzed. The first principal component explains the most variance among the observed variables, the second principal component the next largest amount of variance, and so forth. The end result is the transformation of correlated variables into uncorrelated principal components. The first principal component is often used by researchers as a general index of a construct represented by shared variance among related variables. For example, if one had administered five tests of specific cognitive abilities, the first unrotated principal component extracted from intercorrelations among the five individual ability measures could be viewed as a measure of general ability. Among "true" factor analysis algorithms, principal axis factoring is probably the most common. This technique is quite similar to the linear strategy employed by PCA but uses an iterative procedure whereby estimates of communalities (amount of a variable's variance that is accounted for by common factors) are inserted into the diagonals of the correlation matrix being analyzed.

How Many Factors Are Enough?

One of the challenges of factor analysis is determining the most appropriate number of factors to extract and rotate. Statistical programs can sometimes "trip" the unwary factor analyst by choosing a number of factors to extract based on an arbitrary default setting. The most commonly used default criterion is selecting the number of factors that have eigenvalues (an index of variance accounted for by the factor) over 1.0. Researchers should also evaluate a full plot of eigenvalues for all potentially extracted factors. This scree plot will show a decrease in the amount of variance accounted for by the addition of each new factor, and it has been argued (Cattell, 1966) that at the point when the plot breaks substantially and tails off, no further factors should be extracted. Finally, for exploratory factor analyses, it is recommended that the researcher extract one or more factors *above* and *below* the number of factors suggested by statistical program's default options. This allows for assessment of which extraction appears to provide a clearer "simple structure" (small number of variables with high loadings, relatively few variables with "split" loadings across factors).

To Rotate or Not to Rotate

If the goal of the researcher is pure data reduction of the sort described above, then an unrotated first principal component will do the job nicely. However, it is often the case that researchers are interested in identifying the most interpretable and meaningful structure of a group of variables, perhaps in an attempt to understand better the construct validity of a particular measure. In this case, a variety of factor rotation strategies assist in interpretation of the initially unrotated factor solution. Rotation basically reflects mathematical alignment of a reference axis through points in "factor space" that are held by the variables in the factor model. Variables that cluster closely together on some axis are presumably related to each other. The two principal forms of rotation are orthogonal and oblique. An orthogonal rotation creates factors that are independent of each other (the reference axes are at right angles to each other), whereas an oblique rotation allows for the rotated factors to correlate with each other (reference angles may be at oblique angles). In some cases, there may be a theoretically important reason for picking either a correlated or an uncorrelated factor solution. When there is no such rationale, it may be most prudent to proceed with an oblique solution, given that the constructs encountered most often by behavioral researchers are not independent. It may also be useful in exploratory analyses to use both oblique and orthogonal rotations to explore various ways of bringing meaning to the factors extracted from the observed data.

Conclusion: Cleaning up the Data Requires Getting a Little Dirty

One memorable teacher in the senior author's graduate education, a teacher of statistics, was fond of reminding her class, "Don't be afraid to get your nose dirty in the data." It may seem ironic, but a dirty nose may be the best way to ensure clean data. In general, preliminary analyses are the most legitimate time to commit the statistical sin of data snooping. As much as you may want to quickly check out whether your hypotheses were supported, it is important to remember that the first analyses done on a new data set (or an old one being reanalyzed) should be considered preliminary. By becoming intimately acquainted with such trivial details as the number of subjects on different variables or sets of items, you will be better able to spot problems or discrepancies in the data set and ultimately ensure a study with greater integrity.

Recommended Readings

Readers interested in more detail on the topics of clean data and preliminary analyses should consider the works by Anscombe (1973), Kim and Mueller (1978), and Smith et al. (1986).

References

Anscombe, F. J. (1973). Graphs in statistical analysis. *American Statistician, 27,* 17-21.

Badad, E. Y., Mann, M., & Mar-Hayim, M. (1975). Bias in scoring the WISC subtests. *Journal of Consulting and Clinical Psychology, 43,* 268.

Barber, T. X. (1976). *Pitfalls in human research.* New York: Pergamon.

Barnett, V., & Lewis, T. (1978). *Outliers in statistical data.* New York: John Wiley.

Cattell, R. B. (1966). The scree test for the number of factors. *Multivariate Behavior Research, 1,* 245-276.

Comrey, A. L. (1985). A method for removing outliers to improve factor analytic results. *Multivariate Behavioral Research, 20,* 273-281.

Costa, P. T., & McCrae, R. R. (1992). *The Revised NEO Personality Inventory (NEO-PI-R) and NEO Five-Factor Inventory (NEO-FFI) professional manual.* Odessa, FL: Psychological Assessment Resources.

Harman, H. H. (1967). *Modern factor analysis* (2nd ed.). Chicago: University of Chicago Press.

Hawkins, D. M. (1980). *Identification of outliers*. New York: Chapman & Hall.

Jackson, D. N. (1984). *Personality Research Form manual* (3rd ed.). Port Huron, MI: Research Psychologists Press.

Kaiser, H. F. (1974). An index of factorial simplicity. *Psychometrica, 39,* 31-36.

Kim, J. O., & Mueller, C. W. (1978). *Introduction to factor analysis*. Beverly Hills, CA: Sage.

Roman, R. J., Moskowitz, G. D., Stein, M. I., & Eisenberg, R. F. (1995). Individual differences in experiment participation: Structure, autonomy, and time of the semester. *Journal of Personality, 63,* 113-138.

Rosenthal, R. (1966). *Experimenter effects in behavioral research*. New York: Appleton-Century-Crofts.

Rosenthal, R. (1994). Interpersonal expectancy effects: A 30-year perspective. *Current Directions in Psychological Science, 3,* 176-179.

Rosenthal, R., Friedman, C. J., Johnson, C. A., Fode, K., Schill, T., White, R. C., & Vikan, L. L. (1964). Variables affecting experimenter bias in a group situation. *Genetic Psychology Monographs, 70,* 271-296.

Sattler, J. M., Hillix, W. A., & Neher, L. A. (1970). Halo effect in examiner scoring of intelligence test responses. *Journal of Consulting and Clinical Psychology, 34,* 172-176.

Schultz, D. P. (1969). The human subject in psychological research. *Psychological Bulletin, 72,* 214-228.

Smith, P. C., Budzeika, K. A., Edwards, N. A., Johnson, S. M., & Bearse, L. N. (1986). Guidelines for clean data: Detection of common mistakes. *Journal of Applied Psychology, 71,* 457-460.

Chapter 14

Doing Qualitative Analysis

PAMELA S. HIGHLEN
HEATHER C. FINLEY

Denzin and Lincoln (1994) generically defined *qualitative research* as an interpretive multimethod approach to the study of people in their natural surroundings. Empirical data derived from case studies, interviews, observations, and historical, interactional, and visual texts are examined systematically. Researchers strive to understand or interpret self-ascribed meanings of routine or problematic moments in people's lives. With the exception of the positivist paradigm, qualitative research emphasizes (a) processes and meanings that are not rigorously measured in terms of quantity or intensity, (b) the socially constructed nature of reality, (c) the relationship between the researcher and the researched, and (d) situational constraints that influence inquiry.

Qualitative Paradigms

According to Guba and Lincoln (1994), "Questions of method [and data analysis] are secondary to questions of paradigm, or the basic belief system or worldview that guides the investigator, not only in choices of method but in ontologically and epistemologically fundamental ways" (p. 105). Therefore consideration of basic paradigms used in qualitative research is an essential prerequisite to any discussion of qualitative data analysis. Numerous paradigm classification systems have been proposed (e.g., Denzin & Lincoln, 1994; Guba & Lincoln, 1994; Habermas, 1971; Lather, 1994a). Due to space limitations, five major paradigms will be presented briefly: (a) positivist, (b) postpositivist, (c) interpretive/constructivist, (d) critical, and (e) poststructural. The paradigms will be outlined, with particular emphasis on criteria for evaluating the quality of research within each paradigm. These criteria are often referred to as criteria of *epistemological validity,* or "a set of rules concerning knowledge, its production, and representation" (Lincoln & Denzin, 1994, p. 578). Epistemological validity is important to the design and execution of a qualitative study and the subsequent analysis of data collected.

AUTHORS' NOTE: We wish to thank Marla J. Oberhausen, Mary Hill, and Judy A. Lawton for their comments on this chapter.

For several reasons, this chapter focuses on the postpositivist, interpretive/ constructivist, critical, and poststructural paradigms more than the positivist paradigm. First, most qualitative researchers believe that reality is socially constructed, which is antithetical to the positivist position. Second, most qualitative research is conducted within one of the other four paradigms. The positivist paradigm is briefly noted to acknowledge that qualitative research can be conducted within its parameters.

POSITIVIST PARADIGM

The purpose of the positivist paradigm is explanation that leads to prediction and control. Qualitative research from a positivist perspective assumes the existence of an objective reality that is both verifiable and quantifiable. The positivist perspective utilizes internal validity, external validity, reliability, and objectivity to evaluate the quality of research. Often quantitative and qualitative methods are combined within a positivist paradigm. For example, subjects' responses to open-ended questions at the end of a survey questionnaire would be content-analyzed by having raters independently classify subject responses into categories. Interrater agreement and reliability would be calculated to ensure the consistency of established categories. The categorized data would be presented descriptively as frequency counts and percentages to provide confirmatory support for the study's hypotheses and/or to suggest directions for future quantitative research. Another example of qualitative research within the positivist tradition is counseling process research, in which therapy sessions are transcribed and content-analyzed on the basis of identified dimensions (e.g., type of counselor and client verbal statements) and the data are analyzed using descriptive and other statistical methods. Qualitative research within a positivist paradigm has been criticized for, among other things, stripping the context from the studied participants by sacrificing relevance for rigor (Guba, 1981), excluding meaning from the data gathered, and generalizing nomothetic data inappropriately to specific cases.

POSTPOSITIVIST PARADIGM

The postpositivist paradigm shares the same purpose of the positivist paradigm: explanation that leads to prediction and control. However, postpositivist researchers strive to address some of the criticisms levied at the positivist paradigm. Objective reality is assumed to exist; however, it can be only approximated (a view termed *critical realism* by Cook & Campbell, 1979). Multiple methods are used, although discovery and theory verification are emphasized. Although researchers seek an objective stance, they acknowledge that interactions between investigators and participants affect the data. Grounded theory (Strauss & Corbin, 1990) is the most widely used postpositivist design because it provides a specific set of steps that are closely aligned with positivist science. Researchers using grounded theory generate theory from data or, if theories relevant to the investigation exist, modify these theories as new data are gathered. Researchers schooled in the positivist tradition can accept and adopt this inductive approach to theory building more easily than methods associated with other qualitative paradigms. Interviews and observations are frequently the source of data for grounded-theory research. Multiple perspectives are sought and then are interpreted conceptually by the investigator. "Coding procedures—including the important procedures of constant comparison, theoretical questioning, theoretical sampling, concept development, and their relationships—help to prevent the researcher from accepting any of those voices on their own terms, and to some extent force the researcher's own voice to be questioning, questioned, and provisional" (Strauss & Corbin, 1994, p. 280). Strauss and Corbin (1994) reconfigured "canons of good (i.e., positivist) science" for qualitative research to include significance, theory-observation compatibility, generalizability, consistency, reproducibility, precision, and verification. Although somewhat vague, these tenets are used to assess the quality of postpositivist qualitative research. Rose and Jevne's (1993) study of psychological processes associated with athletic injuries provides an excellent example of grounded-theory research.

INTERPRETIVE/CONSTRUCTIVIST PARADIGM

The main purpose of the interpretive/constructivist paradigm is understanding the participant's world. Reality is constructed through human interaction and is seen as relative (i.e., there is no single, external, objective truth). Therefore multiple realities exist, and the interactions between the investigator and participants create the findings as the investigation unfolds. This process is reflexive; information gathered from participants is fed back to them for verification of its accuracy (i.e., member checks). "Thick description" (Geertz, 1973) is used to bring the context and meaning of participants' lives forward by presenting "detail, context, emotion, and the webs of social relationships that join persons to one another" (Denzin, 1989, p. 83). The use of thick description allows readers to formulate their own interpretations of the results (Patton, 1990). Research within the interpretive/constructivist paradigm uses methods that allow the investigator to record participant observations accurately and to uncover the meanings that participants ascribe to their life experiences (Denzin & Lincoln, 1994).

Constructivism, as formulated by Lincoln and Guba (1985), provides a systematic qualitative method within the interpretive/constructivist paradigm. The researcher as a facilitator and participant attempts to understand and reconstruct individuals' perspectives (constructions). He or she seeks a consensus in meaning while allowing for new interpretations to emerge as information and awareness changes. Initially "trustworthiness" was postulated as a set of correspondence criteria for judging the quality of research (Lincoln & Guba, 1985). Trustworthiness consists of four components that parallel the methodological criteria of positivist science: (a) credibility (internal validity), (b) transferability (external validity), (c) dependability (reliability), and (d) confirmability (objectivity). Credibility is increased through prolonged engagement in the field, persistent observation, triangulation (of sources, methods, and investigators), peer debriefing, negative case analysis, progressive subjectivity (monitoring the researcher's ongoing hypotheses and constructions of the data), and member checks. Use of thick description provides for transferability. Dependability is enhanced by using overlapping methods and dependability audits (documentation of changes in the inquiry process). Confirmability builds on audit trails (multiple records kept during the research investigation such as written field notes, memos, a field diary, process and personal notes, and a reflexive journal).

More recently, Guba and Lincoln (1989) presented authenticity criteria that go beyond the methodological criteria of trustworthiness. They contended that outcome, product, and negotiation criteria are as important as methodological criteria (i.e., trustworthiness) for the evaluation of qualitative research. Authenticity consists of five components: fairness (extent to which different constructions and underlying values are solicited and honored), ontological authenticity (extent to which personal constructions are expanded and elaborated), educative authenticity (extent to which respondents' understanding of others' constructions is enhanced), catalytic authenticity (extent to which respondents are stimulated to action), and tactical authenticity (extent to which participants are empowered to act). Authenticity criteria address concerns involving ethics and empowerment raised by proponents of the critical and poststructural paradigms.

CRITICAL PARADIGM

The purpose of the critical paradigm is emancipation and transformation—to enable participants to gain knowledge and power necessary to be in control of their lives (Gibson, 1986). Critical research is multivocal, collaborative, and grounded in the lived experience of participants, often termed "coinvestigators." It is organized by an interpretive theory, such as feminism, neo-Marxism, or participatory inquiry. Although most qualitative researchers acknowledge that there is no value-free inquiry (Janesick, 1994), critical paradigm investigators openly bring their values and theoretical perspectives to the research process. They engage in dialectical dialogue with coinvestigators to connect meaning to broader structures of social power, control, and history (Lather, 1994a). As noted by Guba and Lincoln (1994), this "dialogue must be dialectical in nature to transform ignorance and misapprehensions (accepting historically mediated structures as immutable) into more informed consciousness (seeing how the structures might be changed and comprehending the actions required to effect change)" (p. 110).

Evaluating critical research is based on the degree to which (a) social, political, ethnic, economic, cultural, and gender elements of the situation studied are taken into account; (b) the investigation eradicates ignorance and misconceptions; and (c) the inquiry creates praxis, or action toward transforming the existing structure (Guba & Lincoln, 1994, p. 114). Jones (1989, cited in Lather, 1992) used a critical research perspective as she examined the interaction of race, class, and gender in the lives of adolescent school girls in New Zealand. Using neo-Marxist social theory, she employed critical ethnography to create emancipatory theory that would stimulate the participants to struggle against their oppression.

POSTSTRUCTURAL PARADIGM

A major purpose of the poststructural paradigm is deconstruction: that is, to destabilize and challenge any given interpretation of socially constructed reality as complete knowledge. Deconstruction is based on the two principles of the "contextual determination of meaning and . . . the infinite extendability of context" (Culler, 1982, p. 215). In the poststructural paradigm, language is considered to be an unstable system of referents, thereby suggesting that the meaning of any action, text, or intention can never be fully captured (Denzin & Lincoln, 1994, p. 15). It is argued that the reflexive nature of all qualitative inquiry is nonobjective, incomplete, and inextricably bound to the researcher's interpretive framework, the context of the phenomenon studied, and the genre or format (e.g. scientific report) used to disseminate findings. The poststructuralist perspective challenges the claim of any text to possess external authority. No text can be authoritative or valid because any text can be deconstructed using its internal structural logic. Values and politics, rather than methodological validity, assume prominence in the evaluation of research. The issue of power as related to culture, gender, ideology, language/text, relevance, and advocacy becomes critical. For example, are the effects of societal factors, such as sexism and racism, acknowledged in the study of participants? Are participants given full voice in the text? Often poststructural research focuses on the unheard voices of those with less power and privilege (e.g., women, people of color). These inquiries investigate how race, class, and gender influence the lives of the people who are studied. From the poststructural perspective, the validity of qualitative research depends on the goals of the research (e.g., emancipation, deconstruction) and the "interpretive communities" (general public, research participants, scientific community) who will read and evaluate the inquiry.

Several authors have reformulated the concept of validity by incorporating the issue of power (culture, race, gender) within the poststructural framework (e.g., Lather, 1993; Scheurich, in press). By offering formulations as beginning, partial practices rather than as immutable, universal tenets, Lather (1993) took an antithetical stance to the constructivist position. *Ironic validity* offers multiple representations of reality showing the strengths and limitations of each; *neopragmatic validity* makes use of differences in the service of disruptive interpretation that destabilize the researcher's position as the master of knowledge; *rhizomatic validity* destabilizes authority from within, using a nonlinear presentation of multiple voices that speak their definition of reality throughout the text; and *situated validity* imagines a feminist validity in opposition to the dominant male voice that excludes the multiplicities of women.

Woodbrook's dissertation research (1991, cited in Lather, 1993) provides an example of poststructural research. She studied African American women in leadership positions in higher education. Through member checks and peer debriefing, she critiqued and reanalyzed the data. The second draft was sent to participants, who were phoned for their reactions. Woodbrook then juxtaposed her voice as a White female researcher with those of the African American female participants. Utilizing Van Maanen's (1988) realist and critical tales approach to ethnographic narratives, she first constructed a realist tale in which the participants' voices were highlighted. She then interrupted this tale with a critical tale that focused on how her theoretical orientation as a feminist shaped her analysis of the data. She concluded with a deconstructive tale in which participants' reactions to her critical tale were highlighted. One conclusion in her deconstructive tale was that feminist consciousness raising "perpetuates feminism as a white middle class project and trivializes the deep emotional ties that black women share with black men" (Woodbrook, 1991, p. 200, cited in Lather, 1993, p. 680). This poststructural research illustrates the use of multiple voices in the text and how ongoing dialogue between researcher and participants decenters the researcher as the master of knowledge.

PARADIGM SUMMARIES

The choice of paradigms will be influenced by researchers' worldviews and the empirical questions of interest. Researchers must be aware of their worldview and choose a qualitative paradigm that is consistent with it. Choice of paradigms will influence the strategy, execution, and data analysis of qualitative inquiry. Positivist researchers view qualitative data as information that can be used for prediction and control. Tenets of quantitative research (e.g., objectivity, reliability, validity) are applied to the collection and analysis of qualitative data.

Postpositivist researchers approach data as information that creates, supports, and/or disconfirms theory that leads to prediction and control. Researchers assume a detached stance similar to that of positivist investigators. Methodological rigor corresponding to the positivist canons of science is employed.

Interpretive/constructivist researchers assume a relativist view of reality in which local and specifically constructed realities exist. Researchers facilitate a "multi-voiced reconstruction" of all participants' constructions as well as their own (Guba & Lincoln, 1994). Researchers and participants are interactively linked so that the results are created as the investigation unfolds. The goal is to create a consensus construction that is more informed than before. Trustworthiness criteria are used to obtain methodological rigor. In addition, authenticity criteria are employed to enhance participants' level of understanding and to empower them to take action.

Critical researchers use data to facilitate change by raising the consciousness of both participants and investigators. According to Giroux (1988), researchers become "transformed intellectuals" who dispel ignorance and stimulate participants to act on the basis of their acquired knowledge. Through open expression of values, researchers engage in dialectic dialogue with coinvestigators to connect meaning to broader structures of social power. The quality of critical research is demonstrated by the degree to which it addresses broader issues of social power that affect participants' lives and the degree to which it eradicates ignorance and leads to action.

Poststructural researchers view data from a philosophical, questioning stance. Researchers become iconoclasts by destabilizing the notion of immutable knowledge. They acknowledge the existence of multiple realities and argue that no research text has external authority. The concept of validity is either discarded or reformulated to reflect the goals of emancipation and deconstruction.

METHODOLOGICAL VARIATIONS ACROSS PARADIGMS

Notable methodological differences exist across these paradigms. The issue of legitimization, or how research makes claims for its authority, is approached differently depending on the paradigm employed. For example, triangulation is one common method used to strengthen qualitative research. Denzin (1978) identified four types of triangulation: (a) data triangulation (using a variety of data sources), (b) researcher triangulation (using multiple investigators to collect and analyze data), (c) theoretical triangulation (using multiple perspectives to interpret the same data), and (d) methodological triangulation (using multiple methods to study the same question). All forms of triangulation are acceptable to positivist and postpositivist researchers, given their ontological belief in realism and critical realism, respectively. In contrast, interpretive/constructivist researchers view data triangulation with skepticism. Because of their belief in the relative nature of reality, interpretive/constructivists reject verifying one participant's account through another source. As Guba and Lincoln (1989) noted, "Triangulation should be thought of as referring to cross-checking specific data items of a factual nature (number of target persons served, number of children enrolled in a school-lunch program" (p. 241). Critical and poststructural researchers reject the use of triangulation because it assumes a fixed point that can then be triangulated. Instead, Richardson (1994) suggested using crystals as a metaphor for the qualitative research process: "Crystals are prisms that reflect externalities and refract within themselves, creating different colors, patterns, arrays, casting off in different directions" (p. 522). Crystallization deconstructs the traditional idea of triangulation in that no single truth or fixed point exists. Poststructural researchers reveal a more partial understanding and then doubt what has been revealed.

The use of *member checks* is another methodological variation. Positivist researchers use member checks to verify the objective accuracy of data obtained from subjects. Postpositivist and interpretive/constructivist researchers use member checks to verify that participants' data accurately represent their construction of reality (Guba & Lincoln, 1989). Typically these member checks involve asking participants to verify that transcripts of their constructions are accurate. Interpretive/constructivist investigators who employ authenticity criteria (Guba & Lincoln, 1989) conduct more extensive and interactive member checks to enhance participants' understanding of other constructions generated by the investigation and their ability to act on the basis of their increased knowledge. As used by critical researchers, member checks are dialectic in nature. Researchers and participants examine their combined perspective to ascertain whether it reflects a more informed view. Member checks conducted by poststructural researchers are more extensive. In addition to verifying the accuracy of their constructions, participants comment on investigator interpretations of all data. These reactions are reported in the text as, for example, a deconstructive tale (e.g., Woodbrook, 1991, cited in Lather, 1993).

Qualitative Strategies

Once researchers select a paradigm that is consistent with their worldview and the empirical questions they wish to address, they select a suitable strategy for operationalizing their inquiry. Qualitative strategies are the practices researchers employ in data collection and analysis. Due to space limitations, qualitative strategies are only briefly mentioned. In Table 14.1, qualitative strategies most relevant to psychological research are identified, along with the focus of each strategy. Refer to Denzin and Lincoln (1994) and Patton (1990) for further information. It is important to note that a strategy may be used within more than one paradigm, although many are associated with a particular paradigm. For example, action inquiry is frequently utilized in the positivist paradigm; grounded theory is most commonly used in the postpositivist paradigm; and phenomenology, heuristics, hermeneutics, and constructivism strategies are typically employed in the interpretivist/constructivist paradigm. Likewise, orientational strategies are usually associated with the critical and poststructural paradigms. Often strategies are based on the context of interest. For example, case studies focus on the individual unit (e.g., person); symbolic interactionism examines interactions among people; ecological studies focus on the interaction between the individual and the environment; and a systems or action inquiry approach focuses on larger units, such as organizations and families. Cultural context is especially important to ethnography, ethnomethodology, and orientational strategies. However, other strategies can be used to investigate issues of culture, such as hermeneutics and constructivism. Clinical inquiry deals with diagnosis and intervention of people seeking medical and/or psychological assistance and may employ various approaches, such as grounded-theory and case study strategies. Suffice it to say that the interrelationships between paradigms and strategies are complex. However, the choice of strategy should be based on the paradigmatic view researchers bring to inquiries along with the research questions they wish to address.

Methodological Commonalities

Although differences among qualitative paradigms and strategies exist, common guidelines have been generated for qualitative inquiry. Numerous texts provide generic methodological guidelines for conducting qualitative research (e.g., Glesne & Peshkin, 1992; Marshall & Rossman, 1995; Morse, 1993; Patton, 1990). Due to space limitations, only one set of guidelines is presented to illustrate methodological commonalities. Kvale (1995) outlined seven stages of the interview process. Each stage deals with an aspect of validity that he referred to as *quality of craftsmanship:*

1. *Thematizing:* Validity hinges on the soundness of theoretical tenets and on the logic of theory application to the study's specific questions.
2. *Designing:* The adequacy of the design and methods must be matched to the study's purpose.
3. *Interviewing:* The trustworthiness of participants' reports and the quality of interviewing are continually checked.
4. *Transcribing:* The choice of linguistic style addresses the question of what is a valid account as data are transformed from oral to written form (e.g., noting loudness of voice by underlining words that were orally emphasized).
5. *Interpreting:* The degree to which the questions asked of the text are valid and the logic of ensuing interpretations are monitored.
6. *Verifying:* Identifying the relevant forms of validation for the study and determining who is the relevant community for a dialogue on validity (e.g., member checks with participants, scientific community, general public) are stressed.
7. *Reporting:* The format and content of the report are a valid representation of the findings. (pp. 8-9)

The remainder of this chapter focuses on a generic approach to qualitative data analysis.

TABLE 14.1 Selective Strategies Used in Psychological Qualitative Research

Strategy	Focus
Case studies	The individual case or unit
Ethnography	The culture of groups of people
Ethnomethodology	The ordinary routine of daily life
Phenomenology	The essence (content) and structure of participants' experience
Heuristics	Self's (researcher's) experience of phenomenon and the perspective of others who have experienced the phenomenon
Hermeneutics	The contextual interpretation of written materials (documents, records, texts)
Constructivism	The reconstruction of realities that participants construct
Grounded theory	The development of theory grounded in systematically collected and analyzed data
Ecological	The specifics of person and environment influencing achievement of participants' goals
Symbolic interactionism	The common set of understanding and symbols that give meaning to human interactions
Systems	The functioning of a system (organization, family) as a whole
Action inquiry	The development of effective action that contributes to transforming organizations and communities
Clinical inquiry	The commitment to change through diagnosis and treatment rather than large-scale social change
Orientational	The application of a perspective (e.g., feminist, ethnic, Afrocentric) to the people studied, often to effect change

Nuts and Bolts
of Qualitative Data Analysis

OVERVIEW

Although data analysis guidelines exist, Patton (1990) stressed that no steadfast rules govern the procedures: "Because qualitative inquiry depends, at every stage, on the skills, training, insights, and capabilities of the researcher, qualitative analysis ultimately depends on the analytical intellect and style of the analyst. *The human factor is the great strength and the fundamental weakness of qualitative inquiry and analysis*" (p. 372, italics added). If we recognize that each qualitative study is unique, the question is not how closely the researcher followed the guidelines, but how fully the data analysis guidelines followed were reported (Patton, 1990).

Data analysis is a nonlinear simultaneous process of bringing order, structure, and meaning to the data in the search for general statements about relationships among categories of data (Marshall & Rossman, 1995, p. 111). Data analysis occurs at every point in the research process: while planning the investigation, during data collection, and after data collection as themes and interpretations are refined (Huberman & Miles, 1994).

A helpful guideline is to divide the research process into thirds. The first two thirds involves simultaneous collection and analysis of data (see Marshall & Rossman, 1995, for collection strategies). While reflecting on the data, investigators concurrently attend to participant reactions, refine methodological strategies, and acknowledge alternative conceptual perspectives from peer reviewers who analyze the data. The final third of the research process is devoted to writing. This framework serves as a guide for investigators to minimize burnout, prevent information overload, and take advantage of the emergent nature of the research process (Lather, 1994b).

Research dialogue (the ongoing discussion of each phase of the study) is of paramount importance throughout the research process. Research dialogue engages various research records, such as note cards, analytic files, tape recordings, monthly reports, and structured research logs (Glesne & Peshkin, 1992; Patton, 1990). A systematic filing system (Glesne & Peshkin, 1992; Patton, 1990) provides a structured method to organize thoughts about the process and outcome of the qualitative study. Using computer files for notes, reports, and logs facilitates the systematic storage and retrieval of these records. Observational, methodological, theoretical, and personal notes reflecting multiple components of the study increase the methodological rigor of the investigation (Schatzman & Strauss, 1973). Examples of *observational notes* include perceptions during naturalistic observation and specific information about participants' nonverbal expressions during interviews. *Methodological notes* focus on the research process (e.g., logistical procedures, interview format) and may be used to refine methods as the study progresses. *Theoretical notes* consist of categories and themes recognized during data collection, as well as information supporting and disconfirming original hypotheses and research questions. *Personal notes,* consisting of the researcher's beliefs and hypotheses, are kept throughout the investigation to document the researcher's perspective and to minimize bias in collecting and interpreting the data (Giorgi, 1970). This technique is often referred to as "bracketing the researcher's perspective" (Husserl, 1913/1962).

DATA ANALYSIS STRATEGIES

Five categories of data analysis strategies are (a) organizing the data; (b) generating categories, themes, and patterns; (c) testing emergent hypotheses against the data; (d) searching for alternate explanations of the data; and (e) writing the research report (Marshall & Rossman, 1995).

Organizing the Data

Systematic data organization allows researchers (a) to obtain high-quality, accessible data, (b) to document analyses as they are conducted, and (c) to retain the data and associated analyses on completion of the investigation (Huberman & Miles, 1994). The format chosen reflects the categories of available data. The following list of data organization formats is extensive but not exhaustive:

1. *Raw material* (field notes, interview tapes)
2. *Partially processed data* (transcriptions, the researcher's reflective remarks)
3. *Coded data* (specific codes describing small chunks of data)
4. *Coding scheme* (extended definitions of codes)
5. *Memos* or other analytic material (researcher's reflections on conceptual meanings of data)
6. *Search and retrieval records* (a system of linking codes and the original data source)
7. *Data displays* (charts or networks displaying information in compressed forms)
8. *Analysis episodes* (documentation of the research process)
9. *Report text* (successive drafts of what is written on the study's design and methods)
10. *General chronological log or documentation* (data collection and analysis work)
11. *Index* of all previously listed material (Huberman & Miles, 1994)

Well-planned and efficient data management practices also include practical attention to detail, such as (a) labeling audiotapes; (b) carrying extra tapes and batteries for the tape recorder; (c) color-coding notes according to names, dates, and events; (d) transcribing data as they are collected; (e) making at least four computer file copies of data—keeping one for backup and using the others for different analyses; (f) concurrently transcribing and analyzing individual cases; (g) identifying common themes across cases; and (h) assessing the research process as it unfolds (Lather, 1994b; Marshall & Rossman, 1995). The importance of seemingly trivial details should not be underestimated. *Attention to minute detail in data collection and management minimizes unproductive digressions during the writing of the research report.*

Generating Categories, Themes, and Patterns

The heart of data analysis consists of identifying categories, recurrent themes, ideas or language, and belief systems that are shared across research participants and settings (Marshall & Rossman, 1995). Glesne and Peshkin (1992) recommended the use of codes when generating themes and emphasized the progressive process of coding: clumping data into major categories, categorizing the data within each clump (i.e., creating subcodes), and placing the various groups of data into a meaningful sequence or interrelated patterns. The purpose of each major code is to identify a central concept or idea, with enough major codes generated to subsume all of the data. A codebook, personally designed to fit the researcher's style, provides a place to initiate, subdivide, and revise codes throughout the research process. A code may be assigned to any amount of text, from a phrase to several pages. Deciding how codes fit into categories and how they are interrelated is exciting and tedious and requires analytical stamina, creativity, and persistence.

Content analysis, a common type of category generation, involves finding patterns in the data and placing each pattern into a category (Patton, 1990, p. 381). The researcher examines portions of the text and gives them labels, as if constructing an index for a book.

These labels or codes that make up the data index are then applied to corresponding passages within the data. This indexing system can be developed either manually, using cut-and-paste methods with index cards and hard copy transcripts, or using computer software specifically designed for qualitative research.

Computer software programs can assist researchers in both data management and analysis. Macintosh software includes HyperQual, Hypersoft, and HyperRESEARCH; MS-DOS programs include AQUAD, The Ethnograph, MAX, QUALPRO, and Textbase Alpha.[1] Although each program is unique, the software programs specialize in descriptive analysis or theory building. Programs focusing primarily on descriptive analysis (The Ethnograph, HyperRESEARCH, MAX, QUALPRO, Textbase Alpha) can (a) import text from word-processing files; (b) code by examining any combination of information sets; (c) group text from various sources that share the same code; (d) incorporate multiple codes to the same text passage; and (e) print any combination of themes, ranging from a specific target to a more general overlay. Programs developed for theory building (e.g., AQUAD) focus on exploring conceptual relationships. Once concepts are identified, researchers can use the software to determine if the concepts are linked, occur in a chronological pattern, have subordinate relationships, co-occur with three or more concepts, or are causally related. See Tesch (1990) and Weitzman and Miles (1995) for more detailed descriptions of computer software.

Suggestions for generating categories, themes, and patterns include the following:

1. Read transcripts as they are completed to identify emerging themes that may modify subsequent data collection (e.g., interview questions) and analysis.
2. Read transcripts three times before coding to identify themes and to avoid getting lost in minutiae.
3. Carry a notebook or tape recorder to record spontaneous analytic thoughts as they emerge.
4. Reread the data and analytic files regularly, adding thoughts, questions, and insights as they surface. (Glesne & Peshkin, 1992; Lather, 1994b)

Testing Emergent Hypotheses Against the Data

Testing research hypotheses primarily refers to data analysis conducted in positivist, postpositivist, and interpretivist studies. As themes and patterns emerge, the researcher sifts through the data to challenge hypotheses by searching for disconfirmatory data and to incorporate supporting data into larger constructs (Marshall & Rossman, 1995). For critical and deconstructive research, the investigator evaluates the quality of data (i.e., adequacy of information, credibility, usefulness, and centrality) to determine how useful the data are in addressing the objectives of the study (Marshall & Rossman, 1995). Suggestions for testing research objectives against data include (a) posting research questions above the investigator's workspace as a visual reminder to maintain analytic focus, (b) comparing themes and subthemes listed in the codebook with each data source, and (c) using simple matrices to summarize themes across data sources (Glesne & Peshkin, 1992). Newsprint posted on a wall in the workspace makes it possible to record multiple data sources, to note emergent themes and disconfirmatory and confirmatory patterns, and to create potential models for the data throughout the analysis process.

Searching for Alternate Explanations of the Data

Multiple perspectives must be incorporated during coding to gain analytic breadth and to check for researcher bias. Multiple perspectives include (a) coding data from different theoretical perspectives; (b) having multiple researchers code the same piece of data, including individuals with different backgrounds (e.g., gender, race/ethnicity); (c) asking participants for feedback about assigned codes and/or suggestions for codes (Glesne & Peshkin, 1992; Lather, 1994b; Marshall & Rossman, 1995). Approaching the data from various perspectives and documenting each component increases the study's trust-worthiness.

Once a set of themes has emerged across the data, it is important to search for disconfirming information in the remaining text. For example, if four of six interviewees emphasize positive early school experiences, the researcher must conduct a negative case analysis to search for contradictory evidence in the other two cases. Reporting themes in the study must take into account all cases and must include qualifying statements when evident (e.g., "four of the six participants reported positive early school experiences"). Attention to disconfirmatory data is necessary to avoid making simplistic interpretations that gloss over the complexity of themes across participants and settings, to allow readers to make their own interpretations of the data, and to maximize the study's trustworthiness (Glesne & Peshkin, 1992; Lather, 1994b; Marshall & Rossman, 1995).

Writing the Research Report

At least three issues must be addressed by researchers as they move from the field (data collection) to the construction of the text (research report): sense making, representation, and legitimization (Denzin, 1994).

First, questions for sense making that must be addressed include "What will be reported?" and "How will it be represented?" Information sources include the data collected from participants; the researchers' theoretical, field, and code notes; and any information obtained through member checks and follow-up interviews.

Second, representation deals with the voice of the text and the text's audience. The participant's voice, often termed the "Other," and the author's role in the reflexive text are important considerations. As Denzin (1994) noted, representation is always self- (researcher) representation because the researcher determines both the content and order of presentation. The creation of multivoiced (versus single-voiced) texts may partially address this concern (e.g., Woodbrook's poststructural research, 1991, cited in Lather, 1993). However, the problem of representation can never be fully resolved because of two irreconcilable issues: first, concern for the text's validity as "a form of isomorphism and authenticity," and second, certainty that all texts are historically, socially, politically, and culturally bound (Lincoln & Denzin, 1994, p. 582).

Third, legitimization is the correspondence of the text to an agreed-upon standard, such as epistemological validity or valid exemplars that are accepted by the scientific community. As noted previously, each paradigm has its own criteria for legitimization. Lincoln and Denzin (1994) raised the following questions related to legitimization: "Is a text . . . faithful to the context and the individuals it is supposed to represent? Does the text have the right to assert that it is a report to the larger world that addresses not only the researcher's interests, but also the interests of those studied?" (p. 578). These three issues must be addressed by investigators as they transform their data and interpretations into texts.

Various forms of text organization and writing style may be chosen, depending on the purpose of a study. Hammersley and Atkinson (1983) suggested the following strategies to organize text: (a) *natural history* (useful for highlighting fieldwork process), (b) *chronology* (especially helpful when passage of time is important to research objectives), (c) *changing focus* (ranging from data description to theoretical abstraction), (d) *separated narration and analysis* (addressing research process and theory in separate dialogues), and (e) *organization of themes or topics* (each theme that emerges from analysis is discussed in depth). Various methods for writing styles, referred to as *tales,* include realist (observational position of authority), confessional (interpretation, emphasizing the researcher's filtered view of the data), impressionist (creative, artistic means of recalling the fieldwork experience), critical (illumination of the social, political, and economic issues in which the study is embedded), and formal (explicit building, testing, or exhibiting of theory) tales (Van Maanen, 1988).

Conclusion

Doing qualitative data analysis involves much more than knowledge of data analysis procedures. All phases of the qualitative research process are linked to each other and hinge on the paradigm that frames the investigation. Therefore qualitative investigators must begin at the macro level because it is the paradigm that will frame the study's design, strategy, data analysis, and report of the results. This chapter provided an overview of the five major paradigms employed in qualitative research and highlighted methodological issues and strategies associated with them. Generic guidelines for collecting and analyzing qualitative data also were offered.

Through qualitative inquiry, researchers can obtain relevance and rigor. Qualitative paradigms offer systematic methods to examine the socially constructed nature of reality, attend to nuances of individual variability and complexity, and offer discovery-based approaches for the acquisition and verification of knowledge and theory. Therefore qualitative research provides a viable approach to the systematic, scientific investigation of the world.

Recommended Readings

Further information about the topic covered in this chapter can be found in the following recommended readings: Denzin and Lincoln (1994), Glesne and Peshkin (1992),

Huberman and Miles (1994), Hill (1994), Van Maanen (1988), and Weitzman and Miles (1995).

Note

1. These programs are available from Qualitative Research Management, 73-425 Hilltop Road, Desert Hot Springs, CA 92240, phone (619) 329-7026.

References

Cook, T., & Campbell, D. T. (1979). *Quasi-experimentation: Design and analysis issues for field settings*. Boston: Houghton Mifflin.

Culler, J. (1982). *On deconstruction*. Ithaca, NY: Cornell University Press.

Denzin, N. K. (1978). *The research act: A theoretical introduction to sociological methods*. New York: McGraw-Hill.

Denzin, N. K. (1989). *Interpretive interactionism*. Newbury Park, CA: Sage.

Denzin, N. K. (1994). The art and politics of interpretation. In N. K. Denzin & Y. S. Lincoln (Eds.), *Handbook of qualitative research* (pp. 500-515). Thousand Oaks, CA: Sage.

Denzin, N. K., & Lincoln, Y. S. (1994). Introduction: Entering the field of qualitative research. In N. K. Denzin & Y. S. Lincoln (Eds.), *Handbook of qualitative research* (pp. 1-17). Thousand Oaks, CA: Sage.

Geertz, C. (1973). *The interpretation of culture*. New York: Basic Books.

Gibson, R. (1986). *Critical theory and education*. London: Hodder & Stoughton.

Giorgi, A. (1970). *Psychology as a human science: A phenomenologically based approach*. New York: Harper & Row.

Giroux, H. (1988). *Schooling and the struggle for public life: Critical pedagogy in the modern age*. Minneapolis: University of Minnesota Press.

Glesne, C., & Peshkin, A. (1992). *Becoming qualitative researchers: An introduction*. White Plains, NY: Longman.

Guba, E. G. (1981). Criteria for assessing the trustworthiness of naturalistic inquiries. *Educational Communication and Technology Journal, 29*, 75-92.

Guba, E. G., & Lincoln, Y. S. (1989). *Fourth generation evaluation*. Newbury Park, CA: Sage.

Guba, E. G., & Lincoln, Y. S. (1994). Competing paradigms in qualitative research. In N. K. Denzin & Y. S. Lincoln (Eds.), *Handbook of qualitative research* (pp. 105-117). Thousand Oaks, CA: Sage.

Habermas, J. (1971). *Knowledge and human interests* (J. Shapiro, Trans.). Boston: Beacon.

Hammersley, M., & Atkinson, P. (1983). *Ethnography: Principles in practice*. New York: Tavistock.

Hill, C. E. (Ed.). (1994). Special section: Qualitative research in counseling process and outcome. *Journal of Counseling Psychology, 41*, 427-512.

Huberman, A. M., & Miles, M. B. (1994). Data management and analysis methods. In N. K. Denzin & Y. S. Lincoln (Eds.), *Qualitative research handbook* (pp. 428-444). Thousand Oaks, CA: Sage.

Husserl, E. (1962). *Ideas*. New York: Colliers. (Original work published 1913)

Janesick, V. J. (1994). The dance of qualitative research design: Metaphor, methodology, and meaning. In N. K. Denzin & Y. S. Lincoln (Eds.), *Handbook of qualitative research* (pp. 209-219). Thousand Oaks, CA: Sage.

Kvale, S. (1995). Validation as communication and action. *Qualitative Inquiry, 1*, 1-19.

Lather, P. (1992). Critical frames in educational research: Feminist and post-structural perspectives. *Theory Into Practice, 31*(2), 87-99.

Lather, P. (1993). Fertile obsession: Validity after poststructuralism. *Sociological Quarterly, 34*, 673-693.

Lather, P. (1994a). Critical inquiry in qualitative research: Feminist and poststructural perspectives: Science "after truth." In B. F. Scrabbler, W. L. Miller, R. B. Addison, V. J. Gilchrist, & A. J. Kuzel (Eds.), *Exploring collaborative research in primary care* (pp. 103-114). Thousand Oaks, CA: Sage.

Lather, P. (1994b). *Introduction to qualitative research in education*. Class lecture, The Ohio State University, Columbus.

Lincoln, Y. S., & Denzin, N. K. (1994). The fifth movement. In N. K. Denzin & Y. S. Lincoln (Eds.), *Handbook of qualitative research* (pp. 575-586). Thousand Oaks, CA: Sage.

Lincoln, Y. S., & Guba, E. G. (1985). *Naturalistic inquiry*. Beverly Hills, CA: Sage.

Morse, J. M. (1993). *Critical issues in qualitative research methods*. Thousand Oaks, CA: Sage.

Marshall, C., & Rossman, G. B. (1995). *Designing qualitative research* (2nd ed.). Thousand Oaks, CA: Sage.

Patton, M. Q. (1990). *Qualitative evaluation and research methods* (2nd ed.). Newbury Park, CA: Sage.

Richardson, L. (1994). Writing: A method of inquiry. In N. K. Denzin & Y. S. Lincoln (Eds.), *Handbook of qualitative research* (pp. 516-529). Thousand Oaks, CA: Sage.

Rose, J., & Jevne, R. F. J. (1993). Psychosocial processes associated with athletic injuries. *Sport Psychologist, 7,* 309-328.

Schatzman, L., & Strauss, A. (1973). *Field research.* Englewood Cliffs, NJ: Prentice Hall.

Scheurich, J. (in press). The masks of validity: A poststructural interrogation. *International Journal of Qualitative Studies and Education, 9*(1).

Strauss, A., & Corbin, J. (1990). *Basics of qualitative research: Grounded theory procedures and techniques.* Newbury Park, CA: Sage.

Strauss, A., & Corbin, J. (1994). Grounded theory methodology. In N. K. Denzin & Y. S. Lincoln (Eds.), *Handbook of qualitative research* (pp. 273-285). Thousand Oaks, CA: Sage.

Tesch, R. (1990). *Qualitative research: Analysis types and software tools.* Philadelphia: Falmer.

Van Maanen, J. (1988). *Tales of the field: On writing ethnography.* Chicago: University of Chicago Press.

Weitzman, E. A., & Miles, M. B. (1995). *Computer programs for qualitative data analysis: A software sourcebook.* Thousand Oaks, CA: Sage.

Chapter 15

A Basic Guide to Statistical Research and Discovery

Planning and Selecting Statistical Analyses

ROBERT A. YAFFEE

When one is designing and conducting research, the choice of appropriate statistical analyses depends on the statistical question and the nature of the variables involved. Whether research is confirmatory or exploratory in nature, researchers should always strive to design their projects before collecting data. As any project is planned, a series of choices must be made. For many of these choices, statistical tests are informative. In planning an empirical study, a researcher should first estimate the pilot study sample size, the survey (or experimental) sample size, the design and weights for the samples, and the statistical test for each conceptual hypothesis. Second, pilot studies permit discovery of response and coverage rates necessary for general sample size planning and assessment of the utility of individual items and sets of items to be used in the survey or experiment. Third, once data are collected and input, data cleaning involves error detection and correction (refer to Dollinger & DiLalla, Chapter 13 of this volume). In the case of missing data, replacement rules need to be established and followed. Finally, the hypotheses can be evaluated. For undergraduate and graduate students of psychology, this chapter serves as a navigational guide through coastal statistical waters.

This chapter addresses the choice of statistical tests to answer research questions. A three-part scheme organizes the analyses into those completed before data collection, those completed before hypothesis testing, and those completed for the purpose of hypothesis testing. Where possible, I refer to such computer packages as SAS (SAS Institute, Inc., 1990), SPSS and SYSTAT (SPSS Inc., 1989, 1990), BMDP (Dixon, 1990), and LIMDEP (Greene, 1992). The remainder of the chapter is structured as follows. After briefly treating analyses conducted before data collection, I address preliminary analyses to be completed before evaluating hypotheses. The bulk of the chapter is aimed at choice of tests to evaluate hypotheses. In this section, I review tests for one dependent variable. These include tests for a single independent variable and tests for multiple independent variables. Then I present tests for multiple dependent variables. Moreover, it is good practice to test assumptions before models are evaluated. Thus I also consider diagnostics and assessment of fit for the different statistical models. Nonparametric analyses can be substituted when violations of parametric assumptions occur. For most analyses, these alternatives will be presented. The relative efficiency of nonparametric tests should be assessed before using them, however, to ensure that the trade-off between assumptions and power is tolerable.

Analyses Conducted Before Collecting Data

Before collecting data, it is important to consider the required sample size, the sampling design, and the weighting of the sample. Issues of sample size and statistical power are discussed here, but sampling design and weighting issues are discussed by McCready (Chapter 8).

SAMPLE SIZE REQUIREMENTS

Researchers should perform a power analysis to estimate sample size requirements. The power of a statistical test is its capability to reject a false null hypothesis. Cohen (1988, pp. 14-16) defined four related factors of statistical inference: power, level of significance (α), sample size (N), and effect size (ES). *Effect size* is defined as the extent to which a psychological phenomenon exists. Other things being equal, the larger the sample size, and the larger the effect size, the more powerful the statistical test. The greater the power of the statistical test, the smaller the effect size that can be reliably detected. With greater power, the test is less likely to suggest accepting an incorrect null hypothesis. For a researcher to have sufficient statistical power, a certain sample size is required (one rule of thumb suggests power of at least .80; Cohen, 1988). When any three factors are fixed, the fourth is determined.

Simpler power/sample size calculations may be made by hand. Assume that several researchers are analyzing proportions and reporting them in percentage terms. They may decide that the amount of error tolerable is no more than 3% of the estimated proportion. The estimated sample size (N) to achieve this error may be determined from the formula for confidence intervals around proportions. For more elaborate assessments of statistical power, tables or computer programs are recommended. The tables provided by Cohen (1988) are the most comprehensive. Borenstein and Cohen (1988), Borenstein, Cohen, Rothstein, Pollack, and Kane (1992), and Lenth (1987) offer such programs, and a more advanced program, STATPOWER (Bavry, 1991) is available from Scientific Software. Goldstein's (1989) comparison of several PC programs for estimating sample size or power should be consulted for further information.

Although the required sample size is determined from the power analyses, the contact sample sizes for the pilot study and general survey (or experiment) need to be estimated in each. The pilot study allows discovery of response and coverage rates by which inverses the reseacher inflates the needed sample size to obtain the contact sample size. The resulting interview or observational sample should have the required size and power (Deming, 1960; Kish, 1965).

Analyses Conducted Before Evaluating Hypotheses

With data in hand but before evaluating hypotheses, researchers should complete data cleaning, univariate item analysis, and scale construction and evaluation. Further, a missing data screening and replacement strategy should be in place. Some of these preliminary analyses are addressed in greater detail by Dollinger and DiLalla in Chapter 13 of this volume. In this section, I present univariate item analysis and scale evaluation.

UNIVARIATE ITEM ANALYSIS

Item inspections are used to evaluate items before the formation of multi-item scales. One rule of thumb is that if an item has over 30% missing values, it should be dropped from the instrument. In addition, missing value substitution may be appropriate. If the distribution of the item is approximately normal, the mean value may be used for missing data replacement. One can also regress the variable with the missing values on other variables in the data set (e.g., using BMDP subprogram AM). A regression equation is used to estimate the new values (Anderson, Basilevsky, & Hum, 1983). If the distribution is non-normal, such as one characterized by outliers, a "trimmed" mean can be calculated by dropping extreme values from both sides. If a distribution is skewed to one tail or the other, a median may be used for missing value replacement.

SCALE/COMPOSITE ANALYSES: RELIABILITY AND VALIDITY

Researchers often aggregate items into scales or composites to analyze data and test hypotheses. After univariate item analysis, researchers use various correlations to evaluate derived composites measured in surveys or in experiments. It is important to distinguish the question of interest to choose among the large number of available correlation coefficients.

Bivariate correlations are a family of measures for estimating the relationship between variables. The choice of coefficient depends on the variables involved. If both variables are continuous and at least interval level, a researcher may wish to plot the joint distribution of the two variables to verify that the relationship is linear. If the relationship appears nonlinear, the researcher may wish to test different functional forms for fit, transform one or both of the two variables according to the best functional fit to linearize the relationship, or use a nonlinear regression approach. The basic coefficient is the Pearson product-moment correlation (PPMC), which measures the magnitude of change in one variable when change occurs in the other variable. A common transformation is Fisher's r to z, which normalizes the sampling distribution of the correlation coefficient. A significance test for the PPMC is the t test, which can be used to evaluate the null hypothesis that the observed coefficient is not significantly different from zero.

When the two variables are not interval, there are several possible situations. First are the situations when both variables are measured at the same level. If both variables are ordinal, if there is no clear independent-dependent variable distinction, or if the researcher has a small sample size (say, with $n < 30$), nonparametric correlations can be used to assess the magnitude of the relationship. *Magnitude* is defined as monotonicity, whether both variables increase or decrease together. Some of the available coefficients include Spearman's rho (ρ), Kendall's τ_a or τ_b, Stuart's τ_c, symmetric lambda (λ), Goodman and Kruskal's gamma (Γ), and the polychoric correlation. Only the τ_a and Γ coefficients do not correct for ties (those situations in which no change occurs for both variables). In general, for the same data, Γ will have the largest value and τ_a will have the smallest value. The τ_b corrects for ties, and the λ and τ_c deal with variables with different numbers of values. The polychoric correlation estimates the relationship between two variables with underlying bivariate normal distributions for which the observed variables are multiple categories (Jöreskog & Sörbom, 1988). Second, if there are clear dependent and independent variables, the researcher must specify which variable is independent and which is dependent. For such asymmetric relationships, Somer's D or asymmetric λ can be used to estimate the association between the two variables.

When both variables are nominal/categorical, Goodman and Kruskal's λ, Cramer's V, or the contingency coefficient may be used. Cramer's V ranges between 0 and 1, whereas the contingency coefficient generally approaches .87 as its maximum value. The λ, which ranges between 0 and 1, indicates the proportional reduction of error in predicting a dependent variable when the values of the independent variable are known. The symmetric λ can be thought of as the average of the two asymmetric versions. If the nominal variables are dichotomous or binary, the phi (ϕ), tetrachoric, or Yule's q may be used to estimate the extent of the relationship. The PPMC coefficient reduces to the ϕ coefficient when applied to binary data. In cohort studies that track a group of persons, relative risk is used to estimate a ratio of incidence rates; in case-control studies, relative risk may be used to indicate the odds ratio of a case over that of a control. A continuity-adjusted χ^2 may be used also to test the significance level. With an unbalanced, skewed, or sparse sample, the Fisher's exact test will yield the exact significance level.

When the two variables differ in measurement level, the choice of correlation coefficient is more complex because it depends on the different measurement levels of the variables as well as on the symmetry of their relationship. Usually, the analyst uses a coefficient designed to deal with the lower level of measurement rather than higher levels of measurement. For example, one of the two variables may be dichotomous, while the other may be interval, ratio, ordinal, or nominal. Suppose the other variable is continuous in nature. If the investigator can argue that the dichotomous variable has an underlying normal distribution, the biserial correlation coefficient is appropriate. Another relevant coefficient is the point-biserial coefficient, which requires that the dichotomous variable represent a true dichotomy (Andrews, Klein, Davidson, O'Malley, & Rodgers, 1981; Jöreskog & Sörbom, 1988). If one variable is dichotomous and the other variable is ordinal, then eta-squared (η^2), epsilon-squared (ε^2), or Hay's omega-squared (ω^2) is appropriate. If one variable is dichotomous and the other is nominal, then the contingency coefficient, Cramer's V, τ_c, or the asymmetric λ coefficient is suggested.

Further, the relationship between dichotomous and other levels of measurement is not the only possible pairing. The relationship may be between an ordinal variable and a continuous variable or a nominal variable. If one variable is ordinal and the other is continuous, then an appropriate coefficient is the polyserial correlation coefficient. The ordinal variable used is assumed to have an underlying normal distribution (Andrews et al., 1981; Jöreskog & Sörbom, 1988). A Spearman's ρ, Kendall's τ_a or τ_b, Stuart's τ_c, or Goodman and Kruskal's Γ coefficient is also appropriate. If the second variable is nominal, then λ, η^2, ω^2, or ε^2 may be used (Kirk, 1994; Winer, Brown, & Michels, 1991). If one of the variables is ordinal and the other is either continuous or integer in nature, the η^2 coefficient is appropriate.

SCALE EVALUATION

Scale development and factor analysis may be used to enhance validity through aggregation. Scales are formed by combining items, each of which measures a part of a construct. A scale may be analyzed in various ways to determine whether the items form one scale or several. First, however, the reliability of scales should always be estimated and reported. *Reliability* is defined as the ratio of true score variance to observed variance. It is measured by coefficients ranging from 0 to 1. The three basic types of reliability are stability, equivalence, and internal consistency. The stability of measurements of items over time may be assessed by test-retest correlations. The intraclass correlation may be used to estimate reliability where there are multiple raters or repeated observations. Cohen's kappa (κ), which controls for chance agreement, may be used to evaluate the consistency of two or more raters. For more than two raters, the multiple-rater κ coefficient must be used. Coefficients of equivalence, usually a PPMC, pertain to the relationship between two subsets of items from a single domain (e.g., job satisfaction). Coefficients of internal consistency, which pertain to a single set of items, include the split-half estimate, Cronbach's alpha (α), Kuder-Richardson KR-20/21, and Cochran's Q (if the items are dichotomous).

Nunnally's earlier work asserted that reliabilities of .50 or .60 or more were required for adequate reliability of a composite, but he later called for reliabilities as high as .70 (Nunnally & Bernstein, 1993). When the assumptions for the correlation are unlikely to be met, then Kendall's coefficient of paired rankings, Kendall's coefficient of agreement, or Kendall's coefficient of concordance may be used (Siegel & Castellan, 1988). The SPSS package has a reliability procedure that provides some of these coefficients, and the SAS package has an option for Cronbach's α in its correlation procedure.

The scale may be evaluated using factor analysis (Rummel, 1970). An alternative is multidimensional scaling, which extracts dimensions from the similarities between variables. In factor analysis, patterns are observed in the number, nature, and correlation among extracted factors (dimensions). Each factor constitutes the basis for a scale, and the factor score for each individual can be saved and used as the scale score. Factor loadings reflect the relationship between the underlying construct and each observable indicator variable. The factor structure, a pattern of intercorrelation among the variables, forms a basis for internal consistency among the items. It represents the homogeneity of the variables highly correlated with one another. Evidence for the construct validity of the theoretical construct is provided by the dimensions or factors extracted (Cook & Campbell, 1979). To the extent that the component dimensions of a construct are not found in the factor structure, some lack of validity is indicated. If factor analysis is used, the factors extracted may or may not corroborate the hypothesized dimensions of the concept. This finding has implications for the support of construct validity. Factor scores may be used to represent an individual's position on a factor. If some items are measured by one means and other items are measured by other means, then convergent and discriminant validity may be established with a multitrait-multimethod correlation matrix.

Another aspect of scale development focuses on external correlates of individual items. This aspect of an item is the extent to which items relate to an external criterion and to which they can be generalized to and across persons, populations, settings, and times (Cook & Campbell, 1979; Pedhazur & Schmelkin, 1991). If the same factor structure is replicable using a different sample, then the scale structure is said to demonstrate external validity. Often such cross-validation is performed by replicating a specific extracted factor structure (construct validation) on a holdout sample to provide evidence of generalizability.

Analyses to Evaluate Hypotheses

After these preliminary analyses have been completed, the conceptual questions driving the research project can finally be addressed. Use of basic and advanced statistical analyses is addressed in greater detail by Dickter and Roznowski in Chapter 16 and by Levy and Steelman in Chapter 17 of this volume. In this section, I cover one-sample, paired-sample, and two-sample tests for single dependent variables; the general linear model including ANOVA, regression, and ANCOVA; and model building and multivariate analyses.

ONE-SAMPLE TESTS

In a number of situations, one would like to determine whether a sample comes from a population with certain parameters (e.g., proportion or mean). Alternatively, the researcher might wish to know whether his or her ordinal or continuous sample came from a normally distributed population. In other words, the sample at hand is assumed to have an underlying continuous normally distribution. A Shapiro-Wilks W or Kolomogorov-Smirnov statistic may be used to test whether the distribution is significantly different from the theoretical normal distribution. Further, a multitude of plots may be used to assess distribution shape graphically—specifically, the histogram with overlaid normal curve (SPSS Frequencies), the box and whisker plot (SAS Univariate, SPSS Explore, SYSTAT Graphs), or the normal probability plot (SAS Univariate; SPSS MANOVA or residual analysis in the Regression routine).

Some measured variables are binary or dichotomous, possessing only two values. One might want to know the probability of obtaining one or the other result. If one is rolling dice, one may determine the probability of obtaining two threes in five rolls of the dice. The test of choice is the binomial test, which gives the probability of obtaining this result. The use of this test for each possibility less than two threes will give the probability of obtaining a result less than or equal to two threes in five rolls of the dice. When the sample size is large, a correction for continuity is suggested.

When the variables are categorical, the researcher may wish to ascertain whether the result is significantly different from what one would expect from a presumed population, then she may use the χ^2 goodness-of-fit test. This test evaluates observed against expected frequencies.

There are times during experimental design that a researcher needs to determine the randomness of assignment to control and experimental groups. A one-sample runs test may be used for this purpose. The longer the run of successive assignments to one group, the less likely the distribution is random. Tabled values show the critical levels for the lengths of different runs. The test is appropriate for samples larger than 20.

PAIRED SINGLE-SAMPLE TESTS

There are a number of circumstances in which a variable is measured repeatedly. A researcher may wish to ascertain whether a change has taken place after some impact or intervention. Often the same group of persons is used before and after some experimental intervention. Sometimes a less preferable method is utilized in which groups are matched on external variables that are expected to influence the outcome variable. Whichever the case, when the variable under examination in the sample is continuous (interval or ratio level) and we are examining the change of its mean from pretest to the postest, then the paired t test is usually the more powerful test. The validity of its test results is based on specific assumptions. Among them are the assumptions of random sampling, normality, and equal variances. If the population is not normally distributed but the sample is large enough, then the sampling distribution of means becomes normal. Sample sizes of approximately 40 are large enough (Hays, 1973).

If the sample is too small or not normally distributed, a nonparametric alternative test should be employed. Six of these tests are discussed in decreasing order of their power-efficiency. The power-efficiency is the number of cases for the most powerful statistical test divided by the number of cases for the test in question to attain the same power. There are six popular nonparametric tests. The Wilcoxon signed-ranks test, which has 95.5% power-efficiency compared to the t test, is preferred. Somewhat less powerful are the McNemar, sign, binomial, Cochran's Q, Kendall's coefficient of concordance, and Friedman's two-way tests.

The six tests differ in their features. The Wilcoxon test is easy to compute. The difference scores between the first and second repetition are ranked. Pluses are assigned to positive ranks, and minuses are assigned to the negative ranks. The mean deviation of the positive total is divided by the standard deviation to get a z score. If the absolute z score exceeds 1.96, the result is significant, with the rejection of the null hypothesis. With a correction for tied ranks, this test is a powerful distribution-free alternative for the paired t test. For assessment of the statistical significance of changes in nominal or ordinal variables, a McNemar distribution-free test may be used. This provides a χ^2 for actual compared to expected changes between the pretest and postest. A correction for continuity is often applied. Therefore the sample size must be large enough so that not too many cells have expected frequencies less than 5. Depending on the sample size, the power-efficiency of this test may vary between 63% and 95%. Two other nonparametric alternative tests are the sign and binomial tests. Their power-efficiency is about 95% when the sample size is six and decreases to about 63% with increases of sample size. Cochran's Q is a test of proportions over k samples to determine whether the proportions defined by the distributions within a nominal or ordinal variable have significantly changed over time. The test is a kind of modified χ^2 test with k columns and n rows that can be used for dichotomous variables as well. Kendall's coefficient of agreement (u) is useful for two judges or paired observations. Kendall's coefficient of concordance (W), which corrects for ties and ranges between 0 and +1, is the nonparametric alternative to the completely within-subjects repeated-measures design.

BIVARIATE DIRECTIONAL MODELS

Apart from the bivariate association models discussed above, there are many circumstances in which the relationship between the dependent variable and an independent variable determines whether the predictor variable is a candidate for a more complex model with multiple independent variables. A series of bivariate tests between the dependent and possibly theoretically related independent variables is sometimes called *variable screening* or *selection.* Only relationships that are found to be significant are used in the larger model. Cross-validation on a holdout or new sample is an obvious requirement.

If the model under consideration is a directional one, the first question is the respective levels of measurement of the dependent and independent variables. Assume that the dependent variable is continuous, and the question arises as to the measurement level of the independent variable. The independent variable may be continuous, ranked, or categorical. Suppose that the independent variable takes two values, say the presence or absence of a treatment/intervention. The more powerful parametric independent samples t test is applied first. This test assumes that the measures of the dependent variable, within levels of the independent variable, are independent and normally distributed. If the variances are equal, the t test may be applied. If the variances are unequal, then a correction for degrees of freedom is used to obtain a separate variances estimate. For the test results to remain valid, the samples should be fairly normally distributed. However, the test is robust to moderate violations of normality if the sample sizes are large enough and the variances are equal.

If the parametric assumptions are substantially violated, a distribution-free nonparametric test may be substituted. If the dependent variable is ordinal or can be treated as ordinal and the independent variable is binary, then the Mann-Whitney U test may be used. Corrections for tied ranks can be made also. Generally, the only assumption of the nonparametric tests is that observations are independent of one another (Siegel & Castellan, 1988).

General Linear Model

The general linear model includes analysis of variance (ANOVA), regression, and analysis of covariance (ANCOVA). If the dependent variable is continuous and the independent variable has three or more levels, a one-way ANOVA may be applied. If there are multiple independent categorical variables, then factorial ANOVA is required to analyze interactions as well as main effects. For valid interpretation, the assumptions of the F test must be fulfilled. Random sampling is often presumed unless the study is a clinical trial in which specific inclusion and exclusion criteria hold. The residuals are assumed to be normally distributed and could be tested for normality by a Shapiro-Wilks test for smaller samples or a Kolmogorov-Smirnov test for larger samples. Because the model can withstand moderate violations of the normality assumption, the normality may be evaluated using a histogram with a superimposed normal curve or by a normal probability plot. An essential third assumption of the model is equal variance of the residuals. The residuals are tested for homogeneity with Hartley's F (larger variance divided by smaller variance) or Levene's test, which is less sensitive to non-normality (Kirk, 1994; Snedecor & Cochran, 1980). The residuals may be graphically viewed with the standardized residuals plotted against the predicted dependent and/or independent variables. If means in the analysis are distorted by outliers, diagnostics such as casewise plots, Mahalanobis, or Cook's distances facilitate detection of problematic cases. Outliers may be "trimmed" from the analysis if circumstances warrant. The BMDP program 7D performs ANOVA with trimmed means. Finally, violations of these assumptions may also be dealt with by transformations of the dependent variable to render the distributions of residuals more normal and/or homogeneous (e.g., Blom, arc-sine, square root).

If the assumptions are fulfilled and the overall test is significant, a researcher must decide which of the group means within the multiple levels of the independent variable are significantly different. Two approaches are available. One approach is to test mean differences with a priori or planned contrasts. For complex orthogonal contrasts, there are the multiple t, multiple F, and robust Behrens-Fisher and Welch tests. For nonorthogonal complex contrasts, the Bonferroni and Dunn-Sidàk tests are appropriate, whereas for pairwise comparisons, Dunnett's test between levels can be used. A second approach is to test mean differences with nonorthogonal multiple comparisons. When using such tests, it behooves the researcher to calculate the experimentwise error rate based on the number of pairwise comparisons performed. Then he or she should plan on employing the Bonferroni or Dunn-Sidàk correction to determine the correct comparisonwise significance level. A conservative test generally used for complex comparisons is the Scheffe S test, which requires homogeneity of variance and tends to be less powerful. The more robust Brown-Forsythe (BF) test may also be used. Neither of these tests requires equal sample sizes. For pairwise comparisons, there is the Fisher least significant difference (LSD) test, Tukey's honest significant difference (HSD) test between the largest and smallest mean, Spjötvoll and Stoline's T test, and the Tukey-Kramer modified honest significant difference test (the latter two are used when the ns are different but the assumption of homogeneous variances holds). The robust procedures developed by Games-Howell/Tamhane from the Behrens-Fisher statistic with the Welch adjustment to the degrees of freedom may be used when the ns differ and homogeneity of variance is lacking. The Newman-Keuls test should be used for stepwise or layered approaches to significance testing (Kirk, 1994). Many subsets of these tests are found in the major statistical computing packages.

If the assumptions are seriously violated, then the researcher may use nonparametric tests. One such test that applies if the independent variable is ordered with two or more levels is the Kruskal Wallis one-way nonparametric ANOVA on ranks, which tests the significance of differences between the average ranks for each of the levels of the independent factor. Provision is made for multiple comparisons between each of the levels by comparing the absolute difference of the average ranks with the interval. This test has 95.5% power-efficiency relative to the F test (Siegel & Castellan, 1988). When there are significant differences between the sum of those ranks, when corrected for ties, a significant difference is indicated.

If the analyst finds that a two-way ANOVA, one-way randomized block design, or split-plot ANOVA is invalid because of violations of underlying assumptions (especially compound symmetry among the repeated measures) or that the proper error terms for the between- and within-subjects effects are not used, he or she may use the Friedman two-way rank ANOVA. These tests are for situations with two ordinal variables or one ordinal and one categorical independent variable.

Regression

If the dependent and independent variables are continuous, the appropriate test is that provided by simple (bivariate) regression. Regression also requires specific assumptions, including random sampling, independent observations, functional linearity, uncorrelated errors, normality of residuals, homogeneity of variance, and no multicollinearity among independent variables. These assumptions may be tested by the above-noted techniques. If the assumptions are not met, researchers may use nonparametric regression analysis (Hollander & Wolfe, 1973; Hettmansperger, 1984). If there are only two independent variables, the analyst may use the partial Kendall correlation. If there are two or more independent variables and they are uncorrelated, he or she may choose the Brown-Mood method for finding the slope and intercept of the separate regression lines based on a median split of the data on each x- and corresponding y-axis (Daniel, 1990) and may choose Theil's estimate of slope and the distribution-free test for its significance (Hollander & Wolfe, 1973). These analyses may be helpful fallbacks from parametric tests when assumptions are unmet.

Model Building and Regression

When the relationship to be developed links a dependent variable with several independent variables, the analysis depends on the measurement levels of the variables. Partial correlations reveal associations between two continuous variables while a third continuous variable is held constant. With one interval dependent variable and several continuous independent variables, a multiple correlation coefficient indicates the magnitude of the relationship. Because this coefficient is inflated by the inclusion of additional independent variables in the model, an adjusted or shrunken multiple correlation coefficient compensates for the change in degrees of freedom. The square of the multiple correlation (SMC) coefficient is known as the coefficient of determination or R^2, which represents the proportion of variance of the dependent variable explained by the variables in the model. A squared semipartial correlation reflects the change in this R^2 from the addition of a new set of variable(s). Variations of the F test are used as significance tests of these omnibus statistics. Ordinary least-squares (OLS) multiple linear regression models are developed often by adding variables that significantly increase the coefficient of determination.

Four computer algorithms are used to select variables for inclusion in OLS models. Specifically, forward, backward, stepwise, and forced-entry selections are employed by statistical computer packages to choose variables for models. Stepwise techniques can erroneously drop components that are necessary for proper specification and interpretation. Forced-entry techniques, on the other hand, are useful for hierarchical modeling, theory building, and hypothesis testing.

In the event that assumptions of the multiple linear regression model are violated, there are also alternatives. If the linearity assumption is violated, transformations may be used to linearize the relationship between the dependent and the respective independent variables. Polynomial or nonlinear regression may be used if the linearity is not eliminated by the transformation, with the different powers indicating specific nonlinear forms. When there is substantial multicollinearity, instrumental variables may be substituted for the correlated independent variables. A principal components analysis among the highly correlated independent variables can generate component scores that may be used as independent variables in the regression analysis. Variance stabilizing and normalizing transformations may be used in the event of violation of the homogeneity and the normality assumptions. If heterogeneity of variance persists, then weighted least squares may be used as the estimation technique. Correlated residuals, diagnosed with the Durbin-Watson test, Durbin's m test, or the autocorrelation function, may require first differencing or other autoregression techniques. However, if none of these techniques suffices to eliminate the problem, then a set of PPMCs may be performed between the dependent variable and each independent variable sequentially.

Model building may promote maximal theoretical scope and power by beginning with a general model including all relevant empirical parameters and continuing with sequential testing and eliminating nonsignificant effects until a parsimonious model is specified (Hendry & Richard, 1982). Model revision generally increases power and eliminates nonsignificant effects, although there are exceptions to this rule. When main effects are necessary to specify interaction effects, suppression of main effect significance by interactions does not justify removal of the component main effects. Component main effects are necessary to specify interactions. For example, lower-level interactions are necessary to specify higher-level ones (Cohen, 1978). Otherwise, nonsignificant effects are pruned from the model.

Path-analytic models may be developed using regression procedures or covariance structure analysis (e.g., using EQS, CALIS, RAMONA, or LISREL). Bivariate relationships may mask antecedent or intervening variables. Path models decompose the total effects of a dependent variable into direct, indirect, and spurious effects. They are able to show how some variables mediate between an antecedent variable and an outcome variable. Path models consist of a series of OLS regression equations, but now with LISREL they can be constructed using ordinal or nominal variables as well. These analyses are useful in developing and evaluating hypothesized models.

Other problems may plague such models. Leamer (1983) noted that misspecification of the model may result in fragile models, in which addition of a variable may cause drastic changes in the magnitudes of regression coefficients of other variables. Leamer suggested focusing on one important variable at a time, adding the less important variables in various combinations and noting changes in the size of the magnitude of regression coefficients of the focus variable. The smallest and largest magnitudes constitute the extreme bounds. If the range spanning these bounds exceeds the confidence interval of the variable in the full model, then the model is fragile and unreliable. Fragile components may be eliminated from the model. In this way, the robustness of the model is enhanced and in conjunction with improving explanation.

Where there is one dependent variable and multiple independent variables (IVs), the measurement level of the dependent variable may be dichotomous, ordinal, or interval. If the dependent variable is dichotomous, then the researcher may use a logit, logistic, probit, or discriminant function model. The logit model has categorical independent variables. Independent ordinal and categorical variables may be dummy-coded for easily interpretable effects and used with continuous variables in logistic regression models. Dummy coding is preferred over effect coding in logistic models to facilitate interpretation. Independent continuous variables may be included in the logistic models without complication. As logit and logistic models are estimated with maximum likelihood, they require large sample sizes. Variables are added that significantly improve the fit between observed and predicted probabilities of the model. Probit analyses involve normal distributional assumptions, yet the probit coefficients are more difficult to interpret than are the logistic regression coefficients. Discriminant function models, which assume equality of the error covariance matrices and multivariate normality, may be used. Box's M test can be used to evaluate equality of the error covariance matrices, and Mardia's test for multivariate normality may be employed. Functions discriminating between the groups of the dependent variable are extracted as long as their minimum eigenvalue is greater than or equal to 1.0. If the dependent variable is ordinal in nature and has only a few values, an ordinal logistic model should be used, utilizing cumulative logits. The SAS, BMDP, and LIMDEP packages perform cumulative logistic regression analysis.

When the dependent variable is a multicategory variable, the analysis of choice is a multinomial logit, a discriminant function analysis, or a discrete-choice model. In the multinomial logit model, one of the categories is taken as a default category, and logits are formed with reference to that default category. There is one less function than there are categories of the dependent variable. These functions serve to classify cases according to the group membership with respect to the default group. The same holds for discriminant function analysis: Either there is one less function formed than there are categories, or there are as many functions as there are significant eigenvalues of the functions extracted. These functions, in maximally discriminating among the groups, serve to classify cases according to dependent variable group membership. With the discrete-choice model, there are a set of attributes of the dependent categories—for example, different modes of transportation—that are the independent variables in the model. Among these predictors might be cost of trip, availability of mode of transportation, and cost of alternative mode of transportation. The LIMDEP (logit), SAS (PHREG), and SPSS (Genmod) packages have procedures for multinomial logit analysis, and LIMDEP has a procedure for the discrete-choice model.

If the dependent variable represents a count or a rare event, then the proper analysis is a Poisson regression. This model is restricted by its peculiar assumption that the mean equals the variance (Maddala, 1983). The SAS, SPSS, and LIMDEP packages perform this analysis. If the dependent variable is truncated (censored) at the bottom, top, or both, then a tobit regression may be appropriate with LIMDEP (TOBIT) or SAS (LIFEREG).

When the dependent variable is continuous and the independent variables are continuous, then the researcher has a multiple linear regression analysis. The assumptions are essentially the same as they are for the ANOVA. If there are both continuous covariates and factors as independent variables, then the model is one of ANCOVA. In addition to the regression and ANOVA assumptions, there is an assumption of homogeneity of regression, with regression slopes essentially equal across the levels of the IV(s). This assumption is tested by assessing the significance of the interaction term between covariates and IVs. If this interaction term is not significant, then the researcher can request the least square or adjusted means from the ANCOVA. Otherwise, he or she might have to model separate regressions, and if these assumptions are violated, then he or she should use nonparametric regression analysis.

Multivariate Analyses

With two or more dependent variables, a multivariate situation arises. Bock (1975) noted that a design may be multivariate in two ways, either with multiple times or with measures. If one is looking at a repeated-measures design of the multivariate ANOVA, or MANOVA, then multiple dependent variables are constructed from the trials. Correlation between repeated trials is adjusted by transformation of the between-groups sum of squares and cross-product matrix. All of the assumptions of the univariate general linear models hold for these multivariate analyses. There is, however, another postulate in need of testing.

If the multiple dependent variables are continuous and correlated (but not repeated observations of one another) and if the model has one or more independent factors, then MANOVA is the procedure to use. The crucial assumption here is one of multivariate homogeneity of variance, which may be evaluated with Box's M test. If the model contains repeated measures treated as multiple dependent variables, then specific assumptions of compound symmetry are made; Mauchley's test for sphericity may be used to evaluate this assumption. If it is violated, the researcher may use the Greenhouse-Geiser or Huyhn-Feldt adjustments. Fulfillment of the other univariate assumptions, including normality of the residuals, needs to be assessed for multivariate models as well.

If the multiple dependent and multiple independent variables are all continuous, then multivariate regression analysis may be employed. If the independent variables are categorical and a continuous control variable is available, then a MANCOVA may be used. In addition to the assumptions of the MANOVA, there must be homogeneity of regression (Tabachnick & Fidell, 1989; Tatsuoka, 1988).

Summary

Finally, the researcher/analyst is in a position to interpret the findings. The statistical conclusion validity of these interpretations depends on selecting the proper tests and understanding their assumptions. Those assumptions need to be tested, and their robustness must be evaluated in face of violation. If the assumptions are fatally violated, the researcher should resort to alternative techniques of analysis while appreciating their relative strengths and weaknesses. Issues such as contribution to prevailing theory, new knowledge developed, knowledge gaps filled, and resolution of theoretical inconsistencies can then be discussed. The analyst can therefore understand and explain the findings, along with explaining their strengths and limitations. Unresolved problems are noted, and directions for future research are presented.

Recommended Readings

In this section, we recommend books for further study. For basic statistics, consult Kachigan (1986) or Berenson, Levine, and Rindskopf (1988). For intermediate discussions, consult Snedecor and Cochran (1980) or Hays (1973). For planning serious research, the treatment of power and effect size by Cohen (1988) is indispensable. Classical texts on research design and validity include Cook and Campbell (1979), Winer et al. (1991), and Keppel (1991). Other sophisticated treatments of correlation, multiple regression, and model building include texts by Pedhazur (1982), Cohen and Cohen (1983), and Draper and Smith (1981), as well as Fox (1984). Excellent yet sophisticated treatments of the other side of the general linear model and experimental design are Winer et al. (1991) and Kirk (1994). These texts cover ANOVA, repeated measures ANOVA, ANCOVA, MANOVA, and MANCOVA. General multivariate analysis texts include Tatsuoka (1988) and Morrison (1976). Comprehensive treatments of measurement, design, and analysis are provided by Kerlinger (1985) and by Pedhazur and Schmelkin (1991).

With respect to more complex procedures, individuals pursuing covariance structure modeling should read Bollen (1989) and Bollen and Long (1993). Students studying limited dependent variables can consult Maddala (1983) and Greene (1993). Readers considering expositions of nonparametric alternatives should study Seigel and Castellan (1988), Daniel (1990), Hollander and Wolfe (1973), or Conover (1980). When the sample sizes are unavoidably small, seriously unbalanced in sample size, or ties, the student may wish to consult Mehta and Patel (1995). By studying these texts, the reader may successfully navigate the coastal waters of contemporary social science research.

References

Anderson, A. B., Basilevsky, A., & Hum, D. P. J. (1983). Missing data: A review of the literature. In P. H. Rossi, J. D. Wright, & A. B. Anderson (Eds.), *Handbook of survey research* (pp. 414-494). Orlando, FL: Academic Press.

Andrews, F. M., Klein, L., Davidson, T. N., O'Malley, P. M., & Rodgers, W. L. (1981). *A guide for selecting statistical techniques for analyzing social science data.* Ann Arbor: University of Michigan, Institute for Social Research, Survey Research Center.

Bavry, J. L. (1991). *STATPOWER: Statistical design analysis system* (2nd ed.) [Computer program]. Chicago: Scientific Software, Inc.

Berenson, M., Levine, D., & Rindskopf, D. (1988). *Applied statistics: A first course.* Englewood Cliffs, NJ: Prentice Hall.

Bock, R. D. (1975). *Multivariate statistical models in behavioral research.* New York: McGraw-Hill.

Bollen, K. A. (1989). *Structural equations with latent variables.* New York: John Wiley.

Bollen, K. A., & Long, J. S. (Eds.). (1993). *Testing structural equation models.* Newbury Park, CA: Sage.

Borenstein, M., & Cohen, J. (1988). *Statistical power analysis: A computer program* [Computer program]. Hillsdale, NJ: Lawrence Erlbaum.

Borenstein, M., Cohen, J., Rothstein, H. R., Pollack, S., & Kane, J. (1992). A visual approach to statistical power analysis on the microcomputer [Computer program]. *Behavior Research Methods, Instrumentation, and Computers, 24*, 565-572.

Cohen, J. (1978). Partialed products are interactions; partialed powers are curve components. *Psychological Bulletin, 85*, 858-866.

Cohen, J. (1988). *Statistical power analysis for the behavioral sciences* (2nd ed.). Hillsdale, NJ: Lawrence Erlbaum.

Cohen, J., & Cohen, P. (1983). *Applied multiple regression/correlation analysis for the behavior sciences* (2nd ed.). Hillsdale, NJ: Lawrence Erlbaum.

Conover, W. J. (1980). *Practical nonparametric statistics* (2nd ed.). New York: John Wiley.

Cook, T. D., & Campbell, D. T. (1979). *Quasi-experimentation: Design and analysis issues for field settings*. Boston: Houghton Mifflin.

Daniel, W. W. (1990). *Applied nonparametric statistics*. Boston: PWS Kent.

Deming, W. E. (1960). *Sample design in business research*. New York: John Wiley.

Dixon, W. J. (Ed.). (1990). *BMDP statistical software manual* (2 vols.). Berkeley: University of California Press.

Draper, H., & Smith, N. (1981). *Applied regression analysis* (2nd ed.). New York: John Wiley.

Fox, J. (1984). *Linear statistical models and related methods*. New York: John Wiley.

Goldstein, R. (1989). Power and sample size via MS/PC-DOS computers. *American Statistician, 43*, 253-260.

Greene, W. H. (1992). *LIMDEP user's manual and reference guide (Ver. 6.0)*. Bellport, NY: Econometric Software.

Greene, W. H. (1993). *Econometric analysis*. New York: Macmillan.

Hays, W. L. (1973). *Statistics for the social sciences*. New York: Holt, Rinehart & Winston.

Hendry, D., & Richard, J.-F. (1982). On the formulation of empirical models in dynamic econometrics. *Journal of Economics, 20*, 3-33.

Hettmansperger, T. (1984). *Statistical inference based on ranks*. New York: John Wiley.

Hollander, M., & Wolfe, D. A. (1973). *Nonparametric statistical methods*. New York: John Wiley.

Jöreskog, K., & Sörbom, D. (1988). *PRELIS: A program for multivariate data screening and data summarization*. Mooresville, IN: Scientific Software.

Kachigan, S. K. (1986). *Statistical analysis: An interdisciplinary introduction to univariate and multivariate methods*. New York: Radius.

Keppel, G. (1991). *Design and analysis: A researcher's handbook* (3rd ed.). Englewood Cliffs, NJ: Prentice Hall.

Kerlinger, F. N. (1985). *Foundations of behavioral research* (3rd ed.). New York: Holt, Rinehart & Winston.

Kirk, R. E. (1994). *Experimental design: Procedures for the behavioral sciences* (3rd ed.). Belmont, CA: Brooks/Cole.

Kish, L. (1965). *Survey sampling*. New York: John Wiley.

Leamer, E. E. (1983). Let's take the con out of econometrics. In C. W. J. Granger (Ed.), *Modeling economic series: Advanced texts in econometrics* (pp. 29-50). New York: Oxford University Press.

Lenth, R. V. (1987). POWERPACK: A microcomputer package for power and sample size problems [computer program]. *American Statistician, 41*, 239-240.

Maddala, G. S. (1983). *Limited-dependent and qualitative variables in econometrics*. New York: Oxford University Press.

Mehta, C. R., & Patel, N. R. (1995). *SPSS Exact Tests 6.1 for Windows*. Chicago: SPSS.

Morrison, D. F. (1976). *Multivariate statistical methods*. New York: McGraw-Hill.

Nunnally, J., & Bernstein, I. (1993). *Psychometric theory* (3rd ed.). New York: McGraw-Hill.

Pedhazur, E. (1982). *Multiple regression in behavioral research* (2nd ed.). New York: Holt, Rinehart & Winston.

Pedhazur, E. J., & Schmelkin, L. P. (1991). *Measurement, design, and analysis: An integrated approach* (student ed.). Hillsdale, NJ: Lawrence Erlbaum.

Rummel, R. J. (1970). *Applied factor analysis*. Evanston, IL: Northwestern University Press.

SAS Institute, Inc. (1990). *SAS/STAT user's guide* (2 vols., Ver. 6). Cary, NC: Author.

Siegel, S., & Castellan, N. J., Jr. (1988). *Nonparametric statistics for the behavioral sciences* (2nd ed.). New York: McGraw-Hill.

Snedecor, G. W., & Cochran, W. G. (1980). *Statistical methods* (7th ed.). Ames: Iowa State University Press.

SPSS Inc. (1989). *SPSS algorithms* (2nd ed.). Chicago: Author.

SPSS Inc. (1990). *SPSS reference*. Chicago: Author.

Tabachnick, B. G., & Fidell, L. S. (1989). *Using multivariate statistics* (2nd ed.). New York: Harper & Row.

Tatsuoka, M. M. (1988). *Multivariate analysis: Techniques for educational and psychological research* (2nd ed.). New York: Macmillan.

Winer, B. J., Brown, D. R., & Michels, K. M. (1991). *Statistical principles of experimental design* (3rd ed.). New York: McGraw-Hill.

Chapter 16

Basic Statistical Analysis

DAVID N. DICKTER
MARY ROZNOWSKI

Generally, it is impossible to sample an entire population for a study. Psychologists obtain data from a sample instead and make conclusions about the population based on these data. However, it is always possible that the study's results were a fluke, and it is incumbent on the researcher to provide statistical evidence to the contrary, showing that it is unlikely that the effects reported in the study could have occurred solely by chance. Thus statistical analysis is indispensable in psychological research.

Basic statistical analysis is a broad topic whose thorough explanation requires more space than is available in this chapter. Therefore this chapter unabashedly takes a cookbook approach to statistical analysis, providing procedural suggestions and encouraging the reader to explore the topic further in additional sources. For more information about the statistical theory behind the methods described here, readers should consult texts such as Hays (1991), Lehman (1995), or Runyon and Haber (1991). This chapter gives readers a good start at data analysis and covers several inferential statistics that psychologists use, from t tests and analysis of variance (ANOVA) to correlations and regression. In addition, the chapter addresses the use of chi-square analysis for frequency data. All of the approaches to analysis discussed will be univariate; the analysis of multiple dependent variables is covered in other chapters in this volume.

Getting Started

Before conducting any analyses, researchers will need to prepare their data files and to select a statistical package. The two most frequently used statistical packages are SAS and SPSS. The packages use similar logic, and user-friendly Windows versions are available for both. However, researchers will need to refer to the manuals for many analyses, and the manuals for SPSS are easier for the beginner to understand than those for SAS. It is often difficult to pick up a SAS manual and find out how to do an analysis without first knowing the name of the procedure, which may not be what one would expect. For instance, the name for the main regression procedure in SAS is PROC GLM, for *general linear model,* rather than REGRESSION. On the other hand, as Levy and Steelman point out (Chapter 17 of this volume), SAS offers flexible procedures for data manipulation, such as combining data sets. For a good reference on basic statistical analysis using SAS, see the handbook *SAS System for Elementary Statistical Analysis* (SAS Institute, Inc., 1987). Kinnear and Gray (1994) have written a good reference on SPSS for Windows.

If the data are on paper, then the researcher will need to enter them into a computer file (preferably with the help of one or more assistants). Some statistical packages can assist in data entry, but many do not. A data file is simply a collection of numbers; researchers can create the file using a word processor or text editor. Typically, each subject in the data file has one or more rows of data, beginning with a subject number and followed by that subject's scores on each variable. Categorical data are often given codes to save space. For instance, the first two lines of the data file might look like this:

001 2 27 4 2 3 5 3 7 2 3 3 5 7 6 3 3 4 2 5 1

002 1 23 7 4 5 5 2 3 1 5 4 5 6 5 4 4 4 3 2 3

The experimenter should keep a list of the values represented by the codes, called a *codebook.* In this example, the first three characters are the subject number. The second entry indicates sex (1 = female, 2 = male), the third entry is age, and the remaining numbers are responses to a questionnaire that uses a Likert rating scale that ranges from 1 to 7.

There are several things one should be sure to do, or to avoid, when creating a data file. Do not enter subjects' data in columns; statistical packages will expect rows, and transposing rows and columns is a difficult and unnecessary complication to data preparation. If there are missing data, indicate them in the file with some code, such as "999" for SPSS or "." (a period) for SAS. For researchers who are new to data entry, it is inadvisable to leave a blank space when there are missing data because the computer will ignore the blank (unless one informs it otherwise) and will mistake the next number down the line for the missing one. As a result, the computer will be one column off after that point, like a student taking a standardized exam who forgets to fill in a bubble for one question and thus answers the rest of the items incorrectly. If one uses a word processor to create the file, one should be sure to save it as "text only" (also known as "ASCII" or DOS text). Otherwise, the file will contain extraneous icons that are invisible on screen but cause statistical packages to reject the data file.

Once the researcher has created the data file, he or she will need to use a statistical package to tell the computer what the numbers in the files mean (i.e., assign variable names to the numbers) before running the analyses. This data preparation is referred to as the "data step" or "input step" in SAS and as "creating an input file" in SPSS. This stage involves stating a command that specifies where each of the data points is located. If any of the variables have been entered without spaces in between (e.g., if Subject 001's data reads "0012274235372335576334251"), then it will be necessary to specify a "fixed" format, indicating which variable is found in which column. Alternatively, if one uses the format given in the earlier example, "free" format, this is not necessary. For more advanced users, SPSS and SAS permit a variety of more complex data structures; the manuals provide adequate guidance for writing the appropriate data preparation commands.

Descriptive Statistics

Once the commands for reading in the data file are written, one should make sure that there are no data entry mistakes and that any inappropriate values have been changed (e.g., using the program or a word processor to recode variable values; see Chapter 13 of this volume, by Dollinger & DiLalla, on cleaning the data). One can use descriptive statistics for this purpose. More important, however, one should use descriptive statistics to summarize the data and to check statistical assumptions.

Means and standard deviations provide important information about representative scores and the amount of variation in the data, respectively. In addition, the researcher can use descriptive statistics and graphics to check for several potentially problematic characteristics of the data set. These include non-normality—a distribution of scores that departs substantially from a bell-shaped curve—and outliers, scores that are highly discrepant from most other scores. A good starting point is a data plot, such as a stem-and-leaf plot or a normal-plot, graphically depicting the distribution of scores in the sample. The former illustrates the frequency distribution and identifies outliers, and the latter is a graph that is a straight line when the data are normally distributed but becomes curved when there is non-normality. Skewness and kurtosis provide further information about the shape of the data, indicating whether values are clustered in particular patterns that may depart from normality. A skewed distribution is asymmetric, with higher frequencies on one side and a long "tail" of low frequencies on the other, and a kurtotic distribution has a high peak and long tails on both sides. Most statistical packages provide simple commands that yield information about a variety of characteristics of the data set (e.g., the descriptive procedure in SPSS and UNIVARIATE procedure in SAS).

Inferential Statistics

It is informative to plot the data and to use other descriptive statistics to get a good sense of what the data distribution looks like. This alone will seldom lead to a publication, however, and the demands of a research assistantship rarely end with descriptive statistics. Researchers need to make *inferences* about the population from which the sample was drawn. This chapter addresses several types of inferential statistics. First, however, a discussion of statistical significance testing is in order.

THE SIGNIFICANCE TEST

This chapter discusses each type of statistical analysis in a consistent format. First, the purpose and underlying assumptions of each test are covered, followed by a brief discussion of one or more statistics calculated for each test and how the statistics are used to decide whether to reject the null hypothesis. Before discussing basic analysis, we wish to devote some space to several important issues about significance tests, as outlined by Cohen (1990, 1994) and others.

Statistical significance tests begin with the supposition that the null hypothesis is true (e.g., that there is no treatment effect, or that the difference between two sample population means is zero) and asks how likely it would be for the observed data to result, given the truth of this supposition. If assuming that the null hypothesis is true makes the results seem unlikely (customarily, less than a 5% p value, or probability of occurring), then the researcher rejects the null hypothesis and concludes that there is support for the alternative, that a treatment effect exists. This notion is simple enough, but unfortunately it is subject to serious misinterpretations. Cohen (1994) pointed out two misconceptions that researchers exhibit about hypothesis testing and p values that should be mentioned here. One misconception is that the p of .05 is the "probability that the null hypothesis is true" and that its complement, .95, indicates the chance that the research hypothesis is "true." On the contrary, the 5% probability refers to the likelihood of obtaining the observed *results* if the null hypothesis is true and does not provide proof of the "truth" or falsity of the null hypothesis or research hypothesis. A second misconception outlined by Cohen (1994) and termed the "replication fallacy" by Rosenthal (1993) is that if a study with results that were significant at $p < .05$ were replicated numerous times, researchers would find a significant result most of the time (in particular, 95%). Unfortunately, the p value says nothing about the chance of replicating the results. Instead, the level of power typical in a given literature provides a better estimate of the likelihood of finding an effect, if there is one to find (see Cohen, 1988; Levy & Steelman, Chapter 17 of this volume).

Cohen (1990, 1994) and others have also emphasized the importance of extending research beyond the significant/nonsignificant dichotomy that characterizes much of the literature in psychology. First, it is important not to limit all research to studies whose results will hinge on a significance test. Valuable contributions to theory should not be hindered by the pervading acceptance of the $p < .05$ requirement. Strict adherence to the .05 value makes an arbitrary cut-off that categorizes potentially important findings as nonsignificant, and therefore nonfindings. In numerous publications, Cohen and other methodologists have argued that researchers should pay attention not just to whether a result is significant but to the size of the effect. Cohen (1994) bemoaned the small effect sizes in many studies. Other researchers (e.g., Schmidt, 1992; Hunter & Schmidt, 1991) have focused on this issue in their work on meta-analysis, a statistical method that involves aggregating the results of multiple studies and calculating an overall effect size. Researchers must bear in mind that statistical significance and effect size are distinct (Rosenthal, 1993). Results that are significant at $p < .05$ are not necessarily "large"; similarly, researchers should avoid the temptation to proclaim that an effect that is significant at a smaller probability (e.g., $p < .001$) is "very large" (Cohen, 1994).

When a significance test is reported, it is most informative to report the confidence interval, which shows the range of values for which the null hypothesis would be retained. A large range may indicate sampling error, such as an inadequate sample size or poor variability in scores, and indicates that it would be difficult to reject the null hypothesis even if it were false (i.e., that there is a substantial "Type II" error).

In summary, researchers can obtain important information about their data by doing more than simply conducting an hypothesis test. Moreover, by being aware of common misconceptions and misstatements about hypothesis tests, they can avoid common pitfalls in their conclusions.

FORMAT OF STATISTICAL TESTS

Statistical tests follow a consistent sequence. A statistical indicator is calculated from the study results and is used to test the null hypothesis that there is no treatment effect. This "test statistic" must meet or exceed some threshold value, known as a "critical" value, ideally determined prior to the study. The critical value is a number taken from a table of statistical distributions. Its magnitude depends on the sample size, the value of p the researcher chooses, and possibly other characteristics as well. The p value is selected depending on the experimenter's tolerance of Type I error, the probability that the observed data will lead the researcher to reject the null hypothesis falsely. If the statistic is equal to or exceeds the critical value, then the researcher rejects the null hypothesis, concluding that there is a treatment effect.

t Tests

One elementary statistical test with several variants is the analysis of the difference between means. This section will focus on the two-sample t test. Suppose that a graduate student collects test scores for a treatment group and a control group. A good way to compare the groups is to find the average test score for each group and to judge whether they are significantly different. Suppose that on a 40-point scale, the treatment group has a score of 20 and the control group has a score of 25. Is this a trivial difference that probably occurred by chance, or is there a treatment effect? Another way of stating this question is, "Do the two sample means come from the same population distribution or two different ones?" By conducting a t test, we can answer this question, judging whether there is a significant difference between these scores. The answer will depend not only on the size of the effect but on the sample size and level of tolerance for Type I error (the "alpha" level).

The t test assumes certain things about the data that researchers should verify before conducting the test. First, do the data in each group follow a normal distribution? If the sample is small, the test may be incorrect because the test statistic calculated from the data may not have the normal distribution that is assumed for the statistical test. However, if the sample size is moderate or large (e.g., 40 to 100 or more), the distribution of the test should closely approximate a normal distribution, and the test will be accurate (Hays, 1991). Second, the t test assumes that the variance for the two groups is about the same. Researchers should check this "homogeneity of variance" assumption. This assumption is more important and can lead to inaccurate results, particularly for small groups with unequal sample sizes. Third, observations are assumed to be independent, such that one subject does not influence another subject's score (e.g., copying a test answer). Researchers should check to be sure that these assumptions are met when conducting a t test.

The t test uses a statistic calculated from the sample means divided by a variance estimate. This obtained t statistic is compared to the critical value obtained from a probability table at the selected p value (usually .05, but possibly .01 or .001). If the t statistic is equal to or exceeds the critical value, then the difference between the group means is significant at the chosen level of alpha. Note that the significance test can be "one-sided" or "two-sided" (also called "one-tailed" or "two-tailed," respectively). The former is used when the mean for a particular group is hypothesized to be higher than the mean for the other group. The latter is used when the means are expected to be different but there is no a priori hypothesis that a particular mean will be higher. For the two-sided test, the alpha level (and therefore the p value) is halved to guard against the increase in Type I error that would accompany such a general hypothesis. As a result, a larger t statistic is necessary if the null hypothesis is to be rejected.

A similar type of t test is the paired-differences test. For instance, suppose that a researcher wants to compare the job performance of a group of employees who receive a 1-week job training course with the performance of a control group that receives no training. The performance of each employee is rated prior to training and several weeks later. For this test, it is assumed that each pair (pre/post) of observations is independent from other pairs. To examine whether the performance ratings of the treatment group improve more than those of the control group, the researcher may perform a one-sided t test on the means of the pre/post difference scores for the two groups.

Analysis of Variance (ANOVA)

The t test is useful for determining whether two means are significantly different. However, there is a Type I error associated with each test that increases as the number of group means being compared increases. For instance, if a researcher conducts five t tests and permits the usual .05 Type I error on each, the error rate will be $1 - .95^5$, or nearly a 23% chance of falsely rejecting the null hypothesis. An alternative to conducting multiple t tests when there are more than a few groups is ANOVA. Like the t test, ANOVA involves a comparison of group means. Unlike the t test, however, there need be no limitation on the number of group comparisons a researcher may make. (Of course, group comparisons should be made on the basis of theoretical predictions rather than by random fishing for differences among the groups.) Researchers use ANOVA to examine the variability of scores within and between groups. Subjects' scores within the same group will vary due to individual differences and random error. If there is a treatment effect, however, there will be more variance between groups than within groups. When there are only two groups, using ANOVA and a t test will produce identical results.

As with the t test, ANOVA assumes that observations are independent, the data are normal, and group variances are equal. A violation of the homogeneity-of-variance assumption can undermine the results, particularly when group sample sizes are unequal. Therefore one should be especially vigilant in spotting this violation.

The first step in conducting an ANOVA is to determine whether any group mean is significantly different from any other group mean. This is called an overall F test. If there are no differences (i.e., if the F test is not significant), then there is no point in comparing any of the two groups. The results have indicated that the researcher should retain the null hypothesis that all group means are equal. On the other hand, if the overall F is significant, the researcher may then make "post hoc" comparisons between group means. A significant F indicates that at least one group mean is significantly different from one other group mean. The researcher should then investigate his or her hypotheses about the groups. For instance, the researcher might have hypothesized that the mean of Group A is significantly different from the means of Groups B, C, and D, or that the means of Groups A and B are significantly different from the means of Groups C and D. It is important to emphasize that these statistical tests must be based on the study hypotheses (e.g., that Groups A and B will have higher exam scores than Groups C and D because Groups A and B received a new type of tutoring and Groups C and D did not). Clearly, the tests must *not* be conducted after looking at all of the group means, taking note of the ones that differ markedly, and conducting statistical comparisons between these groups to "find" a significant result. Researchers must decide on meaningful group comparisons *before* they see the data, rather than hypothesizing after viewing the results and claiming that the results are what they predicted all along.

Researchers can use a variety of statistical tests to compare group means after finding a significant overall *F*. With each test, the researcher runs some risk of making a Type I error. This is least likely for the Tukey and Scheffe tests and more likely with the Fisher and Newman-Keuls tests. With the Tukey and Scheffe tests, however, the reduction of Type I error comes at some expense: increased Type II error, failing to find a treatment effect that is present. Nevertheless, the Tukey test is generally the best choice (Keppel, 1991).

Conducting ANOVA can involve higher levels of complexity. The reader should consult additional sources (e.g., Keppel, 1991) to find out more about when it is appropriate to conduct various kinds of ANOVA. Factorial ANOVA, which includes two or more independent variables, may involve interaction effects. An interaction occurs when the effect of an independent variable on the dependent variable depends on the level of another independent variable. For instance, if students in an experiment who set high goals for themselves can solve more physics problems than students who set low goals, but this difference is observed only for individuals with high cognitive ability, then there is a goal-setting × ability interaction. An interaction indicates that one cannot generalize about physics problem solving that occurs when high and low goal levels are set, for instance, without specifying whether the students have high cognitive ability. The "main" effects of goal level and ability depend on the category of the other variable to which the students belong.

Due to the brevity of this chapter, the reader is urged to consult additional sources of information about ANOVA (and, for that matter, about all of the analyses described in this chapter.) In particular, ANOVA permits analysis of repeated-measures designs, in which subjects receive more than one treatment and effects within a group of subjects are examined. Keppel's (1991) handbook provides a wealth of information on the use of ANOVA for repeated measures and other experimental designs.

Correlations

Before discussing regression, it will be useful to devote some attention to correlations. A correlation is an association between two variables that takes on a value between +1.0 and −1.0. If two variables are positively correlated, then as one increases, the other increases. If they are negatively correlated, then as one variable increases, the other decreases. If they are not associated at all, the correlation is zero. If each subject's scores on the two variables were plotted as a point on an xy axis (i.e., in a "scatter plot"), a zero correlation would appear as a roughly circular field of points with no clear relationship between x and y. A positive correlation would appear approximately linear and increasing, and a negative correlation would appear approximately linear and decreasing. Correlations can be used to make inferences about the associations between two variables in a population, such as by testing the null hypothesis that two variables are unrelated. When such inferences are made, the data are assumed to be normally distributed.

Although it is customary to test the null hypothesis that the population correlation is 0.0, in practice it is somewhat unusual to see many sample correlations that are 0.0. However, even tiny correlations may be statistically significant because the significance of a correlation depends partly on the sample size. Indeed, given a large sample size, one can expect correlations of .001 between theoretically unrelated variables to achieve significance, a phenomenon contemptuously named the "crud factor" (Meehl, 1990, cited in Cohen, 1994). Psychologists typically attach more importance to correlations that are ±.3 or greater. By squaring the correlation between two variables, A and B, one can find how much of the variance in A can be explained by knowing the value of B (and vice versa). Thus a correlation between A and B of .3 means that A explains 9% of the variance in B.

It is important not to make causal statements about the relation between two variables based solely on the correlation between them. People often fall prey to this mistake, proclaiming, for instance, that an observed decline in SAT scores in the United States was due to an increase in the number of hours American youth spent watching television. Just because association is observed does not mean that there is a *causal* relationship. All that a correlation tells is that there is some association, positive or negative, and not that A causes B or B causes A.

Regression

The idea of "variance accounted for" discussed above is an important concept for regression analysis, as will be discussed shortly. Researchers can use regression to do everything ANOVA does and more. ANOVA analyzes mean differences between groups satisfactorily, but what if instead of discrete groups, there is a continuous variable, such as age? The researcher could divide the sample into two discrete groups, such as those over and under 40 years of age, and compare the two, but to do so would place 5-year-olds in the same category as 37-year-olds. The best thing to do would be not to use 2, 3, 10, or any number of categories but to make use of the continuous nature of the age variable. Regression can do this; ANOVA cannot. Regression typically involves creating a linear equation to predict scores on a dependent variable. The equation represents a line that best fits through a scatter plot of points describing the relationship between the dependent variable and one or more independent variables. The beta weights, or coefficients on the independent variables in the equation, provide information about the relationships between the independent variables and the dependent variable. For instance, the beta weight for a regression equation with one independent variable can be understood as follows: Imagine an xy coordinate axis that plots each subject's score on the independent variable versus his or her score on the dependent variable. If one draws a single line to best fit these data, the slope of that line will be the beta weight and will represent the changes in the value of the dependent variable that are associated with each change of one unit in the independent variable.

Like *t* tests and ANOVA, regression analysis assumes independence, normality, and constant variance. In addition, linear relationships between the independent variables and dependent variable are typically assumed. Researchers may wish to test for nonlinear trends in the data to create a regression equation with a better fit to the data (e.g., see Cohen & Cohen, 1983).

Simple linear regression involves a single independent variable that is used to estimate scores in the dependent variable. Regression is used to determine whether the variance accounted for by the continuous independent variable (e.g., GRE score) in the dependent variable (e.g., first-year grade-point average in graduate school) is significant. To do this, one finds the square of the correlation between them (the R^2) and tests whether it is significantly different from zero. If so, then one can make a statement such as the following: "GRE score accounts for 16% of the variance in first-year grades" (if the R^2 is .16). Thus regression analysis provides some index of the magnitude of the association between the independent and dependent variables. Another way of testing the significance of the independent variable is to perform a t test on the estimated value of its beta weight (also known as its "parameter estimate") to determine if it is significantly different from zero.

Multiple linear regression can be used to determine if the amount of variance that a set of independent variables explains in the dependent variable is significantly different from zero. As with factorial ANOVA, interactions are possible because there is more than one independent variable. In addition, one may also want to ask more complex questions, such as what percentage of *unique* variance an independent variable explains in the dependent variable. That is, what explanatory value does the independent variable add over and above the others? This statistic is known as a *squared semipartial correlation.* Note that entering variables into the regression equation in different orderings produces different results. Readers should consult an additional resource such as Cohen and Cohen (1983) for information about partialing out variance and the use of regression procedures such as forward selection, backward elimination, and stepwise regression to evaluate the predictive contributions of particular variables and sets of variables.

Chi-Square Tests

A different type of study might involve analyzing frequencies to see if they differ across some category. For instance, one might want to study whether males and females hold different opinions about a political issue, such as whether smoking should be banned in restaurants. None of the statistical tests discussed above are appropriate because the data are categorical. Moreover, this type of study examines the shape of the entire frequency distributions for each group (e.g., the proportion of people who answer "always," "sometimes," "never," etc.), rather than some summary statistics, such as means or variances. In this example, chi-square analysis can be used to ask the question "Do men and women hold different opinions on this political issue?" The null hypothesis that there is no difference of opinion will be rejected if the proportion of men who believe that smoking should be banned in restaurants is significantly different from the proportion of women who hold this belief.

As with the other statistical tests, several assumptions are made when conducting a chi-square analysis. One assumption is that the observations are independent. That is, one person's response to the smoking ban question should not be influenced by another respondent's. In addition, observations must fall into mutually exclusive categories (e.g., smoker versus nonsmoker), rather than counting toward more than one frequency tabulation. Finally, the expected frequency for a given category (discussed below) should generally not be lower than 5 (see Hays, 1991).

Chi-square analysis uses observed and expected frequencies to test the null hypothesis. Under the null hypothesis, the same proportion of men and women would be in favor (or against) the smoking ban. The expected frequencies of favorable (or unfavorable) responses for men and women are those that would make these proportions the same. To the extent that the observed (actual) frequencies differ from the expected frequencies, the results provide evidence for rejecting the null hypothesis.

The chi-square test follows the same format as other statistical significance tests: If the chi-square value exceeds a threshold, then the researcher rejects the null hypothesis that the groups are the same. In this case, that would mean that men and women hold different opinions about the smoking ban. Chi-square analysis is particularly useful for survey research, which generally involves frequency data that are not appropriate for the other types of basic analysis discussed in this chapter.

Summary

This Reader's Digest outline of chi-square analysis, t tests, ANOVA, and correlation and regression analysis was intended to answer some questions and to create many more. Certainly, the cookbook approach of this chapter cannot serve as a substitute for formal training from a master chef or for personal experience in the kitchen. Try the approaches described in this chapter, consult the texts cited, and confer with your colleagues, professors, and research supervisors. Mastery of basic statistical analysis is an invaluable skill that you will be able to draw on every day in your research.

Recommended Readings

Readers are urged to examine one or more texts for each of the main statistics topics discussed in this chapter (e.g., Cohen & Cohen, 1983, for correlation/regression; Hays, 1991, for chi-square tests; Keppel, 1991, for ANOVA; and Runyon & Haber, 1991, for t tests). It would be helpful as well to examine a recent text that introduces both statistics and the use of SPSS (e.g., Bryman & Cramer, 1994; Rose & Sullivan, 1993; Stevens, 1990) or SAS (e.g., Stevens, 1990). Naturally, it will be necessary to refer repeatedly to the "basics" manuals published by the statistical package companies (e.g., SAS Institute, Inc., 1993; SPSS, Inc., 1993). Both SAS and SPSS publish numerous manuals for their mainframe and PC packages that can be ordered through a college or university bookstore. Other handbooks may be useful supplements, such as Spector's (1993) guide to the SAS programming language and data manipulation and Kinnear and Gray's (1994) guide to SPSS for Windows.

References

Bryman, A., & Cramer, D. (1994). *Quantitative data analysis for social scientists* (Rev. ed.). London: Routledge.

Cohen, J. (1988). *Statistical power analysis for the behavioral sciences* (2nd ed.). Hillsdale, NJ: Lawrence Erlbaum.

Cohen, J. (1990). Things I have learned (so far). *American Psychologist, 45,* 1304-1312.

Cohen, J. (1994). The earth is round *(p < .05). American Psychologist, 49,* 997-1003.

Cohen, J., & Cohen, P. (1983). *Applied multiple regression/correlation analysis for the behavior sciences* (2nd ed.). Hillsdale, NJ: Lawrence Erlbaum.

Hays, W. L. (1991). *Statistics* (5th ed.). New York: Holt, Rinehart & Winston.

Hunter, J. E., & Schmidt, F. L. (1991). Meta-analysis. In R. K. Hambleton & J. N. Zaal (Eds.), *Advances in educational and psychological testing: Theory and applications* (pp. 157-183). Boston: Kluwer.

Keppel, G. (1991). *Design and analysis: A researcher's handbook* (3rd ed.). Englewood Cliffs, NJ: Prentice Hall.

Kinnear, P. R., & Gray, C. D. (1994). *SPSS for Windows made simple.* Hillsdale, NJ: Lawrence Erlbaum.

Lehman, R. S. (1995). *Statistics in the behavioral sciences: A conceptual introduction.* Pacific Grove, CA: Brooks/Cole.

Rose, D., & Sullivan, O. (1993). *Introducing data analysis for social scientists.* Buckingham, UK: Open University Press.

Rosenthal, R. (1993). Cumulating evidence. In G. Keren & C. Lewis (Eds.), *A handbook for data analysis in the behavioral sciences: Methodological issues* (pp. 519-559). Hillsdale, NJ: Lawrence Erlbaum.

Runyon, R. P., & Haber, A. (1991). *Fundamentals of behavioral statistics* (7th ed.). New York: McGraw-Hill.

SAS Institute, Inc. (1987). *SAS system for elementary statistical analysis.* Cary, NC: Author.

SAS Institute, Inc. (1993). *SAS user's guide: Basics.* Cary, NC: Author.

Schmidt, F. L. (1992). What do data really mean? Research findings, meta-analysis, and cumulative knowledge in psychology. *American Psychologist, 47,* 1173-1181.

Spector, P. E. (1993). *SAS programming for researchers and social scientists.* Newbury Park, CA: Sage.

SPSS, Inc. (1993). *SPSS for Windows: Base system user's guide, release 6.0.* Chicago: Author.

Stevens, J. P. (1990). *Intermediate statistics: A modern approach.* Hillsdale, NJ: Lawrence Erlbaum.

Chapter 17

Using Advanced Statistics

PAUL E. LEVY
LISA A. STEELMAN

One's research question should be the key to determining what statistical analyses will be employed in a particular study. Tabachnick and Fidell (1996) suggested that research questions can be placed into one of four categories. We will use their framework as an heuristic guide to using and understanding advanced statistics. Although we will cover each of these, our focus will be on three of these categories: degree of relationship among variables, mean differences across groups, and structure. We want to be clear, however, that for a given study, researchers may ask questions that fall into any or all of the four categories. This, of course, explains why any one particular study may report results from various statistical analyses. Before pursuing these advanced statistical techniques, we want to begin with a primer on statistical power because this is one of the most important issues in research design and analysis, yet one of the most neglected.

Power

The following overview of the factors involved in power can be supplemented by Cohen's (1988) complete and technical discussion of power or Lipsey's (1990) more general but very readable treatment of the subject. The power of a statistical test is the *probability of rejecting a null hypothesis when it is false*. That is, power is the likelihood of correctly rejecting the null hypothesis of no difference between experimental groups when there is in fact a true population difference.

Four major factors determine the power of a statistical test: (a) the statistical test itself, (b) alpha level, (c) sample size, and (d) effect size. First, in any data-analytic procedure, we want to select the most sensitive statistical test for which the assumptions of that particular test can be met. Different statistical tests have different levels of power when applied to the same data. For example, nonparametric tests (e.g., Mann-Whitney U, Kruskal-Wallis) are generally less powerful than are parametric tests (t test, ANOVA) when the assumptions of the latter are met. Violating the assumptions of a statistical test reduces the power of that test, as well as limiting the reliability of the findings. In addition, testing nondirectional hypotheses (two-tailed) is less powerful than testing directional hypotheses (one-tailed). Thus researchers must choose their statistical tests carefully.

The second determinant of power is alpha level (α). This indicates the percentage of time we are willing to reject mistakenly a true null hypothesis or make a *Type I error. Type II error,* or β, is the probability of failing to reject a false null hypothesis. These two definitions imply a trade-off that is very important to the researcher. Type I error rate is inversely related to Type II error rate. If, for instance, a researcher chooses a very small α such as .001, this will protect him or her from making Type I errors (i.e., he or she is not very likely to reject a true null hypothesis) but will inflate β and increase the likelihood of making a Type II error (i.e., he or she will be more likely to accept a false null hypothesis). By setting α, the researcher decides what kind of ratio is acceptable for his or her research. In behavioral research, we are usually more concerned with Type I errors and therefore keep α very low (i.e., .01 or .05).

Power is directly and inversely related to Type II error and is therefore designated $1 - \beta$. This, of course, means that the power of one's test is also indirectly related to α because α, as we mentioned above, is related to β. In other words, the trade-off we mentioned above directly affects the power of one's test as well. Because power is the probability of rejecting a false null hypothesis, any increase in Type II error rate (i.e., probability of accepting a false null hypothesis) lowers power, whereas increasing Type I error rate increases power. This suggests that small α levels reduce power. One way to increase power is to be willing to accept a larger Type I error rate by increasing the level. The bottom line is that the researcher has to make a well-informed judgment call about the relative importance of each type of error for his or her particular study and then set α accordingly.

Sample size is also a critical factor in determining the power of a statistical test. The larger the sample size, the more likely it is that one's statistical test will be able to detect a real treatment effect. This occurs because larger sample sizes, if drawn appropriately, are more likely to be representative of the population and thus are associated with smaller sampling error. A common misconception is that any increase in sample size provides a corresponding increase in power. Schmidt, Hunter, and Urry (1976) empirically demonstrated that the sample size needed to attain adequate power in validation research is substantially greater than most people believe. Therefore one limitation of using sample size to increase power is that you will often need a substantial increase in sample size to effect the desired increase in power. Further, this substantial increase in sample size is generally costly and time consuming for the researcher.

Finally, power is determined by effect size. The effect size indicates the difference between the treatment and control groups and depends on the means and variances of the two groups. The larger the effect size between the two experimental groups, the greater the power. Effect size is related to experimental design because the more error introduced into the experimental design (e.g., sampling error, measurement error, and the quality of the manipulation itself), the smaller the effect size and therefore the lower the power. Thus the clever experimenter initially designs research to minimize as much extraneous error as possible, thereby improving power through the impact on effect size. Thus it should be clear that power is very complex and that it cannot be adequately conceptualized or controlled by focusing on any single element of the research but must be viewed within the experimental design as a whole.

Because power, α level, sample size, and effect size are all interrelated, the power of a particular experimental design can be useful in many ways. A power analysis can be conducted a priori to determine the appropriate sample size needed to detect a given effect size. One can also conduct a post hoc power analysis to determine how powerful the study was or what minimum effect size could have been detected with a sample of the given size. The reader is referred to Lipsey (1990) for a detailed discussion of power issues and instructions on conducting power analyses. Now we will use the Tabachnick and Fidell (1996) scheme to discuss the various statistical approaches available to answer your research questions.

Degree of Relationship Among Variables

Tabachnick and Fidell's (1996) first category includes research questions dealing with the degree of relationship among variables and suggests the use of some form of correlation or regression. Among the common analyses are bivariate/multiple correlation, regression, and chi-square contingency analysis, which were examined in Chapter 16 of this volume. A useful extension of the basic linear regression approach is *canonical correlation*, which examines the relationship between multiple predictors and multiple criteria. For instance, a researcher might be interested in the relationship between socioeconomic status indicators (e.g., income, job level, occupational prestige, assets) and measures of perceived quality of life (e.g., job satisfaction, family satisfaction, contentment, feelings of generativity). The canonical correlation tells the researcher if there is a statistically significant relationship between the two sets of variables and what the nature of that relationship is. Recall that in bivariate or multiple correlation there is one index of the particular relationship. In the canonical correlation extension, there may be multiple pairs of *canonical variates*, indicating a more complex relationship. Bobko (1990), in his chapter on multivariate correlational analysis, covered canonical correlation in more detail and is a very readable resource. He noted that canonical correlation is actually the grandparent of most of the basic, familiar statistical tools, such as simple and multiple correlation and regression; these are just special cases of canonical correlation. Other useful resources include Stevens (1992) and Tabachnick and Fidell (1996), which provide both a conceptual understanding and the technical details of this analytic tool.

Significance of Group Differences

Most experimental research is interested in the differences on some dependent variables (DVs) among those individuals assigned to different conditions. Group differences are also the focus of a great deal of field research that often involves naturally occurring groups. It should be clear that the significance of group differences is one of the most frequent research questions. Dickter and Roznowski (Chapter 16) discussed some of the basic tests for mean differences, such as *t* tests, one-way ANOVAs and ANCOVAs, and factorial ANOVAs and ANCOVAs. A major focus of the current chapter is the multivariate extensions of these analytic strategies. By *multivariate extensions*, we are referring to studies that are interested in group differences on *multiple dependent variables*.

HOTELLING'S T^2

A developmental psychologist might be interested in comparing 10-year-old and 12-year-old children on multiple measures of cognitive functioning (e.g., an IQ test, a reading ability test, a series of Piagetian tasks, practical knowledge). These data could be analyzed by using Hotelling's T^2, which is the multivariate analogue of a *t* test. Hotelling's T^2 tells the researcher whether the two groups differ on the DVs combined. These data could be analyzed by four separate *t* tests, but the problem of *experimentwise error rate* would strongly suggest that this approach not be used. The error rate problem is simply that multiple tests inflate the Type I error rate. Further, these DVs are likely to be related, and this exacerbates the Type I error rate problem. In other words, even if the individual differences (i.e., the separate *t* tests) were tested with an $\alpha = .05$, the experimentwise error rate as a result of the multiple tests might be .20 (see Keppel, 1991, for a detailed discussion of this issue). The researcher might think that his or her α level was .05, but it would really have been inflated to .20. Hotelling's T^2 avoids this problem by doing only one *t* test on the combined DVs.

ONE-WAY MANOVA

An industrial/organizational psychologist might be interested in how different leadership styles (transformational, transactional, or authoritarian) might influence multiple measures of performance (absence rates, coworker ratings of employee performance, quantity/quality of output). Because we have three groups in this example rather than two, Hotelling's T^2 is inappropriate. In a univariate analysis, these data would be analyzed using ANOVA (rather than *t* tests), but with multiple DVs the analogue would be MANOVA (multivariate analysis of variance). In particular, if we were interested only in the effect of leadership style on quality of performance, knowledge from Chapter 16 of this volume would lead one to use a one-way ANOVA. Because we have multiple DVs, the analysis of choice here would probably be a one-way MANOVA.

MANOVA examines differences between two or more groups on two or more DVs combined. In the previous example, we noted the problem of doing multiple *t* tests and inflating our Type I error rate; the same problem would arise if we chose to do an ANOVA on each DV. Rather than taking this approach, the astute researcher would avoid the problem of inflated Type I error rates and choose the more appropriate analytic strategy— MANOVA. There are other benefits of this approach. First, using multiple measures increases the scope of a research project (Spector, 1977) and allows the researcher to look at the set of measures as they represent an underlying construct such as, in our example, performance (Bray & Maxwell, 1982). Second, using multiple measures allows the researcher to examine the relationships among the DVs and to determine how the independent variable relates differentially to those DVs.

A great variety of statistics texts and quantitative journal articles provide thorough treatments of the MANOVA techniques (see Bray & Maxwell, 1982, 1985; Spector, 1977;

Stevens, 1992; Tabachnick & Fidell, 1996). Although our discussion will borrow from these four sources in particular, we will avoid the statistical and computational issues where possible and focus instead on the conceptual issues. MANOVA is a two-step process. The first step is often called the *omnibus test*, meaning that it focuses on testing whether, overall, there are differences between groups on the combined DVs. This is analogous to the overall F test in ANOVA. In our example, the omnibus test tells us whether leadership style has an effect on performance. Of course, an answer in the affirmative to this question (i.e., we reject the null hypothesis of no difference) provides only a partial answer to the researcher. Usually, we want to know where those differences lie. This simple question—where the differences lie—is typically the focus of the analytic approach as well as the real crux of the researcher's interest. Therefore the second step in the process is to conduct follow-up tests to examine these differences.

After finding a significant MANOVA result, the researcher can examine where the differences lie in a number of ways. The reader is referred to the sources listed earlier for a more thorough discussion of the advantages, disadvantages, and procedures involved in these various approaches. We will spend some time here focusing on the two most prevalent approaches in the published literature. Perhaps the most frequent approach used by researchers is to follow up significant MANOVA with univariate ANOVAs. For instance, we could conduct four separate ANOVAs to reveal the DVs on which the groups differ. Perhaps the multivariate effect identified by the MANOVA is driven by group differences on absence rates and performance quantity only. This would be revealed by significant ANOVAs on these two DVs and nonsignificant ANOVAs on the other two DVs. Of course, the ANOVA tells us on what variables the groups differ, but it does not tell us which groups differ on these variables. If we had only two groups, this would not be an issue, because the differences could be only between those two groups. But because we have three groups, the researcher must further explore these differences with one of the available post hoc tests (see Keppel, 1991, for a comprehensive discussion of these tests) to determine which groups (1 vs. 2, 1 vs. 3, and 2 vs. 3) differ on absence rates, for example. Spector (1977) argued that the major advantage of using the ANOVA follow-up procedure is in hypothesis testing. Consistent with our approach emphasizing the use of one's research question to determine the appropriate statistical analysis, Spector (1977) suggested that researchers' choice of follow-up tests to a significant MANOVA should be based on their research questions. If the question has to do with testing hypotheses or theory regarding on which DVs the experimental groups differ, univariate ANOVA is the best approach.

A second common approach to following up MANOVAs is to use discriminant analysis (DA), which specifies a linear combination of the DVs that maximizes the separation between groups (Spector, 1977). Mathematically, it is helpful to conceive of DA as a special type of regression, with group membership being the criterion variable. In this way, DA tells the researcher how well the data predict group membership. In our leadership example, we could examine how well the performance measures predict which leadership style individuals experienced. The discriminant coefficients are analogous to regression weights and reveal the relative contributions of the DVs to the maximum differentiating function. Spector (1977) suggested that using DA as a follow-up is appropriate if the researcher is interested in prediction and classification. Let us assume that our MANOVA was significant and therefore that we concluded that leadership style affects performance.

If we were interested in determining which DVs or what linear combination of the DVs differentiated among group members best, then DA would be a logical approach to answering this question. Tabachnick and Fidell (1996) considered DA to be the main analytic strategy for their third category of research questions, which relate to the prediction of group membership. Although in this chapter we are viewing DA as a follow-up tool to MANOVA, we want to emphasize that DA is a major analytic tool that stands alone. The interested reader should see Tabachnick and Fidell (1996).

A MANOVA EXAMPLE

Of course, a particular research project may be best served by using univariate ANOVA and DA as follow-ups to a significant MANOVA, depending on the research questions. We will present one example from the applied psychology literature to illustrate this approach. Abelson (1987) was interested in determining what variables could predict employee termination—turnover. He argued that individuals might leave for various reasons that can be categorized in at least two ways. First, there are those who leave for reasons that the organization could not control (e.g., spouse gets another job in another location)—*unavoidable leavers.* Second, there are those who leave for reasons that the organization could control (e.g., employee finds a new job with better working conditions and better pay)—*avoidable leavers.* Finally, there are those individuals who do not leave—*stayers.* Abelson's thesis was that stayers would be very much like unavoidable leavers and that these two groups would differ significantly from the avoidable leavers. The rationale was that neither stayers nor unavoidable leavers really wanted to leave their job and certainly would not leave because of anything about the organization. The avoidable leavers, however, were motivated by different issues to leave the organization.

Abelson (1987) conducted a study in an organization using nursing personnel. Among the variables of interest were age, marital status, job satisfaction, organizational commitment, job tension, and perceptions of leaders' sensitivity. The MANOVA revealed a significant effect indicating that, as expected, the groups differed on the combined DV. Univariate ANOVAs were reconducted to examine where the differences lay—in other words, on what variables the groups differed. The univariates were significant for about half of the variables, including job satisfaction and organizational commitment. This indicates that the groups differ on these variables, but we do not know at this point which groups differ. The prediction was that unavoidable leavers would be similar to stayers and these two groups would differ from avoidable leavers. Post hoc tests were used to uncover which groups differed. As predicted, for both job satisfaction and organizational commitment (as well as other variables), unavoidable leavers and stayers did not differ from each other, but both differed significantly from avoidable leavers, who were less satisfied and committed.

In addition to employing the univariate ANOVA approach, Abelson (1987) also employed DA to follow up the significant MANOVA in an attempt to "determine which of the variables best predict(s) membership in the stayers, unavoidable leavers, and avoidable leavers groups" (p. 383). The DA revealed that six of the variables were the best discriminators among the groups and that the analysis discriminated avoidable leavers from both stayers and unavoidable leavers. The DA had a hit rate of 80%; this means that the discriminant function (i.e., individuals' scores on the significant variables) classified 80% of the subjects into their correct groups. The results of the MANOVA, univariate ANOVAs, post hoc tests, and DA supported the a priori predictions.

OTHER EXTENSIONS

We should point out that we have really only opened the door slightly to the world of analyses with multiple DVs. As with ANOVA, MANOVA can be extended to factorial designs with multiple independent variables. Similarly, MANCOVA is the multivariate analogue of ANCOVA and looks at the effect of an independent variable(s) on multiple DVs while controlling for other variables that are predicted to be related to the DVs. For instance, in our leadership example, tenure working for a particular leader could have served as a covariate in our one-way MANOVA design, turning it into a one-way MANCOVA. Keep in mind that the primary objective of covariate designs is to reduce the error term by controlling for the relationship between the covariate and the DV (see Pedhazur & Schmelkin, 1991, for more discussion on the use and misuse of covariate analyses).

Structure

The last of Tabachnick and Fidell's (1996) categories comprises research questions that concern themselves with the latent structure underlying a set of variables. Common analytic tools include *principal components analysis* and *factor analysis*. These approaches are often used for variable reduction purposes or to determine an underlying latent structure that defines the multiple variables. For instance, principal components analysis may be used to reduce subjects' responses to 100 items tapping what they dislike about their jobs into a more workable number of dimensions, such as those dislikes related to their supervisor, the work environment, their coworkers, what they do on their job, and pay/benefits. These five dependent variable composites can then be used in various analyses in a much more useful and manageable way than the 100 original variables. Factor analysis may be used to examine whether a researcher's 10-item scale designed to measure one construct, let us say self-esteem, really measures one construct or more than one. In other words, factor analysis might be used to demonstrate the validity of a particular scale as well as the extent to which a particular construct is uni- or multidimensional.

Path analysis is an extension of multiple regression that also deals with the structure of one's data. Path analysis is useful when researchers want to analyze certain causal structures among variables. For instance, Levy (1993) used path analysis to examine an a priori model that predicted relationships among self-esteem, locus of control, self-assessment, and attributions. The analysis is a straightforward extension of multiple regression with a few extra considerations. The reader is referred to Pedhazur (1982, chap. 15) and James, Mulaik, and Brett (1982) for detailed discussions of the analysis. In general, each DV is regressed on every independent variable that is predicted to affect it. For instance, Levy (1993) predicted that self-assessment would be affected by self-esteem and locus of control and that attributions would be affected by self-assessment and locus of control. One multiple regression was conducted for each of these DVs. The resulting regression weights indicate the strength and direction of the relationships among the hypothesized variables. The predicted model can be examined for fit by recomputing the correlations among the variables and by using Q, a conventional fit index (see Pedhazur, 1982). If the model seems to fit the data well, the researcher can conclude that the data are consistent with the a priori causal model. Please note that this is not the same as saying that the path analysis *proves* causality (see Bobko, 1990). This latter statement cannot be made with any degree of certainty.

One of the fastest growing analytic strategies in the social sciences is *structural equation modeling* (SEM). Pedhazur (1982, chap. 16), in his excellent introduction to SEM, referred to this as a generic term for the various approaches to the analysis of causality (note that path analysis is one of these approaches). He also noted that more powerful approaches than path analysis, such as LISREL, have been developed and that these approaches are based on less restrictive assumptions. LISREL stands for "linear structural relations" and was developed by Jöreskog in the 1970s (see Jöreskog & Sörbom, 1993, for the most recent version of the statistical program and accompanying discussion). It is based on maximum-likelihood statistical theory rather than the more typical least-squares statistical theory, which is the foundation for simple and multiple regression, covered in a previous chapter. Obviously, structural equation modeling (of which LISREL is one approach) is very complex, and we certainly cannot begin to explain it here. In addition to Pedhazur (1982) and Jöreskog and Sörbom (1993), for other good discussions of the general approach, the reader is directed to Bobko (1990), Long (1983), and Pedhazur and Schmelkin (1991, chap. 24).

Bobko (1990) provided one of the better summaries of LISREL when he noted that LISREL is a general combination and extension of path analysis (the structural aspect) and confirmatory factor analysis (the measurement aspect). In fact, in a frequently cited paper, Anderson and Gerbing (1988) suggested that LISREL analyses proceed via a two-step process. The first step relates to factor analysis and is commonly referred to as testing the *measurement model*. After determining the latent constructs, the second step deals with the structural aspect, as in path analysis, and is referred to as testing the *structural model*. LISREL models deal with *latent variables*, or hypothetical constructs, and *manifest variables*, or indicators of the hypothetical constructs. For instance, an educational psychologist may be interested in the relationships among the following latent variables: socioeconomic background, academic achievement, and career success. Let us assume that socioeconomic background is measured by family income during formative years, per-pupil expenditure in elementary school district, and occupational prestige of parents. Academic achievement could be measured by highest level of schooling completed, grade point average, honors/awards, and rank in school. Finally, career success could be measured by income, occupational prestige, job level within organization, and peer ratings of individual's success. All of these specific measures represent indicators of the construct of interest. The extent to which these measures do represent the hypothesized constructs in the way predicted is a test of the measurement model. The structural part of the analysis tests whether the latent variables (as measured by the manifest variables) are related in the way predicted by the researcher. For instance, we might predict that socioeconomic background would be causally related to academic achievement and that both of these variables would have direct effects on career success.

In summary, LISREL estimates the loadings of each indicator on its respective latent variable to provide information about the measurement model. In other words, are these good measures of each construct? If not, then the measurement model requires more work before testing the structural model. If the data indicate support for the measurement model, then the researcher proceeds to examine the structural model. LISREL then tests for the causal relations among the latent variables. Both the measurement model and the structural model should be tested for goodness of fit, using one or more of the many fit indices available. Again, this is a thumbnail sketch of this very complex and potentially useful procedure.

Conclusion

We would like to close with a little information about the common statistical programs available to "run" these and other statistical analyses. Although our statistical analyses have become more complex, students can rejoice in the knowledge that our statistical computer programs have become more user-friendly. The days of factor analyses by hand are long gone and have been efficiently replaced by a handful of mainframe-based computer applications and a plethora of PC-based packages. We will just briefly mention the most commonly used computer programs in this final section of the chapter.

First, there are generally three well-known mainframe computer applications: SPSS, SAS, and BMDP. SAS and SPSS are more commonly used in the social and behavioral sciences. Our experience is that SAS is much better for the management of large data sets (such as combining data sets or moving data around) but that for the actual statistical analyses discussed in this chapter and the previous one they are both excellent programs. Each of these is very comprehensive, and you will probably find that both of them (and perhaps BMDP) are available at your university. You should check with the computer support staff at your university to get more information on the applications available.

The newer approach to data analysis is through the PC environment. Some programs, such as SYSTAT and MYSTAT, are designed to run in the PC environment. These will do much of what you need expediently. More recently, however, SAS and SPSS have developed PC versions of their mainframe applications. These are advertised to do everything the mainframe applications do, but on your very own PC (provided, of course, that you buy the SAS or SPSS software). Experts believe that these programs will revolutionize data analysis and may make the mainframe applications obsolete. Many universities have purchased site licenses for these products and have made them available to faculty and students by loading them onto the computers in the various labs on campus. Our experience is that these programs are designed to be more user-friendly than the mainframe-based applications, which involve more "computer programming." The PC-based programs are more in line with the computer industry's movement toward "point-and-click" applications. Whether you choose mainframe applications or PC programs for your analysis, the analysis of data is one of the most important aspects of the design and conduct of behavioral research. More information on SPSS software can be obtained by calling (312) 329-3500 and on SAS software by calling (919) 677-8000.

Recommended Readings

We hope that this chapter provides an overview of some of the common advanced statistical techniques used in the analysis of data as well as some suggestions as to where to go next for more useful information. Our discussion is certainly not exhaustive either with respect to the different approaches available or with respect to the statistical and conceptual details associated with the procedures covered. Throughout the text, we have referred the reader to other sources, some of which are advanced technical discussions and others of which are more basic introductory discussions focusing on conceptual under-standing. Some excellent sources to begin with are Grimm and Yarnold (1995), Pedhazur and Schmelkin (1991), Stevens (1992), and Tabachnick and Fidell (1996). These references, again, are not exhaustive but should be an excellent way for students to take the next step to familiarize themselves with these various techniques.

References

Abelson, M. A. (1987). Examination of avoidable and unavoidable turnover. *Journal of Applied Psychology, 72,* 382-386.

Anderson, J., & Gerbing, D. (1988). Structural equation modeling in practice: A review and recommended two-step practice. *Psychological Bulletin, 103,* 411-423.

Bobko, P. (1990). Multivariate correlational analysis. In M. D. Dunnette & L. M. Hough (Eds.), *Handbook of industrial and organizational psychology* (Vol. 1, pp. 637-686). Palo Alto, CA: Consulting Psychologists Press.

Bray, J. H., & Maxwell, S. E. (1982). Analyzing and interpreting significant MANOVAs. *Review of Educational Research, 52,* 340-367.

Bray, J. H., & Maxwell, S. E. (1985). *Multivariate analysis of variance.* Beverly Hills, CA: Sage.

Cohen, J. (1988). *Statistical power analysis for the behavioral sciences* (2nd ed.). Hillsdale, NJ: Lawrence Erlbaum.

Grimm, L. G., & Yarnold, P. R. (1995). *Reading and understanding multivariate statistics.* Washington, DC: American Psychological Association.

James, L. R., Mulaik, S. A., & Brett, J. M. (1982). *Causal analysis: Assumptions, models, and data.* Beverly Hills, CA: Sage.

Jöreskog, K., & Sörbom, D. (1993). *LISREL 8: Structural equation modeling with the SIMPLIS command language.* Hillsdale, NJ: Lawrence Erlbaum.

Keppel, G. (1991). *Design and analysis: A researcher's handbook* (3rd ed.). Englewood Cliffs, NJ: Prentice Hall.

Levy, P. E. (1993). Self-appraisal and attributions: A test of a model. *Journal of Management, 19,* 51-62.

Lipsey, M. W. (1990). *Design sensitivity: Statistical power for experimental research.* Newbury Park, CA: Sage.

Long, J. S. (1983). *Covariance structure models: An introduction to LISREL.* Beverly Hills, CA: Sage.

Pedhazur, E. (1982). *Multiple regression in behavioral research* (2nd ed.). New York: Holt, Rinehart & Winston.

Pedhazur, E., & Schmelkin, L. (1991). *Measurement, design, and analysis.* Hillsdale, NJ: Lawrence Erlbaum.

Schmidt, F. L., Hunter, J. E., & Urry, V. W. (1976). Statistical power in criterion-related validation studies. *Journal of Applied Psychology, 61,* 473-485.

Spector, P. E. (1977). What to do with significant multivariate effects in multivariate analyses of variance. *Journal of Applied Psychology, 62,* 158-163.

Stevens, J. (1992). *Applied multivariate statistics for the social sciences* (2nd ed.). Hillsdale, NJ: Lawrence Erlbaum.

Tabachnick, B. G., & Fidell, L. S. (1996). *Using multivariate statistics* (3rd ed.). New York: HarperCollins.

Chapter 18

Conducting a Meta-Analysis

HARRIS COOPER
NANCY DORR

Literature reviews typically serve to summarize results of past studies, suggest potential reasons for inconsistencies in past research findings, and direct future investigations. There are two ways a review of a literature can be conducted: in the traditional narrative manner or by a meta-analysis. The traditional narrative reviewer identifies articles relevant to the topic of interest, examines the results of each article to see whether the hypothesis was supported, and provides overall conclusions. Conclusions are usually drawn in a qualitative manner, and procedures for drawing conclusions are typically left up to the individual reviewer. Traditional narrative reviews have been criticized because they easily allow the reviewer's biases to enter into the conclusions and because information in the original studies can be discarded unconsciously or inconsistently (Cooper & Rosenthal, 1980). A meta-analysis has the same goals as the traditional review. Alternatively, a meta-analysis uses statistical procedures to combine the results of previous studies. One strength of meta-analysis is its specific procedures for how the results of relevant studies are to be combined and how conclusions should be drawn.

The implications of quantitatively (i.e., statistically) combining the results of studies rather than qualitatively drawing conclusions were explored in a study conducted by Cooper and Rosenthal (1980). They asked university professors and graduate students to examine seven studies that tested whether females were more persistent than males. Participants were randomly assigned to one of two conditions: (a) a traditional narrative review condition, in which participants "were asked to employ whatever criteria they would normally use" in drawing conclusions of the results of the seven studies (p. 443), or (b) a statistical review condition, in which participants were taught how to combine statistically the results of the same seven studies. Statistical reviewers concluded that there was more support for the notion that females were more persistent than males and perceived a larger difference between males and females than did traditional narrative reviewers.

With the advent of meta-analysis and the rigorous standards for how literature is to be synthesized, literature reviewing has been elevated to a respected scientific endeavor in

AUTHORS' NOTE: Portions of this chapter were presented at the National Conference on Research Synthesis: Social Science Informing Public Policy, June 21, 1994, Washington, DC.

its own right. This chapter first explores the history of meta-analysis, focusing on the need for its development. Then the major meta-analytic procedures are described.

Brief History of Meta-Analysis

The year 1904 witnessed the earliest known application of what today we call meta-analysis. Karl Pearson (1904), having been asked to review the evidence on a vaccine against typhoid, gathered data from 11 relevant studies. For each study, Pearson calculated a recently developed statistic called the correlation coefficient. He averaged these measures of the treatment's effect across two groups of studies distinguished by the nature of their dependent variable. On the basis of the average correlations, Pearson concluded that other vaccines are more effective and, with political sagaciousness that transcends a century, counseled that "improvement of the serum and method of dosing, with a view to a far higher correlation, should be attempted" (Pearson, 1904, p. 1245).

The scene shifts next to 75 years later. In Cambridge, Massachusetts, Rosenthal and Rubin (1978) undertook a review of research studying the effects of interpersonal expectations on behavior in laboratories, classrooms, and the workplace. They found not 11 but 345 studies that pertained to their hypothesis. In Boulder, Colorado, Glass and Smith (1979) conducted a review of the relation between class size and academic achievement. They found not 345 but 725 estimates of the relation based on data from nearly 900,000 students. The same authors also gathered assessments of the effectiveness of psychotherapy. This literature revealed 833 tests of the treatment (Smith & Glass, 1977). Hunter, Schmidt, and Hunter (1979), working at Michigan State University and the U.S. Office of Personnel Management, uncovered 866 comparisons of the differential validity of employment tests for Black and White workers.

Each of these research teams drew the inescapable conclusion that the days of the traditional research review were over. They realized that the influx of personnel into the social and behavioral sciences at midcentury had had its intended effect. For some topic areas, prodigious amounts of empirical evidence had been amassed on why people act, feel, and think the way they do and on the effectiveness of psychological, social, educational, and medical interventions meant to help people act, feel, and think better. These researchers concluded that the traditional narrative review, involving the selective search for studies, the use of post hoc criteria to exclude studies from consideration, and the application of faulty cognitive algebra to amalgamate statistical results so numerous they are well beyond the capacity of the human mind, simply would not suffice.

Largely independently, the three research teams rediscovered and reinvented Pearson's solution to their problem. They were quickly joined by others. Among these were Richard Light and David Pillemer (1984), who prepared a text that focuses on the use of research reviews in the social policy domain. Hedges and Olkin (1985) provided the rigorous statistical proofs that established quantitative synthesis as an independent specialty within the statistical sciences. Cooper (1982, 1989) proposed that the research synthesis process be conceptualized in the same manner as original data collections. He presented a five-stage model for the integrative research review that paralleled primary research (see Table 18.1). The stages include problem formulation, data collection or the literature search, data evaluation, analysis and interpretation, and public presentation. For each stage, Cooper codified the research question asked, its primary function in the review, and the procedural differences that might cause variation in synthesis conclusions. In addition, Cooper suggested that the notion of threats to inferential validity (such as internal and external validity), introduced by Campbell and Stanley (1966) and expanded by Cook and Campbell (1979), be applied to the evaluation of research synthesis. Cooper also stated the presupposition underlying the efforts of all the research synthesis methodologists: that the second, and later, users of data must be as accountable for the validity of their methods as the original data gatherers.

Procedures of Meta-Analysis

SEARCHING THE LITERATURE AND CODING STUDIES

Let us turn now to the more mundane issue of the procedures that constitute a present-day research synthesis. Suppose we enter the office of Dr. Polly C. Analyst, about to undertake a review of research assessing the effects of remedial education on the self-esteem of adolescents. In addition, suppose that Dr. Analyst has already completed her search for relevant studies. Her search strategy employed computer reference databases (e.g., PsycINFO), convention programs, the reference lists of reports, a search of related journals, inquiries to government agencies, and letters to active researchers (see Chapters 2 and 3 of this volume). Notice that in conducting her search for relevant studies, Polly attempted to uncover both published and unpublished reports. This is important because although there are many reasons for a report not to be published, one reason is that the study failed to reject the null hypothesis (that is, the study did not find a statistically significant difference in self-esteem between participants who received remedial education and those who did not). If Polly did not include unpublished research in her meta-analysis, she would be likely to conclude that education has a greater effect on self-esteem than if she included unpublished research. Thus taking the results of unpublished research into account allows for a more accurate assessment of the relation between education and self-esteem.

Suppose further that Polly's search uncovered 20 reports that include relevant data testing the hypothesis that remedial education increases self-esteem. In glancing at the results of the 20 studies, Dr. Analyst notices that some studies suggested that individuals who received education had higher self-esteem than individuals who did not, some studies showed no difference in self-esteem between individuals who received education and those who did not, and a few studies showed that individuals who received education had lower self-esteem than individuals who did not. Quite appropriately, she decides that she would like to explore potential reasons that the studies have different results. Polly further notes that the 20 studies use a variety of procedures. She thinks about which characteristics of the 20 reports might affect the results of the study. She may wonder, for example, whether remedial education will affect the self-esteem of females and males differently, whether remedial education will affect subjects of varying ages differently, and whether the type or length of the educational program will affect self-esteem. Thus Polly systematically extracts

TABLE 18.1 The Integrative Review Conceptualized as a Research Project

			Stage of Research		
Stage Characteristics	Problem Formulation	Data Collection	Data Evaluation	Analysis and Interpretation	Public Presentation
Research question asked	What evidence should be included in the review?	What procedures should be used to find relevant evidence?	What retrieved evidence should be included in the review?	What procedures should be used to make inferences about the literature as a whole?	What information should be included in the review report?
Primary function in review	Constructing definitions that distinguish relevant from irrelevant studies	Determining which sources of potentially relevant studies to examine	Applying criteria to separate "valid" from "invalid" studies	Synthesizing valid retrieved studies	Applying editorial criteria to separate important from unimportant information
Procedural differences that create variation in review conclusions	Differences in included operational definitions	Differences in the research contained in sources of information	Differences in quality criteria	Differences in rule of inference	Differences in guidelines for editorial judgment
	Differences in operational detail		Differences in the influence of nonquality criteria		
Sources of potential invalidity in review conclusions	Narrow concepts might make review conclusions less definitive and robust	Accessed studies might be qualitatively different from the target population of studies	Nonquality factors might cause improper weighing of study information	Rules for distinguishing patterns from noise might be inappropriate	Omission of review procedures might make conclusions irreproducible
	Superficial operational detail might obscure interacting variables	People sampled in accessible studies might be different from the target population	Omissions in study reports might make conclusions unreliable	Review-based evidence might be used to infer causality	Omissions of review findings and study procedures might make conclusions obsolete

from the Method and Results sections of the reports each piece of information she wants to include in the analysis. Polly also has another individual extract information from a sample of the 20 studies to determine the extent to which she accurately and reliably coded the information from the reports.

VOTE COUNTING

Dr. Analyst's data collection is now complete. Next she must decide how to combine the results of the 20 studies to draw overall conclusions about remedial education's effectiveness. First, she could cull through the 20 reports, isolate those studies that present results counter to her own position, discard these disconfirming studies due to methodo-logical limitations (e.g., no random assignment of participants to educational conditions), and present the remaining supportive studies as representing the truth of the matter. Such a research synthesis is not unheard of. However, its conclusions would be viewed with extreme skepticism. It would contribute little to the public debate.

As an alternative procedure, Polly could take each report and place it into one of three piles: statistically significant findings indicating that education is effective in improving self-esteem, statistically significant findings indicating that education is counterproduc-tive, and nonsignificant findings that do not permit Polly to reject the hypothesis that education has no effect. She could then declare the largest pile the winner.

This vote-counting strategy has much intuitive appeal and has been used quite often. However, the strategy is unacceptably conservative. In research, it is typically accepted that the results of a study are statistically significant when the difference between conditions could have occurred purely by chance only 5% of the time or less (i.e., $p < .05$; see Chapter 15 of this volume). In Dr. Analyst's review, if the null hypothesis is true and remedial education has no effect on self-esteem, then chance alone should produce, out of the 20 studies, only about one (5%) falsely indicating that education is effective. However, by dividing the 20 reports into three piles, the vote-counting strategy requires that a minimum 34% of findings (seven studies) be positive and statistically significant before the program is ruled the "winner." Thus the vote-counting strategy could, and often does, lead to the suggested abandonment of effective programs and to the implication that resources have been wasted when in fact such waste has not occurred. In addition, the vote-counting strategy does not differentially weight studies on the basis of sample size: A study with 100 adolescents is given weight equal to that of a study with 1,000 adolescents. This is a potential problem because large samples are more likely to estimate the precise population value. Therefore effect sizes from larger samples should be given more weight. Another problem with the vote-counting strategy is that the revealed impact of the treatment in each study is not considered: A study showing a slightly lower mean for the individuals who received education as compared to individuals who did not is given weight equal to that of a study showing a much higher mean for individuals who received education as compared to individuals who did not. For these reasons, Polly may report in her meta-analysis the number of studies that fall into each pile, but she decides not to base her conclusions on these data alone.

COMBINING PROBABILITIES

Trying to take these shortcomings into account, Polly next considers combining the precise probabilities of results in each study. Each of the 20 studies tested the null hypothesis (i.e., adolescents receiving education and not receiving education do not differ in self-esteem) by conducting a statistical test and examining its associated probability. To combine the probabilities of results for each study, Dr. Analyst would locate each test of the null hypothesis and extract the probability associated with it. She would then use one of several statistical formulas to generate a single probability that relates to the likelihood of obtaining a run of studies with these results, given that the null hypothesis is true. For example, Polly's results might show that the combined probability of obtaining the results of the 20 studies, assuming that education has no effect on self-esteem, is $p < .03$. Thus she could conclude that education is related to higher self-esteem. Alternatively, if the combined probability of obtaining the results of the 20 studies was $p < .19$, Polly would conclude that there was not evidence to suggest that education is related to self-esteem.

The combining-probabilities procedure overcomes the improper weighting problems of the vote count. However, it has severe limitations of its own. First, whereas the vote-count procedure is overly conservative, the combining-probabilities procedure is extremely powerful. In fact, for treatments that have generated a large number of studies, rejecting the null hypothesis is so likely that testing it becomes a rather uninformative exercise; it is very rare that this procedure does not allow the meta-analyst to reject the null hypothesis and conclude that the treatment had an effect. For Polly, this means that if this were the only meta-analytic procedure she used, she would be very likely to conclude that education is related to self-esteem.

EFFECT SIZE ESTIMATION

The combined probability addresses the question of whether an effect exists; it gives no information on whether that effect is large or small, important or trivial. Therefore Polly decides that answering the question "Does remedial education influence self-esteem?" is not really the question she needs to ask. Instead, she chooses to reframe her question as "How much does remedial education influence self-esteem?" Polly's answer might be zero, or it might be either a positive or a negative value. Positive values typically indicate that the effect size is consistent with the meta-analyst's hypothesis. For example, if Polly's effect size was positive, this would mean that individuals receiving education had higher self-esteem than those who did not. Alternatively, if her effect size was negative, this would mean that individuals receiving education had lower self-esteem than those who did not. Dr. Analyst can then use this effect size to assess whether education's benefits justify its costs. Further, she can ask, "What factors influence the effect of education?" She realizes that the answer to this question could help her make sound recommendations about how to improve and target educational interventions.

Given her new questions, Polly decides to base her conclusions on the calculation of average effect sizes, much like Pearson's. Because her research involves comparing a treatment group with a control group—that is, adolescents receiving and not receiving remedial education—she is likely to describe the magnitude of effect by calculating what

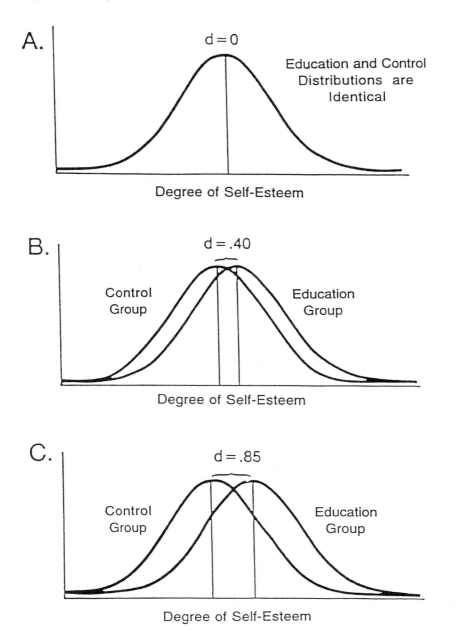

Figure 18.1. Three Hypothetical Relations Between Education and Control Groups in Self-Esteem Experiments

is called a *d* index, or standardized mean difference (Cohen, 1988). The *d* index is a scale-free measure of the separation between two group means. It describes the difference between two group means as a function of their standard deviations. Figure 18.1 presents the results of three hypothetical studies in Polly's review. In Figure 18.1A, education has no effect on adolescents' reported self-esteem; thus $d = 0$. In Figure 18.1B, the average adolescent receiving education has a self-esteem score that is four tenths of a standard deviation above that of the average adolescent not receiving education. Here $d = .40$. In Figure 18.1C, $d = .85$, indicating an even greater separation between the two group means.

Suppose for a moment that Polly's research did not compare two group means but instead explored the relationship between two continuous variables (e.g., suppose Polly wanted to investigate the relationship between extraversion and self-esteem). Instead of calculating a d index, she would simply use Pearson's product-moment correlation coefficient (i.e., r; see Chapter 16 of this volume). Unlike the d index, the r index is typically reported in the primary research report, and additional computation is not required to obtain effect sizes.

Once Polly has calculated a d index for each outcome in each study, she might next average all the d indexes, weighting them by sample size. This would tell her how big of a difference between the education and control condition exists for all 20 studies. This average effect size ignores the characteristics of the studies, such as the sex makeup of the sample and the length of educational program.

INFLUENCES ON EFFECT SIZES

Polly next may decide that she wants different estimates of the effect of education on self-esteem based on certain characteristics of the data. Recall that as Polly was glancing through the results of the studies, she noticed inconsistencies. She can test whether some of the inconsistency is due to different characteristics and procedures of the original studies. To do this, she calculates average d indexes for subsets of studies that have characteristics in common. For example, she might wish to compare the average effect sizes for different educational formats, distinguishing treatments that used large group lectures from treatments that used small group discussions. Polly might also want to look at whether education is differentially effective for different types of adolescents, say males and females. Her ability to broach these questions about whether such variables are related to the size of education's effect reveals one of the major contributions of meta-analysis. Specifically, even if no individual study has compared different educational formats or types of adolescents, by comparing results across studies, Polly's synthesis can give a first hint about whether these factors would be important to look at as guides to theory and policy.

Next, Polly will statistically test whether these factors are reliably associated with different magnitudes of effect—that is, different average d indexes (Cooper & Hedges, 1994; Hedges & Olkin, 1985). This is sometimes called a *homogeneity analysis*, and it is likely to provide the most interesting results of Polly's synthesis. Because effect sizes are imprecise, they will vary somewhat even if they all estimate the same underlying population value. Homogeneity analysis allows Polly to test whether sampling error alone accounts for this variation or whether features of studies, samples, treatment designs, or outcome measures also play a role. Polly will group studies according to potentially important characteristics and test for between-group differences. If she finds that differences exist, her average effect sizes corresponding to these differences will take on added meaning and will help her make recommendations concerning whether, and especially which, educational programs should be continued for whom, when, and for how long. For example, Polly could conduct a homogeneity analysis to test whether studies with a 1-month educational program produced a larger effect of education on self-esteem than studies with a 1-week program.

If the homogeneity analysis was significant, Polly could suggest that the differences in effect sizes between studies employing 1-month or 1-week programs was not due to sampling error alone. Polly might then calculate the average effect size (weighted by sample size) for 1-month programs to be higher than the average effect size for 1-week programs (e.g., $d = .55$ vs. $d = .05$, respectively). This would provide an initial hint that the length of the educational program is related to self-esteem and that perhaps longer programs are more beneficial. However, the results of Polly's homogeneity analysis do not permit her to make causal statements. That is, Polly cannot conclude that longer programs cause an increase in self-esteem. The reasoning behind this lies in random assignment: A meta-analyst cannot randomly assign studies to procedures. In research, unless the investigator randomly assigns participants to conditions (e.g., 1-week vs. 1-month programs), causality cannot be assessed. Without random assignment, the possibility that a third variable is the true cause is always present. Nevertheless, Dr. Analyst's homogeneity analyses are still beneficial in summarizing past research and directing future research, especially if none of the original 20 studies examined the impact of program length.

Conclusion

In describing Dr. Analyst's pursuit of the perfect research synthesis, we have made her task appear simpler than it is. Polly will encounter missing information, coding ambiguities, correlated data points, and a host of other problems. How she chooses to handle these problems will influence the trustworthiness of her results and the value that others place on her conclusions. However, if social science research is to contribute to rational decision making, then research synthesis is a most critical component in our methodological arsenal, and it needs to be held to the same standards of rigor and systematicity as the primary research on which it is based. Meta-analysis helps us meet these standards.

Recommended Readings

For more information on conducting a meta-analysis, we recommend starting with Cooper's *Integrating Research: A Guide for Literature Reviews* (1989) and Rosenthal's *Meta-Analytic Procedures for Social Research* (1984). For further information on more advanced meta-analytic issues, we recommend consulting Cooper and Hedges' *Handbook of Research Synthesis* (1994).

References

Campbell, D. T., & Stanley, J. C. (1966). *Experimental and quasi-experimental designs for research.* Chicago: Rand McNally.

Cohen, J. (1988). *Statistical power analysis for the behavioral sciences* (2nd ed.). Hillsdale, NJ: Lawrence Erlbaum.

Cook, T. D., & Campbell, D. T. (1979). *Quasi-experimentation: Design and analysis issues for field setting.* Chicago: Rand McNally.

Cooper, H. (1982). Scientific guidelines for conducting integrative research reviews. *Review of Educational Research, 52,* 291-302.

Cooper, H. (1989). *Integrating research: A guide for literature reviews* (2nd ed.). Newbury Park, CA: Sage.

Cooper, H., & Hedges, L. V. (1994). *The handbook of research synthesis.* New York: Russell Sage.

Cooper, H. M., & Rosenthal, R. (1980). Statistical versus traditional procedures for summarizing research findings. *Psychological Bulletin, 87,* 442-449.

Glass, G. V., & Smith, M. L. (1979). Meta-analysis of research on class size and achievement. *Educational Evaluation and Policy Analysis, 1,* 2-16.

Hedges, L. V., & Olkin, I. (1985). *Statistical methods for meta-analysis.* Orlando, FL: Academic Press.

Hunter, J. E., Schmidt, F. L., & Hunter, R. (1979). Differential validity of employment tests by race: A comprehensive review and analysis. *Psychological Bulletin, 86,* 721-735.

Light, R. J., & Pillemer, D. B. (1984). *Summing up: The science of reviewing research.* Cambridge, MA: Harvard University Press.

Pearson, K. (1904). Report on certain enteric fever inoculation statistics. *British Medical Journal, 2,* 1243-1246.

Rosenthal, R. (1984). *Meta-analytic procedures for social research.* Beverly Hills, CA: Sage.

Rosenthal, R., & Rubin, D. B. (1978). Interpersonal expectancy effects: The first 345 studies. *Behavioral and Brain Sciences, 3,* 377-386.

Smith, M. L., & Glass, G. V. (1977). Meta-analysis of psychotherapy outcome studies. *American Psychologist, 32,* 752-760.

Chapter 19

Test Construction

NANCY E. BETZ

This chapter will begin by discussing the reasons that a psychologist or graduate student might decide to develop a new test or measure, rather than using one of the many existing tests and measures. Then the chapter will provide a detailed discussion of one of the major approaches to test construction, the "construct-based" approach. As will be discussed, this method is widely applicable and, if done properly, can result in high-quality tests. Other useful approaches of test construction will be mentioned, but in less detail, in the last section. The chapter ends with "Recommended Readings" that provide additional information regarding these methods.

Why Develop a Test?

In doing research, the psychologist or graduate student frequently needs to measure some unobservable but important characteristic or attribute of people. For example, a study of the relationship between ordinal rank (birth order) and intelligence would require a measure of intelligence, which is not a directly observable construct. Other major attributes include abilities, personality traits, and attitudes. These constructs are hypothetical entities: That is, we cannot actually see or touch them. One's IQ is stamped neither on one's forehead nor on one's social security card; in other words, we cannot directly observe intelligence. Rather, we develop tests that we think reflect a person's intelligence in an indirect way.

Because our research ideas usually build on previous studies in the area of study, there are likely to be existing measures of these constructs that have been used in previous studies. Assuming that these measures have been shown to be of adequate quality (see below), it is almost always preferable to use existing measures rather than to develop new ones. This is because each study adds to the knowledge base around a given psychological test and makes subsequent studies more easily comparable to previous ones. Overall, contributions to theory and general knowledge are facilitated when measures of high quality are used in a series of studies. Further, it takes several studies to demonstrate that an instrument possesses adequate levels of reliability and validity; to continually validate new measures is a waste of researchers' time and intellectual effort. Only when new theories and/or constructs needing measures are proposed, or when no high-quality measure of a given construct exists in the literature, should the researcher proceed to develop his or her own.

To make sure that a useful measure does not exist, the researcher should carefully review test "dictionaries" and "encyclopedias" such as the *Mental Measurements Yearbook Series* (e.g., see Kramer & Conoley, 1992), Beere's (1990a, 1990b) compendia of measures related to gender roles and women's issues, and Robinson, Shaver, and Wrightsman's *Measures of Personality and Social Psychological Attitudes* (1991).

Evaluating Test Quality

As mentioned above, the general recommendation here to use an existing test or scale rests on the presumption that it is of high quality. Quality in psychological tests and measures is mandated by and exhaustively reviewed in *Standards for Educational and Psychological Testing,* prepared by a joint commission of the American Educational Research Association (AERA), American Psychological Association (APA), and National Council on Measurement in Education (NCME; AERA, 1985). Because a more detailed discussion of methods of evaluating this quality can be found in Chapter 6 of this volume, only brief reviews are provided here.

Because we therefore develop tests as indicators of hypothetical constructs, we need to demonstrate that the tests are measuring what we think they are measuring; this is the process of evaluating the psychometric quality of our tests, most importantly their reliability and validity. *Reliability* refers to the extent to which we are measuring some attribute in a consistent and repeatable way. *Internal consistency reliability* refers to the consistency of information across stimuli presumed to measure the same thing (i.e., two test items or two forms of a test). *Test-retest reliability,* or *stability,* refers to consistency of measurement over time (e.g., a retest occurring 2 weeks after the initial testing).

Validity refers to the extent to which the test is measuring what we say it is measuring. There are many types of validity (see Walsh & Betz, 1995, for a more complete review), but the major types are content validity, criterion-related validity, and construct validity. The term *content validity* refers to how well the particular sampling of behaviors used to measure a characteristic reflects performance in the entire domain of behaviors that constitutes that characteristic. That is, we are interested in the behavior of a person as expressed in a variety of situations or toward a universe of possible "items." Although we are interested in, and wish to generalize to, an entire domain of behaviors, it is rarely feasible to include on a test all possible situations or items that might be relevant to that domain. Content validation, however, allows us to judge whether the content of a test is representative of the desired universe of content.

The term *criterion-related validity* usually refers to the extent to which a measure of an attribute demonstrates an association with some independent or external indicator of the same attribute. This external indicator, called the *criterion,* may represent the behavior we are actually interested in, and we wish to use test scores or other measurements to predict status or performance on the criterion. For example, scholastic aptitude tests are used to predict success (grade point average [GPA]) in college course work. Success in college is the behavior of interest, and the magnitude of the correlation between test scores and GPA is an important index of the applied usefulness of the test.

Although content and criterion-related validity are useful in addressing the question "Does the test measure what it is intended to measure?", the type of validity most directly addressing this question is *construct validity*. Construct validation occurs within the context of a theory or set of hypotheses concerning the construct in which we are interested. The constructs of the theory are made *observable*, or operationalized, through tests or assessments, and then the hypothesized relationships among variables can be studied through studies of the relationship between the tests/assessments that are thought to indicate them. Once the constructs can be operationalized, or *measured*, studies of their interrelationships can take place. In the present example, we have postulated that intelligence should be related to school performance and learning ability. We could also postulate that intelligence, as we conceptualize it, should not be related to height, eye color, or the state in which one was born. Examination of the relationships of scores on our intelligence test to these other variables is the means by which we would evaluate the construct validity of our intelligence test. Only when the observed pattern of relationships corresponds with predictions based on our understanding of the construct can it be said that the construct validity of the test is supported. Although the reliability and validity of a test are evaluated after the test is constructed, the best way (probably the only way) to ensure a high-quality test is through proper and careful methods of test construction. If a test was well constructed in the first place, chances are good that it will be found to be reliable and valid. High-quality test construction is the focus of this chapter.

Procedures in Test Construction

Before proceeding, two terms must be defined. First, strictly speaking, the word *test* refers to a measure on which there are correct and incorrect answers, usually an ability or achievement test. For example, few would disagree with "4" as the correct answer to the question "What is 2 + 2?" In an exam for an introductory psychology course, "B. F. Skinner" would be a correct answer to the question "What psychologist is associated with the initial research on operant conditioning?" In contrast to a test, a *scale* or *inventory* or *questionnaire* does not have correct answers, only answers that are descriptive of the stimulus (person) being measured. These include personality and vocational interest inventories as well as measures of attitudes, preferences, and values. There are some differences in how tests versus scales are evaluated, and these differences will be mentioned in the following discussion. However, unless indicated otherwise, the following procedures for test construction will refer to both tests and scales.

In general, test construction should proceed with the following steps:

1. Careful definition of the attribute or construct to be measured
2. Development of a large pool of items logically related to the attribute of interest
3. Administration of the items to a large sample of subjects, often called the "development sample"
4. Refinement of the original item pool through item analyses and expert judgment

5. Administration of the revised test to a new sample of subjects
6. Based on the new samples, examination of evidence for reliability and validity and compilation of normative data

Each of these steps will be discussed in the sections below.

DEFINITION OF THE CONSTRUCT

Test construction begins with a careful, detailed definition of the characteristic to be measured. This definition should include both what the attribute is and what it is not; it should include a specification of both behaviors/tasks included in the definition and those not included.

If we are constructing the midterm exam for an introductory psychology class, we begin by defining which book chapters and/or lectures the exam is to cover and then specify relative weighting, if any, of different content areas. But defining the domain of content for a personality or attitude measure is less straightforward. It begins with careful thought about what our attribute is intended to represent. For example, here is a definition for the construct of *unconditional self-regard*, a type of self-esteem postulated by Betz, Serling, Wohlgemuth, Harshbarger, and Klein (1995):

> *Unconditional self-regard* refers to the extent to which an individual perceives him- or herself as a person of worth and places standards of evaluation within the self. This valuing and acceptance of oneself is noncontingent. In other words, self-liking or self-acceptance is not contingent on one's own performances in various behavioral domains (e.g., athletic, academic, social), although the individual may strive to improve his or her levels of performance in one or more of those areas.

We would write test items that reflect part of all of this definition, for example, "I like who I am" and "Even though I make mistakes, I still feel good about myself as a person."

WRITING TEST ITEMS

Tests and scales constructed in psychology should have several items. Multi-item scales are used for several reasons. First, items usually have considerable specificity: Whether a child can spell *umpire* or *carburetor* may depend on specific background experiences or be gender related. Most applicants to graduate school would object if one item on the Graduate Record Exam determined acceptance to graduate school. Second, one item can distinguish people in only a limited way. For example, "true/false" or "right/wrong" can distinguish only two levels, and the commonly-used 5-point Likert scale can distinguish five levels. However, if we use six 5-point Likert scales, our score range is from 1 to 30 (5×6), permitting 30 levels of distinction.

Third, we cannot compute the internal consistency reliability of a one-item scale. More limited score ranges reduce the possible value of correlations with other variables, thus reducing our validity coefficients.

Once the dimension or construct of interest is defined, the test constructor develops test items that are related to the *content* (i.e., the definition) of that dimension. This kind of item development requires that the test developer carefully examine the definition of the construct and then infer specific behaviors or responses that should reflect components of that definition.

In writing test items, we must decide on both the content of the item and the method of obtaining responses. In ability and achievement testing, the most frequently used item type is multiple-choice, though others, such as true/false and matching, are also used. For scales—that is, for measures on which there are no correct or incorrect answers—there are a variety of methods of obtaining responses. The most frequently used is known as *summated ratings* or *Likert scales* (see Spector, 1992), which ask the respondent to select one position on a continuous series of responses that best reflects his or her position. The three most common types of response choices in Likert scales are agreement, evaluation, and frequency. Agreement is generally indicated on a 5- or 7-point continuum ranging from *strongly agree* to *strongly disagree*. Evaluation can include such continua as *not at all descriptive* to *very descriptive* and *not at all confident* to *very confident*. Frequency uses such response choices as *rarely* to *most of the time* and *never or almost never true* to *almost always or always true*.

Numbers must be assigned to response choices, and usually this is done so that higher numbers indicate *more* of the attribute (e.g., greater self-esteem, higher levels of anxiety). Because roughly half the items should be negatively worded to minimize response sets such as overall positivity or negativity, negatively worded items are reverse-scored when one is computing total scores. For example, degrees of disagreement versus agreement with the statement "I rarely feel anxious" would be an example of a Likert scale, as would degrees of descriptiveness or nondescriptiveness of the personality trait "Anxious." Generally, from 3 to 11 response alternatives are used in a Likert scale, but most measurement specialists agree that between 5 and 7 is the optimal number. A commonly used Likert scale is *strongly agree, agree, neutral, disagree,* and *strongly disagree*), with scores from 5 to 1 (or vice versa) assigned to the five response alternatives, respectively.

Thus test items should bear a logical or rational relationship to the construct as defined by the test constructor. The test constructor should develop (i.e., write or adapt from previously available tests or other materials) a pool of items larger than that needed in the final version of the test. A large pool of items is necessary so that items that do not relate as postulated to the dimension of interest may be eliminated. In other words, although an item may appear to the test constructor to be logically related to the dimension, the item analysis procedures to be discussed next may suggest that it is not highly related to the dimension.

ADMINISTRATION OF TEST ITEMS TO A DEVELOPMENT SAMPLE

The next stage of test construction involves administration of the items to a preliminary sample of subjects (often referred to as the *development sample*). The subjects in this group should be representative of the population of subjects for whom the test itself is intended. In other words, if the test is designed to measure school achievement in Grades 7 through 9, the subjects should be representative of students in Grades 7 through 9.

Similarly, if the test is designed to measure personality characteristics of adults, then a representative sample of adults should be used. Subjects in the development sample are administered the test under conditions identical to those that will be used in the administration of the completed test, and the responses obtained from this pilot testing are used in the item analyses to be discussed next.

REFINEMENT OF THE ITEM POOL THROUGH
ITEM ANALYSES AND EXPERT JUDGMENT

Although definition of the construct and development of relevant test items are intended to ensure that the items in the initial item pool are reasonably good representatives of the construct, knowledge of other properties of the test items is used in *refining* the item pool. By "refining an item pool," we mean eliminating items that, when actually administered in the development sample, do not have the properties we had hoped for or, conversely, selecting items that have particularly desirable properties. In the case of ability and achievement tests, the two most important characteristics are item difficulty and item discrimination.

Item Difficulty

The concept of item difficulty was originally developed for use with test items on which there are right and wrong answers, as in the assessment of ability and achievement. With items of this kind, *item difficulty* is usually defined statistically as the percentage of persons who respond correctly to an item. The higher the percentage of people who answer an item correctly, the easier the item is considered to be, and vice versa. Item difficulty levels are usually expressed as p values: An item answered correctly by 70% of subjects has a p of 0.70, whereas an item answered correctly by only 20% of subjects has a p of 0.20. (Some formulas for the calculation of item difficulty include corrections for guessing; see, for example, Nunnally & Bernstein, 1993.)

Methods of selecting test items on the basis of their p values depend considerably on the purposes for which the test is constructed, but it should be apparent to the reader that the difficulty of the test is a direct function of the difficulty of the test items we choose. If we include only very difficult items, the test will be very difficult; likewise, if all the items we include are relatively easy, the test will also be easy.

We want to select test items such that the overall level of difficulty is appropriate for the groups with whom the test is to be used and such that the test yields a relatively wide range of scores, preferably having a normal distribution. If a test does not yield a range of scores, it does not provide us with information about individual differences in the attribute or trait of interest.

To illustrate how item difficulty influences the characteristics of the resulting test scores, consider, first, an item that everyone in our standardization or normative sample answered correctly. The difficulty or p value of the item is 1.0, as 100% of the examinees answered it correctly. This item is too easy for the group and does not distinguish between individuals in the group; thus it provides us with no new information about individuals. A test constructed using too many easy items would result in a skewed score distribution with too little of what has been called "ceiling": that is, the capacity to discriminate individuals at the upper end of the distribution.

Assume, on the other hand, that we have an item that everyone in our normative sample answers incorrectly; this item has a difficulty or p value of 0.0. This item is too difficult for the group and, like the item that was too easy, provides us with no new information about individual differences. A test constructed with items that are too difficult yields a skewed distribution of scores, which is said to "have too little floor," meaning that it does a very poor job of distinguishing individuals at the lower end of the score distribution.

Generally, a set of test items should include items with a range of difficulties, varying, for example, from $p = 0.10$ to $p = 0.90$. This will produce a test of appropriate difficulty yielding a range of scores. This selection of test items will also ensure that even the least able examinees will be able to answer a few items correctly.

Item Discrimination

The property of item discrimination is important for almost all types of tests designed to assess some unitary attribute. *Item discrimination* refers to the extent to which people's responses to a given item measuring a construct are related to their scores on the measure as a whole. If item responses do not relate to performance on the scale as a whole, we have reason to suspect that the item is not measuring what it was intended to measure. Assume, for example, that the brightest child in the class scores 99 on an achievement test and that the one item answered incorrectly was an item that the poorest student (who got only 10 right altogether) answered correctly: We would wonder about the extent to which that item was actually measuring achievement in the subject matter. Or assume that on one of the items we developed to measure anxiety, the examinees scoring highest (most anxious) on the anxiety test as a whole responded negatively to that item: Again, we would question the effectiveness of that item as a measure of anxiety. The discriminatory power of test items is directly related to the resulting internal consistency reliability. Reliable tests result from items that discriminate well.

Items such as these may be *poorly discriminating* because they are not clearly worded, are ambiguous in meaning, or simply are not related to the dimension of interest. Indices of item discrimination allow the test constructor to select the "good" items (i.e., those that actually appear to measure the dimension of interest) and to eliminate from the test the "bad" items.

There are many indices of item discrimination. Two correlation coefficients used extensively in the examination of discriminating power are the biserial and point-biserial coefficients. The point-biserial r_{pb}, which is a Pearson product-moment correlation coefficient, describes the relationship between a dichotomous variable (e.g., true/false, right/wrong, male/female), and a continuous variable, such as total score on a test. The biserial r_{bis}, on the other hand, describes the relationship between a *dichotomized* variable (a dichotomous item response assumed to summarize an underlying normal distribution) and a continuous variable. The computation of both r_{pb} and r_{bis} is based on comparing the mean test scores of those who pass the item and of those who fail it in relationship to the difficulty of the item itself (see Glass & Hopkins, 1984, for more information regarding these and other correlation coefficients). Evidence for item discrimination requires that the overall test scores of those who respond correctly to an item be higher than the mean scores of those who respond incorrectly to the item.

With ability tests for which item difficulty is also relevant, a good item selection strategy would be to select the n most highly discriminating items within each range of difficulty. Assuming we have 10 difficulty ranges ($p = .01$ to $.01$, $p = .11$ to $.20$, ... $p = .90$ to $.99$) and the desire for a 100-item test, we would use the 10 most discriminating items at each level.

SELECTING ITEMS FOR A SCALE

The most important criterion for selection versus elimination of items for a nonability measure is generally item discrimination, as operationalized by the item-total score correlation (usually a Pearson r). Let us go back to the measure of unconditional self-regard discussed earlier, on which we obtained responses on a 5-point Likert scale: *strongly agree* (5), *agree* (4), *not sure* (3), *disagree* (2), and *strongly disagree* (1). If the *strongly agree* response is reflective of highest self-esteem, we would hope that people who give that response also have higher scores on the total scale (added across all the items in the scale). Thus we compute the correlation between the item "score" (1 to 5) and the total score. A general rule of thumb is that item-total correlations below .30 (or at the *least* .20) indicate poorly discriminating items.

Other criteria for selecting items include mean "score" on the item (analogous to item difficulty), variability in *response* to the item (if everyone responds "strongly agree" to an item, then it is not reflecting individual differences on the attribute in question), and correlation (hopefully *low*) with a measure of "social desirability."

THE USE OF FACTOR ANALYSIS IN SCALE CONSTRUCTION

Factor analysis is used when we wish to investigate the underlying structure or basic dimensions of a set of variables or when we wish to reduce a set of variables to a smaller set. For example, researchers interested in personality may wish to understand whether there are key underlying dimensions to 20 or 30 tests of different aspects of personality. Or assume that a business uses 20 different tests to select employees for a certain job; factor analysis can be used to identify perhaps four or five basic dimensions measured by those 20 tests, so that tests of those four or five basic dimensions can make predictions as accurately and efficiently as the 20 original tests.

In test construction, factor analysis is used in two major ways. If a construct is postulated to be unidimensional (one single dimension), then factor analysis should yield one and only one factor, or, in the language of factor analysis, one large general factor even in the presence of one or more smaller factors as well. In other cases, a researcher may wish to investigate the nature of the underlying dimensions of an existing or new scale. In these cases, too, factor analysis is a useful technique. In some instances, the factor structure is used to support the calculation of subscale scores that provide additional information about the individual being tested: for example, subscales for multiplication, division, and fractions in a test of elementary mathematics knowledge.

TABLE 19.1 Hypothetical Factor Matrix From an Analysis of Scores on Six Different Tests

Test	Factor I	Factor II
Vocabulary	0.90	0.40
Verbal Analogies	0.80	0.30
Reading Comprehension	0.75	0.35
Addition	0.30	0.80
Multiplication	0.35	0.85
Fractions	0.33	0.70

NOTE: The variables loading most strongly on each factor are underlined.

Factor analysis begins with a table of the correlations between all the variables of interest, a table known as a *correlation matrix*. The result of a factor analysis is a *factor matrix*, showing the number of important underlying factors and the "loading," or weight, of each original variable on the resulting factors. A factor loading is like a correlation coefficient: The larger it is (in either a positive or a negative direction), the stronger the relationship of the variable to the factor. In factor-analytic terms, the loading can also be viewed as related to the proportion of the variable's variance explained by the underlying factor. The square of the factor loading is the proportion of common variance between the test and the factor.

Table 19.1 shows a hypothetical factor matrix resulting from a factor analysis of an intelligence test containing six types of items. The first three tests (Vocabulary, Verbal Analogies, and Reading Comprehension) load strongly on Factor I; we might call the underlying ability measured by these tests "Verbal Ability." The next three tests (Addition, Multiplication, and Fractions) load highly on Factor II, which we might label "Ability to Use Arithmetic." For further information about factor analysis, see Chapter 17 of this volume and Tinsley and Tinsley (1987).

Other Approaches to Scale Construction

Because of the short length of this chapter, several other approaches to test or scale construction could not be covered. What follows is brief mention of these, along with resources for interested readers. Generally, textbooks in psychological measurement and testing will expand on these areas: For example, see Nunnally and Bernstein (1993) and Walsh and Betz (1995).

EMPIRICAL SCALE CONSTRUCTION

In contrast to the rational approach to scale construction, empirical scale construction is based on the differences in the responses of people postulated or found to vary on the dimension of interest, rather than on item content itself. In other words, test construction begins with a search for items that will *predict* a criterion measure or status. For example, the Minnesota Multiphasic Personality Inventory (MMPI) was originally designed to permit clinicians to detect persons suffering from serious forms of psychological disorder (e.g., schizophrenia); the responses of diagnosed schizophrenics to a large number of items were compared to the responses of "normal" individuals—in this case, visitors to the same hospital in which the schizophrenic individuals were patients. Items on which the responses of the patient group were significantly different from those of normal individuals were used in constructing the schizophrenia scale of the MMPI. Other examples of empirical test construction are the occupational scales of the Strong Interest Inventory (SII). In this case, the criterion groups were people satisfied in various occupations (e.g., physicians). Items on which the responses of people in a given occupation differed from the responses of people in general were used in constructing the occupational scale.

ATTITUDE SCALE CONSTRUCTION

An *attitude* can be defined as one's view of or reactions toward a given class of stimuli. The stimuli can vary widely and may include such things as attitudes toward political candidates, racial/ethnic groups, women's roles in society, religion, gay lifestyles, or abortion. Although the full range of techniques of attitude scale construction are beyond the scope of this chapter, interested readers may wish to consult Dawis (1987), Fitzgerald and Hubert (1987), and Maranell (1974). Four well-known techniques are the Thurstone, Likert (discussed earlier), and Guttman scales and the method of paired comparisons. See also Edwards's (1957) classic work *Techniques of Attitude Scale Construction*.

ITEM RESPONSE THEORY

Most of the discussion of test construction to this point is based on the assumptions of what is called *classical test theory*. Classical test theory assumes the existence of a "true score" on a test for each individual and assumes that the observed or obtained test score represents the true score plus a certain amount of error in measurement. We assume a linear relationship between the true score and the observed score, and the reliability coefficient indicates the percentage of observed score variance that can be attributed to true scores.

Although classical test theory is still in wide use today, a more recent development in test theory is what has been called *latent trait theory, item response theory (IRT)*, or *item characteristic curve (ICC) theory*. (See Weiss, 1983, and Hambleton, 1989, for excellent reviews.) The theory uses information about item difficulty and item discrimination in mathematical equations, which then guide test construction.

More specifically, latent trait theory (or IT or ICC) is based, not surprisingly, on the assumption that test scores reflect the amount of a "latent trait" possessed by the individual. A latent trait, symbolized by the Greek letter theta (θ), is similar to a hypothetical construct, as described in the discussion of construct validity. Items, on the other hand, can be described using one or more of three properties: item difficulty, item discrimination, and the probability of a correct response as a result of guessing on a multiple-choice test. The theory provides mathematical models or equations expressing the relationship between responses to a given test item and the amount of the latent trait the person is estimated to have. The equations use information about item difficulty, discrimination, and probability of guessing correctly to estimate the amount of the trait possessed by individuals making a given response.

Many advantages accrue to the use of latent trait theory in test construction. For example, each test item can provide an estimate of ability for any individual, and the use of more test items provides more precise estimates. What this means in practical terms is that individuals may be tested with different items and even different numbers of items, yet the same "latent trait" can be measured, and the scores will be on the same numerical scale and thus comparable to one another.

This concept has been used in what is called "adaptive" testing of ability (Wainer, 1990; Weiss, 1974, 1982), in which examinees receive a set of items "tailored" or customized to their ability levels. For example, in the two-stage test (Betz & Weiss, 1973), a preliminary "routing test" is computer administered and scored, and then the scores are used to assign examinees to a more or less difficult second-stage test. Thus examinees doing poorly on the routing test receive an easier set of second-stage items than examinees doing well on the routing test. Adaptive testing procedures can maximize the reliability of measurement while minimizing the number of items that need to be administered to any given examinee.

In summary, although latent trait theories and adaptive testing are relatively new in test construction, they hold great promise for the future. Some of the major tests, such as the Armed Services Aptitude Battery (ASVAB) are already available in computer-administered adaptive form (Moreno, Wetzel, McBride, & Weiss, 1984).

Summary

This chapter has attempted to review basic principles of test construction, but length restrictions prevent as thorough a discussion as the topic warrants. It is recommended that students wishing to construct tests or scales for research or applied purposes take courses in measurement theory and methods and/or consult the many references provided here. Scale construction can advance scientific understanding by providing the means to operationalize important psychological constructs, but it can only advance this understanding if it is done carefully and knowledgeably.

Recommended Readings

Readers who are interested in further information about this topic may refer to *Standards for Educational and Psychological Tests* (AERA, 1985) and Cronbach and Meehl (1955); Nunnally and Bernstein's *Psychometric Theory* (1993) and Spector's *Summated Rating Scale Construction* (1992) are also useful.

References

American Educational Research Association, American Psychological Association, National Council on Measurement in Education. (1985). *Standards for educational and psychological testing.* Washington, DC: Author.

Beere, C. (1990a). *Gender roles.* Westport, CT: Greenwood.

Beere, C. (1990b). *Sex and gender issues.* Westport, CT: Greenwood.

Betz, N. E., Serling, D., Wohlgemuth, E., Harshbarger, J., & Klein, K. (1995). Evaluation of a measure of self-esteem based on the concept of unconditional self-regard. *Journal of Counseling and Development, 74,* 76-83.

Betz, N., & Weiss, D. J. (1973). *An empirical study of two-stage ability testing* (Research Rep. No. 73-4). Minneapolis: University of Minnesota, Psychometric Methods Program.

Cronbach, L. J., & Meehl, P. E. (1955). Construct validity in psychological tests. *Psychological Bulletin, 52,* 281-302.

Dawis, R. V. (1987). Scale construction. *Journal of Counseling Psychology, 34,* 481-489.

Edwards, A. L. (1957). *Techniques of attitude scale construction.* New York: Appleton-Century-Crofts.

Fitzgerald, L. F., & Hubert, L. (1987). Multidimensional scaling: Some possibilities for counseling psychology. *Journal of Counseling Psychology, 34,* 469-480.

Glass, G. V., & Hopkins, K. D. (1984). *Statistical methods in education and psychology.* Englewood Cliffs, NJ: Prentice Hall.

Hambleton, R. K. (1989). Principles and selected applications of item response theory. In R. L. Linn (Ed.), *Educational measurement* (3rd ed., pp. 147-200). New York: Macmillan.

Kramer, J. J., & Conoley, J. C. (Eds.). (1992). *The eleventh mental measurements yearbook.* Lincoln, NE: Buros Institute of Mental Measurements.

Maranell, G. (Ed.). (1974). *Scaling: A sourcebook for behavioral scientists.* Chicago: Aldine.

Moreno, K. E., Wetzel, C. D., McBride, J. R., & Weiss, D. J. (1984). Relationship between corresponding ASVAB and computerized adaptive testing (CAT) subtests. *Applied Psychological Measurement, 8,* 155-163.

Nunnally, J., & Bernstein, I. (1993). *Psychometric theory* (3rd ed.). New York: McGraw-Hill.

Robinson, J. P., Shaver, P. R., & Wrightsman, L. S. (1991). *Measures of personality and social psychological attitudes.* San Diego: Academic Press.

Spector, P. (1992). *Summated rating scale construction.* Newbury Park, CA: Sage.

Tinsley, H. E. A., & Tinsley, D. J. (1987). Use of factor analysis in counseling psychology research. *Journal of Counseling Psychology, 34,* 414-424.

Wainer, H. (Ed.). (1990). *Computerized adaptive testing: A primer.* Hillsdale, NJ: Lawrence Erlbaum.

Walsh, W. B., & Betz, N. E. (1995). *Tests and assessment.* (3rd ed.). Englewood Cliffs, NJ: Prentice Hall.

Weiss, D. J. (1974). *Strategies of adaptive ability measurement* (Research Rep. No. 74-5). Minneapolis: University of Minnesota, Psychometric Methods Program.

Weiss, D. J. (1982). Improving measurement quality and efficiency with adaptive testing. *Applied Psychological Measurement, 6,* 473-492.

Weiss, D. J. (Ed.). (1983). *Latent trait test theory and computerized adaptive testing.* New York: Academic Press.

Chapter 20

Using Archival Data Sets

BARBARA H. ZAITZOW
CHARLES B. FIELDS

What Are Archival Data Sets?

Often a social scientist can answer pressing research questions through the analysis of secondary data sets. Secondary data sets are published data that were "collected for some general information need or as a part of a research effort designed to answer a specific question" (Stewart & Kamins, 1993, p. 2). Using archival data sets is considered a nonreactive data collection method because the researcher does not come into contact with the subjects under investigation; thus the potential error that may result from the effects of a researcher's activities on those studied is eliminated (Webb, Campbell, Schwartz, Sechrest, & Grove, 1981). However, only through the efforts of primary data collection do secondary data sets exist. Thus the extent to which secondary data sets are affected by the methodology employed by the initial investigator is one of several issues to be addressed in this chapter. The purpose of this chapter is to provide an overview on the use of archival data sets for social science research.

One of the first to utilize information collected by others was Emile Durkheim, a founder of the sociological discipline. In his late-19th-century study entitled *Suicide* (1897/1966), he used existing records of approximately 26,000 reports from various countries to examine variation in rates of suicide between "mechanical" (small, rural) and "anomic" (large, urban) societies. Today we may draw on the materials published by the U.S. Bureau of the Census to talk about trends in population growth and decline, or we may use world statistics gathered by the United Nations to study patterns in world economic change and development.

We may also study novels, songs, television programs, and other mass media productions to understand our society better. We can delve into the past, using records kept by historical societies or the diaries and letters of pioneer mothers and fathers to ask questions about the differences between today's families and those of the last century. The groundbreaking work of the Terman "Studies of Genius" at Stanford University, which followed some 1,600 gifted California children from 1922 to the present, in concert with several well-known longitudinal studies at the Institute of Human Development at the University of California, Berkeley, launched a life study approach to data archives that has enabled researchers to examine historical influences on the lives of people from different birth cohorts.

When Should You Consider Using Archival Data?

Archival data sets can be used in a multitude of ways and for a variety of research questions. Aggregate data can be used to focus on the social forces that affect crime. For example, to study the relationship between crime and poverty, criminologists make use of Census Bureau data on income and the number of people on welfare and single-parent families in an urban area and then cross-reference this information with official crime statistics from the same locality (Blau & Blau, 1982; Messner, 1983; Sampson, 1985). The use of these two sources of archival data provides enhanced understanding about the effect of overall social trends and patterns on the crime rate. Archival data may also be used to compare socioeconomic characteristics of different ethnic or racial groups over 10-year intervals to determine if gaps in their socioeconomic status are widening or declining or to examine the suburbanization of industrial activity since World War II and analyze its impact on minority unemployment in the central cities.

Social scientists have at their disposal data from public opinion polls, which are conducted and disseminated on a regular basis. Many survey organizations, such as the American Institute for Public Opinion, which conducts the Gallup polls, the Roper Organization, and Louis Harris and Associates, have conducted literally hundreds of polls over the past few decades. Data from these and similar polls are particularly useful for studying social change and habits. So extensive are the data provided in the various censuses that opportunities for secondary analysis seem to be limited only by the imagination of the researcher.

DISADVANTAGES

Secondary analysis is very closely related to survey analysis (see Goddard & Villanova, Chapter 7 of this volume). The basic difference between survey research and secondary analysis is that in the latter the data have been collected by someone else for some other purpose. This means that the researcher has little control over the nature of the data or of the data collection process. As a result, it is sometimes difficult to formulate appropriate operational definitions because the data have not been collected in the appropriate form. Emile Durkheim's 19th-century study of suicide illustrates some of the dangers of this approach. He relied on official death records to investigate suicide rates among various types of people. But he had no way to check how many accidents were incorrectly classified as suicides or what number of suicides were recorded as accidents or deaths due to some other cause. Thus the researcher must beware of distortions.

Questions may have been phrased and presented to respondents in a way not exactly suited to the current researcher's goals, or the subjects who responded may not have been the ones the researcher would have chosen. "Careful attention must be given to what information actually was obtained in a particular study" (Stewart & Kamins, 1993, p. 23). Knowledge of the methodology employed during the data collection procedure (e.g., sample characteristics, response rates, interview or survey protocol, measurement instruments, coding forms) is necessary to ensure the validity and generalizability of conclusions based on the use of secondary data sources.

Perhaps the major shortcoming of census data in particular for social science research is that many variables of interest to social scientists are not reported in the censuses. For example, no information is collected about sentiments, attitudes, values, or beliefs. Researchers interested in social psychological studies must therefore look elsewhere for secondary sources of data or conduct their own field studies or experiments.

"Secondary data are, by definition, old data" (Stewart & Kamins, 1993, p. 6). Census publication delays, for example, will affect the temporal boundaries from which measurements are taken, results are obtained, and generalizations are put forth. For example, if you are using archival data to study changes in Americans' premarital sexual behavior, results will have to be interpreted in light of several sociohistorical events. Clearly, the reasons for older Americans "waiting until marriage" are qualitatively distinct from more recent respondents' concerns that "the first time may result in a death sentence via HIV/AIDs." In both scenarios, the responses may express celibate intentions, yet the reasons for this in the two eras may be very different! Again, one must be alert to these sociohistorical issues when using archival data sets (Gergen, 1973). Obviously, we are dealing with a trade-off here; the usefulness of the data must be balanced against the ease with which they can be obtained. Therefore, whenever researchers use information collected by others, they must interpret the data with care and in a way suitable for their goals.

ADVANTAGES

On the other hand, it can be argued that secondary analysis frees researchers from the responsibility and the time and expense of collecting and coding their own data. The use of archival data sets enables social scientists with low budgets to undertake research that might otherwise be impossible. Furthermore, sampling and measurement error in U.S. censuses, for example, is among the lowest of all sources of survey data. Nevertheless, human and mechanical errors do occur that reduce the accuracy of some reported data. In the words of the U.S. Bureau of the Census (1964):

> Such errors include failure to obtain required information from respondents, obtaining inconsistent information, recording information in the wrong place or incorrectly, and otherwise producing inconsistencies between entries or interrelated items on the field documents. Sampling biases occur because some of the enumerators fail to follow the sampling instructions. Clerical coding and editing errors occur, and errors occur in electronic processing. (p. lxxxv)

To mitigate these errors, Bureau of the Census personnel review enumerators' work, verify the manual coding and editing, check the tabulated figures, and utilize statistical techniques such as ratio estimation of sample data to control totals in the complete count. Through such efforts, errors in the printed reports are usually kept at an acceptably low level so that secondary analysis of these data will not generally yield misleading results.

What makes archival data particularly useful for secondary analysis is that most variables are available not only cross-sectionally (at one point in time) but also on a longitudinal basis (at a number of different occasions). This enables researchers to measure particular social relationships and examine their historical trends. For example, criminologists make extensive use of official statistics—especially the Uniform Crime Reports prepared and distributed by the Federal Bureau of Investigation—concerning the frequency of various crimes in the United States, yet they are always on guard against distortions in these statistics. We know, for example, that many crimes (e.g., illegal drug use) are not reported to the police; and to make this problem more complex, the rate of reporting varies according to the type of crime. Homicides are very likely to come to the attention of police, whereas rapes have traditionally been underreported. One attempt to correct for this discrepancy entails researchers' collecting their own data to check the accuracy of official crime statistics. The value of available data is clearly enhanced if we have some idea of how accurate they are. Moreover, the use of multiple sources of information may be the best strategy to overcome some of the problems that may be present in secondary data.

On a more practical or applied level, additional considerations that must be weighed in your decision to use archival data include the following: (a) Will the data be transferable to your computer system? (b) Will the documentation (which may not be provided at all) be sufficient to carry out the analyses? and (c) Do you have the expertise and patience to deal with conflicts arising from differing levels of aggregation, classification schemas, and appropriate software to facilitate analyses?

In their work with archival data, Elder, Pavalko, and Clipp (1993) noted the following themes recurring:

1. Archival data are never precisely what one wants or expects. Given this, the investigator is challenged to do what is possible, given time and resources, in shaping the data according to needs.
2. The data at hand often reflect the perspectives of the original investigators, as expressed in research questions, data collection procedures, and analytic techniques.
3. Longitudinal data archives do not guarantee life-record or longitudinal data analysis. Cross-sectional data entries and storage are far more common than temporal records of information on people's lives, and often these cross-sectional records have to be converted to a life-record format.
4. . . . [These] studies can draw on quantitative and qualitative data and analysis. Effective use of both kinds of data requires careful planning to permit their application to identical topics or problems.
5. The rationale for using archival data should be based on strengths of the data. It should not be defended through attempts to disarm or ignore the weaknesses. (p. 11)

Careful consideration of these points is necessary to determine the usefulness of archival data for your particular research question. For the data to be usable, you must know exactly what you are dealing with.

Archival Data Accessibility

As you are probably aware, thousands of surveys have been conducted in recent decades by college- and university-based researchers, private organizations and corporations, and various government agencies. Most of these surveys have resulted in computerized data archives, many of which are available to researchers (an excellent review of such resources is provided by Stewart & Kamins, 1993). There are currently three main sources of existing data: (a) various public and private data archives, (b) the U.S. Census and related sources, and (c) published or broadcast media suitable for content analysis. The following discussion will focus on the first two categories as they typify "already collected" data.

PUBLIC AND PRIVATE DATA ARCHIVES

Many college professors conducting research are willing to share their data with others whose research interests are slightly different from their own. In fact, some do this on a regular basis through organizations such as the Henry A. Murray Research Center of Radcliffe College, which serves as a "national repository for data in the fields of psychology, psychiatry, sociology, anthropology, economics, political science, and education" and contains much useful information for secondary analysis (Elder et al., 1993, p. 83). Similarly, the Inter-University Consortium for Political and Social Research (ICPSR) is a national organization in which most major universities participate.

Inter-University Consortium for Political and Social Research

Founded in 1962 as a partnership between the University of Michigan's Survey Research Center and 21 research universities around the country, the ICPSR currently has a membership of 325 colleges and universities in the United States and Canada and several hundred additional institutions around the world. The ICPSR, through its archive, receives, processes, and distributes machine-readable data on social phenomena obtained from a variety of sources. Data ranging from American election information from the 1790s (the largest collection) to recent United Nations session materials are available.

Data and supporting documentation are available at no (or nominal) cost through member institutions; nonmembers may also obtain ICPSR data, but it can be more expensive. Four "classes" of data are available, and collections are categorized according to the level and extent of processing necessary by the ICPSR:

> *Class I:* Datasets have been checked, corrected if necessary, and formatted to ICPSR specifications. Also, the data may have been recoded and reorganized in consultation with the investigator to maximize their utilization and accessibility. A codebook, often capable of being read by a computer, is available.
>
> *Class II:* These studies have been checked and formatted to ICPSR specifications. Most non-numeric codes have been removed. A copy of the documentation (codebook) is supplied when the data are requested.

Class III: These have also been checked by the ICPSR staff for the appropriate number of data records and accurate data locations as specified by the investigator's codebook. The data themselves usually are available only in the format provided by the Principal Investigator.

Class IV: These studies are distributed in the form received by ICPSR from the original investigator. The documentation is reproduced from the material originally received (ICPSR, 1994, p. xxiii)

The ICPSR also provides various kinds of assistance in using their data sets effectively. For example, assistance in selecting equipment and data storage media, identification of appropriate software, and utilization of computer networking technology is available to members through written materials, special workshops and seminars, and telephone consultation. A major concern is to assist in the use of new technologies that "are radically changing the potentialities for social science instruction and research (ICPSR, 1994, p. viii).

A few of the many data sets available from the ICPSR that may be of interest to psychology students include the following:

- *Americans View Their Mental Health, 1976* (ICPSR 7948)—Contains the data from a nationwide survey sponsored by the National Institute of Mental Health. The survey (sample of 2,264,850 variables) focused on the areas of marriage, parenthood, employment, leisure time, motives for achievement and power, and general social relationships. In addition, extensive information was collected in the areas of help seeking, the readiness of people to use professional help, referral mechanisms, and evaluation of help received.

- *Marital Instability Over the Life Course* (U.S.): A Three-Wave Panel Study, 1980-1988 (ICPSR 9747)—This data collection attempts to identify the causes of marital instability throughout the life course. A national sample ($N = 2,033$) of married individuals 55 or younger were interviewed by telephone in 1980, then reinterviewed in 1983 and 1988. Questions dealing with economic resources, employment, children, and life goals were asked to determine links that tend to cause divorce.

- *Survey of Parents and Children, 1990* (ICPSR 9595)—Conducted by the National Commission on Children. This collection was designed to assess the attitudes, well-being, and life circumstances of American families. The sample consisted of 1,738 parents and 929 children aged 10 to 17, and households with Black and Hispanic children were oversampled.

- *Project TALENT Public Use File, 1960-1976* (ICPSR 7823)—A longitudinal survey assessing the personal, educational, and educational factors promoting or inhibiting the development of human talents. In 1960, 400,000 (subsample of 4,000 included here) students in Grades 9 through 12 were surveyed on interests, plans, family background, cognitive skills, etc. Follow-up surveys conducted 1 year, 5 years, and 11 years after graduation produced information regarding post-high-school education, family development, plans and aspirations, and life satisfaction.

Other Government Documents

Many government agencies conduct surveys and other forms of research and then sell computer archives of the data at cost. One example of such a source is the FBI's well-known Uniform Crime Reports (UCR). The UCR is one of the most commonly used official data sources in America today and has been extremely influential in guiding policy decisions regarding crime prevention and control. However, some limitations must be considered when selecting and using this and similar databases, and these should be examined thoroughly before considering use. For example, the UCR has been based on voluntary reporting by local police departments. Here, reporting differences have been noted between urban and rural precincts, with the latter group reporting less frequently. Perhaps a more serious flaw is that surveys of crime victims (the National Crime Surveys [NCS] published by the Bureau of Justice Statistics) reveal that fewer than 50% of all serious crimes are reported to the police (Bastian & DeBerry, 1994). The use of multiple data sources is recommended to provide a more accurate picture of the phenomenon being investigated.

Although the Bureau of the Census (discussed below) is probably the best source for archival data, a wide range of information is available from other government agencies. Government agencies at the federal, state, and local levels, the judicial system, and various legislative and administrative bodies continue to produce vast quantities of information. Though much of this has traditionally been unavailable for various reasons, the Freedom of Information Act of 1966 opened numerous avenues for the public to get this information.

The U.S. government also has a registration system that records births, deaths, marriages, and divorces as they occur. The Department of Health and Human Services publishes the *Monthly Vital Statistics Report* as well as an annual summary that is an important source for researchers interested in these topics.

U.S. CENSUS DATA

A major source of data, available to anyone with access to a good library, is the U.S. census. The census, conducted every 10 years, includes comprehensive data on a wide range of population and housing characteristics for areas as small as a city block and as big as the entire country. A glance through any major sociological journal will reveal that the census is one of the most important sources of data for sociological research. In addition to population and housing, regular censuses are also conducted on manufacturing, wholesale trade, retail trade, service industries, agriculture, mineral industries, and government. The results of all of these censuses can be looked up at any major library or purchased on computer tape or CD-ROM from the Census Bureau or any number of universities and private firms.

The population census is conducted only every 10 years, however, and there is a need for more current data. This need is met by the Current Population Survey. This survey, conducted on an ongoing basis by the Census Bureau for the Bureau of Labor Statistics, provides annual updates on such things as population size, age structure, racial composition, income, education, and employment and unemployment. In addition, regular and special (e.g., one-time) supplements are available in specific areas. If you need up-to-date data on any of these issues, the Current Population Survey is the place to look.

Also, keep in mind that the ICPSR archives contain many of the Census of Population data sets available to researchers. The complete 1970, 1980, and 1990 census data are accessible, as are a variety of representative sample collections derived from the original census questionnaires. Incomplete census data are available from 1860 (Urban Household Sample), 1880, 1910 (Oversample of Black-Headed Households), and up through the 1960 series.

A word of caution: Although the Bureau of the Census and other government agencies have a tradition of being protected from political interference, various administrations can influence what topics are covered by special reports and how often certain kinds of data are published. For example, the Reagan administration unsuccessfully tried to stop publishing the government's yearly report on after-tax income (which showed the rich getting richer, contrary to administration claims). The 10-year census has also been subject to political influence regarding what questions are asked and how answers are interpreted (Alonso & Starr, 1986). More recently, the commissioner of the Social Security Administration resigned after admitting that the agency had run verification checks of social security numbers for a credit company; the privacy of these records is basic to maintaining trust in the entire social security system.

Steps in the Research Process

In looking for an optimum fit between your research questions and the archival data, the following steps are suggested.

STEP 1: PROBLEM SPECIFICATION

In secondary analysis, research questions are often less specific than in research by the more traditional methods. Often the data themselves dictate what questions can be asked and how to ask them. The first thing to do is to identify what you know about your topic, as well as what you want to know.

STEP 2: SEARCH FOR APPROPRIATE DATA

Always keep in mind that not all information collected from secondary sources is equally reliable or valid. You must evaluate the data carefully to see if they are indeed appropriate for your needs. Stewart and Kamins (1993, pp. 17-30) identified six questions that should be asked when you are evaluating the data you want to use:

1. What was the purpose of the study?
2. Who collected the information?
3. What information was actually collected?
4. When was the information collected?
5. How was the information collected?
6. How consistent is the information with other sources?

Remember that these may not be the only questions that will come up when you are searching for the data for your study. The authors suggested keeping an attitude of "healthy skepticism" (p. 31) when using secondary sources; other constraints may exist as well. Access to the data may be limited, for example. Sometimes the original collector (or owner) may require approval before allowing use of data.

STEP 3: PREPARATION OF THE RESEARCH PROPOSAL

Preparation of the research proposal for secondary analysis is very similar to that done in other types of research. Organization of research proposals/reports will vary by the specifications of the audience (e.g., university professor vs. professional journal). A comprehensive literature review of existing theoretical and empirical work that is of relevance to the research problem at hand will result in criticisms of past efforts as well as the discovery of new frontiers that beckon for inquiry. It is during the preparation of the research proposal that the information provided by others will assist you in selecting a research methodology (i.e., developing measurement techniques, deciding on relevant samples, choosing analytic strategies) and in the avoidance of pitfalls noted in previous efforts. As with any research methodology, the advantages of the data collection strategy are weighed against the disadvantages. As Elder et al. (1993) noted, "The most effective strategy is to make a case for the advantages of the data" (p. 21).

STEP 4: INITIAL ANALYSIS AND RECASTING OF ARCHIVAL DATA

Once you decide on what data to use, then you must determine how to use them. More often than not, the data as they were originally measured will not be entirely suitable for the researcher's current needs; it sometimes must be reformulated for your specific purposes. This reformulation, sometimes called *recasting*, is a process in which some variables may be recategorized and those with inadequate data may be eliminated altogether (McCall & Appelbaum, 1991).

STEP 5: ANALYSIS

Obviously, the methods used to analyze data must fit the question(s), the measures, and the characteristics of the original sample. But many times, questions do not get asked unless the researcher knows how to answer them statistically (McCall & Appelbaum, 1991, p. 916).

Conclusion

Although one can list the ideals of research, real-life situations often force social scientists to settle for something that falls short of the ideal. Consequently, the typical dilemma that social researchers confront is either not to study what they want to study or to study it under less than ideal conditions. Researchers' choice of methodology is dependent on available resources. For example, although they prefer to conduct a survey, they may find that finances will not permit it and instead turn to the study of documents or utilize an already collected data archive. Each method is better for answering some questions than for others. If you wish to study the causes of revolution in an underdeveloped country, you do not necessarily need to become a participant observer among the guerrillas. You might be able, instead, to use existing documents and records to relate revolution to such factors as poverty.

Archival data provide an efficient, cost-effective, and timely way for researchers to pursue important theoretical and policy-related questions about a variety of issues. Perhaps the greatest scientific value of archival data lies in the potential for replication by other researchers. Confidence in the validity of a relationship increases as it can be reproduced in a variety of settings. And, as Traugott (1990) noted:

> The resulting data may lend themselves to other analyses which were never anticipated by the original researchers. A secondary analysis effort may arise because a researcher has a different set of theoretical interests or reconceptualizes the problem. Or it may result from the accumulation of data in an archive. Multiple data sets, each originally collected for a different purpose, may take on new analytical utility based upon their possible combinations or a series of complementary analyses which none of the principal investigators could have contemplated. (p. 146)

More researchers are working with better data than would be available if they had to organize and administer their own data collection projects. And they are devoting more of their effort to analysis than to the necessarily time-consuming administrative tasks associated with managing large-scale data collection projects. Although care must be taken in reviewing the principal investigator's decisions about conceptualization and operationalization, secondary analysis has increased research opportunities and hence has resulted in an extension of our understanding of a multitude of topics and issues. And that is exactly what science needs more of—imaginative, and sometimes daring, research conducted in an imperfect world under less than ideal conditions. This is what it is all about. The application of research methods takes us beyond common sense and allows us to penetrate surface realities so we can better understand social life.

Recommended Readings

In this section we present several sources for further study and advanced reading, drawn from psychological and sociological research literature. Barrett (1994) and Davis and Smith (1991) present comprehensive but readable treatments of using the U.S. Census and the National Opinion Research Corporation (NORC) General Social Survey, respectively. Both of these archival datasets are available for researchers, and they present the advantage of repeated measurements on the general population of the United States. Brooks-Gunn, Phelps, and Elder (1991) present a treatment of secondary (i.e., archival) data sources for developmental psychologists as part of a special issue of *Developmental Psychology* that contains other articles of interest (e.g., Cherlin, 1991; McCall and Appelbaum, 1991). A classic archival and longitudinal data source is Terman and coworkers' massive study of high-IQ children in California, which started in the 1920s and continues to this day (Craven, 1992). Terman (1925), the earliest in the series, and Terman and Oden (1959), the fifth volume, would make useful sources. Finally, an inventory of longitudinal studies across the social sciences is provided by Young, Savela, and Phelps (1991).

References

Alonso, W., & Starr, P. (1986). *The politics of numbers.* New York: Russell Sage.

Barrett, R. E., (1994). *Using the 1990 U.S. Census for Research.* Thousand Oaks, CA: Sage.

Bastian, L., & DeBerry, M., Jr. (1994). *Criminal victimization, 1992.* Washington, DC: Bureau of Justice Statistics.

Blau, J., & Blau, P. (1982). The cost of inequality: Metropolitan structure and violent crime. *American Sociological Review, 47,* 114-129.

Brooks-Gunn, J., Phelps, E., & Elder, G. H., Jr. (1991). Studying lives through time: Secondary data analyses in developmental psychology. *Developmental Psychology, 27,* 899-910.

Cherlin, A. (1991). On analyzing other people's data. *Developmental Psychology, 27,* 946-948.

Craven, H. J., (1992). A scientific project locked in time: The Terman genetic studies of genius, 1920s-1950s. *American Psychologist, 47,* 183-189.

Davis, J. A., & Smith, T. W. (1992). *The NORC General Social Survey: A user's guide.* Newbury Park, CA: Sage.

Duncan, G. J. (1991). Made in heaven: Secondary data analysis and interdisciplinary collaborators. *Developmental Psychology, 27,* 949-961.

Durkheim, E. (1966). *Suicide.* New York: Free Press. (Original work published 1897)

Elder, G. H., Jr., Pavalko, E. K., & Clipp, E. C. (1993). *Working with archival data.* Newbury Park, CA: Sage.

Gergen, K. (1973). Social psychology as history. *Journal of Personality and Social Psychology, 26,* 309-320.

Inter-University Consortium for Political and Social Research. (1994). *Guide to resources and services, 1994-1995.* Ann Arbor, MI: Author.

Kiecolt, K. J., & Nathan, L. E. (1985). *Secondary analysis of survey data.* Newbury Park, CA: Sage.

McCall, R. B., & Appelbaum, M. I. (1991). Some issues of conducting secondary analysis. *Developmental Psychology, 27,* 911-917.

Messner, S. (1983). Regional and racial effects on the urban homicide rate: The subculture of violence revisited. *American Journal of Sociology, 88,* 997-1007.

Sampson, R. J. (1985). Structural sources of variation in race-age specific rates of offending across major U.S. cities. *Criminology, 23,* 647-673.

Scott, J. (1990). *A matter of record: Documentary sources in social research.* Cambridge, UK: Polity.

Stewart, D. W., & Kamins, M. A. (1993). *Secondary research: Information sources and methods.* Newbury Park, CA: Sage.

Terman, L. M. (With others). (1925). *Genetic studies of genius, Vol. 1: Mental and physical traits of a thousand gifted children.* Stanford, CA: Stanford University Press.

Terman, L. M., & Oden, M. H. (1959). *Genetic studies of genius, Vol. 5: The gifted group at mid-life: Thirty-five years of follow-up of the superior child.* Stanford, CA: Stanford University Press.

Traugott, M. W. (1990). Using archival data for the secondary analysis of criminal justice issues. In D. L. MacKenzie, P. J. Baunach, & R. R. Roberg (Eds.), *Measuring crime: Large-scale, long-range efforts* (pp. 145-155). Albany: State University of New York Press.

U.S. Bureau of the Census. (1964). *U.S. census of population: 1960, United States summary, characteristics of the population* (Vol. 1, Pt. 1). Washington, DC: Government Printing Office.

Webb. E. T., Campbell, D. T., Schwartz, R. D., Sechrest, L., & Grove, J. B. (1981). *Nonreactive measures in the social sciences.* Boston: Houghton Mifflin.

Young, C. H., Savela, K. L., & Phelps, E. (1991). *Inventory of longitudinal studies in the social sciences.* Newbury Park, CA: Sage.

PART V

Research Writing

Chapter 21

Writing in APA Style

Why and How

JAMES T. AUSTIN
ROBERT F. CALDERÓN

The importance of communicating research findings through publication cannot be overemphasized within science. Valuable research findings, if not communicated, may fail to influence science and society. Scholarly communication (Hills, 1983) ensures that the results of research are not isolated within individuals or research teams. The functions served by the review-publication process include conveying information, defining the field, setting quality standards, certifying individual merit, storing information, contributing to intellectual life, and protecting the public. Undergraduate and graduate students are often asked to prepare lab and research reports. Writing up early graduate and undergraduate research (theses and dissertations) is another step in learning to communicate research findings. Thus writing is a component of a researcher's higher-order repertoire at all career stages.

Writing for scientific audiences is different from other writing styles taught in schools (Lannon, 1988; Sides, 1989; Woodford, 1967). Therefore students of psychology may have difficulties in acquiring this skill. Realizing this difficulty and wishing to standardize communication within the psychological research community, the American Psychological Association (APA) requires a specific format and style for researchers to follow in preparing research reports, grants, or other communications (APA, 1994) and has for some time (Anderson & Valentine, 1944). Although this style may seem alien as you start to learn it, it is a standard format that transmits conceptual arguments and empirical results in a logical and concise manner.

This chapter addresses basic requirements for format and style defined by the latest APA *Publication Manual* (4th ed.; APA, 1994). After discussing the parts of the empirical research report, APA format and word-processing technology are integrated, given the increasing importance of the computer in publication (APA, 1994; Standera, 1987; Wright, 1987). Appendix 21.1 at the end of this chapter provides a metatemplate for preparing/evaluating draft manuscripts with respect to their match to the *Publication Manual*. Note that we treat writing stylistically rather than substantively. Other chapters in this book address preparing drafts (Peterson, Chapter 22) and revising manuscripts (Nagata &

Trierweiler, Chapter 23), and elsewhere, Becker (1986), Runkel and Runkel (1984), and Jones (1976) specifically address scientific and technical writing.

Writing in APA style and format is not the same as writing well, although both involve elements of self-discipline. The *Publication Manual* provides advice within a dual framework of specificity and sensitivity (APA, 1994, p. xxvi). *Specificity* is the standard that research be described in sufficient detail to permit replication. *Sensitivity* is the standard that language be free from bias against societal groups. Specific recommendations for reducing language bias include choice of appropriate level of specificity, sensitivity to labels and labeling processes, and acknowledgment of participation. Choice of precise words, avoidance of ambiguity, order and sequence of ideas, and consideration of your reader are additional guidelines. All are useful recommendations, but writing and how to do it better are best treated by other sources, listed near the end of this chapter. One method for improving writing style and substance is practice. When considering a research topic, prepare miniproposals (two to three pages) to help automate the components of this skill. The *Publication Manual* identifies empirical, review, and theoretical types of manuscripts. It is unlikely that you, as a research assistant, will be asked to prepare the latter two types of manuscripts; thus the empirical manuscript is the primary focus of this chapter.

Components of the Empirical Manuscript

Manuscripts generally consist of three parts. *Front matter* consists of the title page and abstract. The *body* of the empirical manuscript consists of the Introduction, Method, Results, and Discussion sections. *Back matter* includes supporting material: references, notes, tables and figures, and appendixes. Not all of these back matter elements will be required for every manuscript, but it is useful to have a working knowledge of each part and to refer to the *Publication Manual* for more detailed descriptions. In addition, there may be subsections within the four major parts of the body (e.g., the Method section may have subsections for participants, apparatus/measures, and procedures). Below we describe each of the components in order.

INTRODUCTION

The introduction informs the reader of the specific problem under study and how that problem is related to prior research. In writing the introduction, attempt to answer four questions for the reader: (a) What is the point of the study? (b) What is the relation of the study to previous work? (c) What is the rationale that links the study and the research design? and (d) What are the theoretical limitations of the study? The most difficult part of writing the introduction is to develop explicitly the logical connection between your research question, the work in the literature, and your research design. Clarify these matters for the reader as you write.

Writers should list hypotheses or research questions at or near the end of their introductory section. Hypotheses are specific predictions about expected results; research questions are general and indicate more of an exploratory focus. A separate heading might be used for this section of the introduction, and justification for each hypothesis might be placed in the text immediately before or after the statement of hypothesis.

In sum, the introduction gives readers a method of judging whether the purposes of the study are related to the empirical literature. It sets the stage for the rest of the body of text, consisting of the Method, Results, and Discussion sections. If this section is poorly written, readers may lose interest or develop a negative perception of the research. Because the initial readers of a manuscript are often editors and reviewers, it is wise to avoid such negative perceptions.

METHOD

The Method section of an empirical manuscript details what was done to collect the data to be analyzed. It has several subsections, with the exact number depending on the complexity of the study. In general, it informs readers about the participants (also called *subjects*), what procedures were used, the design, and any apparatus/equipment that was used. A competent researcher should be able to evaluate the quality of the research and replicate the study after reading this section alone. Moreover, you can and should apply this "test" yourself when reading an article's Method section.

A Participants subsection should provide clear answers to three questions: (a) Who took part in the study? (b) How many participants were there? and (c) How were participants selected? (Are they representative of a defined population?) In addition, you may provide major demographic characteristics of the sample and the number assigned to experimental groups or condition. Last, always report any inducements for participation (monetary, extra credit).

In the Apparatus subsection, describe the major devices or materials used in the study. If you constructed the apparatus yourself, you may have to provide greater detail so that a reader can comprehend exactly what the device was. Appendixes or a separate technical report may be required. Any questionnaire measures should be referenced here, and deviations from the original scales or instructions should be described. Some writers provide the psychometric characteristics (e.g., reliability estimates, standard errors of measurement) in this section, whereas others provide such details in the Results section.

A Procedures subsection presents the steps in the actual running of the study. It may include instructions to participants, formation of groups, and any specific experimental manipulations. Describe subject assignment, counterbalancing, and other control features. This section should inform the reader what was done, how it was done, and in what order. Again, it does so in sufficient detail to permit replication. Informed consent, debriefing, and other ethical requirements must be mentioned in this section. In summary, then, the Method section details participants, apparatus and measures, and the procedures used to present stimuli and measure responses.

RESULTS

The Results section summarizes the collected data and their statistical treatment. Briefly state the main types of analyses to begin. Detail is needed only for the more esoteric statistical tests. Then report those analyses in detail so that you can justify conclusions you intend to make in later sections. State the results, and do not discuss their implications or make inferences until the Discussion section. Report all relevant results, even those counter to your hypotheses (this is important!).

In this section, you may choose to present results using graphs or tables, but consider the value of this mode of presentation carefully, as tables and figures are expensive to typeset (figures are more difficult to typeset than tables). On the other hand, the saying that "one picture is worth a thousand words," is also applicable. If you do use tables or figures, refer to graphs, pictures, or drawings as *figures* and to tables as *tables*. For example, you could say in the text, "Figure 1 depicts the goal acceptance levels for each of the experimental groups." If you include tables and figures, place them together at the end of the manuscript (after the references). Tables should have the running head and page number, whereas figures should not. On the other hand, figures do require a caption on a separate page immediately preceding the figure (which does have the running head and page number). The *Publication Manual* gives additional details on tables and figures (Table Checklist, Section 3.74, pp. 140-141; Figure Checklist, Section 3.86, pp. 162-163).

The statistical presentation of data should include sufficient information so that the reader can confirm that appropriate analyses were conducted. Therefore all inferential statistics (e.g., t tests, F tests, chi-square tests) *must* include information concerning the means, variability measures (e.g., variance, standard deviation), obtained magnitude of the test statistic, the degrees of freedom, the probability of observing such a test statistic given a true null hypothesis, and the direction of the effect. Here are examples: "As predicted, females ($M = 9.55$, $SD = 1.67$) reported greater liking for school than did males ($M = 7.62$, $SD = 1.22$), $t(22) = 2.62$, $p < .01$," and "The ANOVA indicated significant differences in latency of response for participants not provided with training, $F(1,34) = 123.78, p < .001$)." However, if exact probabilities are presented, then an a priori probability level (i.e., alpha level) must be stated before specific results are reported. Here are examples: "An alpha level of .01 was used for all statistical analyses" and "With an alpha level of .01, the effect of gender was statistically significant, $t(22) = 2.62$, $p = .006$." Furthermore, if descriptive statistics are provided in a table or figure, they do not need to be repeated in the text unless they are supporting/rejecting a hypothesis or research question. The *Publication Manual* gives additional details on sufficient statistics and statistical presentation (Section 1.10, pp. 15-16; Sections 3.53-3.61, pp. 111-119).

Increasingly, statistical power associated with the tests of hypotheses is also included in this section (Yaffee, Chapter 15 of this volume). Statistical power pertains to the likelihood of correctly rejecting the hypotheses of interest and is dependent on the chosen alpha level, effect size, and sample size (all of these values should also be reported in a summary of research). Further, statistical power should be considered during the design phase of a study so that necessary changes (e.g., larger N, increased number of trials) can be made to ensure that sufficient power can be achieved in the study. Methods for calculating both statistical power and effect size are presented in various statistics classes.

At the novice level, common analyses include t tests on means for two groups, one-way analysis of variance for three or more groups, and simple and multiple regression to study interrelationships among larger sets of measures (Dickter & Roznowski, Chapter 16 of this volume). Complex and sophisticated techniques, including multivariate ones, become common with greater exposure to research or in graduate education (Levy &

Steelman, Chapter 17 of this volume). In summary, then, the Results section includes summary statistics and statistical significance tests of a priori hypotheses and any hypotheses that may emerge from your planned analyses.

DISCUSSION

The Discussion section is where authors elaborate their results. One way to begin the discussion is to open with a statement on the support of your original hypotheses or research questions. In addition, you may examine, interpret, and qualify your results, as well as advance generalizations. Be guided by questions such as these: (a) What is the contribution of this research? (b) How has this study helped to resolve issues in this content area? (c) Can a clear conclusion be drawn from this study? and (d) What further research could be done in this specific topic area? Some attention to the soundness of the results, perhaps by applying Cook and Campbell's (1979) validity taxonomy of internal, external, statistical conclusion, and construct types, is often useful for self-evaluation. In summary, the Discussion section includes a synopsis of the results, their significance, and self-criticism.

Word Processing and APA Style

Because of the widespread and increasing usage of computerized text/word processing, we offer comments on establishing default formatting. Smith (1992), for example, provided commands for users of WordPerfect 5.1. Although the commands may vary from program to program (e.g., WP to MS-Word), several major program features to consider are line spacing, page margins, running headers, justification and hyphenation, and spell-checking. First, manuscripts should always and entirely be double-spaced, even the references and tables, to permit comments from editors/reviewers or copy editors. Page margins should be set at least 1.0 inch all around, with one exception being the top margin. This exception occurs because the margin should be 1.0" from top to the first line, not to the running head. Therefore a top margin of approximately .50" inch or .60" inch works best. Running headers are usually set up in the formatting section of the word-processing program. There are two requirements for the running head: top/flush right placement and a page number (now placed on the same line as the short title). Manuscripts should be left-justified only, meaning that the right edges should be "ragged" and not straight. Further, hyphenation should be turned off from the beginning of the manuscript. Last, using the set of writing tools provided by computer packages is highly recommended. Primarily, spell-checking a document during its preparation and definitely before sending it out for comments or review is mandatory. Remember that it is not necessarily your spelling that is problematic, but rather your psychomotor (typing) skills. A thesaurus is useful when trying to avoid overuse of certain words. A final feature is a grammar checker, which yields valuable information on such common errors as the overuse of passive voice. It also provides helpful statistics (e.g., reading-ease formulas, number of characters/words/paragraphs). Our advice is to learn APA format from the beginning of your word-processing days and to practice until it becomes automatic.

Several commercial programs offer more specialized writing functions. Some maintain a bibliography and provide references in correct APA style (e.g., End Note Plus, Niles & Associates, 1993; WPCitation, Oberon Resources, Inc., 1989), whereas others provide a shell for the entire document (e.g., Manuscript Manager, Pergamon Press, Inc., 1988).

Summary

In summary, APA style and format is easy to learn and follow with the proper effort. Automating this format endears you to teachers and fellow researchers alike. As well, following a style demonstrates your professional self-discipline. This chapter provided a basic discussion of some elements of the fourth edition of the APA *Publication Manual*, organized around the empirical manuscript, and a job aid in the form of Appendix 21.1. There is no substitute, obviously, for careful examination of the *Publication Manual* and related materials. Obviously, repetition will enhance anyone's style of writing. Get used to iterating or cycling as you write for class and for your lab groups. Specifically, rewrite your papers for classes, prepare miniproposals, and practice, practice, practice!

Recommended Readings

Our last section provides recommended sources for following up on this chapter. They include the *Publication Manual* itself, easily the most important and final arbiter (Knapp, Storandt, & Jackson, 1995). Hummel and Kaeck (1995) provide a short treatment of the essentials of APA format that for the most part conforms to the *Publication Manual*. However, Chapell (1995) critiqued the format for references presented by Hummel and Kaeck (1995), noting that it was incorrect because of use of the third edition format. More generally, three classic sources of information on writing style include *The Elements of Style* (3rd ed.; Strunk & White, 1979), *The Chicago Manual of Style* (14th ed.; University of Chicago Press, 1993), and *The Manual of Style* (Government Printing Office, 1986). Other book-length treatments for the social sciences include Becker (1986), Jones (1976), Runkel and Runkel (1984), and Sternberg (1993). Rubens (1991) presents a manual of style specifically for scientific-technical writing. Last, Sternberg's (1992) article develops a framework about writing for psychological journals. His complete organization scheme includes (a) what you say, (b) how you say it, (c) what to do with what you say, and (d) what to do with what others say (e.g., colleagues, reviewers).

References

American Psychological Association. (1994). *Publication manual of the American Psychological Association* (4th ed.). Washington, DC: Author.

Anderson, J. E., & Valentine, W. L. (1944). The preparation of articles for publication in the journals of the American Psychological Association. *Psychological Bulletin, 41*, 345-376.

Becker, H. S. (1986). *Writing for social scientists: How to start and finish your thesis, book, or article*. Chicago: University of Chicago Press.

Chapell, M. S. (1995). Correction to APA style. *American Psychological Society Observer, 8*(6), 33.

Cook, T. D., & Campbell, D. T. (1979). *Quasi-experimentation: Design and analysis issues for field settings.* Boston: Houghton Mifflin.

Hills, P. J. (1983). The scholarly communication process. *Annual Review of Information Science and Technology, 18,* 99-125.

Hummel, J. H., & Kaeck, D. J. (1995). How to use the '94 APA style guide. *American Psychological Society Observer, 8*(4), 16-22.

Jones, W. P. (1976). *Writing scientific papers and reports* (7th ed.). Dubuque, IA: William C. Brown.

Knapp, S., Storandt, M., & Jackson, D. (1995). Fourth edition of the *Publication Manual. American Psychologist, 50,* 581-583.

Lannon, J. M. (1988). *Technical writing* (4th ed.). Glenview, IL: Scott, Foresman.

Niles & Associates, Inc. (1993). *End Note Plus* [Computer program]. Berkeley, CA: Author.

Oberon Resources, Inc. (1989). *WPCitation* [Computer program]. Columbus, OH: Author.

Pergamon Press, Inc. (1988). *Manuscript manager* [Computer program]. Elmsford, NY: Author.

Rubens, P. (Ed.). (1991). *Science and technical writing: A manual of style.* New York: Holt.

Runkel, P. J., & Runkel, M. (1984). *A guide to usage for writers and students in the social sciences.* Totowa, NJ: Rowan & Allanheld.

Sides, C. H. (Ed.). (1989). *Technical and business communication: Bibliographic essays for teachers and corporate trainers.* Urbana, IL: National Council of Teachers of English, Society for Technical Communication.

Smith, R. (1992). Formatting APA pages in WordPerfect 5.1. *Teaching of Psychology, 19,* 190-191.

Standera, O. (1987). *The electronic era of publishing.* New York: Elsevier.

Sternberg, R. J. (1992). How to win acceptances by psychology journals: 21 tips for better writing. *American Psychological Society Observer, 5*(5), 12.

Sternberg, R. J. (1993). *The psychologist's companion: A guide to scientific writing for students and researchers* (3rd ed.). New York: Cambridge University Press.

Strunk, W., & White, E. B. (1979). *The elements of style* (3rd ed.). New York: Macmillan.

University of Chicago Press. (1993). *The Chicago manual of style* (14th ed.). Chicago: Author.

Woodford, F. P. (1967). Sounder thinking through clearer writing. *Science, 156,* 743-745.

Wright, P. (1987). Reading and writing for electronic journals. In B. K. Britton & S. M. Glynn (Eds.), *Executive control processes in reading* (pp. 107-144). Hillsdale, NJ: Lawrence Erlbaum.

Appendix 21.1

A Job Aid for Writing in APA Format

The following pages present a two-level template for writing in APA style, derived from earlier versions prepared by Dr. Evan Mendes (George Mason University) and Dr. Peter Villanova (Appalachian State University). This appendix works at two levels. The first, that of physical features, pertains to the actual layout of a manuscript written in current APA format (1994). Thus the document in this appendix is set up in the format of the empirical research report. The second level, that of cognitive features, pertains to elaboration of the physical features. For example, the abstract contained in the template provides a rationale for any abstract and also provides details of its preparation. Thus the document in this appendix both discusses APA format and is formatted correctly. Note two things about this appendix. All possible features of an empirical manuscript could not be incorporated, so the *Publication Manual* is still the final and best arbiter. Also, the page numbering begins at 1 for correctness.

1

Running head: SHORT TITLE OF YOUR CHOICE (ALL CAPS)

Title of Your Manuscript
(Typed in Mixed Case and Centered on the Page)

Your Name

Organizational Affiliation

(Prepared by James T. Austin)

Correspondence:

Name

Address

Phone and E-Mail Address (Optional but Helpful)

Abstract

This job aid teaches you American Psychological Association (APA) style in two ways. The text explains the elements and organization of a typical empirical research report and is also formatted in proper APA style. The section you are reading, the abstract, is written on a separate page immediately after the title page. (Underlining, in a manuscript, tells copy editors and typesetters that the underlined section should be set in italics; do not use the italics function key of your word-processing program.) This page must have the running head in the upper right corner of the page, with the page number following it ("page 2"), and the word Abstract centered on the page. The abstract is written in block form: a single paragraph with no indentation. The abstract contains a brief summary of the article. It should inform intelligent readers so that they can decide whether the article is relevant to their interests. In many cases, the abstract determines whether the article will be read in its entirety. Thus it should present information about the problem, the method, and the results, as well as implications and conclusions. Typically, the length for an empirical article is 100 to 150 words, not to exceed 960 characters (this specific abstract has 205 words and is thus slightly long). In summary, the abstract should be short and informative.

Title of Your Manuscript
(Typed in Mixed Case and Centered on the Page)

The introduction starts a fresh page after the title and abstract pages. Note that the running head and the full title are on the top of the first page of the introduction, but there is no subheading. Also note that the entire text is typed without right justification and hyphenation. Other information about manuscript preparation can be obtained by consulting the American Psychological Association <u>Publication Manual</u> (4th ed.; APA, 1994). Other specific treatments of social science writing may be found in Sternberg (1993) and Becker (1986). A useful source of general style information is <u>The Elements of Style</u> by Strunk and White (1984). These writing sources are cited in the Reference section of this chapter.

Because the function of the introduction is obvious, a heading is not needed. Specifically, the introduction informs the reader of the specific problem under study and how that problem is related to prior scientific work. In writing the introduction, keep these four questions in mind: (a) What is the point of the study? (b) What is the relation of the study to previous work in the area? (c) What is the rationale or logical link between the study and the research design? and (d) What are the theoretical limitations of the study? The most difficult part of writing the introduction is to develop explicitly the logical connection between your research question, the work in the literature, and your research design. Clarify these matters as you write a manuscript.

The introduction does discuss the literature, but it need not be an exhaustive review. If you have completed an exhaustive review, consider writing it up as a review/theoretical article, a quantitative review (or meta-analysis), an annotated bibliography, or perhaps a technical report. When writing an empirical report, try to cite only those studies pertinent to specific issues under investigation. When selecting studies for your literature review, include recent literature as well as any classic citations, the former to ensure that you are not reinventing the wheel and the latter to demonstrate your grasp of the history of the phenomenon. Consider including meta-analyses (quantitative reviews) of the research domain if they are available (and they usually are). Do not completely describe the studies you cite; often all that is needed is a brief description of the variables, procedures, analyses and findings, and conclusions. Finally, avoid tangential or general references unless they buttress your arguments.

In the body of the paper, articles and books are cited by the last name(s) of the author(s) and the year of publication. This form of citation is termed <u>scientific</u> to distinguish it from citations in literary writing, which follow the style guide of the Modern Language Association (MLA). For example, you might say, "Distinctions between operant and classical conditioning, originally stated by Skinner (1938), have recently been challenged (Rescorla & Wagner, 1969)." Notice that when a reference is enclosed completely within parentheses the ampersand (&) is used instead of the word <u>and.</u> However, <u>and</u> is used outside of parentheses. In citing more than one work by the same author(s) in one year, the suffixes <u>a, b, c,</u> etc., are added after the year. These suffixes are also used in the Reference section. For instance, you might say, "Recent studies by Smith (1965, 1975, 1978a, 1978b) have shown support for the expectancy interpretation." If different authors are cited simultaneously at the same point in the text, the citations are always arranged alphabetically by the authors' surnames, separated by semicolons, and enclosed in parentheses: "Recent studies dispute the behaviorist position (Smith, 1983; Smith & Jones, 1984; Toffler, 1979)."

Try to avoid footnotes and quotations. The literature you cite should be from original work and should be your interpretation of it. Plagiarism is extremely dishonest and is severely punished by most schools and professions. However, sometimes you have no choice but to rely on secondary sources, which are someone else's interpretation of a study. Then you should cite the secondary source in the text. Place the source in the text as "Heider (1958) reported that Asch observed. . . ." In the Reference section, list Heider, not Asch, even though it is the work of Asch that is of interest.

Try to write with clarity, and do not use flowery language. For example, "The eminent American clinical psychologist, Dr. George Kelly, is credited with the first portrayal of individuals as naive scientists" could be better stated as "Kelly (1955) was the first to portray persons as naive scientists." Three simple principles are to know your audience, know your communication goals, and be simple, brief, and concise. Outlines can help clarify your thinking and can be constructed either after you finish writing (a reverse outline) or before you start.

Hypotheses

Authors should list hypotheses or research questions at the end of the introductory section. Hypotheses are specific predictions about expected results; research questions are general and indicate an exploratory study. A third-level heading might be used for this section of the introduction.

In summary, the introduction tells readers, within the framework of the existing research, why this study is being conducted. It sets the stage for the manuscript, which consists of the Method, Results, Discussion, and Reference sections.

Method

The Method section is headed with the word <u>Method</u>—in mixed case and centered. This is an example of a first-level heading and immediately follows the Introduction section and any hypotheses or research questions. The Method section generally has several subsections, with the exact number depending on the complexity of the study. Its purpose is to inform readers about the participants, what procedures were used, and what apparatus was used so that competent researchers can evaluate the quality of the research and replicate the study.

Participants

Note that the subsections of the Method section, such as Participants, have capitalized headings, are underlined, and are flush left. These are called <u>third-level headings</u> in the APA's style guide. The Participants subsection should provide clear answers to three questions: (a) Who participated in the study? (b) How many participants were there? and (c) How were the participants selected? (Are they representative of a defined population?) In addition, you should give the major demographic characteristics and the number assigned to each experimental group or condition. Report any inducements, whether monetary or otherwise, that were offered for participation. Finally, the word <u>subjects</u> is sometimes considered to be derogatory, so the word <u>participants</u> is one alternative.

Apparatus/Measures

In this subsection, give brief descriptions of the major apparatus or materials used in the study and their functions.

If you constructed the apparatus yourself, you may have to go into greater detail so that readers can comprehend exactly what the apparatus was. Perhaps an appendix or a separate technical report will be required. Questionnaire measures, whether homemade or off the shelf, should be referenced here, and all deviations from the original scales or instructions should be described.

Procedure

This subsection should present each step in the actual execution of the study. It should include initial instructions to participants (informed consent), formation of the groups, and the specific experimental manipulations, if any. Describe randomization, counterbalancing, and other control features of the research design. Describe debriefing of participants in accordance with APA ethical guidelines. In general, this section informs the reader what was done, how it was done, and in what order, in sufficient detail to permit replication.

Results

The Results section immediately follows the Method section. The word <u>Results</u> is centered and in mixed case as a first-level heading. The purpose of this section is to summarize the collected data and the statistical treatment of those data. First, briefly state the main thrust of your results or findings. Second, report the analyses in detail so that you can justify conclusions you intend to make in later sections. State the results only, and do not discuss implications or make inferences until the Discussion section. Report all relevant results, even any that may be counter to your hypotheses (this is important!).

You may choose to present data or results in the form of graphs or tables, but consider the value of this mode of presentation carefully, as tables and figures are expensive to typeset. On the other hand, the saying that "one picture is worth a thousand words," is also applicable. If you do use tables or figures, refer to graphs, pictures, or drawings as <u>figures</u> and to tables as <u>tables.</u> For example, you could say, "Figure 1 graphs the goal acceptance levels for each of the experimental groups." If you include tables and figures, they are <u>placed together at the end of the manuscript.</u> Figures require a caption on a separate page immediately preceding the figure. Examples of a table and figure are given at the end of

this guide. However, do indicate where the table or figure
should fit into the text as follows.

             Insert Table (or Figure) 1 about here

When you report the results of a test of statistical
significance, you must include information concerning the
means, measures of variability (e.g., variance, standard
deviation), obtained magnitude of the test statistic, the
degrees of freedom, the probability of observing such a test
ratio given a true null hypothesis, and the direction of the
effect. Here are several examples: "As predicted, females (M =
9.55, SD = 1.67) reported greater liking for school than did
males (M = 7.62, SD = 1.22), $t(22)$ = 2.62, p < .01," and "The
analysis of variance indicated significant differences in
latency of response for subjects not provided with training,
$F(1,34)$ = 123.78, p < .001)." Some of the conventions for
reporting statistical significance and the effect size are
presented in classes on statistics and research methods.
Further, tables are often used to present the results of
complex analyses such as factor analysis, multiple regression,
or factorial analysis of variance.

At the undergraduate level, the most common statistical
analyses to be reported include t tests on dependent variable
means for two groups, one-way analysis of variance to compare
the means of three or more groups on a single manipulated
factor, simple correlation and regression to relate two
measured variables, and multiple regression to examine
interrelationships among multiple measured variables. More
sophisticated techniques are used at later stages of exposure
to psychological research.

Discussion

The Discussion section follows immediately after the
Results section. Note the mixed case and the centering of the
section heading. One way to begin the discussion is to open
with a statement on the support of your original hypotheses or
research questions. In addition, you may examine, interpret,
and qualify your results, as well as advance generalizations.
Be guided by questions such as these: (a) What have I
contributed in this research? (b) How has my study helped to
resolve issues in this content area? (c) Can I draw a clear

conclusion from this study? and (d) What further research could
be done in this specific topic area?

In sum, note that the research report is a logical flow of
information from how the problem was stated to how the problem
was conceptualized to how the problem was researched, how the
data were analyzed, what the findings were, how the findings
were interpreted, and some suggestions for new studies. Last,
the best way to improve your writing is to practice, practice,
practice!

[Begin Reference section on new page]

References

Psychological writing places references in one place at the
end of the text so that they do not interfere with reading of
the manuscript. There is generally little use of notes in the
text (they too are placed in the Reference section immediately
before the references). The section starts on a new page
immediately after the discussion section. The purpose of the
references is to allow a reader to obtain the sources used in
the writing of an article. The heading References is typed in
mixed case and centered. Below are examples of the format
required for common manuscript references. Further information
and examples pertaining to references can be obtained by
consulting the APA Publication Manual (1994, Appendix 3-A,
pp. 189-222). Additional material on citing legal materials is
provided in the latest revision (Appendix 3-B, pp. 223-234).

Adams, J. E., & Aronfreed, J. L. (1971). Group dynamics in
the prison community. Journal of Experimental Social
Psychology, 42, 17-21. (example of an article)

American Psychological Association. (1994). Publication
manual of the American Psychological Association (4th ed.).
Washington, DC: Author. (APA Style Guide—the "Bible")

Riesen, A. H. (1966). Sensory deprivation. In E. Stellar &
J. M. Sprague (Eds.), Progress in physiological psychology
(Vol. 1, pp. xxx-xxx). New York: Academic Press. (example of a
book chapter)

Stogdill, R. M. (1974). Handbook of leadership. New York:
Free Press. (example of a book)

Appendix A

Informative Title of Your Choice
(Centered, Mixed Case)

   An appendix presents additional material of interest to the
reviewer or reader. The material may not fit conveniently into
the body of the paper but is important in reading or reviewing
the manuscript. Examples of such material include
questionnaires developed by the author specifically for the
research project (e.g., for a senior honors thesis), computer
program listings, a list of stimulus materials (e.g., for
verbal learning experiments), or a complicated mathematical
proof. It should be double-spaced and should begin on a new
page following the references. Letters are used to identify
each appendix. If only one appendix is used, no identifying
letter is required.

Author Notes

   In a typical empirical paper, there are three components of
author notes. The first provides the departmental affiliations
of the authors. The second acknowledges help or assistance the
author has received, whether from colleagues, from external
funding sources, or from research assistants. The final part
indicates where the author may be contacted for reprints,
including standard and electronic addresses. Author notes are
not numbered.

Table 1

Average Maze Performance for Prenatally Malnourished and
Control Rats

_____

_____

Table notes go here

[statistical significance followed by other explanations]

Figure 1.

(Compose a brief and informative title for the figure)

Mean body weight for the prenatally malnourished (X--------X)
and control groups (O--------O) from birth through 200 days of
age.

[The actual figure should be on the page following the caption]

Chapter 22

Writing Rough Drafts

CHRISTOPHER PETERSON

All who give advice to would-be writers stress that final products are virtually impossible to create without going through a series of drafts. Despite the universality of this advice, drafting imperfect versions of a final product is not part of the writing repertoire of many graduate and undergraduate students. My purpose in this chapter is not to extol the value of rough drafts; I take that as a given. Rather, I provide some concrete steps involved in writing drafts.

Magical Thinking

Like many self-defeating behaviors, not being able to write is caused in part by deeply held but poorly examined beliefs (Beck, 1976). Individuals can be tyrannized by *automatic thoughts*, rigid and overly simple beliefs that come unbidden to mind, producing emotional and behavioral difficulties. These thoughts are maintained by *magical thinking* that keeps them immune to reality testing. In terms of writing, a magical belief system interferes with the business of beginning and finishing because it leaves no room for what happens in between. Writing is often spoken of in terms of art, inspiration, genius, and the like. Writing in actuality is a mundane activity that takes place over time. Repetitive actions are the essence of writing.

Let me be concrete. An aspiring writer may believe, for example, that writing should be effortless. When it proves otherwise, the conclusion may follow that he or she is incapable of writing. Not helpful here is the way that students are socialized early in their school careers. We somehow learn that "good" students do not sweat, that "effort" trades off with ability, that *quick* is a synonym for *smart*, that things come easily or not at all. None of these stereotypes has anything to do with actual writing.

Or a writer may believe that there is a perfect way to phrase sentences. Again, when sentences do not take immediate and immortal form, the conclusion may follow that one is not ready to begin writing. Perhaps one never will be ready until one knows exactly what is to be said. How can this be accomplished? One "strategy" is to read everything ever

AUTHOR'S NOTE: I thank James T. Austin and Lisa M. Bossio for their comments on rough drafts of this chapter.

written on a given topic. The student disappears to the library and postpones writing indefinitely (see Chapter 2 of this volume).

I often ask would-be writers who sits on their shoulders while they write. Sometimes it is a critical parent. Sometimes it is a seventh-grade teacher who presented writing solely in terms of participles, pluperfect tenses, and diagrammed sentences. Sometimes it is an admired figure who has unwittingly mystified the process of writing. And most commonly, it is an unidentified yet omniscient "they" passing harsh judgment on one's intelligence and ability.

Most students eventually do write, but because writing is fraught with supposed implications for self-esteem and competence, their final product is far from satisfactory. Getting in the way of writing are rituals and superstitions that students believe are necessary for the process to occur (Becker, 1986). I am not railing against routines in writing, for they are obviously needed. But I am criticizing magical routines because they prevent the would-be writer from beginning to work.

Perhaps the most critical determinant of whether one can write a useful rough draft is the belief that this can be done. Several influences on this belief in one's own efficacy with regard to drafts can be specified, notably prior success in producing rough drafts, examples by others that this can be done, and verbal persuasion that drafts are possible (see Bandura, 1986). The present chapter is specifically an instance of this latter influence on self-efficacy vis-à-vis rough drafts, but the reader should know as well that what appears here is the sixth draft of what began in rough form.

Taking Ownership

Students often have a confused view of why they are writing. On one level, of course, a person writes for an audience and usually because of an external demand. Teachers assign essays. Graduate school admission committees ask for personal statements. Research supervisors request proposals. The academic profession requires published journal articles and books. But the most immediate reason for writing must be located within one's self, and the would-be writer has to think in these terms (see Chapter 1 of this volume).

I try to encourage the student to take ownership of what he or she is doing. The most important part of taking ownership of a written product is to take responsibility for doing it. *Writing* is a verb, and it refers to something that a specific person does. If it is your paper, then you are that person. This reframing becomes increasingly necessary as the eventual written product becomes lengthy and/or important.

My doctoral students almost always fall into a way of speaking about their dissertations as "*the*" dissertation. Goodness. It is one thing to speak about "*the*" weather or "*the*" government; these are matters over which we expect no control and assume no ownership. But to move one's writing into this category is to undercut any role of personal agency in the process.

I insist that my doctoral students stop referring to their dissertations with definite articles and instead start using personal pronouns. I even tell them not to use the word *dissertation* at all because it sounds so imposing. One does not really write a dissertation per se. One writes words and sentences and chapters; when a student presents these in an appropriate fashion, then we call it a dissertation. When my students start to talk about writing up their research, I know the process has begun. When they start to talk about writing up their hypotheses, their methods, and their results, I know the process is all but over.

There is a myth that some academics write only outstanding papers. A corollary of this myth is that some of the very best academics write just a handful of influential articles and books. The evidence does not bear this out. Those who write frequently cited papers are those who write many papers (Merton, 1968). Some prove influential and some not. Consider Freud, Lewin, and Skinner—among the most important figures in psychology. Some of their papers are awkward, incoherent, and inconsequential. But we honor their good papers. I am sure that none of these individuals set out to write classic papers. They simply wrote.

My point is that the writer should not simultaneously take on the role of critic or historian. Yes, the writer should try to do a good job while writing, but this means putting in time and effort, not trying to match some abstract template concerning profundity and impact. There are limits to what the writer should attempt to own.

Spewing It Out

The most obvious thing about a rough draft is that it is rough. It *should* be rough: preliminary, incomplete, even stupid and contradictory. Yet many students do not want to write a rough draft because *rough* has such negative connotations. As a result, when a writer starts a paper, he or she may try to begin with a finished product. Every sentence must be grammatical, every example apt, and every transition seamless. These are daunting goals, and the writer who tries to write perfect prose from the start ends up editing as he or she goes along and may never get as far as the second sentence.

The more realistic alternative is to separate writing from rewriting. Writers should adopt the *spew method*, letting their words and sentences tumble out in a first draft. The only rule governing the spew method is not to rewrite as one goes along. Some common sense must be employed, of course, because the writer has to stay within the demands of the given product, but otherwise, anything goes.

To put it another way, a writer starting a rough draft needs to have only an approximate idea of what is to be written. I think the notion of planning out one's writing before one starts has been given too much emphasis. To be sure, a *general* outline is a good idea, and I use one when I write. But if a writer tries to create too detailed an outline before actually writing, then the tendencies to perfectionism that handicap writing rough drafts are displaced to writing outlines, and the writer is another step further from being done.

Much of what we write in psychology has an accepted format. A research report, for example, consists of Introduction, Method, Results, and Discussion sections. There is a prescribed way of organizing ideas within each of these sections. Once a writer has this general organization in mind, how much of a further outline is really needed before he or she begins?

With regard to writing a literature review, I often advise my students to alternate between reading and writing. They must have some familiarity with a topic before they begin to write about it, but they need not have read everything before writing. A strong argument can be made in favor of *not* reading everything, just enough to get started with the writing. In the course of writing, it becomes evident where more information is needed, and these places can be marked with an asterisk or parenthetical comment. But writers should keep spewing and only later track down needed details.

As part of my background research for something I am writing, I often take notes. And I invariably have a pile of pertinent articles and books. However, when spewing out a rough draft, I do not consult these sources unless the essential meaning of what I want to say is in doubt. They come into play when I rewrite and polish the rough draft.

One need not spew in any particular order. Final versions of an article or book may be read from start to finish, but they do not have to be written this way. I often begin by writing the sections with which I am most familiar and comfortable. Getting something on a page, wherever that particular page will eventually appear, is a good way to begin a rough draft.

For example, it is often easiest to write the Methods section of a research article first. I usually do this because it is the most formulaic section. Then I jump to the end of the introduction and specify my hypotheses. Next it is time—at least for me—to draft the Results section, and I usually do this before I have completed the data analyses. I find this efficient because as I try to describe what a study showed, I am reminded of just which empirical details are needed. These may not be immediately evident if one tries to do "all" the analyses before writing about them. Often what happens is that the data are overanalyzed; this wastes a lot of time, not to mention computer funds.

There are many ways to put the spew method into action. Early in graduate school, I put aside pens and pencils and wrote first drafts on a typewriter. Even though I am a two-finger typist, I could type more quickly than I could write, and I made a deliberate effort to avoid x-ing out words and sentences while spewing. With the advent of word processors, spewing became even easier for me, although word processors bring with them an even stronger temptation to fiddle with spelling and phrasing instead of writing.

If a writer cannot resist the temptation of rewriting, one extreme measure is to spew into a computer after turning off the video monitor. What you cannot see, you cannot rewrite. Needless to say, make sure your word processing program is not set on its overwriting option! Another extreme technique of spewing is to dictate your ideas into a tape recorder for later transcription. This is time consuming, but it can be a useful short-term solution if you have inordinate trouble writing a first draft.

Some teachers react negatively when students ask how long a paper should be. I find this misguided. Writing in the real world needs to fit within a page limit, and nothing could be more reasonable than knowing how long a written product should be. Although the exact content of what I write may not be clear when I begin a draft, the length is never a mystery to me. The same is true for the sections of what I plan to write. Word-processing programs can be helpful here in keeping track of written volume because they typically provide a character, word, or page count.

Letting It Sit

Once a rough draft has been written, it needs to be rewritten. But there is an important step in between: doing nothing with it. Letting it sit for a day or two or even longer allows the writer to approach his or her work with a fresh eye. Sometimes ideas and their expression need to incubate (see Poincaré, 1913). In my own writing, I have had the frequent experience of coming back to a draft and not knowing why I said certain things or why I failed to say others.

Another benefit of letting a draft sit is that a writer may realize when returning to it that it is more complete than it originally seemed. I tend to have problems with introductions, particularly those that begin lengthy literature reviews (see Chapter 24 of this volume). I try to foreshadow what will follow, but I often overdo it. One solution I have devised is to write a very brief introduction with the intent to expand on it when I am rewriting. More often than not, I end up deciding that the brief introduction is sufficient.

Time constraints dictate the length of the period between successive drafts, and here we are reminded of the maxim about starting projects early and the threat posed by procrastination. A discussion of procrastination is beyond my scope here (see Silver & Sabini, 1981), but one way to get started early enough to allow the rough draft time to sit is to plan to show it to one or more people. The writer should establish a deadline by which to show the draft to them, and this deadline should be taken as seriously as the "final" deadline for the written product.

Rewriting

Time has presumably passed, and the writer returns to his or her rough draft to rewrite it. There should be a plan about what to do with the next draft. Perhaps more material should be spewed out. Perhaps gaps need to be filled and missing information provided. Perhaps grammar, punctuation, and spelling should be checked. A given draft may be too rough to do all of these things at the same time, and if the writer attempts to turn a very rough draft into a final product in one swoop, he or she will probably become bogged down.

As people write more and more, they usually become aware of their idiosyncratic foibles, and these should receive special attention while one is rewriting. For example, while spewing, I often write passive sentences, and I look for these when I rewrite, turning them into active ones. I also start lots of sentences with *thus* and *indeed*, and at least in my usage, these words usually occupy empty space. When I rewrite, I search for these words and delete most of them.

Other foibles are more structural in nature but should be treated in the same way. Writers may consistently write too much or too little in a rough draft. They may neglect to use examples or transitions. They may fail to be explicit about the import of conclusions. Writers should make a list of such common problems and put extra effort into correcting these flaws while they are rewriting drafts. In many cases, the process will eventually become automatic and part of how one spews.

Although I have de-emphasized the importance of outlines for first drafts, they can prove quite helpful for subsequent drafts (see Chapter 23 of this volume). In a strategy called *reverse outlining,* the writer outlines what he or she has already written. Reverse outlining allows misplaced paragraphs and sections to be identified and uneven coverage to be corrected.

Let me comment here on the need to strike a balance between holding onto copies of early drafts and getting rid of them. Some writers who use a word processor end up with dozens of versions of the same paper on a disk and then get mixed up about what is what. Students with some frequency have given me the "wrong" draft of a paper. Sometimes they save an early draft over a later draft. And sometimes different versions of the same paper become jumbled together.

My own style of writing is *not* to keep copies of drafts that I have rewritten because I have learned that I never go back to them. To be sure, if there is a paragraph or page that I think might someday be useful but does not fit in the current draft, I keep it at the end of my manuscript in a separate section. But I see no reason to keep a copy of a draft filled with awkwardness once I have smoothed it out. If you wish not to follow my lead, at least be sure to keep successive drafts clearly identified, perhaps labeling them with the draft number or the date they were completed.

Receiving (and Following) Advice

Writing is not as solitary an endeavor as popular stereotypes suggest. Someone will read most of what is written, and perhaps the best way to satisfy the eventual audience is to involve other people while one is working on the manuscript. Many resist this because drafts seem embarrassing, and we hesitate to reveal ourselves to others. But receiving (and following) useful advice from another person is a critical step in writing.

The would-be writer must struggle with fear of feedback, realizing that it is much preferable to be criticized at a time when change is possible than when it is too late. Most teachers would rather teach than assign grades, and they are usually happy to comment on a draft. So too are research supervisors, and I have on occasion had success running early versions of what I have written past journal editors and granting agencies. Fellow students and researchers may often be the most suitable individuals for advice. I regularly rely on a colleague to advise me on what I have written, and I reciprocate the favor. To repeat: I think every would-be writer should solicit advice on rough drafts.

Not all to whom you show your drafts are helpful; they may be too late, too critical, or too cursory in their suggestions. Critics may advise you that a sentence is awkward or unclear but not explain why. A would-be writer may have to shop around a bit for a good critic and take responsibility here by being explicit about the sort of advice that is needed. And beware the overly positive reader; unconditional praise makes a writer feel good, but it does not improve his or her writing.

Once you find someone who will read and comment on your drafts, what can you do to make the process palatable to your advisor? To begin with, do not rely on someone else to do what you can do for yourself. For example, it is insulting and wasteful to use another person as a spell-check program. He or she may spend a lot of time correcting your spelling errors at the expense of more substantive advice.

Students sometimes give me a rough draft and ask for advice, but the manuscript they hand over is single-spaced and printed with a condensed typeface and minimal margins. Not only do I have trouble reading it, I have no room to note suggested changes. On purely physical grounds, drafts vary in how amenable they are to advice. Similarly, do not hand a potential advisor a computer disk containing your draft and expect him or her to print it before making comments, unless the two of you have agreed that this is how to proceed. Again, this can be time consuming for your advisor, if not impossible given the variety of operating systems and word-processing programs available.

Although drafts are not expected to be complete, too preliminary a draft does not lend itself to comments. It must have at least some content. Students sometimes show me a bare-bones outline of what they wish to write—beginning, middle, and ending—and I am usually at a loss to say anything. If a writer wants substantive comments on the Results section of a potential journal article, essential tables and figures need to be included. I rarely find an abstract included as part of a rough draft given to me for comments, but an abstract is as helpful to the reader of a preliminary draft as it is to the reader of a final product, perhaps even more so.

As mentioned earlier, tell the person the sort of advice you most need. The more specific you can be, the better. A deadline for returning comments should be agreed on. You may not be able to control your advisor's end of the agreement, but do not ask for comments to be left for you on Monday and then not pick them up until Friday.

When advice is given to you about your draft, be sure to abstract the gist of the suggestion and follow it, not just where it is indicated on your manuscript but elsewhere as appropriate. I remember suggesting the identical word change 20 times in someone's dissertation. The student diligently made the suggested changes in the given 20 locations and not at all anyplace else. In other words, think about the advice, and if it is useful, learn a general lesson from it that you can apply broadly.

You should, of course, thank the person who gives you advice, and perhaps the best way to express gratitude is by offering to review your critic's own drafts and then following through if your offer is accepted. And speaking of following through, it is imperative that you take advice seriously. This need not mean doing everything that is suggested, but neither does it mean finding reasons not to do so (see Chapter 25 of this volume). At the very least, if someone suggests that a draft be changed in a given way, the writer should usually change it in some way. There must have been something amiss to elicit criticism in the first place.

I ask those who read my drafts to make as many changes as they can in the text: reorganization, word choice, punctuation, and the like. I almost always incorporate these changes, but when I do not, I ponder the material in question and figure out how to revise it. If somebody does not like a word I chose, and I do not like his or her suggested word, then I find a third word. The recipient of advice is not a participant in a debate; the writer who fails to follow sincere suggestions is not triumphing over an opponent.

If you are fortunate, you have several people on whom to rely for advice about your writing. Time permitting, the best way to make use of multiple sources of suggestions is successively. Simultaneous advice can be contradictory and overwhelming. Like writing and rewriting, responding to suggestions is most likely to be successful when it can be spread out.

Conclusions

In sum, I have described writing rough drafts as a process that necessarily extends over time. Several steps in writing a rough draft need to be distinguished and enacted. First, the writer must take ownership of what is to be written, assuming responsibility for what must follow. Second, the writer needs to get his or her preliminary ideas on paper. Third, the writer should, if possible, let the rough draft sit for a period of time. Fourth, the draft must be rewritten, perhaps several times if revisions are extensive. Fifth, the writer should solicit (and follow) advice from others.

The writing of rough drafts needs to be separated from their polishing at a later date. Counterproductive assumptions and habits can inhibit the writing of rough drafts, and these should be monitored and challenged on an ongoing basis. But with all this said and done, the fact remains that the final step in writing anything is deciding that it is done.

A writer should not become so smitten with writing and revising drafts that a product is never deemed complete. He or she must be willing to recognize that a written product cannot be perfect, that there is a time to say enough is enough. A paper or book that no one ever reads is a wasted opportunity to participate in one's chosen field. Get it out the door!

Recommended Readings

Consistent disagreement between you and someone who reads your drafts may mean that there is a technical misunderstanding about the right way to describe, for example, complex data analyses. It might also mean that you have different writing styles, although this should not be offered glibly as a reason not to follow suggestions (see Chapter 26 of this volume). The APA *Publication Manual* (APA, 1994) and *The Elements of Style* (Strunk & White, 1979) are explicit in many cases about correct and incorrect ways of writing. These should be consulted when the two of you begin to butt heads about style (see Chapter 21 of this volume).

Other useful sources on writing include Gelfand and Walker's *Mastering APA Style* (1984), Runkel and Runkel's *Guide to Usage for Writers and Students in the Social Sciences* (1984), and Becker's *Writing for Social Scientists* (1986). Swan and Gopen (1990) discussed the "science" of scientific writing, and Sternberg (1992) offered a brief set of tips about how to write better papers. Most generally, I recommend that aspiring writers read a variety of well-written articles and books with the goal of abstracting effective strategies.

References

American Psychological Association. (1994). *Publication manual of the American Psychological Association* (4th ed.). Washington, DC: Author.

Bandura, A. (1986). *The social foundations of thought and action: A social cognitive theory.* Englewood Cliffs, NJ: Prentice Hall.

Beck, A. T. (1976). *Cognitive therapy and the emotional disorders.* New York: Harper & Row.

Becker, H. S. (1986). *Writing for social scientists: How to start and finish your thesis, book, or article.* Chicago: University of Chicago Press.

Gelfand, H., & Walker, C. J. (1994). *Mastering APA style.* Washington, DC: American Psychological Association.

Merton, R. K. (1968). The Matthew effect in science: The reward and communication systems of science are considered. *Science, 159,* 56-63.

Poincaré, H. (1913). *The foundations of science.* New York: Science Press.

Runkel, P. J., & Runkel, M. (1984). *A guide to usage for writers and students in the social sciences.* Totowa, NJ: Rowan & Allanheld.

Silver, M., & Sabini, J. (1981). Procrastinating. *Journal for the Theory of Social Behaviour, 11,* 207-221.

Sternberg, R. J. (1992). How to win acceptances by psychology journals: 21 tips for better writing. *American Psychological Society Observer, 5*(5), 12.

Strunk, W., & White, E. B. (1979). *The elements of style* (3rd ed.). New York: Macmillan.

Swan, J. A., & Gopen, G. D. (1990). The science of scientific writing. *American Scientist, 78,* 550-558.

Chapter 23

Revising a Research Manuscript

DONNA K. NAGATA
STEVEN J. TRIERWEILER

Most authors would agree that there is a great feeling of relief and satisfaction after sending your final manuscript off to the journal editor. By that point, you have expended considerable energy into the paper's conceptualization, analyses, and write-up. (See Parts 2, 4, and 5 of this text for guidelines in each of these areas respectively.) Now the manuscript moves into the review process. The American Psychological Association (APA) *Publication Manual* (APA, 1994) describes this process and includes a useful flowchart (p. 303) delineating each step along the way. Several months after submission, you will receive feedback from the editor about the acceptance or rejection of the paper, as well as reviewer comments about your work. (The APA *Publication Manual* notes that although editors are not required to provide reviewer comments, they do so frequently.) This chapter describes how one goes about revising a research manuscript once it has been submitted for publication. It begins with a discussion of journal reviewer comments and how an author might respond to such comments. Next, the chapter illustrates various decision points in the rewriting process. Finally, concrete suggestions are made for resubmitting the paper for further review.

Although this chapter focuses on authors who decide to revise and resubmit their research manuscript to the same journal, one should keep in mind that this is not the only option. After carefully reading the review comments and suggestions, you may feel that the requested changes are not appropriate and decide not to resubmit your paper. The "fit" between your manuscript and the journal may be too discrepant, and you may wish to submit your work to another journal. (It should be noted, however, that such a decision might also require revision of the manuscript.) Therefore issues relevant to evaluating the fit between a paper and journal will also be discussed.

Who Are the Reviewers?

Peer review is a major mechanism for establishing the legitimacy of a research finding and the overall acceptability of an author's interpretation and conclusions. Several works discuss aspects of the editorial and review process (e.g., APA, 1994; Ceci & Peters, 1984; Cofer, 1985; Daft, 1985; Peters & Ceci, 1985; Roediger, 1987). It is a critical part of academic scholarship because the quality of a science is as dependent on the rigor and accuracy of reviewer scrutiny as it is on the methods of science themselves. Typically, reviewers are researchers and scholars whom editors have identified as experts in the area of research addressed in your manuscript. In all the effort that is required to prepare a manuscript, it is easy to forget that the individuals reading and evaluating your work are highly accomplished individuals in their own right and may be the foremost experts available anywhere in the country or even in the world. Their work usually is anonymous and completely voluntary. Rarely do such individuals treat their responsibility lightly, although the effort they give the task of reviewing may vary considerably from time to time. When functioning properly, there is tradition and integrity in this system that merits respect. Major publications receive hundreds of submissions in a given year in the service of relatively few pages available in the actual publications. One can refer to the *Journals in Psychology: A Resource Listing for Authors* (APA, 1993) to obtain information on the editorial policies of specific journals as well as the number of published pages per year for each of those journals. The high ratio of submissions relative to the low rate of published articles means that if you get a thorough review, whether it is positive or negative, someone has put a good deal of work into looking at your paper.

Throughout your work with the publication process, keep in mind that editors and reviewers operate from a systems-level perspective, whereas you will generally be completely wrapped up in your own research. This means that those evaluating the manuscript will be exposed to and affected by comparative information—such as other manuscripts in related areas and their overall sense of the field—to which you will have no access. This is particularly an issue for beginning authors. As part of the general consensus-building process of science, authors must strive to discern how their work fits into this system. The better you become at managing your relationship to the system, the broader will be your opportunities to communicate with others through publication of your work.

Receiving Review Comments

Notification from a journal editor will typically include a cover letter from the editor summarizing the editor's recommendation for acceptance, rejection, or suggestions for revision of your paper based on a summary and interpretation of reviewers' comments. The length and level of detail in editors' letters vary a great deal, although the majority will provide a restatement of reviewer comments (Fiske & Fogg, 1990). (In some cases, the editor also serves as a reviewer; see Fiske & Fogg, 1990.) Copies of comments from two or more reviewers who have read your manuscript are typically included. The editor's cover letter is important. It should give you a sense as to whether a manuscript revision and resubmission to the journal are encouraged or feasible. It can also highlight the major concerns that would need to be addressed in a rewrite. Some journals also provide an indication as to whether the manuscript requires major versus minor revisions prior to reconsideration. This, in turn, can help you determine the amount of work that you would need to do to resubmit.

There is understandably a level of apprehension regarding rejection of a manuscript. Similarly, researchers may have concern regarding critical comments from the individual reviewers (Fiske & Fogg, 1990). Such comments play a major role in a decision about resubmitting an article or about submitting it elsewhere. They also provide the author with guidelines for revising the manuscript because in most cases revisions are requested by the editor before a final decision to accept an article is made. First readings of review comments can be emotional: As an author, you may feel that criticisms from a review are misdirected, unhelpful, or incorrect from your perspective. Alternatively, comments may seem helpful and justified, spurring you to notice aspects of the paper that slipped your attention before. For example, a reviewer might provide specific references that expand your thinking on a particular analysis, conceptualization, or interpretation. Two points should be noted here. First, reviewers vary in the tone of their feedback. Some may be bluntly critical, whereas others may raise the same concerns in a more positive manner. Reviewers also vary in the length and detail of their reviews. Second, as Fiske and Fogg (1990) noted, the typical reviewer spends little time providing positive feedback. Therefore authors should be prepared for this.

There can be an initial reaction of frustration and disappointment on first reading of the criticisms raised in one's reviews. This is understandable because you have no way of immediately responding to or rebutting the reviewers' remarks. Such an emotional response need not be negative. It can bolster a sense of commitment to refining the paper and addressing the questions raised. The goal of any revision should be a stronger presentation of one's research. To this end, one strategy for dealing with the initial receipt of reviews is to read them through, then put them aside for a period of time before rewriting. This can be helpful in allowing you to "step back" from a potentially emotional first response. Often, in rereading a review, you will find comments to be less negative than initially felt or will come to realize that positive indications in the reviews have been overlooked. These realizations can help you achieve the sense of confidence and efficacy required to approach the task of rewriting.

Applying a specific step-by-step, problem-focused strategy can also help you manage the emotion associated with evaluation and increase a sense of efficacy. Priority tasks should include the following: (a) Evaluate how serious the questions raised by reviewers are; (b) weigh how adequately they can be addressed by revision; (c) determine if revision seems an appropriate course of action; and, if so, (d) develop a plan for revision, including a time frame for its execution.

If there are multiple criticisms to be addressed in a rewrite, it can be helpful for the author simply to begin by listing reactions to those criticisms along one side of a paper and tentative strategies for addressing them on the other side of the paper. In so doing, carefully consider the following questions and strategies. Is something basic to the major message of the study being questioned? If so, can it be addressed? Alternatively, has the reviewer somehow misunderstood something? If so, how might that have happened? Never assume that your writing is as clear as it can be; sometimes relatively minor changes in writing can get a message across that reviewers could not discern during their examination of the manuscript. Consider carefully your message at each point in the manuscript receiving commentary from the reviewers. However, just because reviewers do not comment on particular sections does not mean that those sections cannot be improved. Imagine a conversation with the reviewer, responding to what he or she seems to be saying and anticipating what his or her response might be if he or she were to react to your revision. Address each reviewer point, one at a time. Do not ignore or take lightly any comment, however off the mark it may seem from your perspective. Because of time and communication constraints, reviewers will not always be able to articulate thoroughly what is troubling them. Some will tell you this directly; others may express their concern by concentrating on relatively minor specifics, but in a tone that sounds more condemnatory than the crime. Try to read past this unclarity to discern the source of the reviewer's concern. You are far more the expert on your paper than the reviewers can ever be. If there is a point of disagreement, then it must be addressed directly if the revision is to succeed. Recognize that ultimately the task is to convince reviewers, and particularly the editor, that their concerns have been adequately addressed. Always operate from a position of balance and clarity; the reviewers are windows to your audience, and heeding their feedback, even when it is vague and uncertain, can greatly improve the presentation of your research.

Do not expect multiple reviewers to provide consensus in their comments. Fiske and Fogg (1990) noted that agreement between reviewer general recommendations typically correlates around .3. In their study of over 400 "free-response" comments of reviewers for 153 papers submitted to 12 editors of journals published by the APA, they found that "rarely did one reviewer make the same point as any other reviewer of that paper" (p. 593). This means that you should carefully consider the full range of issues raised before attempting to rewrite your paper.

Despite the lack of consensus about particular points, certain areas of weakness appear in reviewer comments frequently. Fiske and Fogg (1990) examined the distribution of manuscript weaknesses reported by their sample of reviewers across 10 categories: presentation of conceptual work prior to execution, linkage of conceptual work to execution, design, procedures, measurement, statistical analyses, results, interpretations and conclusions, editorial and writing, and general weaknesses. Of these 10, the most frequently cited locus was "interpretations and conclusions," followed by, in order, presentation of conceptual work prior to execution, results, procedures, and design. One can also refer to Daft's (1985) chapter entitled "Why I Recommended That Your Manuscript Be Rejected and What You Can Do About It," in which he identified frequent problems encountered in over 100 of his own reviews. An additional resource cited by Fiske and Fogg (1990) is Smigel and Ross's (1970) presentation of reasons for acceptance/rejection from the perspective of associate editors.

Common Areas for Revision of a Research Manuscript

The particular areas requiring revision for a given paper will, of course, vary. Reviewers may urge an author to expand their coverage of literature in the introductory portion of the paper and/or in the interpretations and conclusions. The editor/reviewers can also suggest the need for additional or different statistical analyses in the study. In that case, the revision requires not only running more analyses but also changing the Results and Interpretation/Conclusion sections to reflect those findings. Consistent with the 10 categories of manuscript weakness used by Fiske and Fogg (1990), we can divide reviewer comments into five overarching areas of concern: (a) substantive/theoretical, (b) methodological, (c) data analytic, (d) interpretive, and (e) fit with the publication. In this section, we provide an overview of some common ways in which these areas of critique interact with the structure of the research report and discuss their implications for revising the manuscript. When reviewer comments are nonspecific, it is especially important for authors to consider the possibility that portions of the manuscript other than those discussed by reviewers might be strengthened, thereby reducing the probability of additional questions down the line.

REVISING THE FRONT MATTER

The front matter of a manuscript will set the reviewers' expectations for the article and the research it describes. Even a small oversight or unclarity here can make a huge difference in reviewer response to your article. By the same token, a small change can sometimes completely eliminate reviewers' concerns. Never underestimate the possibility that your title and abstract have led reviewers to expect something you have not delivered in the body of your manuscript. Does your title contain words and phrases that link directly to the central themes of your report? Does the abstract tell the story in a way that is logically consistent with your more detailed development in the body of the article? If not, then consider changing them or rewriting parts of the manuscript so as to strengthen the logical ties between the front matter and the body of the article.

REVISING THE INTRODUCTION

The introduction consists of three major components: a statement of the research problem, a literature review, and an elaboration of a basic theoretical framework. Fiske and Fogg (1990), consistent with our own experience as reviewers and authors, suggested that any one or all of these can be a source of reviewer concern. These different elements are usually strongly linked. As with the front matter, the statement of the problem will lead reviewers to have expectations about what follows. The literature discussed should be directly focused on the research problem and provide the reader with a sense of the state of the field with respect to the problem. Reviewers, as experts in relevant areas, may notice problems in the completeness, appropriateness, and accuracy of your presentation of the literature. Sometimes, these concerns can be handled by adding, or even eliminating, references. Usually, however, they revolve around the more central issue of elaborating a theoretical framework: Too often this is left implicit in the presentation as authors pay too much attention to what others have said and shy away from the problem of justifying and rendering comprehensible their own research. Good literature reviews for research reports stay strongly focused on the problem at hand and provide only enough detail to inform the current study. Theoretical frameworks guiding the research should be as specific as possible given the area of research. They are evaluated in terms of appropriateness, adequacy, the extent to which they justify the method and results to follow, and the clarity and logic with which they link what is known in the literature to the findings of your study. A well-designed figure provides an excellent visual presentation of a theory's key constructs and their interrelationships. Because of their great power in summarizing complex information, we recommend that authors include such displays whenever feasible, for both qualitative and quantitative information (Tufte, 1990).

REVISING THE METHOD SECTION

If reviewers find something basic to be wrong with the design or execution of the study, say a confound, additional data collection may be the only way to correct it. Less severe reviewer concerns about the method usually will involve questions about clarity. The focus will be on matters such as the participant sample, study design, measures, and procedures. In a well-designed study and successful research report, these elements will be clear and obviously linked to the overall goals of the research. The aim is to get the reviewers nodding as they read, so that all makes sense and there are few, or no, surprises. Good reviewers and good readers will notice if you fail to report material such as relevant reliability coefficients, so a policy of full and unabashed disclosure is a must. Even problematic research situations can play well with reviewers when handled appropriately by authors. On revision, attend to and correct any situation that may have led the reviewer to doubt that the manuscript is a complete account of what was done; such doubts can quickly generalize to other aspects of the manuscript and can greatly impede the success of the report. Of course, it is possible that reviewers will identify design flaws or weaknesses in the study that are insurmountable in a revision. If so, one should look again at the study and try to establish the level of conclusion that is supported in the work. It still may be possible to publish the results if the interpretation and conclusions are developed at a level consistent with the strengths and weaknesses of the study. Alternatively, reviewers may have given a clear indication of what additional work is needed to achieve a publishable product.

REVISING THE RESULTS SECTION

For many studies, results are altogether harder to report than scientists care to admit. Beginning authors often miss the subtlety of good presentation of research findings, particularly the subtlety of balancing everything one looked at with the practical matter of making a focused and compelling case for what your study reveals about the research problem. The trick is to find the proper level of focus in the results—neither too detailed nor too general—and to organize the presentation in such a way that the reader is taken to ground level in your research and back up again so as to be ready for the conclusions to be drawn in the discussion. The logical ties between the research question, the design of the study, and the major results to be considered should be carried in both the way the results are presented and the order of the presentation. Secondary but important matters are held apart from the central development and presented as such with the promise of later interpretation in the Discussion section. Again, thoroughness is extremely important, but reviewers will not appreciate unnecessary and distracting detail. It is also extremely important to be accurate and thorough in presenting statistical findings, but do not succumb to the trap of depending too heavily on statistical sophistication to impress reviewers. Studies need to be up to date and sophisticated, but ultimately reviewers want to know how the data from this study inform the research question. Consider that statistical tests address the probability that differences observed in your results might occur by chance; once dealt with, this problem is of little substantive significance to your presentation (Cohen, 1994). The essence of your study is in the structure of the data, as in the size of mean differences observed between groups in your design. You will never be faulted for presenting basic descriptive and summary information along with the higher-level statistical analyses—these can be easily removed if not required—but you may well be faulted if you do not. If the Results section requires revision, efforts designed to make clear the interesting and informative aspects of your data, including addition of or editing of tables and figures, are the most likely to be successful. Similarly, be sure there is a logical order in the presentation that helps the reader quickly grasp what is being examined and how. The tighter this organization, the less likely that reviewers will be led to questions they might not have otherwise considered.

REVISING THE DISCUSSION

Discussion sections can also be difficult to write, and it is here that reviewers often find inadequacies in first submissions. The objectives of a good discussion are to unravel the major themes of the research, drawing out their implications for theory and research, and to elaborate conclusions that are appropriately sensitive to the strengths and limitations of the study. Reviewers are looking for it all to come together in the discussion, and they are not expecting to have to expend much effort to understand how it comes together—that is the job of the author. Unfortunately, in our experience as reviewers, too often one finds that the discussion trails off inconclusively or that the theoretical implications of the work are minimally dealt with, even in otherwise strong research projects. One often gets the impression that authors have not thought seriously about the larger implications of their work. Or worse, it can seem as if they are waiting to see what reviewers say before committing themselves. Although this might be a good—albeit Machiavellian— strategy for getting a paper published, it is extremely bad form to leave it to reviewers to figure out how to explain what they believe the paper needs. Thus revisions of Discussion sections are typically oriented toward broadening the interpretation of the results to place them in the context of the larger theoretical problems addressed by the project, to correct any tendencies to draw conclusions that are too strong or too weak given the limitations for the study design, and to link the results to other areas that are theoretically or empirically related to the study. Because discussions are interpretive, there are no simple rules governing their production and revision. It is useful, however, to keep in mind a goal of striking a balance between staying close to the data in your interpretations and fairly discussing the broader implications of the work.

Important future research can emerge from a well-constructed Discussion section, so carefully consider what you would like your reader audience left with as your paper comes to a conclusion. The more explicitly and incisively you can articulate these thoughts, the more affirmative will be reviewer response. Alternatively, if reviewers find points for disagreement, your clarity will have established the basis for productive dialogue with reviewers in defense (or modification) of your position that can greatly improve both your paper and your understanding of your research area. Remember, a major ideal in science is to establish a consensus around an area of study and to establish unequivocally the empirical basis for that consensus. In working toward this goal, you will note that some concrete ways of interpreting your results are fairly noncontroversial. The problem, however, comes in linking these basics to higher-level theoretical interpretations (e.g., Cronbach & Meehl, 1955). This is an art form that is often best learned and exercised in revision of a scientific report based on reviewer response.

EVALUATING FIT WITH THE JOURNAL

In many cases, it is clear that the journal to which you have chosen to submit your work is the right one for its ultimate publication. Nonetheless, it is important to be aware that the fit of a manuscript with the journal's usual type and quality of article is regularly assessed by reviewers. The APA *Publication Manual* (APA, 1994) lists summaries of policy statements on its journals and descriptions of the kinds of articles they publish. Many of the descriptions indicate the major criteria for acceptance as well as the content areas deemed appropriate. Authors may also consult the *Journals in Psychology: A Resource Listing for Authors* (APA, 1993) and the *Author's Guide to Journals in the Behavioral Sciences* (Wang, 1989) for additional journal information. However, the APA *Publication Manual* suggests that authors always refer to the policy statements published in the most recent edition of the particular journal to which they are submitting because that is where any changes in current editorial policies will be documented.

Reviewers will be judging the extent to which your research is of interest to the journal's readership and the overall importance of the work in advancing knowledge in your area. These are obviously comparative judgments, depending as much on the pool of submissions to a journal as on the merits of any given manuscript—this is true of publishing in general. Journals will vary in the extent to which they seek only the most advanced level of research product. Depending on the type of feedback you get from reviewers, you might use the opportunity to revise to reassess whether you have submitted your manuscript to the best journal. What constitutes the "best" journal? Many feel publication is most desirable in an APA journal. However, whether an APA journal provides the best outlet and readership for your particular work is a personal decision. Therefore you may wish to examine other journals as well, although there is general agreement that you should, if at all possible, keep to a peer-reviewed journal rather than a journal that does not apply review standards.

In their letter of response, editors will be tentative about the extent to which a revision will be successful; after all, they cannot know how effectively you will be able to handle the revision. Generally, however, the suggestion that an author "revise and resubmit" is positive feedback, suggesting at least the possibility that an article appropriate for the journal can be produced from your research. In all this, keep in mind that once you have produced a successful manuscript, your interest will immediately transform to a focus on whether the work is getting adequate exposure in the journal. Use the revision time to reconsider this issue carefully.

ADDITIONAL POINTS TO CONSIDER
IN EXECUTING THE REVISION

So far we have focused largely on the feedback from journal editors and reviewers as key in revising a research manuscript. Attention to such feedback is essential if one wishes to have work published in a refereed journal. However, the revision process is much broader than this. To revise is, quite literally, to "re-see" one's work. An author may, on the basis of feedback from the reviewers and his or her own rereading of the paper, wish to incorporate additional new material. In this sense, a reviewer's comments can offer the author an outside view of his or her paper. As reviewer criticisms are addressed, authors gain a new perspective on their work. Similarly, it is useful to have revisions read by colleagues before resubmission to the journal because authors can become so involved in the rewrite that it becomes difficult to identify flaws in the paper.

In fact, one challenge in rewriting a research manuscript stems from the incorporation of changes while maintaining a coherent, logical writing style. Although the "cut-and-paste" functions of word processing are enormously helpful, they can lead to choppy manuscripts. Authors should carefully review their own papers during the revision process, paying attention to their writing, grammar, and punctuation. Fiske and Fogg (1990) noted that "it is impressive that the reviewers saw as many problems in the presentation—exposition and description—as in the actual research activities" (p. 592) of the papers reviewed in their study. Clearly, editors and reviewers would pay equal or perhaps even more attention to this issue when reviewing a resubmitted manuscript.

In writing your manuscript, and once again in preparing your revision, pay special attention to the overall unity and tightness of the writing. These qualities of good writing can be difficult to achieve, but they will become increasingly apparent as your revision develops. Basically, they give readers a sense of everything fitting together in a lucid and seamless manner; readers are effectively pulled along by the writing, with relative ease, through even the most complicated sections. This does not mean that you cannot write about complicated topics, but rather that effort is made to anticipate where readers are as they enter a section and that provision is made to help them move quickly through it. Economy is of the essence. A few well-chosen transitions or subheadings can work wonders in this regard, and wise revising authors are ever on the lookout for improving this aspect of a manuscript, for it is a virtual certainty that reviewers will respond positively to their efforts.

Once you feel your revised manuscript is ready for resubmission, you should prepare a cover letter to accompany the rewritten paper when it is sent to the journal editor. In addition to specifying the paper as a resubmission, it is often helpful to describe how the various points raised in the editor's feedback and reviewer comments have been addressed in the revision. If there are points that you decided not to change or address, you should articulate your reasons for doing so. This alerts the editor to the fact that you have not missed a reviewer's suggestions and provides a rationale for the decisions reflected in the rewrite. Overall, such a letter clarifies in summary form the significant ways in which the revised manuscript has taken into account previous concerns. (See Chapter 26 of this book for additional information on dealing with editors and reviewers.)

Two final thoughts in closing. If reviewers have worked for you, whether their work has seemed easy or difficult, fair or misguided, it is likely that your manuscript is better at resubmission than before. The effort of reviewers deserves recognition in the acknowledgments for the paper. Also, we have presented revision as a common and workable step in the process of publishing research findings. Nonetheless, it is not without its pitfalls: For example, the added clarity of a revision can, on occasion, raise new, unanticipated questions for reviewers. Editors are generally not inclined to put authors in double jeopardy, but neither are they inclined to ignore serious doubts legitimately raised in the review process. It is important for authors to recognize that this is simply a part of the consensus-generating system, however arduous it may seem. It is useful always to consider yourself in a learning process, learning new things about how your research might be conceptualized, perhaps about how to communicate in the peer review system, perhaps about yourself and your work. Such attitudes may help you accept the discipline and humility required to publish your work and perhaps will make the problem of manuscript revision a bit more palatable. In any case, standing with your conclusions in the presence of your peers is a big part of what science is all about, and few aspects of the process will put you there quite like revising your work. As with the initial submission, there is relief again when the revision is complete and comfort in the sense that the manuscript has improved. However, it should be remembered that revision does not guarantee acceptance, although the probability of acceptance can improve with revision. Fiske and Fogg (1990) pointed out that whereas only 2% of initial submissions are accepted (Eichorn & VandenBos, 1985), between 20% and 40% of revised manuscripts are accepted. The process of review and publication is an imperfect art form (Kupfersmid, 1988; Sussman, 1993), and the reliability between reviewers has been questioned (Peters & Ceci, 1982; Spencer, Hartnett, & Mahoney, 1986). Nonetheless, peer review remains the standard in science, and this is unlikely to change anytime soon. With luck and diligence, your effort will pay off, your manuscript will be accepted, and you will see work you can be proud of go to print.

Recommended Readings

The APA *Publication Manual* (APA, 1994) provides an excellent overview of many of the issues covered in this chapter, including specifics on manuscript preparation, an overview of the editorial and review process, and general writing guidelines. Additional readings that cover more specific issues related to editorial and review procedures include Cummings and Frost's *Publishing in the Organizational Sciences* (1985), Jackson and Rushton's *Scientific Excellence: Origins and Assessment* (1987), and DeBakey's *The Scientific Journal: Editorial Policies and Practices* (1976). For a recent perspective on these issues, one may also refer to Sussman's (1993) article "The Charybdis of Publishing in Academia." There are also several excellent books that discuss the construction of figures, graphs, and visual displays of information. These include two volumes by Tufte, *Envisioning Information* (1990) and *The Visual Display of Quantitative Information* (1983). Additional sources are Kosslyn's *Elements of Graph Design* (1994) and Wilkinson, Hill, and Vang's *Graphics* (1992).

References

American Psychological Association. (1993). *Journals in psychology: A resource listing for authors.* Washington, DC: Author.

American Psychological Association. (1994). *Publication manual of the American Psychological Association* (4th ed.). Washington, DC: Author.

Ceci, S. J., & Peters, D. (1984). How blind is blind review? *American Psychologist, 39,* 1491-1494.

Cofer, C. N. (1985). Some reactions to manuscript review from a questionnaire study. *Behavioral and Brain Sciences, 8,* 745-746.

Cohen, J. (1994). The earth is round *(p* < .05). *American Psychologist, 49,* 997-1003.

Cronbach, L. J., & Meehl, P. E. (1955). Construct validity in psychological tests. *Psychological Bulletin, 52,* 281-302.

Cummings, L. L., & Frost, P. J. (Eds.). (1985). *Publishing in the organizational sciences.* Homewood, IL: Richard D. Irwin.

Daft, R. L. (1985). Why I recommended that your manuscript be rejected and what you can do about it. In L. L. Cummings & P. J. Frost (Eds.), *Publishing in the organizational sciences* (pp. 193-204). Homewood, IL: Richard D. Irwin.

DeBakey, L. (1976). *The scientific journal: Editorial policies and practices.* St. Louis, MO: C. V. Mosby.

Eichorn, D. H., & VandenBos, G. R. (1985). Dissemination of scientific and professional knowledge: Journal publication within the APA. *American Psychologist, 40,* 1309-1316.

Fiske, D. W., & Fogg, L. (1990). But the reviewers are making different criticisms of my paper! Diversity and uniqueness in reviewer comments. *American Psychologist, 45,* 591-598.

Jackson, D. N., & Rushton, J. P. (Eds.). (1987). *Scientific excellence: Origins and assessment.* Newbury Park, CA: Sage.

Kosslyn, S. M. (1994). *Elements of graph design.* New York: W. H. Freeman.

Kupfersmid, J. (1988). Improving what is published: A model in search of an editor. *American Psychologist, 43,* 635-642.

Peters, D., & Ceci, S. J. (1982). Peer-review practices of psychological journals: The fate of published articles submitted again. *Behavioral and Brain Sciences, 5,* 187-255.

Peters, D., & Ceci, S. J. (1985). Peer review: Beauty is in the eye of the beholder. *Behavioral and Brain Sciences, 8,* 747-750.

Roediger, H. L., III. (1987). The role of journal editors in the scientific process. In D. N. Jackson & J. P. Rushton (Eds.), *Scientific excellence: Origins and assessment* (pp. 222-252). Newbury Park, CA: Sage.

Smigel, E. D., & Ross, H. L. (1970). Factors in the editorial decision. *American Sociologist, 5,* 19-21.

Spencer, N. J., Hartnett, J., & Mahoney, J. (1986). Problems with review in the standard editorial practice. *Journal of Social Behavior and Personality, 1,* 21-36.

Sussman, M. B. (1993). The Charybdis of publishing in academia. *Marriage and Family Review, 18,* 161-169.

Tufte, E. R. (1983). *The visual display of quantitative information.* Cheshire, CT: Graphics Press.

Tufte, E. R. (1990). *Envisioning information.* Cheshire, CT: Graphics Press.

Wang, A. Y. (1989). *Author's guide to journals in the behavioral sciences.* Hillsdale, NJ: Lawrence Erlbaum.

Wilkinson, L., Hill, M., & Vang, E. (1992). *Graphics.* Evanston, IL: Systat Inc.

Chapter 24

Dealing With Journal Editors
and Reviewers

SAMUEL H. OSIPOW

After all the work on a research project has been completed, it is logical to pursue publication, for after all, part of the scientist's obligation is to share results with a wide audience. However, many potential barriers exist to thwart reaching this objective. Not the least of these barriers are those thrown up by the editor and reviewers of periodicals to which one submits the work. In what follows, some fundamental procedures are presented that may reduce the frustration that attempts to publish may cause and possibly even enhance the success of the publication effort.

Preparing the Manuscript

The first step starts long before the research has been completed. It is imperative to begin with a good (read "important and interesting to your field") research idea and a sound research design. (See Wampold, Chapter 5 of this volume.) Next, the data must be based on a sample that is appropriate and large enough to test the hypotheses. These hypotheses, in turn, should be clearly stated, and their source—that is, the theory or empirical findings of others—should be identified and illustrated. A thorough literature review should be conducted to enable the author to be satisfied that the study is either sufficiently different from those that have gone before or an accurate replication. (See Stockdale and Kenny, Chapter 3 of this volume.) Last in this early stage is the adequate analysis of the data, using appropriate statistics interpreted properly. In other words, there is no substitute for good work in enhancing the probability of successful publication in journals. (See Dollinger & DiLalla, Chapter 13 of this volume, and Levy & Steelman, Chapter 17 of this volume.)

Selecting an Outlet

Good work alone, however, though necessary, is not sufficient to achieve publication. With your research results in hand and your research report in front of you, the next task is to identify the appropriate publication outlets for your work. The easiest way to accomplish this is to read or skim several issues of the journals you think might be appropriate outlets. Most periodicals have a statement of goals and definitions as part of their masthead. Read these statements carefully to satisfy yourself, at least at a preliminary level, that the journal has possibilities as an outlet for your research. You should also look at the table of contents of several recent issues to see what has recently been judged to be appropriate. If you are still uncertain, drafting a letter of inquiry summarizing your study briefly (in a page) to the editor and asking for an opinion of the appropriateness of its submission may be helpful. Most editors will respond to such an inquiry because it can save hours of wasted editorial and reviewer time. One of the more annoying things an editor experiences is receiving a manuscript from someone who obviously has never seen the periodical because if he or she had, he or she would have known better than to submit it.

Also be sure that you look at the most recent issues in considering topical appropriateness. Even though the mission statement on the masthead may be constant over several years, there is often a "drift" of topical importance as interests in different topics under the general topic of the journal wax and wane. It is also important to send the manuscript to the current editor, so check carefully the name and address to which it should be sent.

While reading the masthead statement, determine several other important mechanical pieces of information that can cost you time (and the good will of the editor) if not followed. Make yourself aware of such simple things as how many copies to submit, whether the manuscript should be prepared to expedite "blind" review, and manuscript style and format requirements. "Blind" review permits the author to be anonymous to the reviewers. This has the advantage to a young investigator of permitting your manuscript to be judged on its own merits and not on the author's reputation.

At this stage, prepare your manuscript in the proper format. Important here is the need to avoid falling in love with your words. Often manuscripts submitted for publication are based on thesis or dissertation research. An editor can almost always tell if that is so, partly because the manuscript is probably too long, provides a more comprehensive literature review than is necessary or appropriate, and goes into more detail in the presentation of results and discussion than is necessary in journal publication. You must learn to take a heavy hand with the "blue pencil," cutting down your paper to journal length while maintaining the important methodological details and results so that the article is comprehensible to a reader who is relatively unfamiliar with your topic. You have probably grown so intimate with your study that you cannot always see where gaps may exist in your presentation.

A word about the presentation of tables and figures is in order. Detailed instructions in the American Psychological Association (APA) *Publication Manual* (1994) describe the format of tables and figures and should be carefully followed. However, it is important to emphasize that the author must use good judgment in deciding what is appropriately presented in a tabular or pictorial manner. If the information is readily presented in the text, a table or figure is probably unnecessary.

After you have produced a draft that you think is reasonably good, turn it over to a colleague or professor and ask for critical comment. The pain of receiving criticism is more than offset by the value such feedback provides. A "naive" (to your paper, anyway) reader can perceive flaws that you, as the author, will gloss over because of your familiarity with the topic and paper. Thus such outside friendly readers may find poor sentences, vague antecedents, poor organization, sentences that are not clear, gaps in information provided, confusing tables and figures, and many other shortcomings. Remember that it is far better to get this critique from a sympathetic reader than from an editor or reviewer, whose critical words may be far harsher.

Some Typical Editorial Responses

After you are sure that the manuscript is typed accurately and attractively and that the tables and figures are properly presented, you are ready to mail your manuscript to the editor for review. Then the long wait for word about the outcome begins. Most psychology journals hope to have reviews back to authors in about 2 months, but sometimes it takes far longer because of tardy reviewers or editorial workload. If you have received no word after more than 3 months, it is reasonable to inquire about the status of the manuscript.

When you finally get the editorial response, it may take various forms, each of which stimulates its own distinctive author reaction. By far the best outcome is for the editor to say the paper is wonderful and is accepted as submitted. To give the reader an idea how rare that outcome is, in my experience as a journal editor, in which I have made editorial decisions on close to 3,000 manuscripts, only three times have I accepted a paper as it was submitted originally, and two of those times the paper was by the same author.

The worst outcome, of course, is outright rejection. Your feelings as an author will be hurt. There is a predictable sequence of emotions that authors experience after a paper is summarily rejected. First is shock: How could this happen after all my work? Then, anger: Those readers and the editor are fools, or they are prejudiced against me or my topic or both. These stages last different lengths of time in different people. An experienced author, sure of him- or herself, will experience less extreme reactions of shorter duration because such an author has a context within which to evaluate the decision and more self-confidence in his or her ability to write for professional publication. During the anger stage, it is important to do nothing either to change the manuscript or to write or call the editor, lest poor decisions make the matter even worse.

After the first two stages have passed, a more rational reaction begins to emerge. The author can read the comments and evaluate them with better judgment. Sometimes it will become clear that the paper would go better elsewhere. Other times, the comments will lead the author to develop alternative ways of presentation that might be more publishable or to identify flaws in the study or analysis that can be corrected through conducting another study. Sometimes an author will gradually get to the point where he or she might want to thank the editor and reviewers for rejecting the paper because it has spared the author the embarrassment of publishing something with serious defects for all the world to see.

Whatever the outcome, remember that many journals in psychology reject 85% to 90% of the manuscripts submitted, so do not overreact to a rejection. If you believe that your paper fundamentally has merit despite the rejection, think of ways to revise and new places to submit the paper. A persistent author is usually successful in achieving publication, although perhaps not in the outlet of first choice.

Two other editorial decisions frequently occur. The editor may write, "This manuscript is not publishable as submitted, but if you are willing to make the changes suggested by the reviewers (see enclosed), we will be willing to consider a revised manuscript." The key word in this situation is *consider*. Here, you must realize, the editor is not making a commitment to publish if you change the paper, only a commitment to rereview, something not ordinarily done by editors. This type of decision can be discouraging and contains certain pitfalls. An author may spend a great deal of time reworking the manuscript, only to find that on resubmission, the editor sends the manuscript to one or more new reviewers, who then find different "flaws." Following this scenario, revision can proceed ad infinitum without reaching closure. If this happens to you, you would be wise to impose a limit on the number of times you will revise the paper.

A better outcome is when the editor tells you that the paper is publishable provided you are willing to make certain changes in the presentation, and then tells you what must be changed and/or where the shortcomings of the paper lie. Here it is important for the author to understand clearly the changes desired before proceeding. If the changes are not clear to you, feel free to ask questions of the editor.

Revising the Manuscript

Ordinarily, when the "accept with revision" option is offered, the author has a limited amount of time to make the changes. (See Nagata & Trierweiler, Chapter 23 of this volume.) If you do not think the editor has given you enough time, either because the changes will take you more time and effort to make than the editor estimates or because your own schedule is very hectic and will delay your paying attention to the manuscript, then write or call the editor and ask for more time, and indicate how much more time you will need. Most editors will grant such extensions if the request is made in a timely fashion and seems reasonable.

Another point to remember is that editorial feedback can and should be educational. If it is possible for you, assume the attitude that the editor and the reviewers are trying to help you and are on your side. Many if not all editors perceive part of their job as editor to teach neophytes how to publish.

Regardless of which of the three above-described outcomes occurs, there will be detailed and substantive feedback from which the author can learn more about conducting research and writing about its results. Of course, this educational phase cannot occur until the shock and anger have passed.

Dealing With Critical Feedback

One of the most difficult features of reading feedback about a manuscript is the tone of the reviewers' comments. Very often the editor encloses uncut copies of the criticisms made by the reviewers. As an author, you may sometimes get the feeling that the review and editorial process is adversarial in nature. Unfortunately, the comments are often extremely hostile and derogatory. All too often, they pass beyond the realm of genuine constructive criticism and enter into the realm of ad hominem attacks. Usually the editor is more tactful in giving feedback, but sometimes editors, too, slip into that angry and demeaning style. In the periodical that I currently edit (*Applied and Preventive Psychology*), the reviewers are instructed to avoid taking an adversarial approach and instead to view their role to be making the manuscript the best it can be. Experience with that approach has shown not only that the authors appreciate that style but that the reviewers do as well. Unfortunately, that procedure might not work with a different kind of journal.

One might think that such angry, hostile comments would be connected exclusively with manuscripts that are rejected. However, one is likely to find them in connection with manuscripts that are accepted with revision or invited for a resubmission. This factor makes it all the more difficult for the author to pass through the angry reactive stage and into a constructive, revising stage. The best thing an author can do is, first, to put the comments aside for a day or two. The comments will still look bad in a few days, but usually the author is calmer. Then abstract the main features of the needed revisions so that it will not be necessary to keep rereading the irritating comments, which will only rekindle the unconstructive, angry feelings.

Disagreeing With Editorial Recommendations

At this point, the author can set about the task of revising the manuscript on the merits of the comments. As noted earlier, after a short time has passed, the comments are likely to look less intimidating, and the author's emotion about them has probably drained away to a manageable level. It is likely that the author will have good arguments to use in rebuttal about one or more of the suggested changes. These counterarguments can be made in a cover letter with the resubmitted manuscript.

In fact, it is useful to write an explanation about how each of the editorial concerns raised was resolved. Thus, where it is appropriate to make your counterpoints, they can be made in a naturally flowing manner. Some editors actually require authors to write such a letter detailing their treatment of each of the needed changes. Such a letter serves the purposes of both the editor and the author. For the editor, the letter serves as a quick summary of changes needed and made, enabling the editor to make a faster decision about whether this version is now satisfactory. For the author, the letter can serve a similar purpose. It can serve as a checklist that the author can use to see whether all the changes have been made.

When the editorial recommendations seem patently incorrect to you, it may be tempting to argue with the editor. This option should be approached with caution because such behavior could antagonize an editor and could also be a waste of your own time.

TABLE 24.1 Important Points in Dealing With Editors and Reviewers

1. Do a thorough literature review.

2. Ensure the importance of your research.

3. Prepare a sound research design and appropriate statistics.

4. Identify appropriate publication outlets.

5. Prepare the manuscript using the proper format.

6. Do not react emotionally to editorial feedback and decisions.

7. Be sure you clearly understand the revisions the editor requires.

8. Write an explanatory letter about the changes you have made.

However, if you cannot accept a major recommended change and your arguments cannot easily be incorporated into the cover letter approach described earlier, the most likely way to present an effective rebuttal is to use the literature, existing data as well as your own, and, above all, logic in attempting to persuade the editor to your point of view.

A related issue is when, if ever, it is appropriate to challenge a rejection. My personal opinion is never, but many authors have had success with their challenges. To challenge, use the same points mentioned above (literature, data, and logic) to make your case. It is likely that the best outcome you will achieve is a fresh review by two different editorial consultants, a not altogether trivial result.

Table 24.1 summarizes the points made in this chapter about how to deal with editors and reviewers.

I have left unsaid the importance of learning the skills involved in effective writing. These skills are necessary before even the first step in publishing your research can be taken.

Recommended Readings

We recommend that the reader consult the following sources for more in-depth information about the topics covered in this chapter: Daft (1985), Frost (1985), Weick (1985), and Dorn's *Publishing for Professional Development* (1985), especially the chapter by Gelso and Osipow (1985).

References

American Psychological Association (1994). *Publication manual of the American Psychological Association* (4th ed.). Washington, DC: Author.

Daft, R. L. (1985). Why I recommended that your manuscript be rejected and what you can do about it. In L. L. Cummings & P. J. Frost (Eds.), *Publishing in the organizational sciences* (pp. 193-204). Homewood, IL; Richard D. Irwin.

Dorn, F. J. (Ed.). (1985). *Publishing for professional development*. Muncie, IN: Accelerated Development.

Frost, P. J. (1985). Responding to rejection: An author's view of the rejection of an academic manuscript. In L. L. Cummings & P. J. Frost (Eds.), *Publishing in the organizational sciences* (pp. 766-773). Homewood, IL: Richard D. Irwin.

Gelso, C. J., & Osipow, S. H. (1985). Guidelines for effective manuscript evaluation. In F. J. Dorn (Ed.), *Publishing for professional development* (pp. 68-69). Muncie, IN: Accelerated Development.

Weick, K. E. (1985). Editing a rejection: A case study. In L. L. Cummings & P. J. Frost (Eds.), *Publishing in the organizational sciences* (pp. 774-780). Homewood, IL: Richard D. Irwin.

PART VI

Special Topics

Chapter 25

Coordinating a Research Team

Maintaining and Developing a Good Working Laboratory

DENNIS L. MOLFESE
KRISTEN L. MURRAY
TINA B. MARTIN
CINDY J. PETERS
ARLENE A. TAN
LESLIE A. GILL
PANAGIOTIS A. SIMOS

In today's complex world of science, investigators find themselves increasingly working in research teams to pool resources and talent. Scientific areas have become complex to the point that it is difficult for one individual to possess all of the expertise and acumen (not to mention time) to carry out an extensive set of experiments. Given such limits, the research team is one particularly effective means to deal with the rapid pace of developments within and across fields and the increasingly complex and wide range of skills needed to address these developments. In a sense, the training students receive in graduate school is a microcosm of their future in science—as part of a scientific research team. Students who can participate in such an experience during graduate training will learn a great number of skills that will be helpful to them in their careers. At the same time, the success of a research group depends greatly on the initiative and expertise of the research members. This means that even the newest member of the research team is an important component in its success. The purpose of this chapter is to review a number of factors that are likely to contribute to the effectiveness of a strong research team (see also the recommended readings at the end of the chapter).

Initiative

The most significant way that students can have a positive impact on their research environment is through their own initiative. Their education and what they will learn through their research training depends foremost on the amount of time and energy that they commit to this process. The process is not a one-way street in which students simply absorb information. Rather, it requires a major commitment of their time and resources. Students must actively participate and aggressively pursue their training. If they make a major commitment, they are likely to experience major gains. If they commit little of their time, on the other hand, their gains will be considerably less. The opportunities for major gains in knowledge and experience are certainly there if the student is part of a research team. How the student makes use of those opportunities and what can be gained from them, however, depends on what the student chooses to do in this setting.

Initiative, then, is very important to the training process and to the success of the research team. Consequently, the usual rules regarding initiative certainly apply. If something needs to be done, do not wait for someone else to do it. Rather, if you know how, do it. Do not put tasks off. Instead, deal with them as demands arise. But research initiative goes beyond simply carrying out necessary or assigned duties. The research activities in which you are involved are for your benefit. You have the opportunity to learn skills that will remain with you for a lifetime and will shape your future career. Such skills also influence the way that the scientific community will view you and your potential impact. Consequently, you should immerse yourself in the lab activities. You should not wait for someone else to set each of your training goals; rather, you should actively help to set them. If the director cannot meet with you for a training or check session, you should take the initiative, checking back with the director to schedule a new time.

Read widely. Ask the research director for additional readings beyond those normally assigned. Develop reading habits to scan relevant journals routinely on a weekly basis. Do not read too narrowly. One never knows in advance how little or how much information is necessary to accomplish some goal. Consequently, you should never limit yourself by studying only within a narrow topic. Correspond with other experts beyond the lab, institute, or university to obtain reprints or address questions regarding their work. Take advantage of guest colloquium series and conferences to learn more about a wide range of more general work as well as that related to your more focused interests and the limited range of activities ongoing within the lab. As new information is gathered, share it with the lab director and other students. They will appreciate this initiative and the shared information. If, in your readings and discussions, you develop ideas for a study, you should organize the study design in a systematic fashion, present a proposal to your lab director, and then work to set it in motion. Just do it! This, after all, is what science education is all about—the acquisition of information and skills so that you will become an independent investigator. You may never have another opportunity as rich in research training possibilities as the one you experience in graduate school. The faculty are there specifically to train you. You should feel that you can approach any of them to take advantage of this wealth of expertise that is available to you. Whereas scientific colleagues must wait for special conferences to meet with your advisor or attend seminars at significant financial costs, you can walk down the halls of your department and, with relatively little preparation, make similar demands on a professor's time. Take advantage of this expertise. Clearly, initiative is a major continuing asset for your education. It is a key element not only in being trained but in being trained extremely well. Yet success in this endeavor requires other factors, such as the expertise and cooperation of the research team leader or lab director.

Team Director

The team director could be your lab director who has a Ph.D. or M.D. degree (whether a faculty member or a postdoctoral fellow) or, in some cases, a senior-level graduate student. Four factors are especially important to the effectiveness of the team director and ultimately to the success of the team's efforts: (a) a clear set of specific goals; (b) clearly defined expectations; (c) effective and continuous two-way communication between the team and the director, as well as good communication within the team itself; and (d) a set of shared values and concerns.

First, the team director should project a clear set of goals for the project and state explicitly his or her expectations for the team members. If the project is funded through a grant, then the objectives outlined in the grant can become the team's goals. However, these objectives will need to be translated into very specific goals and presented in a concrete manner to the team. For example, if one of the project goals is to test 40 individuals over a 6-month period, a testing schedule should be developed in advance that sets weekly test targets: how many individuals will be tested that week. Second, the leader must present a clear set of expectations for the team members to meet. Such expectations could encompass factors such as how the team members will approach their assignments, their level of professionalism during testing, and so forth. The third point, communication, is vital to the success of the project and involves both the director and the members of the team. The team director must communicate effectively and readily with the team members. Likewise, the team members must be able to communicate readily with each other and with the team director. If, for whatever reason, this communication is stymied, or if communication occurs only in one direction, the success of the project will be markedly impeded or even endangered. If a long-term project is involved, communication becomes even more critical to avoid experimental drift and unplanned but potentially devastating alterations in procedures. Flexibility on the part of the lab director and older students is very important. An open mind regarding the suggestions and concerns of each other can set the stage for better communication and experimentation. This point is closely related to the fourth factor—shared values. If the team members and director do not agree on procedures or goals, the data can be compromised. For example, if one team member does not agree that a certain procedure is the best to use during data collection, that individual may not adhere to this procedure with the same enthusiasm as the others. Instead, he or she may accept some compromise in his or her work that would be unacceptable to the rest of the team. This could also lead to a breakdown in communication and the lack of willingness to discuss disagreements openly. Obviously, if this happens, the results can be devastating to the future success of the project. It is critically important that all facets of the project be discussed *and* agreed on by all members of the team, director and students alike.

Communication

To help establish a communicative "routine," each new member in the lab should be provided weekly or biweekly supervisory sessions by the team leader. This step is important because it quickly establishes a means to examine individual progress in terms of lab goals and a way for each member to come to understand his or her role in the lab. These supervisory sessions are best conducted on an individual basis. This allows each member to deal directly and privately with the supervisor in developing his or her role in the lab. It also can facilitate problem solving in a nonthreatening manner.

If the team leader's schedule is very limited as to time that can be set aside for supervisory sessions, perhaps some of the sessions could be provided by another senior lab supervisor (e.g., a postdoctoral fellow). In such cases, the two supervisors must allow some time to discuss student development and information to coordinate overall supervision and direction of the lab members. One important point of these individual sessions is to provide a sense of laboratory continuity. In this way, some sense of the "big picture" regarding the lab and its goals can be established with new members. This should also facilitate their understanding of how their own goals fit within those conveyed by the team leader. In fact, such supervision may provide the opportunity to develop both students' goals and the lab goals in mutually supporting ways. People who are achieving their individual goals within the context of the lab are more likely to contribute effectively to lab goals.

A second way to model healthy communication is within the weekly lab meetings with all staff members. These meetings are necessary to maintain consistent goals over time and to discuss systematically and solve problems confronting the lab. Such problems may be practical ones concerned with equipment breakdowns or more interpersonal ones, such as the distribution of workloads. All of these require an open forum. It is imperative that there be honest and efficient recognition and discussion of problems to prevent them from becoming larger and potentially damaging to the research enterprise.

Finally, shame tactics to bring about changes in particular lab members are usually not useful forms of communication, whether used in the form of "peer pressure" or at an individual level. Situations that cannot be dealt with assertively and directly cannot be improved by humiliating another person.

Research Ethics for the Team

This volume is written to provide information to research assistants as they develop through their training into more accomplished scientists and scholars. An important part of this process is the recognition by all involved that trainees are likely to make mistakes along the way. The critical point here is that students come to recognize their mistakes and communicate them readily with the project director and the research team so that procedures can be developed to avoid or lessen the likelihood of those mistakes in the future. To accomplish this, students and the project director must both recognize and accept that mistakes will occur. At the same time, both must be committed to guarding and improving the quality of their work. One factor that can greatly facilitate this process is for the director to make it clear to the team that although mistakes are undesirable, they are a natural and inevitable part of the training process. It would be a mistake in this regard for the research director to mete out heavy penalties or social embarrassment to a student who makes a mistake. Rather, the director should be concerned with teaching students about potential mistakes that might occur in different situations and how to avoid them or detect and correct them. This can be done in a nonthreatening manner by asking students to trouble-shoot experimental procedures or to check databases while encouraging them to discuss openly mistakes they discover or make during the process. Having students report errors to the lab director in private eliminates the additional embarrassment of reporting in front of one's peers. The student and lab director are then freer to discuss issues and perhaps develop strategies for both correcting and avoiding future problems. The results of this meeting can then be discussed within the larger format of the lab meeting, a step that hopefully creates an open atmosphere in which students feel freer to discuss both the positive and the negative aspects of the research process. Students should also come to appreciate that although mistakes are to be avoided, they can and will occur during the research process. Given such occurrences, the student must learn that the researcher has a responsibility to identify, admit, and correct these errors. At the same time, however, it is imperative that the lab director recognize that admitting any fault is extremely uncomfortable for new team members. Public admission of fault from senior members of the team and even the lab director can help these new members learn to overcome their embarrassment and fear.

Recruitment of Research Assistants

The project director is faced with the same issue that any prospective employer faces—how to evaluate the suitability of prospective employees and how to predict their success in this research environment. Whether recruiting graduate or undergraduate students, five factors are very helpful in a successful recruitment: (a) personal interview, (b) an explicit set of evaluation criteria, (c) a review of duties to be performed, (d) length of the assignment, and (e) diversity.

The personal interview allows the director and the prospective student to meet one on one to discuss the assignment and communicate their own expectations regarding the assignment. This provides the director with the opportunity to learn about the student's background, experience, current skill levels, and interests. The director must also describe the research project, its goals, and her or his expectations regarding the student's role in this project. While this discussion proceeds, the director can determine whether the student's credentials meet some basic criteria for participating in the research. The personal interview allows the director to outline lab expectations for the student in terms of hours per week, level of expectations regarding the quality of work, supplementary readings that may help the student learn more about the project, and so forth. Finally, by recruiting students with different academic backgrounds and levels of experience, the director ensures a group of individuals who will bring different orientations and expertise to the research lab. This diversity can greatly enhance discussions and even improve possibilities for designing research projects.

UNDERGRADUATE ASSISTANTS

Whereas graduate students, as part of their admission to a graduate program, may have already met some set of expectations or standards for research assistants that are acceptable for most labs, criteria for determining which undergraduates should be allowed to participate may be more varied. We usually require undergraduate assistants to maintain at least an overall grade point average (GPA) of 3.5 on a 4.0 scale and to commit to at least

10 hours per week for a two-semester period. The GPA establishes a basic level of competency expected of students and hopefully ensures that their research participation will not jeopardize their other course work and academic performance. The requirement of a two-semester commitment on the part of the student allows the student time for lab involvement beyond just his or her training period, as well as providing for some continuity in assistants to the lab across an extended time period. The latter allows the student to be helpful to the project beyond his or her training period.

GRADUATE ASSISTANTS

As noted above, graduate assistants have most likely already gone through an extensive screening procedure. They have most likely already worked as undergraduate assistants in some laboratory and have performed very well in fairly competitive situations. The lab director has the added advantage of access to letters of recommendation written by other professors who have spent time with the student and are willing to share their own evaluations of the student's present ability and potential. At the same time, just because a student has been admitted to graduate school does not necessarily mean that he or she has the skills, temperament, or interest needed to function well in all research settings. The interview, then, provides an excellent opportunity for the lab director and student to meet and discuss issues and supplement their information about each other.

Training and Reliability Checks

Of major importance to any lab are efforts to maintain consistency in lab testing protocols, data entry, scoring, analyses, and so forth. Consistency in training students must be a high priority of the lab director and research assistants. Such training is greatly enhanced by a written protocol that lists the objectives of the training and training targets, both for skills and for training time dates.

If attempts at training are inconsistent or not repeated periodically, even with already trained staff, experimental drift is likely to result. If procedures do change over time in an uncontrolled fashion, consistency in research findings may drop. With such drift comes the increasing likelihood that other confounds may enter the study, further detracting from the study's effectiveness. Such drift in experimental procedures can increase as time passes from the initial training period. The result is that people may begin to modify their procedures over time, treating subjects who participate early in the study differently from those who are tested later. Judgments regarding evaluations of study participants may also change. These are obviously serious problems that can greatly compromise the research study. The use of the lab manual along with periodic and regularly scheduled and independent evaluations of testing protocols can essentially eliminate this danger if carefully exercised.

Lab Manuals

One easy way to communicate goals and expectations is through the development and use of a lab manual (see Appendix 25.1 at the end of this chapter for a sample table of contents). The manual can also facilitate training by listing accepted procedures and forms in a single resource that everyone can access. By reading and referring to the manual, students can identify areas they understand as well as those that seem less clear. Furthermore, the manual can help them to focus their questions better. It also provides an authoritative source for students to go to when they have questions and the lab director or senior lab members are not available. If a lab manual does not currently exist, students or the lab director (or both working together) might consider developing one to help them organize duties, responsibilities, and procedures better.

The manual should include *detailed* information concerning lab philosophy, test objectives, testing priorities, and testing and analysis protocols. Further, it should convey information regarding research ethics and acceptable behavior, demeanor, and dress. Presentation of this information in a manual permits the student to learn about the expected mode of conduct and presentation during various laboratory activities. In addition, the manual should include copies of all test instruments, with annotations concerning special test situations or procedures. The purpose of the manual is to provide a written record that can be readily referenced. The use of such a manual can greatly facilitate training as well as document the standardization of test procedures. Students can read over the manual prior to and during the training process. The manual can also benefit the more experienced students by preventing other dangers that can seep into the research—experimental drift. If procedures outlined in a manual are available to all lab staff, staff can go to the manual to check situations that appear ambiguous or about which older students are unsure. One drawback to a lab manual is the time required to maintain and update it continuously. However, the time demands of this task can be reduced if certain students assume responsibilities for updating or developing different sections that are reviewed by the entire lab team prior to inclusion in the manual. Such participation in updating the manual also gives all involved in the process a sense of ownership over the document and may further encourage participants to update sections of the manual.

Lab Meetings

Lab meetings can be a very effective way to establish strong lines of communication within the laboratory. Such meetings provide an excellent forum from which to coordinate the research group, share information regarding ongoing projects, and resolve difficulties that arise as part of the research process. However, they can vary in their effectiveness and in the way that they are organized. How often should they meet? What activities should they cover? How can discussions during these meetings be kept on target? These are only a few of the questions that arise concerning such meetings. By and large, weekly meetings are very useful for discussing efforts over the previous week that might include equipment problems and training issues, as well as test schedules for the coming week. A written agenda is helpful because it focuses everyone's attention on a set of issues and provides a focal point if discussion moves off the agenda. This agenda could be developed by the more experienced students with input from the lab director or by the lab director. Often the issues or topics will be the same from week to week.

In cases in which the lab may begin a new project, it is both important and useful to provide relevant readings or a bibliography and to establish additional meeting times to discuss previous related work and theoretical issues relevant to this new project. Given the press of business within the regularly scheduled lab meeting (which will most likely have a specific time limit), time constraints may not allow such additional discussions to occur within the structure of the normally scheduled lab meeting. Time must also be set aside to discuss in a systematic fashion the results of completed lab projects on which students have worked. It is important for students to see some closure to their work, as opposed to an endless stream of "ongoing" studies. For new students at the beginning of their lab assignment, the presentation, by the director and involved students, of an overview of past lab studies is very important. Such an overview is a great aid in providing these students (and reminding the more seasoned ones as well) with the framework for understanding the current research program and ongoing studies in which they will participate.

Specific times should also be set aside for lab presentations by students of their honors theses or master's or doctoral studies prior to meetings with their formal committees. These presentations give the student an opportunity to prepare and try out in a fairly supportive environment the materials (i.e., presentation outline, tables, graphs, etc.) and presentation strategies that they plan to use in the upcoming meeting with faculty. Questions or issues that come out in such a practice session can then be developed and dealt with by the student to prepare better for the research presentation defense. When poster or platform presentations are being considered for submission to a conference or professional meeting, discussions can be organized at times outside of the lab meeting to facilitate the development of the materials for these presentations.

Data Checks

Any active laboratory will accumulate various types of data from experiments that are ongoing in the lab. As data accumulate, the research staff are faced with a number of issues that could endanger the integrity of these data. Obviously, data analyses reflect a culmination of the research process. How well the data set is managed and protected can make or break a research project. The data must be as accurate as possible; otherwise all the time and effort that have gone into the project will be lost. By spending extra time to ensure the quality of the data set, the researchers are preserving their earlier efforts. Spending extra time on data checks is a very small price to pay to produce a high-quality product, especially considering all the time and effort already expended to contact subjects and arrange for their tests, the time required for setup and test times, and the anticipated hours to be spent in data analysis, manuscript development, and eventual publication of the research work.

Data can take the form of paper copies of questionnaires or experimenter ratings of subject performance, computer files of subject responses, and materials such as the signed informed consent forms required by the Institutional Review Board if the study involved human subjects. Because a number of records may be kept for each study participant, the lab staff are confronted by the nontrivial but frequently unstandardized tasks of keeping the materials for each subject together and keeping track of them, checking the recorded data for errors made by staff (such as test date, time, and condition assignment), entering the data into computers for data analysis, and then checking the data entries to verify that they accurately reflect the actual recorded data. All of these steps require a great deal of time, care, and precision. The more complex the study or the greater the number of study participants, the greater the time demands for this phase of the research. In fact, with the collection of longitudinal data sets, researchers may find that they spend up to 70% to 80% of their time outside testing simply managing and checking the integrity of their data.

Procedures for checking data should be well described in the lab manual or agreed on at lab meetings with all present. If there is no lab manual, a written record of these discussions must be kept for future reference. Vigilance is a key component for this process. One procedure found to be especially helpful is to have one individual collect the data while a second person independently rechecks the collected data. Computer programs that verify data entry are very useful. Such programs often require individuals to enter the data twice before it is stored into the master data set. The program searches for discrepancies across the two entries and then points those out to the individual responsible for data entry so that conflicts or inconsistencies can be resolved. If possible, random checks conducted by a third individual may also be useful. Duplicate copies of data must *always* be kept and updated accordingly.

There is always a question about who should collect and then enter and manipulate data in the database. Usually, more senior students tend to be primarily responsible for data entry and manipulation because they have developed more skill with the procedures involved. However, training new students on already entered data and comparing their results with the previously checked results is one easy way to train them on these procedures. In addition, these students can watch the activities of the more experienced students on these tasks to develop ideas about how these activities should occur in "real time." When mistakes are made, the director or supervising student can point out these errors and discuss how to avoid or correct them. Discussions at lab meetings of errors in data collection, reduction, or analysis can provide an excellent forum for both training students on how to detect and avoid errors and provide an opportunity for the group as a whole to brainstorm new and better ways to enter data correctly and avoid errors. Obviously, as noted earlier, it is important to convey to all the importance of admitting mistakes without attaching a stigma to the admission. What you are seeking, after all, is to produce the best scientific product possible, and that requires a genuine openness and frankness among the participants in this endeavor.

Stress in the Lab

Regardless of how well a lab is run and the openness of the director and lab personnel to questions and criticism, tensions are bound to arise. Such tensions can develop from a convergence of deadlines, as in cases when student term papers, exams, preparations for poster presentations at conferences, and manuscript or grant deadlines all become due at about the same time. Obviously, prior planning can help reduce some of this stress. With stress and schedule conflicts also come factors that can directly reduce the effectiveness of the lab in terms of training and research quality. People under stress are apt to make more mistakes and to miss appointments. Consequently, although a certain level of stress can generally be expected to occur at different times during the year, it is important for the lab director and personnel to deal with the stress directly and, if possible, to avoid or remove factors that produce or increase stress. By maintaining lab calendars that list subject test dates/times, conference or grant deadlines, and exam and paper deadline dates, the entire lab has the opportunity to discuss work schedules and personal needs to meet the host of deadlines that invariably come at otherwise inopportune times or all at once. Discussions of these potential conflicts at lab meetings, hopefully before they occur, should produce strategies that all or nearly all personnel can use to avoid conflicts.

Another source of stress can develop from interpersonal conflicts. Sometimes people do not like working with certain other individuals. That is a normal part of the human condition. On the other hand, few individuals have the luxury of working only with close friends. A part of any scientist's career will inevitably require him or her to work with someone with whom he or she has some conflict. Yet for the scientific process to survive and move forward, he or she must work efficiently and professionally with such individuals. It is important for such issues to be discussed by the director and students. The director should take a strong stand on this issue and set clear guidelines for behaviors and levels of efficiency that are expected. This situation offers an opportunity to train students on how professionals should behave in such situations. In cases in which disputes occur between students, the director should give them some space to work out their disagreements. However, invariably there are points or situations at which the director must step in for the sake of the students' development and the quality of the research experience. In such cases, it is again important that the director set clear-cut guidelines for discussion and resolution of these problems. Obviously, students will learn from the director's example and that of other professionals. When conflicts arise, the director should deal with these expeditiously, professionally, and in private with the concerned individuals. Airing these issues at a public forum such as the lab meeting may produce unwanted results such as forcing the involved parties to become intransigent or creating more discord at the cost of all concerned. Finally, one would hope that the director would make it very clear at the outset of the training experience that a range of behaviors such as sex, age, or race discrimination are unacceptable. Having explicitly stated codes of behavior can often reduce the likelihood that conflicts related to these issues will arise.

Lab Hierarchy

Invariably in situations in which new assistants come into a functioning lab, they meet up with the "old hands," and some type of hierarchy develops, with the older students taking the lead in training the newer students. This offers an excellent opportunity for older students to learn about mentoring and the responsibilities as well as the satisfaction that can come from it. Sometimes, however, some stress may develop because the newer students do not like being "told what to do" by the more experienced ones, whom they view, after all, as peers. The director can reduce some of this tension by communicating during lab meetings about the mentoring role that the older students are expected to assume and by modeling this mentoring behavior to both new and more experienced students. Further, the clinical model of shared supervision (e.g., of a newer member by both the director and a senior member) can serve both purposes and serve to further differentiate roles within the lab. This makes it clear to all students that some level of direction by more experienced students is expected.

Maintaining a Good Laboratory

Once the lab is operating with trained personnel, a standard set of lab procedures, and established research traditions, many factors fall into place to help the work advance more smoothly. However, a number of factors should be monitored to continue this operation. First, it is important for the research team to maintain a clearly defined set of procedures, duties, and goals. The fewer ambiguities, the better the research. Ambiguities in procedures, when they do arise, can result in decisions that at some level are arbitrary and not guided by established principles. The goals for the research must be reasonable ones that can be reached within a specified time range. Even long-term projects can have a set of goals with interim completion dates. Second, supervision must be personalized. Students must feel that they are an integral part of the research process and that their contributions are important. It is important for the director to provide individual feedback, encouragement, and correction (if needed) on a one-to-one basis. One cannot overestimate the importance and the power of positive feedback on students' work quality and long-range development. We all work better when we are supported and encouraged in our work. This also contributes to our enjoyment of the task. At the same time, the director must feel free to identify areas in which students require more supervision or training. In situations in which a student has not met his or her responsibilities or some errors have persisted, the director should meet with the student in private to discuss these issues. The director should be very explicit about concerns and honest in his or her evaluation, while being supportive of and fair to the student. Together the student and the director should then work out a plan to correct the situation. In some cases, it is possible that a student cannot adapt to the expectations of the lab requirements or is unable to handle the technical aspects of the work. In these situations, the director should identify these problems to the student and, if necessary, discuss with the student other training options, either within the lab or in another context. Perhaps one of the greatest disservices a director can do is to force a student into a line of work in which he or she lacks the intellectual interest or social or technical expertise to function well. Obviously, the director needs to guard against such lapses in judgment.

A final point in developing a strong lab environment is to provide multiple opportunities for students to demonstrate their own initiative and to contribute to the research process. Get students involved in designing research projects as early as possible in their research training. Encourage them to read related papers and try out preliminary research ideas. As opportunities develop, guide the students to participate in conferences, first as coauthors and later as sole authors. As they progress, give them opportunities to make platform presentations. Such opportunities can only help to further immerse students in their research training and enhance the gains they will make in their chosen field of study.

Another way to further develop a healthy lab environment is by encouraging wide-ranging student interests. Students may be more interested in some aspects of the work more than other aspects or in some projects more than other projects. The director and more experienced students should be sensitive to these interests and encourage individuals to pursue these within the lab environment. This often is easier to do if multiple projects are underway.

Summary

This chapter has attempted to touch on topics important for maintaining an effective research team. Topics have included the role of the team director, communication of research ethics to lab personnel, recruitment strategies, the development of lab manuals, student initiative, the importance of data checks for safeguarding the quality of the research enterprise, problems that may produce stress in the lab, how lab hierarchies may develop and influence the research activities within the lab, the importance of regularly scheduled lab meetings, and finally issues important for the maintenance of an effective research team. Although some of the measures discussed have been found to be effective in the successful coordination of a research team, the solutions to problems offered here are by no means exhaustive. Furthermore, although they may work in some situations, they may not be as effective in other environments. Consequently, there is a real need for flexibility on the part of the research director and the team members for the lab to function successfully. Though the reputation of a lab is usually based on the work and prestige of the research director, ultimately the success of the entire enterprise depends on the ability of all members of the research team to work successfully together in a united enterprise.

Recommended Readings

Useful works on communication, teamwork, and training include Tindall (1995), Bormaster and Treat (1994), Johnson (1991), Harris (1993), Wheelan (1990), Larson and LaFasto (1989), Grasha (1987), and Johnson and Johnson (1987).

References

Bormaster, J. S., & Treat, C. (1994). *Building interpersonal relationships through talking, listening, communicating* (2nd ed.). Austin, TX: Pro-Ed.

Grasha, A. F. (1987). *Practical applications of psychology* (3rd ed.). Boston: Little, Brown.

Harris, T. E. (1993). *Applied organizational communication: Perspectives, principles, and pragmatics.* Hillsdale, NJ: Lawrence Erlbaum.

Johnson, D. W. (1991). *Human relations and your career* (3rd ed). Englewood Cliffs, NJ: Prentice Hall.

Johnson, D. W., & Johnson, F. P. (1987). *Joining together: Group theory and group skills.* Englewood Cliffs, NJ: Prentice Hall.

Larson, C. E., & LaFasto, F. M. J. (1989). *Teamwork: What must go right/what can go wrong.* Newbury Park, CA: Sage.

Tindall, J. A. (1995). *Peer programs: An in-depth look at peer helping. Planning, implementation, and administration.* Bristol, PA: Accelerated Development, Inc.

Wheelan, S. A. (1990). *Facilitating training groups: A guide to leadership and verbal intervention skills.* New York: Praeger.

Appendix 25.1

Sample Table of Contents for a Lab Manual

I. Introduction
   A. Lab Philosophy
      1. Positive Interaction
      2. Dress Code
II. Overview of Test Procedures
   A. Subject Solicitation
   B. Prior to the Test Day
   C. Test Day
III. Subject Recruitment
   A. Contacts
      1. Psychology Undergraduate Students
         a. GEB 202
         b. Other Students
      2. Courthouse (Including Tandy Operation)
         a. County Clerk's Office
         b. Tandy 102 to Macintosh Transfer
      3. Hospital
         a. Subject Selection
         b. Subject Information
         c. Subject Solicitation
         d. Check the Following Things at Special Care Nursery (SCN) Each Day
         e. To Recruit Infants From the Special Care Nursery or Referrals
         f. Sample Recruitment Talk
      4. Repeated Testing
      5. Night Before Calling and Protocol
      6. Procedures for Follow-up Testing of Infants
         a. Initial Contact
         b. Calling the Night Before
         c. No Phone Letters
         d. Declines
         e. No-Shows/Cancellations
         f. Updating the Green Book
         g. Sending Cards to the Children in Our Studies
      7. Referrals
         a. Infants
         b. Older Subjects
         c. Medical Data
         d. Referral Reports
IV. Behavioral Tests
   A. The Bayley Scale of Infant Development
      1. Order of Presentation
      2. General Testing Hints
      3. Some Specifics for Testing 1-Year-Olds
      4. Some Specifics for Testing 2-Year-Olds
V. Record Keeping
   A. Files
      1. Medical Records
      2. Consent Forms
      3. Handedness Forms
      4. Impedance Sheets
      5. Behavioral Score Sheets
      6. Pediatric Complication Forms
      7. Checklists
      8. Written Communication
      9. Data Analysis Records
      10. Neurological Data Form (for Adult Subjects)
      11. Hearing Screening Threshold Form (for Adult Subjects)

Chapter 26

Diversity in Work Styles

ELKE BRENSTEIN

A Different Kind of Diversity

Although we are making progress toward honoring diversity with regard to gender, ethnic background, age, religious beliefs, and sexual orientation, we have yet to learn to appreciate interpersonal differences in how people think, act, feel, and deal with tasks and other people. This "psychological diversity," which constitutes an equally important part of a person's individuality, is often glossed over because it is not as easily apparent. Yet it plays an important part in our everyday interactions with friends and family, fellow students, coworkers, and superiors. Take the following situation, for example:

> At a meeting, four people are planning an intervention to improve the delivery of counseling services on campus. John has made a flowchart of how services are currently being rendered. Kim thinks it makes more sense to sit and talk first and brainstorm about problems and possible solutions. June believes that what is most needed is a detailed task analysis of everybody's job duties and service requirements. Alan wants to interview former clients and service personnel to get their input. He thinks that a personal viewpoint is going to provide more information than objective analyses of tasks or abstract flowcharts. John counters that people can only function if the system is set up right. Because he is leading the discussion, he wants the others to follow the agenda he has set for the meeting. At some point, he gets upset that Kim keeps "going off on tangents," as he puts it. Kim thinks that her points are very relevant and that he should not be so "dogmatic."

An outside observer may see that each of them has a valid point. The group members, however, were getting aggravated with each other because they did not quite appreciate the way the others wanted to tackle the problem. Such situations can easily result in a breakdown in communication, and great thinking and action potential may be wasted. Instead, differences in looking at things, conceptualizing problems, and finding solutions could be seen as representing diverse problem-solving approaches with inherent strengths and weaknesses such that one way is not intrinsically "better" or "worse" than another. Their respective worth can be assessed only in terms of how well they serve a given purpose.

June could be accused of being a stickler for details. Or the others could make use of her eye for detail and talent for keeping all the facts straight. Because she is very persistent and conscientious, she has done a great job going through records and compiling patient and service delivery statistics. Instead of blaming Kim for going off on tangents, the others could benefit from her perceptive, big-picture analysis of the situation and her ability to come up with innovative and creative solutions. John may appear rigid at times, but he is very good at objectively and critically evaluating the pros and cons of an issue. In this case, he managed to disentangle those problems caused by personality conflicts between the service providers from other problem areas because he did not get so emotionally involved as some of the others (who were concerned not to hurt a particular person's feelings). Of course, Alan is right in saying that flowcharts and statistics and innovative ideas are fine but that one also needs to consider the ideas and feelings of the people involved to create a system that can work in practice. Because he is very personable, he was instrumental in getting at some "dirty details" that revealed important problems with the way things were currently being done from otherwise reluctant informants.

As this example shows, each person's contribution is important for accomplishing a complex cooperative task. Recognizing that people are different allows us to be more tolerant and fair. Understanding *how* people differ enables us to make constructive use of individual differences and appreciate the value and positive potential of different perspectives. The purpose of this chapter is to provide a brief and not too theoretical introduction to the old and new topic of psychological diversity by answering the following questions regarding individual differences in psychological functioning:

- Where do they come from?
- What are the main dimensions?
- How can I learn about *my* preferences?
- How are preferences manifested?
- How do they develop?

After a brief overview of relevant dimensions and instruments, the impact of individual differences is discussed with regard to several areas of application: learning, working, and communicating with others, as well as time management and organization. Each section contains examples, practical suggestions, and exercises. This is followed by a Reminders section on how to use knowledge about individual differences judiciously without stereotyping. An annotated list of recommended readings at the end of the chapter provides references for those who want more detailed information on theory or different areas of practical application.

Origins of Psychological Diversity

People come not only in all sorts of shapes, colors, and sizes, but also with all sorts of "personalities." However, although most of us do not have a problem accepting that some people are physically better equipped to be runners or high jumpers or that some have better fine or gross motor control, we may find it harder to accept that people have different abilities and preferences in the ways they go about learning, working, or communicating with others, which are an equally important part of who they are as a person.

Early psychological theories (behaviorism, psychoanalysis) underscored the importance of environmental influences. The famous statement by Watson that he could make any given child into a criminal or a scientist reflects the behaviorist assumption that environmental input is responsible for all behavioral variation. However, more recently, advances in the biological sciences have been shedding new light on the biological bases for behavior. For example, research with monozygotic twins reared apart has been providing compelling evidence that behavioral patterns develop according to a genetic blueprint to a larger extent than previously thought (see, e.g., Tellegen et al., 1988, and Neubauer & Neubauer, 1990). Thus, in every person, there are certain physiological and psychological "givens" that provide the person with a *range* of potential for development. We can achieve much if we put our mind to it, but we have different inherent qualities that will influence the direction and the extent of that development.

Of course, this new perspective on the nature/nurture controversy does not imply genetic determinism or diminish the role of outside influences. However, "the environment" is no longer viewed as a static entity but as a changing force in dynamic interaction with the individual. To some extent, "the environment" is what we perceive it to be. Furthermore, our social environment may *react* to how we act toward it and is thus in part determined by us. For example, a mother may be quite different with each of her children because of how they act toward her. In this way, people actively determine or may in fact alter their environment rather than being unilaterally influenced by it. Consequently, more emphasis is now being placed on the *degree of fit* and *specific interactions* among persons and their environments. This "fit" can be assessed with the help of personality measures.

Theories and Measures

Although psychology has a long-standing tradition of research in human variation, individual differences have generally not attracted much attention outside of personality and ability research. On the contrary, in basic psychological and educational research aimed at specific content areas, individual differences have often been considered "nuisance factors" subsumed under the error term. Researchers have mostly focused on developing general models or theories of reading comprehension or creative problem solving rather than also exploring how different people possibly read or solve problems in different ways. Cognitive style research, which did examine *qualitative* differences in perceiving and processing information, often proved inconclusive. The lack of clear predictive results is not surprising, for cognitive style variables measure preferences that may or may not be behaviorally manifested. Also, the dimensions used were often too general to yield interpretable results. Last, the lack of an integrative theoretical framework made it difficult to assess the significance of individual findings. The result was a vicious cycle in which the exclusion of individual differences from research and practice led to theories and findings that failed to take into account the possible impact of these variables.

THE "BIG FIVE"

In recent years, a framework for conceptualizing individual differences in personality started to emerge from the research of Costa and McCrae (1992). Their work toward creating a taxonomy of personality dimensions has its roots in lexical analyses of personality descriptors in the English languages based on the assumption that all relevant dimensions for describing differences among persons would have one or more linguistic representations (Digman, 1990). Five factors were identified and proved robust with numerous "normal" as well as clinical populations of different ages and occupations, using a variety of assessment methods. The NEO-Personality Inventory that was developed as part of this research measures Neuroticism (degree of emotional stability in normal populations), Extraversion, Openness to Experience, Agreeableness, and Conscientiousness. NEO-PI scores are presented in terms of profiles. Although the NEO-PI does not represent a particular personality theory, high intercorrelation with other measures based on theory (e.g., the Myers-Briggs Type Indicator and interest, value, or cognitive style instruments) provides evidence for its construct validity and attests to the fundamental importance and pervasiveness of its dimensions. Because Costa and McCrae's work is based on longitudinal data, there is also growing evidence for the relative stability of these dimensions at a macro level of analysis.

PSYCHOLOGICAL TYPE

A similar framework had been developed earlier by Isabel Myers on the basis of Jungian theory. The resulting instrument, the Myers-Briggs Type Indicator (MBTI), is firmly grounded in theory.[1] The NEO-PI and the MBTI share the notion that functional differences are, to some extent, genetically influenced and therefore show a certain stability across time and situations. This means that people have certain functional preferences (similar to handedness) that they may choose to act on or not. With increasing age and maturity, preferences are said to become more clear, yet actual behavior may become more versatile. The MBTI has been widely used in research and practice.[2] It is also one of the most popular instruments in applied settings. Although it has been extensively validated, the MBTI has not always been favorably received in scientific circles (possibly because it was developed by a lay person). The instrument has also been deemed problematic by some because its scoring system results in a typology.[3] In the MBTI scoring system, individuals are assigned to one of 16 types based on preference scores on four bipolar dimensions: Extraversion-Introversion, Sensing-Intuition, Thinking-Feeling, and Judging-Perceiving (with individual dimensions in the four-letter combination being labeled *dominant, auxiliary, tertiary,* and *inferior*).

Although the NEO-PI and MBTI have been found to intercorrelate highly, they differ somewhat in their definition of the dimensions. Also, the standard form of the MBTI does not assess Neuroticism, as it stresses mostly the positive aspects of individual differences; however, an alternative scoring of the MBTI provides a similar dimension labeled *Comfort-Discomfort*. It should be kept in mind that complex systems such as the MBTI or the NEO-PI, which describe a person in terms of a constellation of scores on various dimensions, are more likely to provide ecologically valid and personally meaningful information than two-dimensional category systems. Moreover, both the MBTI and NEO-PI provide scoring with subscales for each of the main dimensions, thus offering opportunities for further differentiation at a lower level of analysis.

Learning About Your Own Preferences

Do you know what you like doing? Do you know what you are good at or would like to be good at? Whether it is painting, playing chess, helping people, or dealing with numbers, you should find out what you feel passionate about and pursue it, use it, practice it, have fun with it, and derive satisfaction from it in your academic, professional, and personal life. You may already know what your special qualities and strong points are—then again, you may not. However, you can only use them consciously to your best advantage if you know what they are.

SELF-OBSERVATION

When it comes to your working and learning behavior, motivations, and interests, you are the foremost expert. Think about what you do, how you do it, why you do it, and whether it is working for you. You can make a list of strong points and weak points, likes and dislikes. Maybe you want to keep a journal to help you remember, for example, how you felt when you were working on a paper, what particular problems you encountered, how long it took for individual steps to get accomplished, or what interpersonal issues surfaced when you were collaborating with a fellow student or a coworker. You may also want to think why you get along better with some people than with others, why you prefer certain instructors, or what interests you in particular in the field of psychology.

GETTING FEEDBACK FROM OTHERS

Your friends, family, or instructors may also help you to get a more complete picture of who you are. Besides knowing yourself, it is also important to know how your actions are perceived by others. The social mirror may reveal some blind spots or let things appear in a different light. For example, someone may pride him- or herself on being objective and fair because he or she looks at things logically without getting too emotionally involved in an issue, remaining "practical" about it. However, the behaviors associated with this attitude may be perceived as cold or callous, lacking in empathy. Thus our (good) intentions are one thing—how they come across to others is another.

OTHER SOURCES

Several good books are available on psychological type (see the Recommended Readings section at the end of this chapter). Some of these books have quick diagnostic tests, which you may find helpful in the process of becoming more aware of your personal preferences. Of course, they are less accurate and valid than established tests administered by a qualified professional. If you want to explore your preferences in more detail, you can turn to a professional for psychological testing or individualized counseling. Many college counseling centers offer career or lifestyle counseling.

For now, Table 26.1 may help you get started. The described dimensions are based on the MBTI scales mentioned above (similar to the NEO-PI dimensions). They have been adapted from the published literature for this purpose. To avoid the confusion that may result from the use of either the MBTI or NEO-PI scale labels, more general terms were chosen to describe the essential characteristics of each dimension as they are manifested in different contexts.

It is important to keep in mind that the descriptions are meant as a rough framework for developing a better understanding of differences among people, starting with a better understanding of your own preferences. They cannot take the place of more thorough and in-depth evaluations. Most important, they are not meant to be used to "pigeonhole" or label individuals. People are very complex beings with a variety of interests and abilities. Having certain preferences does not mean that we cannot use the less preferred function. It just means that it may require more attention and effort.

Areas of Application

Personality differences and the interests, values, and skills that go with certain functional preferences have an impact on many aspects of everyday functioning, ranging from how we function when we learn, work, and interact with others to how we prioritize tasks and organize our time. The following areas of application will be discussed in more detail below:

- Learning and working
- Communicating with others
- Time management and organization

Personality dimensions are at the core of individual differences in psychological functioning in different areas. As Curry's (1983) "onion model" suggests, learning behavior is fundamentally controlled by the central personality dimensions, which are translated into information-processing dimensions and then manifested through interaction with environmental factors (the outer layers of the onion). Research has also shown that learning behavior and personality dimensions (as measured by independently developed instruments) show a great deal of shared variance (Geisler-Brenstein & Schmeck, 1996; Geisler-Brenstein, Schmeck, & Hetherington, 1996). Even particular skills or abilities are related to personality dimensions. In that case, it is difficult to say whether basic abilities (e.g., Gardner's multiple intelligences) result in the development of corresponding personality "traits" or whether preferences related to personality channel the development of skills in a certain direction. More likely, they jointly influence each other in continuous interaction with environmental factors.

TABLE 26.1 Preference Table

People Who Prefer . . .	*People Who Prefer . . .*
The External World of People and Action	*The Internal World of Thoughts and Ideas*
Are energetic, enthusiastic, and sociable on a large scale, like variety and action, participate in class, like learning from experience, tend to think aloud, and like to think "on their feet," like formulating ideas by discussing them with others, tackle tasks with little planning, welcome distractions, tend to prefer face-to face communication	Are calm and reserved, prefer to socialize one-on-one, like quiet and concentration, sit back and listen, like learning from theory, prefer to have time to think and prepare before talking, need solitude for concentrated work, think carefully before acting, do not like distractions, tend to prefer written communication
Concrete Facts, Details, and Present Reality	*Intuition, Vision, and Future Possibilities*
Rely on direct experience, focus on the here and now, proceed step-by-step (stick to the topic at hand), like information to be precise and factual (look at the trees, not the forest), therefore tend to be good at memorizing facts and prefer facts to be presented first, are guided by practical considerations, may have a don't-fix-it-if-it-ain't-broke attitude, preferring to rely on tried and true procedures for solving problems and applying what they have learned, are good at making smaller changes to an existing system (create by improving)	Have faith in their intuition, like to think of future possibilities, think globally and associatively (easily deviate from the topic at hand), rely on insight and imagination (look at the forest, not the trees), are good at seeing how things connect and interrelate, may be guided by theoretical considerations, want to have the "big picture" presented first, like to solve problems in innovative ways, enjoy learning a new skill more than applying it, sometimes like to make radical changes and invent a new way of doing things (create by inventing)
Objective Thought and Logical Analysis	*Subjective Values and Personal Involvement*
Are task-focused, look at pros and cons of an issue with objectivity and detachment, often base decisions on logical analysis of facts, can argue a point without getting personally involved, may appear tough and critical, value principles, take pride in competence and demonstrating mastery	Are people-focused, consider the human impact and look for personal relevance of an issue, often base decisions on subjective values and intuition, argue points with personal conviction and enthusiasm, value harmony, take pride in advancing a personal cause or communicating deeply held beliefs
Structure and Decisiveness	*Flexibility and Alternatives*
Like to schedule and plan activities, tend to adhere to a set agenda focusing on what needs to be done, use lists as guides for action, dislike surprises, want to follow through, are result-oriented, value purposiveness, state their objectives decisively and clearly, work toward the accomplishment of quantifiable goals, strive for closure, feel satisfied when something has been decided or finished	Value flexibility in planning, dislike narrow time lines, may deviate from a planned course of action, use lists as points of departure for new ideas, are open to alternatives and can adapt to changing demands, are process-oriented, value autonomy, present their views as open for discussion, often incorporating different points of view, work for qualitative improvement, consider most tasks "a work in progress"

NOTE: How to use the table: You should first read through the descriptions on both sides of the table. They provide a rough sketch of polarized characteristics, by presenting the extremes of each scale. You will find that you can agree to statements on either side because you probably act differently depending on situational and task requirements; nevertheless, you should have a preference for the way of functioning described on one side or the other. If you have a clear preference (which may be different from the way you behave in actual situations), you should make a note for each pair of opposites. It is OK if you feel undecided. A personality profile results from the combination of all four preferences. It should be noted that each preference takes on somewhat different qualities in combination with other preferences.

LEARNING AND WORKING

As the example at the beginning of this chapter showed, tasks can be approached in a number of ways. Generally speaking, one way of doing things (which may be an expression of a personal "style") is not in itself better than another. Actually, it is best not to have a fixed style and use instead whatever approach best fits the specific requirements of the task and the situation. Still, most of us *do* have a preference for doing things one way or another, either because this is part of who we are as a person or because we have developed certain habits. Thus learning or working styles are individual preferences in how one generally goes about studying and dealing with tasks and other people.

You may get an idea about your learning preferences by asking yourself questions such as the following: Do you usually work on several projects at the same time, or do you always like to finish one task before starting something else? Do you usually start with the details of a project, or do you prefer to look at the big picture first? Do you like learning about things theoretically, or do you prefer to learn from practical experience? Do you value harmony with your coworkers above all, or do you easily stay objectively detached?

There Is More Than One Way to Write a Paper

Although good teachers try to bring out individual talents, interest, and abilities in their students, most school environments make few provisions for their students' individuality, and educators often unknowingly discriminate against those who do not fit into the role of the proverbial "good student." Thus students who can sit quietly for several hours are favored over those who prefer a more active, expressive, and participative way of learning. Curricula value abstract, symbolic knowledge over concrete, practical experience and emphasize logical analysis more than intuition and personal involvement in learning. Students are often made to follow narrowly prescribed paths to discovery, only seldom being allowed to explore topics in personally meaningful ways. Worse yet, students are sometimes ridiculed or even penalized for doing things differently, such as adding numbers by first finding and checking off pairs that add up to 10 and then adding the remaining ones rather than following "the old-fashioned way" of adding the numbers sequentially.

Thus teaching practices often reflect the belief that there is one best approach to writing a paper, solving a math problem, or doing an assignment. Of course, there are certain "objective" criteria that most people agree on. For example, a good paper or report has to be organized, have a logical flow of argument, have examples, support ideas with evidence, and so forth. However, as the following cases are meant to illustrate, there are different ways of getting there.

In writing a paper, Daryl is very methodical. He usually starts by getting all the relevant information from the library, goes over his notes, makes a thorough outline, and then starts thinking about the issues to be addressed, what they mean theoretically, and what their practical implications are.

Carrie, who feels very strongly about a particular topic, starts by jotting down general thoughts and ideas in a brainstorming session. The structure of the paper is not clear from the beginning but emerges as she follows her intuitive vision of what she wants to write. The organization and details are added later.

Use Your Strong Suit First

As can be seen from the above examples, tasks or even long-range goals can be accomplished in very different ways. The important thing is to find the way that works best for you. When you approach a task, you should rely on the style or strategy that works best for you because that is the engine that drives your work. Most likely you have developed special skills that will make it easier and more fun to tackle a problem your way. Once you have started, it is, of course, important not to forget the other aspects. A project well done is one in which all the bases have been covered—in other words, all of the following aspects have been considered:

- Theories and ideas
- Logical analysis and criticism
- Personal relevance
- Concrete examples
- Organization and structure
- Specific facts and details
- Procedural aspects

COMMUNICATING WITH OTHERS

When two people do not seem to understand each other, the problem does not necessarily lie in *what* is being said but often has to do with *how* it is being conveyed. This does not simply refer to the tone of the message but to more fundamental interpersonal differences that may be at the root of a "communication problem."

George, who worked in the student affairs office, was quite frustrated due to a "communication problem" with his boss. He would occasionally come into her office and "bounce off" some innovative ideas. The trouble was that his suggestions literally seemed to bounce off her, as she never really seemed to listen carefully to what he had to say. On the other hand, he had many informal discussions with his colleague Jarret during which these ideas took concrete form as the two of them talked and brainstormed about the possibilities. Why could his boss not see the merit of his ideas? After attending an MBTI workshop with her, George understood more clearly that she is a person who prefers written communication, likes to have time to think things through in private, is very structured, and is, at the same time, logical and detail oriented. Consequently, from then on, he made a point to write down his ideas, making sure they were well thought out. He made a logical outline of different possibilities and provided the necessary facts that helped to judge the feasibility of his suggestion. Suddenly, his boss was very enthusiastic about his ideas and called a meeting to discuss how they could be implemented.

A "communication problem" such as the one described above may seriously affect the working climate in a group and negatively influence productivity. In this case, it was possible to avoid a potential falling out between George and his boss because George realized why his boss possibly failed to respond to his enthusiastically presented ideas. Thus the quality of communication can be greatly improved if we understand our own way of functioning but also realize "where the other person is coming from." Although this understanding does not solve the problem by itself, it provides both parties with a basis for discussing their differences or disagreements with some objectivity and allows them to take steps to avoid them.

Awareness and appreciation of differences are especially valuable in teamwork because each team member can offer his or her unique perspective and skills. As mentioned above, we have to try to "cover all the bases" when working alone. When we work as a team, we can divide the tasks and let each member tackle different aspects:

- Taking stock

   1. What is the problem?
   2. What are the facts in the current situation?

- Developing a vision of the future

   1. What do the facts imply?
   2. What are the different possibilities to solve the problem?

- Critically evaluating different alternatives

   1. What are the pros and cons of each alternative?
   2. What are the logical consequences of each alternative?

- Considering the human impact

   1. How much do different people value each alternative?
   2. How will people react to each outcome?

The synergy that results when people use their talents constructively and cooperatively can greatly improve the quality of the product *and* the process that has led to this outcome. The heightened sensitivity that comes from the realization that there are different ways of looking at things, each valuable in its own right, may be the first step toward avoiding a "communication" problem. If this awareness keeps the channels of communication open, much is gained already.

The second step is to understand *how* two or more people see a problem. The knowledge of underlying personality differences provides us with a value-free framework to discuss such differences constructively (however, it should be noted that trying to diagnose people can be difficult and bears the risk of labeling; see the Reminders section at the end of this chapter). To that effect, it might be beneficial to have each participant put something down in writing and then discuss the different perspectives. If "the problem" has already moved away from the issue at hand into the personal arena ("You always go off on tangents, you always nitpick on details"), it might also be helpful to hear how other people perceive what they say or do to get a better idea where the differences lie. At this point, it might be helpful to do the following exercise:

You're Sometimes OK and I'm Not Perfect Either

1. Name the qualities that you appreciate in the other person. Try to address different aspects.

2. Take a moment and think about how the way you approach a task or people may be a problem.

3. Share your results with your partner.

Much can be gained by improving listening skills and opening one's eyes to other perspectives. Understanding where the other person is coming from makes it easier to "agree to disagree." If the discussion following such an exercise does not help, it may be worthwhile to attend a workshop presented by a professional or use the help of a skilled mediator.

It is important to remember that favoring a particular way of doing things (for example, paying attention to the big picture) does *not* mean that you are not able to pay attention to details. It means only that it is easier for you to use your preferred style and that it may require more effort and maybe some "tricks" to use your nonpreferred style. For example, you may have to make a special effort to keep track of specifics by writing everything down in a daily planner. The first step to solving a "problem" is understanding what exactly the problem is. With time and practice, a more balanced way of functioning can be achieved.

TIME MANAGEMENT AND ORGANIZATION

Time management is easy! All one has to do is figure out what needs to be done and in which order, assign a priority code to each task, and then just do it. Items get checked off in logical order and things get done quickly and efficiently. Well, at least that is what the authors of time management books tell us. However, if it were that easy, there would not be so many books on this subject.

Interestingly, most of those books were written by people who find it easy to function this way and want to show others how to do it. They often do not acknowledge that some people have fundamentally different ways of approaching a task that may serve them equally well (or even better, for *their* purposes). Also, they seldom mention that efficient, task-focused, results-oriented functioning comes at a price. For example, the narrow focus and decisiveness that are necessary to get a task accomplished fast often leave little room for examining alternatives, paying attention to the process, or considering people's feelings in addition to examining rational task objectives.

To get a handle on your time management problem, it may be helpful to analyze where you fail in the logical sequence mentioned above and why. Then, instead of blaming yourself for not being able to fulfill seemingly reasonable demands, you can get started devising a personalized plan of action. Although some people have an easier time structuring their work and sticking to time lines, most of us procrastinate for one reason or another or put off certain aspects of a task. As you might have guessed, there are different reasons for doing so. Take the people described in the following:

Julie, whom people easily characterize as an extravert, is motivated when she can work with others and can be actively involved in a task. She has a tendency to put off "quiet" tasks such as reading or studying. Because she likes to think on her feet, she also avoids planning ahead. Her roommate Sylvia, more of an introvert, takes more time to think about what she wants to do and often delays acting on her ideas.

Howard is a hands-on person. When studying, he often gets bored with readings that are too theoretical. On the other hand, he does not mind doing routine tasks such as typing references. In his work group, he has sometimes been accused of spending too much time on details and getting stuck in a certain way of doing things. In contrast, his buddy Jose, when writing a paper, gets very excited about a new subject and loves to brainstorm and discuss the ideas with his friend. However, he puts off the more mundane tasks involved with implementing his ideas. He hates detail work, so he sometimes asks his friend to proofread his papers and help him get the references organized.

Alice is fairly good at figuring out what needs to be done in which order. She does not get easily distracted because she is very logical and sensible. Her friends sometimes tell her to loosen up and stop being so serious all the time. She rarely leaves herself time to play. Her friend Ellen also makes lists of things to be done but often gets "sidetracked." The other day she was studying for an exam when a friend called with a personal problem. Ellen and her friend had a long talk, leaving little time for Ellen to prepare for the exam. In such moments, Ellen's priorities get easily rearranged. In this case, she may not have gotten an A, but she felt it was more important to help her friend when she needed it.

Tammy is known for being a good organizer. She is very planful and decisive. When she has a task to accomplish, she just works on one part at a time, doing what needs to be done, and makes a point of finishing this task before starting another. That usually serves her well. Sometimes, her coworkers complain, however, that she decides too quickly without having looked at some other relevant issues. Also, when the situation changes suddenly, she has trouble adapting to new circumstances. Her boyfriend tells her that she should sometimes "schedule to be spontaneous"! Her friend Sara is just the opposite. She is always juggling a number of different projects at the same time—she likes it that way. She is interested in many different things. She is generally a big-picture kind of person and likes to look at how things interrelate. She has been praised by her professors for her thorough research and in-depth presentation of an issue. Because she is interested in a variety of things, she often has trouble prioritizing her work and getting closure on an issue.

As these examples show, there is no one best way of organizing time and personal resources. More important, each way of functioning has its pros and cons that need to be considered.

Coming back to the recipe provided by time management experts, it is clear that we each have to find our own system that fits in with our values and ways of doing things.

As with time management, there seem to be generally accepted standards of organization such as being able to find something when you need it. However, it is important to realize that there are also different ways to get organized. For example, you may know a professor who has piles of books and papers on his desk and the floor of his office. Yet when you ask for a paper that you wrote two semesters ago, he may reach into one of those piles and pull out your paper. Research has confirmed that some people just cannot find things in a filing cabinet because their mind is not organized that way. When they file something away, they often cannot remember what label something was filed under. The Recommended Readings section below lists some books that address the special organizational needs of those who do not fit the traditional picture of a "well-organized person."

Growth and Change

TYPE PATRIOTISM

Myers has coined the term *type patriotism* to underscore the importance of being proud of one's individuality. The first step on the path to becoming a mature and well-rounded person is focusing on and developing our strong points. If we are allowed to follow our personal preferences and practice the skills that go with them, we learn to use our strengths to their best advantage. The confidence gained in the process gives us the energy to tackle challenges that involve the less preferred functions. On the other hand, if we are not allowed to "be ourselves" in our personal or professional relationships (referred to as "falsification of type" in psychological type theory), this energy is diminished, and self-confidence may suffer. For example, an extraverted child who is constantly scolded by his introverted parents for being too loud and active and denied opportunities to express himself may grow up thinking that there is "something wrong" with him. Similarly, a student with a high need for flexibility and a bent toward intuitive, associative thinking may suffer in a school environment that is very structured, rigidly adheres to a curriculum, and does not provide an outlet for the creative interests and abilities of the students.

LIFE CHOICES

When we are older, we are usually in a better position to select consciously environments that are consonant with our preferences. Research has shown, for example, that people with certain personality, interest, and value profiles gravitate toward certain occupational fields. That, of course, only indicates who is attracted to certain professions. In practice, people with a variety of personality profiles are found to be successful in any given profession. Knowledge of personality preferences has proven most helpful for finding the right environment within an occupational field because many professions, such as psychology or medicine, are very diverse and offer a wide range of possibilities for different interests and abilities. Thus some people are more likely to choose certain specialties, such as counseling, clinical, or experimental psychology, or certain areas of application within those specialties, such as working theoretically or working with clients (see Leong & Geisler-Brenstein, 1991).

Instead of focusing on the problems that may result from dealing with people who think differently or environments that do not agree with us, we can put these differences to constructive use. Once we have identified less preferred functions, we can make a conscious effort to compensate for them. For example:

> An instructor who does well in small groups but has trouble being spontaneously entertaining and witty in front of 300 students may spend some extra time thinking of interesting examples or anecdotes to incorporate into an otherwise potentially boring lecture. He may bring a video or have members of the class prepare something to share with others.
>
> An introverted parent who can only handle so much commotion may make sure that her extraverted child gets enough time with friends and doing activities.
>
> In a relationship, the partner who organized a whole vacation to the minute may leave a few days without a program to accommodate the other's need for doing things spontaneously.
>
> Somebody who tends to be very theoretical and abstract can make a conscious effort to think of practical examples when presenting information.

WORK AND PLAY

Experience shows that we work best when we can use our preferred functions. As suggested above, if we are not happy with what we are doing, we need to sit down and examine to what extent what we like doing and are good at is similar to what we actually do in everyday life. Another reason for dissatisfaction with work maybe that we have not been able to strike the right balance between work and play. The best sign that we are having fun at work is when work becomes play.

Csikszentmihalyi (1990) coined the term *flow* for a special kind of experience that people may encounter during a wide range of activities. A surgeon may experience flow during an operation, a statistician may become completely absorbed doing data analysis, and others may completely lose their sense of time when writing a paper, teaching a class, climbing a mountain, reading a book, or weeding a garden. The flow experience is an interesting mix of intense effort and concentration and a feeling of self-absorption and pleasure. Most flow experiences occur when one is able to work without interruptions and when tasks have open-ended outcomes and involve repetitive activities that lead the focus away from the self. The tasks also have to be at the right level of difficulty so that they can be mastered. A task that is too easy would not be a challenge and would hence lead to boredom. On the other hand, a task that is too difficult could result in frustration.

Flow can also occur when one is using a less preferred function during play or when pursuing a hobby. For example, a "people person" who relies more on personal values than on logical analysis in everyday life may find great enjoyment in playing strategic games such as chess in her leisure time. Someone who works in a high-structure profession that requires great precision and attention to detail may find pleasure in painting with watercolors as an outlet for creativity. In summary, it is important to find the right balance between work and play between preferred and less preferred functions. Developing the ability to be "multifunctional" enables us to adjust to the varied demands we encounter when learning, working, and communicating with others.

Reminders

The following are a few points to remember:

- We all can and do act in many different ways, depending on what the task or the situation requires. However, most of us have a preference for a certain mode of functioning (see Table 26.1).
- A personality "type" or "profile" comes from the *combination* of several different preferences. For example, characterizing a person as an introvert or extravert is far too simplistic.
- Although there is evidence that certain characteristics are rather stable over time, they should never be used as an excuse for doing or not doing something. Rather, we should try to work on developing the lesser preferred functions as we grow and develop.
- The categories should not be used for stereotyping. Even people who share most of the broad characteristics (a certain personality "type") are different in many other ways.
- There is no right or wrong way of functioning; a particular way may, however, be more appropriate in a given situation.
- You should be proud of your strengths and make the most of them.
- You should be aware of your less preferred functions, try to strengthen those areas, and find ways to compensate for your weak points.
- Although we cannot easily change some of our habitual preferences, we do have choices and can develop a full range of varied talents.

Recommended Readings

The NEO-PI manual (1994) is a good starting point for those who want to know more about the "Big Five" personality dimensions. It explains the constructs and scoring procedures and provides examples from different areas of application. It also provides a long list of references for those who want to read more on the topic. For a life-span perspective on personality development, see McCrae and Costa's (1990) book *Personality in Adulthood.*

For those interested further in genetics and personality, Neubauer and Neubauer (1990) present a wealth of research findings on monozygotic twins reared apart in their book *Nature's Thumbprint: The New Genetics of Personality.*

There are several introductory books on psychological type theory. Myers and Myers' (1980) book *Gifts Differing* has become a classic among those interested in type. It explains the theory underlying the MBTI and provides information about the distribution of different types in a variety of fields. More recently, Hirsh and Kummerow's *Life Types* (1989) has made the concept of psychological type accessible to a broader public. Their book provides a short diagnostic test as well as many examples of the manifestations of type in different areas of life. An in-depth review of research findings on the MBTI and how it relates to other measures can be found in the *MBTI Manual* by Myers and McCaulley (1985) and Thorne and Gough's (1991) book *Portraits of Type: An MBTI Research Compendium.* Finally, it should be mentioned that some authors, such as Keirsey and Bates (1984) in their book *Please Understand Me*, have a different perspective on psychological type in that they discuss temperament differences (based on combinations of type preference functions). For a critical perspective on the MBTI, see Pittinger (1993) and McCrae and Costa (1989).

Several books have been written on how type theory and the MBTI can be utilized in different applied settings. For example, Provost and Anchors' (1987) book *Applications of the Myers-Briggs Type Indicator in Higher Education* discusses how type knowledge can be used in different areas ranging from student advising to determining individual learning styles. Provost's (1990) book *Work, Play, and Type* examines the delicate balance between work and play and shows, with the help of many exercises and examples, what role type knowledge can play in the process of achieving more personal satisfaction in both areas. In *Do What You Are*, Tieger and Barron-Tieger (1992) examine the implications of psychological type for choosing a career and finding the right niche within an occupational field. The book provides a short test and contains many practical tips and suggestions.

In addition to the many traditional books on time management and organization, some have been written for "the rest of us." Although the following books were not written from a psychological type perspective, they address the special needs of those who think about organization in a different way. For example, Lehmkuhl and Lamping's *Organizing for the Creative Person* (1993) distinguishes between the organizational style of "Arbies" (right-brain creative, divergent-thinking types) and "Elbies" (left-brain, sensible, and convergent-thinking types). Similarly, McGee-Cooper (1992) tells us that *You Don't Have to Go Home From Work Exhausted!* and provides practical suggestions on getting work done while leaving room for creativity and play.

Notes

1. See Myers and Myers (1980) for an introduction.
2. See Myers and McCaulley (1985) and Thorne and Gough (1991) for an overview of research results.
3. For a theoretical debate on the appropriateness of typologies, see McCrae and Costa (1989).

References

Costa, P. T., & McCrae, R. R. (1992). *The Revised NEO Personality Inventory (NEO-PI-R) and NEO Five-Factor Inventory (NEO-FFI) professional manual.* Odessa, FL: Psychological Assessment Resources.

Csikszentmihalyi, M. (1990). *Flow: The psychology of optimal experience.* New York: Harper & Row.

Curry, L. (1983). *An organisation of learning styles theory and constructs.* ERIC Document, 235 185.

Digman, J. M. (1990). Personality structure: Emergence of the five-factor model. *Annual Review of Psychology, 41,* 417-440.

Geisler-Brenstein, E., & Schmeck, R. R. (1996). The Revised Inventory of Learning Processes: A multifaceted perspective on individual differences in learning. In M. Birenbaum & F. J. R. C. Dochy (Eds.), *Alternatives in assessment of achievements, learning processes and prior knowledge: A European perspective* (pp. 283-318). Boston: Kluwer.

Geisler-Brenstein, E., Schmeck, R. R., & Hetherington, J. (1996). An individual difference perspective on student diversity. *Higher Education, 31,* 73-96.

Hirsh, S., & Kummerow, J. (1989). *Life types.* New York: Warner.

Keirsey, D., & Bates, M. (1984). *Please understand me: Character and temperament types.* Del Mar, CA: Prometheus Nemesis.

Lehmkuhl, D., & Lamping, D. (1993). *Organizing for the creative person.* New York: Crown.

Leong, F. T. L., & Geisler-Brenstein, E. (1991). Assessment of career specialty interests in business and medicine. *Career Planning and Adult Development Journal, 7,* 37-44.

McCrae, R. R., & Costa, P. T. (1989). Reinterpreting the Myers-Briggs Type Indicator from the perspective of the five-factor model of personality. *Journal of Personality, 57,* 17-40.

McCrae, R. R., & Costa, P. T., Jr. (1990). *Personality in adulthood.* New York London: Guilford.

McGee-Cooper, A. (1992). *You don't have to go home from work exhausted!* New York: Bantam.

Myers, I. B., & McCaulley, M. H. (1985). *Manual for the Myers-Briggs Type Indicator: A guide to development and use of the MBTI.* Palo Alto, CA: Consulting Psychologists Press.

Myers, I. B., & Myers, P. B. (1980). *Gifts differing.* Palo Alto, CA: Consulting Psychologists Press.

Neubauer, P. B., & Neubauer, A. (1990). *Nature's thumbprint: The new genetics of personality.* New York: Addison-Wesley.

Pittinger, D. J. (1993). The utility of the Meyers-Briggs Type Indicator. *Review of Educational Research, 63*(4), 467-488.

Provost, J. A. (1990). *Work, play, and type.* Palo Alto, CA: Consulting Psychologists Press.

Provost, J. A., & Anchors, S. (1987). *Applications of the Myers-Briggs Type Indicator in higher education.* Palo Alto, CA: Consulting Psychologists Press.

Tellegen, A., Lykken, D. T., Bouchard, T. J., Wilcox, K. J., Segal, N. L., & Rich, S. (1988). Personality similarity in twins reared apart and together. *Journal of Personality and Social Psychology, 54,* 1031-1039.

Thorne, A., & Gough, H. (1991). *Portraits of type: An MBTI research compendium.* Palo Alto, CA: Consulting Psychologists Press.

Tieger, P. T., & Barron-Tieger, B. (1992). *Do what you are.* Boston: Little, Brown.

Chapter 27

Applying for Research Grants

JOHN G. BORKOWSKI

It is easy to win research grants. Simply form a good idea, develop a plan of action, be willing to expend highly focused effort, find several appropriate funding agencies, be willing to tolerate initial setbacks, and then persevere until you receive the award.

Despite the ease of winning grants, most young scholars fail to seek research grants primarily because they fear failure, not because of the shallowness of their ideas. Those who do seek grant support usually do not succeed because they lack perseverance in the face of their initial failure. Hence the major reason for not winning in the game of grantsmanship is rooted in the personal-motivational aspects of scholarship, not the intellectual.

This chapter provides hints on the process of applying for research grants and the motivation to follow through until you encounter success. First, a rationale for submitting research grants is developed, and then practical suggestions are presented that provide direction in writing your first grant or doing a better job the second time around.

Why Write a Research Grant?

I doubt if there will be a single young Ph.D. in the United States in the decade ahead, aspiring to succeed in academia or in professional life, whose career will not be significantly advanced by writing, and winning, a research grant. The case in the academy is straight-forward: Tenure committees are impressed by assistant professors who have developed a track record in the area of grantsmanship. Some will maintain that a successful grant record is as important as a solid record of research. This is often true for your dean, whose financial flexibility is enhanced in some small measure by the return of indirect costs associated with your grant, and certainly for the vice president for research, whose research portfolio will bulge a bit more if it contains your award.

More important, a research grant gives you the capacity to carry out a long-term research plan that is more sustained and systematic than would otherwise be the case. You will find that you have more time for research; hence your research will reflect higher levels of commitment and competence because of your increased investment in it. For instance, you might "buy off" a course each semester for three consecutive years. Certainly, you will benefit from hiring more "helping hands." The additional graduate and undergraduate students budgeted in your grant will provide new blood, not only for carrying out the research plan but, more important, for revising, rethinking, and charting new research directions. You will also have additional flexibility and control in your professional life, in that you no longer will need to ask your department chair for funds for computers, supplies, and travel costs. But most important of all, you will gain the additional self-confidence necessary to enter the "invisible collage of scholars" in your area. This entrance will build, or strengthen, your scholarly networks and enhance collaborative possibilities. Your sense of self-efficacy will increase. All of these positive offshoots from your first research grant should augment your short-term research program as well as contribute significantly to your long-term scholarly life.

A final reason for applying for a research grant is related to the quality and scope of your idea. There are very few simple ideas left to pursue in most areas of contemporary psychology. More than likely, your idea is theoretically complex, multifaceted, process oriented, and perhaps longitudinal in nature. If this is the case, its corresponding research program will be a large undertaking, with many parts and many people involved. It may well become an undertaking so large in scope that it necessitates grant support for successful completion. Although in some areas of psychology it is still possible to mount a sustained research campaign without external grant support, there is no doubt that the energy and competence you bring to the project will be enhanced through grant support.

Many young, aspiring clinicians and counselors believe that a chapter on grant writing is irrelevant for their future careers. I disagree, in large part because I have seen so many professionals move rapidly up the administrative ladder in mental health organizations when they have the skills necessary to obtain grant support for their organization's demonstration, planning, and evaluation programs. Every new idea for treating patients or preventing problems in the home, school, or clinic needs careful documentation in terms of implementation, accuracy, and the range of resulting outcomes.

Possessing the skills (and the will) necessary to write a research grant is a major advantage for almost all professional psychologists. I always recommend that talented students in training to become counselors and clinicians take the full complement of statistics and research methods courses (not the bare minimum, as is often the case) and that they learn the art of grant writing. Forewarned is forearmed: It is often too late to return to graduate school to pick up "missing" computer, quantitative, and research methods courses. Yet for many, this knowledge and these skills, together with an understanding of the grant writing process, will be useful, perhaps essential, for career advancement.

Seek and You Shall Find

CREATING GOOD IDEAS

If I could tell you how to develop an interesting and theoretically important idea, I would probably be a millionaire, or at least have formulated a few more good ideas in my own research career. The problem is, of course, that good research ideas emerge through some unknown combination of existing knowledge within a domain, knowledge in adjacent domains, and technical skills—all welded together by inspiration, imagination, and luck. How these ingredients, which are necessary to form a solid and important researchable idea, come together in each scientist's mind is something only you can experience firsthand. I do know, however, that a sincere commitment to expanding your field, a willingness to explore the forefronts of its boundaries for its sake (not yours), a determined sense of perseverance, and an understanding that the game of science is fun will put you in a good position for preparation and inspiration to unite with luck in creating an original and significant research idea.

Remember that raw ideas need to be sharpened and reshaped to be transformed into researchable hypotheses. All too often, young scholars outline premature ideas in their grants, not theoretically refined and validated ideas supported by the pilot data that demonstrate their plausibility. Do not be afraid to let your ideas ferment, to share them with others, and sometimes to admit grudgingly that what you first thought was a great idea is not a researchable idea or perhaps not a significant one. Continue to struggle, over time, to come up with your best, sharpest idea, and then pursue its implementation with vigor and determination in a series of studies designed to test interrelated hypotheses.

THE AUDIENCE AND THE IDEA

Rarely will you develop a research grant, whether designed to test a theory or an intervention program, without a specific granting agency in mind. You should match your idea not only to a specific funding agency but also to potential reviewers. That is, you should ascertain, with some certainty, that your proposal falls within the objectives of a targeted foundation or granting agency, and if possible you should attempt to discover who will review, and ultimately judge, your grant: Write with a specific audience in mind, if at all possible.

If your project falls within the auspices of a major federal agency, such as the National Science Foundation (NSF), the National Institutes of Health (NIH), or the National Institute of Mental Health (NIMH), then existing brochures and/or program officers will be available to provide the necessary mission statements. If you are responding to a special initiative—called a "request for proposals" (RFP)—then the Federal Register is likely to provide detailed information; your institution's grants office probably subscribes to the Federal Register service. Your grant's officer will also have available a volume describing the range of private granting agencies relevant to your project.

If your proposal is headed to a private foundation, you should take several steps: (a) Ensure that their priorities match your research interests by reviewing a recent annual report as to the foundation's most recent funding decisions; (b) develop a short two- or three-page abstract that outlines your proposal in relation to the foundation's objectives; and (c), most important of all, try to "get your foot in the door." That is, have a friend or colleague initiate phone contact with the relevant program officer to whet the foundation's appetite prior to the arrival of your abstract. *It is rare that unsolicited grants, presented without prior personal contact, are awarded by a foundation.* If you have no direct connection to the foundation, it may be worth paying a firsthand visit so that officers can get to know you and hear the enthusiasm you have for your idea.

The point of this discussion is to make you aware of the need to shape your general idea in such a way as to make it appealing to the reviewers. You need to follow the agency's guidelines without deviation (e.g., do not exceed page limits for any section; do not burden reviewers with excessive materials in an appendix). Remember to present your ideas in accord with the wishes and peculiarities of the granting agency, not your own.

FRAMING THE RESEARCH PLAN

Generally, research plans evolve in your mind over time. Start with a tentative outline of the body of the proposal early in the game. Modify it frequently as you churn the idea, and its ramifications, over and over in your mind. Be flexible in your attempts to locate your project in terms of a narrow context (e.g., testing a specific theory), as well as a context that reveals its long-term applied or practical significance. As socially oriented priorities emerge from federal agencies as well as private foundations that formerly funded only basic research, the day may come when it is simply impossible to fund theoretically oriented research ideas without adequate discussion of their potential long-term applied significance.

Of the two goals in your research plan—*theoretical importance* and *potential significance*—the former should be of greater concern. You simply must convince the reviewers that your research will advance the current state of knowledge in a specific domain. You do this in at least three ways: (a) Present a logical and coherent argument for your theoretical position, showing clearly how it differs from the prevailing view(s); (b) discuss your aims, objectives, and general hypotheses in sufficient detail and with a clear sense of how they interrelate; and (c) present the background literature, especially your own recent work in this area. Chapters 3 and 6 of this volume should prove helpful in this regard.

The final step—showing your research competence—is essential because you must present convincing evidence of the quality of your own scholarship (e.g., recent, relevant publications) or at least strong pilot data showing your experimental savvy. In the case of a large-scale clinical demonstration or intervention project, the documentation of your scholarship might consist of a pilot study dealing with a miniversion of the proposed intervention or individual case studies demonstrating that the full program can indeed be implemented, with good potential for changing deviant or delayed behaviors. As you end this section of the proposal, be sure to outline specific hypotheses (although only the major ones), as well as corresponding predictions about major outcomes that are expected to result from your studies or intervention.

THE RESEARCH SPECIFICS

The second major section of most grants is the Proposed Research section. It mirrors, in many respects, the Methods section of a journal article and is made up of the following subsections: Subjects, Design, Materials, Procedures, and Proposed Statistical Analyses. If the proposal contains multiple experiments, you will need to repeat similar procedural and analytic information for each study unless there is redundancy across the series of studies.

Subjects

The number of subjects and their most important characteristics need to be described, often in considerable detail. For instance, if the population under study is composed of juniors and seniors from a particular college, then little additional information will be needed except the number of subjects, gender distribution, and any special considerations about their abilities or academic achievements. On the other hand, if you are studying children with mental retardation, then you should probably include the number of participants, their sex, age, mental age (or IQ), type of retardation, relevant motor or visual disabilities, years of institutionalization, grade level or reading capacity, medication history, and any other essential characteristics.

Remember to describe the subject characteristics in sufficient detail to enable the reviewer to generalize from your sample to the appropriate population. Often the method of obtaining subjects—whether volunteer or paid, of normal intelligence, or from a clinically defined population—will affect the experimental outcomes; hence such information should be provided in the proposal. Also, whether the subjects are highly trained for the task, have previous experimental participation in similar tasks, or are naive are important considerations that should be included in the Subjects section. Chapter 9, on applying for permission to use human subjects, should be helpful in outlining the range of details needed.

Design

If your study includes a number of independent variables, each having various levels, then it is sometimes wise to refer the reviewer to the entire set of variables that make up the design. Mention not only a description of your variables but also whether they represent within- or between-subjects manipulations. The Design section is commonly omitted if the independent variables have been fully spelled out elsewhere or are few in number. However, usually in a grant proposal, you have developed a novel and complex design. If this is the case, it should be highlighted as a major aspect of the proposal. Power calculations, which reveal the number of subjects needed to detect reasonable effects, will also strengthen this section of the proposal.

Apparatus and/or Materials

The Apparatus section should describe either the type of apparatus (brand name) or, if it is not commercially available, its essential features and dimensions. The Apparatus section should tell what the equipment does rather than how it was put together. Include key dimensions and functional operations instead of a picture or diagram. If the to-be-presented materials are complex—such as the number and size of categorically related words in a free-recall list of 30 items—then their specifications should be presented in detail in a separate Materials section.

Procedures

The best way to handle the Procedures section is to place the reader in the position of the subject. Treat first things first, proceeding from the point at which the subject begins the experiment to the point of the final to-be-recorded behavior. A flowchart will be helpful in organizing the sequence of events. The Procedures section should describe exactly what the subject will be shown and what he or she will be asked to do. Generally, it is best to focus on the subject's activities rather than on the movements of the experimenter. For instance, in a reaction-time study, assume that the experimenter will need to reset the clock after each trial. Critical details necessary for replication, such as the order of events, their timing, the instructions to subjects (paraphrased rather than reported verbatim unless the instructions represent one of the manipulated variables), the type of response measurements, and the controlled events, should all be reported in the Procedures section. But remember to report only those details essential for replication. Avoid redundancies in the Procedures section as well as redundancies across studies in your project.

Analyses and Predictions

Remember that this section is a verbal statement of the expected outcomes backed up by the statistics you need to analyze the data. Use statistical techniques that are state of the art, but at the lowest level of complexity necessary to analyze your data set. In other words, do not try to be too sophisticated unless such treatment is called for by your design and hypotheses. Be sure to focus on the key comparisons among treatment means as well as on individual difference analyses (where theoretically appropriate). Individual difference analyses often provide secondary support for a major hypothesis that itself centers on comparisons among group means. Because most review panels will have a sophisticated statistician on board, it is important for this section to be competently crafted and reviewed by your "in-house" statistician.

Additional Points to Include

The final part of the Proposed Research section is likely to contain a statement about the use of human subjects (including a reference to consent forms that can be found in an appendix and the appropriate inclusion of women and minorities as subjects; the latter is required by agencies such as NIH). See Chapter 9 for more information on the use of human subjects.

The final subsection in the body of the proposal is likely to be entitled "Research Significance." It represents your last chance to show the potential long-range impact of your work on the field and why it would be a wise decision to fund your project to benefit science and/or society. Of course, the Bibliography section will conclude the body of your grant proposal. This section should be complete, accurate, and faithful to current American Psychological Association (APA) style (APA, 1994; also see Chapter 21 of this volume on the use of APA style). A "sloppy" bibliography may be viewed as an indication of a potentially "sloppy" researcher.

The Most Important Part of the Grant: The Abstract

The abstract represents the initial section of the research proposal. It should summarize the manipulated or correlated variables, major tasks, key procedural features, theoretical relevance, and potential significance. I intentionally saved the discussion of this first section of the grant until last to emphasize that in practice, the writing of the abstract is the final order of business in grant writing, but one of the most important. Also, it is easier to write after all else is completed.

Conciseness, precision, and theoretical significance are the chief ingredients that characterize a successful abstract. Of all the information contained in a well-written abstract, the main hypotheses and how they are to be addressed are the most critical. It is difficult to accomplish this goal and simultaneously to include the essential features of the design, the major variables, and their significance in a space of no more than 250 words. Finally, do not overlook the fact that a good abstract, much like the title itself, is likely to induce the reader to peruse your proposal in greater depth and with greater seriousness of purpose. Hence you should construct the abstract with carefully chosen words, sentences, and transitional phrases. It should be the most interesting, and carefully constructed, part of the grant proposal. Remember that some reviewers on your panel will not be directly assigned your proposal; they are likely to read only your abstract in detail. Do not miss the chance to impress them with the importance and scope of your project.

Preparing a Budget

Most young investigators spend an unduly large amount of time in budget preparation. Budgets should be adequate but not excessive: Your salary (for both the academic year and the summer), staff salaries, equipment, supplies, travel, and participant costs are typical items in the direct-costs portion of the budget; a reasonable increase due to inflation (e.g., 4%) is often used to form the budgets for additional years. Indirect costs, as determined by your university or agency, are added to the direct cost to form the total costs of the grant for each year; indirect costs for projects funded by foundations are usually negotiable with your office of grants and contracts but are usually never more than 10%. Any unusual item in the budget (such as the amount of professional assistance needed for collecting data) needs to be justified fully. If in doubt, spend extra time justifying budget items rather than leaving the reviewers with possible unanswered budgetary questions.

Useful Tips in the Art of Grantsmanship

HOW TO GET STARTED

Grant preparation should be a constant part of your daily professional life. Keep a notebook on your desk in which new ideas can be quickly recorded for posterity and old entries reshaped and expanded. Begin modestly, submitting your first grant to an internal unit of your university or to a local agency. A quick reading of Sternberg's (1992) comments on winning acceptance by a psychological journal will be helpful at this point in the process. Your first grant should not be time consuming and should have a high probability of funding.

Build on your first award by publishing two or three research papers in respected journals. You will then be in a good position to seek your first major external award. My advice is to write this first grant proposal very quickly (e.g., in 1 or 2 weeks). First of all, you will be building on an existing base of scholarship that is both theoretical and empirical. Hence the first half of the grant (Aims, Literature Review and Background Research, and Hypotheses) will flow fast, given that you have preexisting written materials to draw on. More time, perhaps, will be required for the Proposed Research section, although I suspect most of the individual studies will have already been outlined in your "little black book." The reason that you should get this first grant done quickly, but competently, is that you will most likely not be funded in this first attempt at securing external funding for your research.

THE NEED FOR PERSEVERANCE

Roughly 80% of reasonably good grants are initially rejected by both federal agencies and foundations. Hence rejection is a fact of grant-related life that you must learn to expect, accept, and tolerate. To paint an even bleaker picture, consider this fact: Of the 20% of grants approved by most agencies, relatively few will have been approved on the occasion of their initial submission. That is, most funded proposals are resubmissions. For instance, within NIH, about 75% of funded grants occur in the second or third rounds of the submissions process. This means that although you will, in some sense, "fail" in your initial submission, you will receive valuable feedback necessary to correct and strengthen your to-be-revised proposal. If you address these criticisms earnestly and thoroughly, your chances of success will improve dramatically the second time around. If not, the third time around might well be your "charm." Hence a major secret—often kept hushed among successful grant getters—is that failures breed success. But perseverance is required!

LOCATING MULTIPLE FUNDING SOURCES

Although journal articles are submitted to only one journal at a time, grants can and should be submitted simultaneously to multiple funding sources. For instance, it would not be unusual for the same grant (with minor modifications to meet specific formatting requirements) to be under review at the same time at NSF, NIH, and a private foundation. Of course, if a positive decision is received from one agency, the grant should be withdrawn immediately from further consideration at the other agencies. Sometimes portions of your grant will be funded by one agency and the remaining parts by another agency. Of course, this requires a great degree of serendipity, but being in the right place at the right time is an essential aspect of winning in grant competition.

ON THE IMPORTANCE OF WRITING STYLE

A research grant should enable the reader to comprehend and evaluate your ideas, without requiring a monumental struggle. To understand the project, the reviewer must be led through the initial comments on the general hypothesis to the final statements about research significance. If you are genuinely concerned with making the task of reading your proposal more manageable, you must interest and motivate the reviewer. Initially, a reader's attention is drawn to your study because of its title and then by its abstract. Your reviewer may be doing similar research or may find your title and general idea intriguing, although he or she may know absolutely nothing about the specific background literature or proposed methodology.

You can make the reader's job easier by writing the proposal for the person who is not terribly well informed about your topic rather than for the most knowledgeable person in your research area. You must lead the reviewer from a general statement of the idea to the relevant issues and literature, to the specific research hypothesis, to the design and procedures, and finally to the proposed analyses and the long-range significance of the data. Good grammar, an interesting style, and neither too much nor too little detail are likely to result in a high level of readability. A readable proposal will interest and attract your audience, whereas a dull or unintelligible proposal might well result in a negative judgment. A member of the National Academy of Science, the chemist Ernest Eliel, one of the most published scientists in America, once said, "It's not so much that I'm a better scientist than the rest, it's just that I'm a better writer." Your grant proposal must be readable if it is to attract and influence its target audience, the panel of reviewers.

Skills in communication, both oral and written, usually are not developed simply within the confines of your scientific training but rather are acquired and refined during the early years of your liberal education—in grade school, high school, college composition classes, or journalism activities. I find it surprising that so many aspiring young psychologists are not informed about, or do not avail themselves of, opportunities to develop general writing skills, both prior to and during graduate training. These skills are essential for winning research grants, which after all must be accurate, informative, and interesting to read to be successful.

Recommended Readings

This chapter has laid out some tips about grant writing. A more complete description of the grant-writing process can be obtained in such recent excellent texts as Ries and Leukefeld's *Applying for Research Funding* (1995) and Locke, Spirduso, and Silverman's *Proposals That Work* (1993). These books elaborate on themes only briefly sketched in this chapter: how to get the process started, what and when to write, checking for infractions, specific contents, and the decision-making process. Many parts of the Ries and Leukefeld (1995) text will prove helpful to you in grant preparation and development.

In the end, the entire process boils down to three simple rules: (a) Form an idea you are proud of, (b) make a concentrated effort to write about your idea and its research implications, and (c) persevere until others see its merits. At that point, you will experience a great intellectual satisfaction: winning your first research grant.

References

American Psychological Association. (1994). *Publication manual of the American Psychological Association.* (4th ed.). Washington, DC: Author.

Locke, L. F., Spirduso, W. W., & Silverman, S. J. (1993). *Proposals that work.* Thousand Oaks, CA: Sage.

Ries, J. B., & Leukefeld, C. G. (1995). *Applying for research funding.* Thousand Oaks, CA: Sage.

Sternberg, R. J. (1992). How to win acceptances by psychology journals: 21 tips for better writing. *American Psychological Society Observer, 5*(5), 12.

Chapter 28

Cross-Cultural
Research Methodology

KWOK LEUNG

FONS VAN DE VIJVER

The world is becoming a truly global village. Globalization of businesses has resulted in workplaces in which people of different nationalities work under the same roof. Migration patterns have rapidly changed the ethnic composition of once relatively homogeneous societies. For instance, Hispanics in the United States are forecast to be the largest minority group in the United States in the near future. Furthermore, challenges such as global warming and arms control require the cooperation of many nations.

The globalization trend has led to a vast increase in intercultural contacts. As a consequence, there is a pressing need to understand similarities and differences across cultures and to distinguish cultural stereotypes from real cross-cultural differences. Psychological research can give us these insights. The goal of this chapter is to provide a comprehensive overview of issues in cross-cultural research methodology.

Characteristics of Cross-Cultural Research

In "true experiments" participants are randomly assigned to different experimental conditions, such as the experimental and control groups (see also Chapter 5 by Wampold, this volume). However, one independent variable in cross-cultural research is culture, and we cannot randomly assign participants to different cultures. We cannot assign, say, a person from Japan an American identity. Culture is an experimental variable that is beyond the control of a researcher, and this inherent reality makes it difficult to evaluate causal relationships in cross-cultural studies. When we discover a difference between two cultural groups, it is difficult to conclude that a *proposed* cause is the *actual* cause of the observed cultural difference. For instance, if we discover that American college students score higher than farmers from Vietnam on reasoning tests, there may be numerous explanations for this difference. The Vietnamese farmers may be less educated than American college students or less familiar with such tests, which causes them to perform poorly. If test familiarity causes the difference, an instrument that uses questions less foreign to Vietnam-

351

ese farmers may result in higher scores for this group. It is a major challenge for cross-cultural researchers to identify the most plausible explanation for cross-cultural differences observed.

Another challenge of cross-cultural research is that the concept of *culture* is global and difficult to define. When we observe that Chinese regard effort as more important for educational achievement than do Americans (Hess, Chang, & McDevitt, 1987), we may be tempted to attribute the difference to culture. But culture includes so many elements that using it as an explanation for observed differences is almost meaningless. The difference may be caused by, among other things, socialization, parental styles, and educational systems. We need to "unpackage" culture into a set of elements and verify which particular element is responsible for the cultural differences observed (Whiting, 1976).

Cross-Cultural Equivalence

Most cross-cultural studies involve at least two cultural groups, but some studies are monocultural and rely on results from previous studies for cross-cultural comparisons. When we try to compare two or more cultures, the comparison may take two forms: *structure oriented* or *level oriented*. Structure-oriented studies examine relationships between variables and attempt to identify similarities and differences in these relationships across cultures. For example, is the structure of values similar across cultures? Level-oriented studies, on the other hand, focus on differences in the magnitude of variables across cultures. For example, do members of Culture A have a higher level of self-esteem than members of Culture B?

In both types of studies, equivalence provides the basis for cross-cultural comparisons, because we cannot compare apples with oranges. Similarity of meaning is called *conceptual* or *structural equivalence*, an essential element in structure-oriented studies. It is possible that a concept has different meanings in different cultures. For instance, the concept of depression may have different meanings in China and in the United States. Chinese tend to describe psychological problems in terms of physical symptoms, a process called *somatization*. Thus, whereas depression is mostly concerned with psychological problems in the United States, the concept of depression among Chinese may include somatic complaints.

There are a number of ways to ascertain conceptual equivalence. We may examine the psychometric properties of the instrument used to measure a concept. Assume that we measure depression in China and the United States with a certain scale: Conceptual equivalence is supported if the scale has similar internal psychometric properties, such as similar levels of internal consistency in the two cultures as measured by Cronbach's alpha or similar factor structures based on factor analysis. Conceptual equivalence is also supported if similar relationships between depression and other variables can be demonstrated in the two cultures. For instance, if depression is correlated with adverse life events in the two cultures, we are more certain that depression has a similar meaning in the two cultures. More generally, conceptual equivalence is supported if our measure of depression shows an expected pattern of correlations with a variety of measures. Various statistical techniques—such as regression analysis, multidimensional scaling, factor analysis, and the analysis of covariance structures (structural equations)—are commonly employed to study conceptual equivalence.

In level-oriented studies, we want to go beyond conceptual equivalence and find out whether cultural groups studied differ in their average scores on a target variable. Unfortunately, even if conceptual equivalence is established, we still cannot be sure that scores derived from an instrument can be directly compared across cultures. When we measure body length in inches in one group and in centimeters in another group, the same concept is measured in the two groups, but the scores cannot be directly compared. In a similar vein, suppose that Japanese and Chinese report a lower level of self-esteem than do Americans, we cannot take this difference as real without further evidence. For instance, response sets may bias the responses of Japanese and Chinese. They may tend to use the middle of a rating scale, or they may report a lower level of self-esteem because of a humility norm, which discourages people from bragging about their abilities.

We need to establish *scalar equivalence* or *full-score comparability* before we can compare scores obtained from different cultures. Examples of variables that show scalar equivalence include weight and height. It is often difficult to establish scalar equivalence for psychological constructs, but we must be aware of this issue in comparing cultural groups. When we claim that one cultural group scores higher than another group on a given variable, we must demonstrate that a reasonably high level of scalar equivalence has been achieved. See the recommended readings in the last section of this chapter for the procedures commonly used for establishing scalar equivalence.

Design of a Cross-Cultural Study

It is often easy to identify significant cultural differences, but difficult to interpret them. Cultural groups differ in many respects, and many of these differences can be advanced as plausible explanations for cultural differences observed. In the design of cross-cultural studies, effort must be made to enhance the interpretability of cultural differences that may be obtained. One solution is to include *covariates,* unintended variables such as educational level, that may produce cultural differences. The inclusion of covariates can help evaluate the proposed explanation for the observed cross-cultural differences and rule out alternative explanations. A good example is Earley's (1989) study on social loafing, which refers to the phenomenon that people work less when they are in a group than when they do the same task individually. Americans were found to show a higher level of social loafing than Chinese subjects. A measure of the individualism-collectivism of subjects was used as a covariate. Individualism refers to a weaker emphasis on one's ingroups, such as one's family, whereas collectivism refers to a stronger emphasis (Hofstede, 1980). After controlling for cross-cultural differences in individualism-collectivism, the cross-cultural differences in social loafing disappeared. The covariance analysis provided strong evidence for individualism-collectivism as the explanation for the observed cross-cultural difference in social loafing.

Leung and Zhang (1996) argue that many studies have been exported from the West to non-Western countries, but some of the issues examined in these studies are of little relevance to the local culture. It is also possible that results obtained in some of these studies are influenced by the cultural background of the researchers. Different results may be obtained if these studies are designed by researchers from different cultural backgrounds. Two approaches can be adopted to avoid the possibility that one single culture will dominate the research questions explored and bias the results obtained. First, in the *decentered approach*, a culturally diverse perspective is taken in the conceptualization and design of a study. For instance, Schwartz (1992) encouraged researchers from different cultures to add culture-specific value items to his pan-cultural set when examining the structure of values.

In the *convergence approach*, the basic idea is to design a study that is as culturally distant as possible from existing studies and see if the results obtained converge with existing results. If convergence is obtained, it is unlikely that the cultural origin of existing studies have biased the results obtained. If different results are obtained, however, the cultural origin of existing studies may have biased the results obtained. A good example to illustrate this approach is provided by Bond and his colleagues, who designed a value survey based entirely on Chinese values and administered it in 22 countries (Chinese Culture Connection, 1987). It was found that three factors overlapped with factors identified by Hofstede (1980), whose results were based on a Western instrument. A new factor was also found, termed Confucian work dynamism, which correlated highly with economic growth of a nation.

Sampling of Cultures

The selection of cultures is often essential in evaluating the cross-cultural hypotheses proposed. *Systematic sampling*, in which cultures are selected in a theory-guided fashion, is a frequently adopted strategy. The classic study by Berry (1966) provides an example of this approach. Two groups were studied—one agricultural and one hunting. It was hypothesized that agricultural societies impose stronger pressure on conformity and hence will lead to field dependence, which refers to the tendency to be more influenced by the background of an object when perceiving this object. Hunting societies encourage their members to be autonomous and hence are conducive to a lower level of field dependence. These two types of societies were selected systematically to evaluate this hypothesis.

In *random sampling*, a large number of cultures are randomly sampled, usually for evaluating the universal structure of a construct or a pan-cultural theory. It is almost impossible to obtain a truly random sample, but the sampling procedure of several large-scale studies may approximate a random sampling procedure. For instance, Schwartz (1992) sampled 20 cultures to evaluate the structure of human values.

Sampling of Participants

To make valid cross-cultural comparisons, the participants from different cultural groups must be similar in their background characteristics. Otherwise, it is difficult to conclude whether the differences observed are due to cultural differences or to sample-specific differences. If we compare illiterate subjects from one culture to highly educated subjects from another culture, the differences observed are likely to be explainable by educational differences rather than differences in other aspects of their cultures. One approach to overcome this problem is to match the samples in terms of demographic characteristics so that sample differences can be ruled out as alternative explanations (see also chapter by McCready, this volume). College students from different cultures are often compared, and it is usually assumed that they have similar demographic characteristics. In a similar vein, Hofstede (1980) reduced the influence of background variables by sampling respondents from 40 countries in a single multinational organization.

It is sometimes impossible to match samples from different cultures because of practical reasons or because there are sharp cross-cultural differences in their demographic profiles. One solution is to measure the relevant demographic variables as covariates. For instance, in a study comparing the delinquent behaviors of adolescents in the United States, Australia, and Hong Kong, it was found that the educational level of the fathers of the Hong Kong subjects was significantly lower than that of the fathers of the American and Australian subjects (Feldman, Rosenthal, Mont-Reynaud, Leung, & Lau, 1991). To overcome this problem, an analysis of covariance was used to compare the three cultural groups, with the father's educational standing equated statistically.

Data Collection

Before we try to gather data from different cultural groups with an instrument, we need to decide whether the instrument is applicable to the cultural groups (see also chapter by Ponterotto, this volume). For instance, some items of the instrument may not make sense in some cultures. When the Minnesota Multiphasic Personality Inventory (MMPI) was applied in China, some items were found to be meaningless in the Chinese context and had to be modified (Cheung, 1989). When too many items are inappropriate, an entirely new instrument may even need to be constructed. Church (1987) argued that Western personality instruments are unable to capture many of the indigenous personality constructs of the Filipino culture. He proposed a number of directions for the construction of a new personality instrument for the Filipino culture.

We may also need to translate an instrument used in a cross-cultural study. The translation-backtranslation method is probably the most widely adopted procedure (Brislin, 1980). An instrument is translated from one language to another and then back-translated to the original language by a different translator. This method is usually adequate; backtranslation can provide researchers who lack proficiency in the target language control of the adequacy of the translation. The method also has a drawback: it may produce a stilted language that reproduces the original language well but is not easily comprehensible. This problem is particularly serious when test items contain idioms that are difficult to translate.

Werner and Campbell (1970) have proposed a *decentering process* in translating instruments—to adjust both the original and the translated versions simultaneously. The aim of decentering is not the mechanical reproduction of the original instrument in a different language but the enhancement of the convergence and readability of the versions in all target languages simultaneously.

When we administer an instrument to participants from different cultures, we need to pay attention to the personal characteristics of the experimenter or interviewer. The presence of an experimenter or interviewer may affect the responses of the participants, particularly when the experimenter and the participants come from different cultural backgrounds. In intelligence testing, the influence of racial differences between the tester and the examinee has been studied systematically. The interaction and communication between the tester and the respondent may also be a source of bias. The experimenter may inadvertently affect the responses of participants by unintended signals or cues, such as appearance and demeanor. Finally, the stimuli and response procedures involved may be a source of bias. For instance, participants who are not familiar with questionnaires may take them as an examination with true and false answers. A study by Deregowski and Serpell (1971) illustrates the importance of stimulus familiarity. Scottish and Zambian children were asked to sort miniature models of animals and motor vehicles in one experimental condition and their photographs in another one. No cultural differences were found when models were sorted, but the Scottish children obtained higher scores than the Zambian children when photos were sorted.

Four Common Types of Cross-Cultural Studies

Four types of cross-cultural studies can be distinguished, depending on whether the orientation is exploratory or hypothesis testing, and on whether or not contextual or cultural factors are considered. The first two types emphasize hypothesis testing. *Generalizability studies* attempt to establish the generalizability of research findings obtained in one, typically Western, group to other Western or non-Western groups. In general, these studies make little or no reference to local cultural elements. For instance, Schwartz (1992) collected data from various countries to evaluate the universality of the structure of human values.

In *theory-driven studies*, cultural factors constitute the core of the theoretical framework. Theory-driven studies test the predictions about a particular relationship between cultural variables and a psychological outcome. This approach involves the sampling of various cultures that differ on some focal dimension and the confirmation of expected cultural differences derived from the theoretical framework. For instance, Leung (1987) predicted that cultural collectivism should be associated with the use of mediation in conflict resolution. Chinese and Americans were sampled to represent two levels of collectivism, and the expected cultural difference in the preference for mediation in conflict resolution was found. The study by Berry (1967) on field dependence described earlier is another example of this approach.

Hypothesis testing is de-emphasized in the following two types of cross-cultural research. In *psychological differences studies*, an instrument is applied in at least two cultures and the focus is on whether there are any differences in averages, standard deviations, reliability coefficients, or other psychometric properties of the instrument across cultural groups. There is often no compelling theory about the nature of the cross-cultural differences to be expected. Contextual factors are typically not included in the design, and post hoc explanations are invoked to interpret the cross-cultural differences observed. For instance, Guida and Ludlow (1989) compared the test anxiety of American and Chilean school children and found that for upper- and middle-class subjects, American subjects reported a lower level of test anxiety than Chilean subjects. As commonly done in this type of research, post hoc explanations were given to explain this finding.

The last type of cross-cultural research, *external validation,* attempts to explore the meaning and causes of cross-cultural differences with the aid of contextual factors. In this type of study, specific *a priori* hypotheses are absent and a large set of contextual variables that may explain an observed cultural difference are included in an exploratory manner. This type of exploration does not target conceptual or scalar equivalence but seeks an empirically derived interpretation of observed cross-cultural differences. For instance, Bond (1991) examined the relationships between the values endorsed by various national groups on a variety of health-related measures and found that values are related to some specific health-related variable.

Conclusion

In cross-cultural research, the interpretation of the meaning of research findings is crucial but evasive, because cross-cultural research is essentially different from true experiments. Typically, many interpretations can be generated to explain a cross-cultural difference. In our opinion, the best approach is to formulate a number of rival hypotheses on an a priori basis and design studies that can rule out alternative explanations. Cross-cultural research may demand a higher level of methodological sophistication than a conventional monocultural study, but in this globalizing world, we cannot afford to be blind to cultural similarities and differences. A carefully planned, competently conducted cross-cultural study is not only rewarding but highly useful for bringing about productive and enjoyable intercultural contact.

Recommended Readings

For a detailed discussion of the various methodological issues encountered in cross-cultural research, consult Brislin, Lonner, and Thorndike (1973). For a detailed discussion of methods and data analysis for cross-cultural research, consult Van de Vijver and Leung (in press). For methodological issues encountered in field research, the book edited by Lonner and Berry (1986) is highly useful.

References

Berry, J. W. (1966). Temne and Eskimo perceptual skills. *International Journal of Psychology, 1,* 207-229.
Bond, M. H. (1991). Chinese values and health: A cross-cultural examination. *Psychology and Health, 5,* 137-152.
Brislin, R. W. (1980). Translation and content analysis of oral and written material. In H. C. Triandis & J. W. Berry (Eds.), *Handbook of cross-cultural psychology* (Vol. 1, pp. 389-444). Boston: Allyn & Bacon.
Brislin, R. W., Lonner, W. J., & Thorndike, R. (1973). *Cross-cultural research methods.* New York: John Wiley.

Cheung, F. M. (1989). A review on the clinical applications of the Chinese MMPI. *Psychological Assessment, 3,* 230-237.

Chinese Culture Connection. (1987). Chinese values and the search for culture-free dimensions of culture. *Journal of Cross-Cultural Psychology, 18,* 143-164.

Church, T. A. (1987). Personality research in a non-Western setting: The Philippines. *Psychological Bulletin, 102,* 272-292.

Deregowski, J. B., & Serpell, R. (1971). Performance on a sorting task: A cross-cultural experiment. *International Journal of Psychology, 6,* 273-281.

Earley, C. (1989). Social loafing and collectivism: A comparison of the United States and the People's Republic of China. *Administrative Science Quarterly, 34,* 565-581.

Feldman, S. S., Rosenthal, D. A., Mont-Reynaud, R., Leung, K., & Lau, S. (1991). Ain't misbehavin': Adolescent values and family environments as correlates of misconduct in Australia, Hong Kong, and the United States. *Journal of Research on Adolescence, 1,* 109-134.

Guida, F. V., & Ludlow, L. H. (1989). A cross-cultural study of test anxiety. *Journal of Cross-Cultural Psychology, 20,* 178-190.

Hess, R. D., Chang, C. M., & McDevitt, T. M. (1987). Cultural variations in family beliefs about children's performance in mathematics: Comparisons among People's Republic of China, Chinese-American, and Caucasian-American families. *Journal of Educational Psychology, 79,* 179-188.

Hofstede, G. (1980). *Culture's consequences: International differences in work-related values.* Beverly Hills, CA: Sage.

Leung, K. (1987). Some determinants of reactions to procedural models for conflict resolution. *Journal of Personality and Social Psychology, 53,* 898-908.

Leung, K., & Zhang, J. X. (1996). Systemic considerations: Factors facilitating and impeding the development of psychology in developing countries. *International Journal of Psychology, 30,* 693-706.

Lonner, W. J., & Berry, J. W. (Eds.). (1986). *Field methods in cross-cultural psychology.* Beverly Hills, CA: Sage.

Schwartz, S. H. (1992). Universals in the content and structure of values: Theoretical advances and empirical tests in 20 countries. In M. Zanna (Ed.), *Advances in experimental social psychology* (Vol. 25, pp. 1-65). Orlando, FL: Academic Press.

Van de Vijver, F. J. R., & Leung, K. (in press). *Methods and data analysis for cross-cultural research.* Beverly Hills, CA: Sage.

Werner, O., & Campbell, D. T. (1970). Translating, working through interpreters, and the problem of decentering. In R. Naroll & R. Cohen (Eds.), *A handbook of cultural anthropology* (pp. 398-419). New York: American Museum of Natural History.

Whiting, B. B. (1976). The problem of the packaged variable. In K. Riegel & J. Meacham (Eds.), *The developing individual in a changing world* (Vol. 1, pp. 303-309). The Hague: Mouton.

Chapter 29

Applying Theories in Research

The Interplay of Theory and Research in Science

CHARLES J. GELSO

Ask your typical undergraduate psychology major (who tends to be a good student) what constitutes psychological science, and the reply will almost always include a bottom-line reference to controlled research. Few if any will mention theory. In fact, I must confess that when I was a graduate student, research and science were pretty much the same thing for me. My only consolation in this wrongmindedness is that I was not alone. Buttressed by the radical behaviorism that was ruling the roost in American psychology in the 1960s, many students and even seasoned scholars equated research and science and, implicitly if not explicitly, viewed theory as unnecessary, even impeding, in our search for laws of behavior.

Even though things are quite different in the 1990s in psychology, there still tends to be a residue of belief that theory is a second-class citizen in the scientific process. By contrast, in this chapter, I shall argue that there is a profound and inevitable connection between theory and research and that science would be impoverished if either were to be relegated to the back seat. Both theory and research are vital and necessary elements of science. Science without controlled, empirical research would consist of only untested ideas and biases, and it would be hard even to think of the result as scientific any more than, for example, witchcraft or astrology are scientific. At the same time, science without theory would consist of an array of disconnected observations (that some might call facts) rather than meaningful understandings of the psychological world.

Not only is the role of theory in psychological science too often minimized, but what actually constitutes theory is often misunderstood. Because of this misunderstanding, in this chapter I first summarize what I believe to be a useful way of thinking about theory: its definition, its elements, and just what constitutes good scientific theory. Then I examine how theory and research are used in science, how each draws on the other, and how they reciprocally relate to each other.

What Is a Scientific Theory?

One of the greatest impediments to appreciating the research-theory link in science is the tendency to misunderstand what constitutes theory itself. Many students equate theory with the grand theoretical systems that have been present in psychology for many years, such as psychoanalysis, behaviorism, and humanism. Also, in practice-oriented fields of psychology, theories are often equated with broad therapy systems such as person-centered therapy, cognitive therapy, and psychoanalytic therapy. As I have elsewhere discussed, these large-scale theories of therapy and the personality theories to which they are wedded are all too often "broad concatenations of (untestable) philosophies of life and humankind, statements of faith, and in some cases loosely stated propositions that were not developed with testability in mind" (Gelso, 1991, p. 212). Such extraordinarily comprehensive theories can probably never be disproved; aspects of them may be disconfirmed, but never the entire theory. Overall, these extremely broad theories are not very scientifically useful. They do not generate research that in turn tests their validity.

More useful are what tend to be labeled *minitheories*. These may be parts of the broader systems, or they may be theoretical statements that are separate from existing systems. An example of a theory embedded in a broader system is Carl Rogers' famous statement of the necessary and sufficient conditions for effective counseling and therapy. After years of research and practice, Rogers made a bold, even audacious, theoretical statement that subsequently proved to have enormous heuristic value. He posited that there were certain client and therapist conditions that were both necessary and sufficient for constructive client change. The three conditions that pertained to therapist attitudes of empathic understanding toward the client, unconditional positive regard for the client, and congruence with the client generated scores of studies over at least three decades. Rogers' theory was embedded in his theory of client-centered therapy, which in turn was embedded within the even broader humanistic approach to conceptualizing human behavior and counseling.

As I have noted, such minitheories need not be embedded in larger systems. They can stand on their own. A theory emerging from my research program on therapist countertransference management is an example of such a minitheory, and I shall discuss this particular theory later in the chapter. Currently in the field of therapy, Bordin's (1979) minitheory of the components and role of the working alliance in therapy has generated a great deal of research, thus displaying the heuristic value that is so central to good scientific theories (see below). It should be noted, however, that even minitheories appearing to stand alone often are connected at a general level to broader theories. Our countertransference management theory and Bordin's theory of the working alliance are, at a very general level, embedded in psychodynamic theory.

So what is a theory? At the most liberal definitional level:

A *theory* may be thought of as a series of two or more constructions (abstractions), which have been hypothesized, assumed, or even factually demonstrated to bear a certain relationship, one with the other. A theoretical proposition, which defines the relationship between constructions (now termed "variables"), becomes a fact when that proposition is no longer contested by those individuals best informed on the nature of the theory, and dedicated to study in the area of knowledge for which the theory has relevance. Theories vary in their levels of abstraction, objectivity-subjectivity, realism-idealism, perspective, and formality-informality. (Rychlak, 1968, p. 42)

In essence, then, a theory is a statement of the suspected relationship between and among variables. From this viewpoint, there is a theory behind virtually all of what we do, all of our research. That is, there is some expectation of how the variables in our research ought to relate to each other. As indicated in the above quote, however, theories vary in their degree of formality/informality. Informal theories are those that are not stated explicitly and do not have as a goal "the formulation of a logically consistent and mutually interdependent body of knowledge" (Rychlak, 1968, p. 35). Our goal as scientists ought to be to make our theories explicit, to put them to the test of empirical research, and thus to stimulate research.

FUNCTIONS AND QUALITIES OF THEORIES

I suggest that for a theory to have much value scientifically, it must go beyond this simple propositional level. A theory ought to tell us *why* the variables or constructs are expected to relate to or influence one another. There must be good reasoning, so to speak, behind the expectation of how variables will be interrelated.

It is also useful to think of any theory as serving certain functions, more or less effectively. Rychlak suggests four such functions: descriptive, delimiting, generative, and integrative. It is worth taking at least a brief look at each of these. Regarding the *descriptive function*, most fundamentally any theory will serve to describe phenomena. The fuller the description of the conditions under which the phenomena are said to occur, the closer we get to what is called *explanation* in science. Good theories explain—the "why" of things, what causes what. Indeed, full description may be seen as tantamount to a causal explanation. Good theories appear to explain effectively. They have a high degree of what may be termed *explanatory power.*

Theories also *delimit.* In effect, they place limits on what is looked at and seen. To limit is to place boundaries, which also means that there are certain things that any theory will not allow us to see. Limits are necessary, however, for they serve as guides to what may be examined. Perhaps most important, theories serve to *generate* further ideas and examination. Highly generative theories are given the venerable label *heuristic*. Such theories stimulate investigation; they stimulate research aimed at testing them. Theories that do not have heuristic value tend to stagnate. They essentially have no scientific value. This point, of course, underscores the integral relationship of theory to empirical research.

Finally, theories have an *integrative function*. By this we mean that the theory seeks to bring together propositions and constructs in a consistent, unified picture. In other words, good theories pull together diverse and at times seemingly disparate, even contradictory, facts into a picture that has coherence and a high degree of *internal consistency.*

One type of integration is particularly worthy of note, both because of its importance and because it is all too often forgotten in the current scene. *Parsimony,* a type of theoretical integration, may be seen as an effort by the theorist to introduce *only* as many constructs and propositions as are necessary to explain the phenomena under consideration. In a recent discussion of the concept of parsimony, I asked a group of counseling psychology graduate students how many had heard of "Ockham's razor." Only one of the eight who were present responded affirmatively. This term, dating back to William of Ockham in the 14th century, implies that the constructs and propositions within a theory that go beyond what is needed to explain the phenomena the theory seeks to explain are "excess baggage." We need to take the razor to them, shaving away the needless excess. Modern-day psychologists would do well to keep Ockham's razor in hand as they construct theories.

THE GOOD SCIENTIFIC THEORY

Within the above discussion of the functions of a scientific theory appear several of what may be seen as the necessary ingredients of a good theory. These are now summarized, and a few additional ingredients are also noted.

As implied, the good scientific theory might be said to be *internally consistent, integrative,* and *parsimonious.* It possesses a high degree of *explanatory power.* Within a domain that is *clearly delimited,* a good theory ought to be *comprehensive.* That is, it should thoroughly specify the important relationships within its domain of inquiry. Furthermore, for a theory to be of optimum value scientifically, it should be stated *explicitly* and *clearly* so that its propositions are high in *testability.* A theory that is testable is capable of disconfirmation. If you cannot disconfirm a theory, its scientific value is severely limited. In fact, each and every empirical study that tests the theory ought to place it in grave danger. In this sense, an endangered theory is a good one! Referring back to a point made earlier, one of the major limitations of the large-scale theories of personality and therapy is that they are not endangered. As Mahrer (1988) noted, this makes theory-testing efforts in relation to such theories next to useless.

Finally, as we have discussed, a bottom line for a good theory is *heuristic value.* The good scientific theory must stimulate inquiry, in the form of both empirical research and further theory. As you can see, when we discuss the parameters of theory and the qualities of "good theory," the inherent importance of research to theory becomes evident. As a way of clarifying the roles of these two elements, theory and research, I shall address the question of where scientific ideas come from. Then I shall examine the "cycle of science"—the synergistic relationship of theory and research. In the final section, I shall discuss and exemplify how theories are used early and late in the life of a research piece—in generating ideas and hypotheses and in seeking to explain and interpret findings.

Throughout much of what follows, as a way of personalizing the discussion, I shall use examples drawn from my own research and theory construction in the area of therapist countertransference. *Countertransference,* as used in this chapter, refers to a counselor or psychotherapist's emotional reaction to a client or patient that is based on the therapist's issues, often tied to earlier, unresolved conflicts—for example, with parents.

The Origin of Ideas

To begin, let us examine where research ideas come from. In the first study of our countertransference research program at the University of Maryland, Ann Peabody, a graduate student at the time, became interested in the connection of counselor empathy to countertransference, defined as emotional withdrawal from the client. We had examined psychoanalytic theories about these two constructs, and on the basis of the theories, along with our own impressions as counselors, we reasoned that the more empathic the therapist, the less likely that he (male counselor) would withdraw from or avoid the material presented by a female client who behaved in an aggressive or seductive manner (which theoretically ought to be threatening to the counselor). We expected that the more empathic counselor would also experience countertransference feelings, but the key difference was that he was expected to be more aware of them and consequently to act them out less with the client. When we used taped actresses playing the role of client, with counselors responding to the "client" at certain stopping points on the tape, our hypotheses were generally confirmed (see Peabody & Gelso, 1982). The main point, however, is that the hypotheses came from theory (as well as clinical experience). Although no theory stated the precise hypotheses of our research, these hypotheses were logically derived from theory. The hypotheses would not have been possible if it were not for theories of empathy and theories of countertransference.

We may also ask where theoretical ideas come from. In more recent work, my collaborators and I reasoned that although all counselors experienced what could be called countertransference feelings, the most important thing in therapy was how effectively counselors were able control or manage those feelings. Countertransference feelings could help therapy if managed effectively or hinder therapy if managed poorly. On the basis of this theory, we constructed a theory of the components of therapists' ability to manage their countertransference reactions to clients effectively (Hayes, Gelso, VanWagoner, & Diemer, 1991; VanWagoner, Gelso, Hayes, & Diemer, 1991). The theory drew substantially from the Peabody and Gelso study as described above, studies that built on that initial one, and other studies that were not connected to this program. It posited that countertransference management ability consisted of five interrelated factors (empirical research informing each factor is cited): counselor self-insight (Peabody & Gelso, 1982; Robbins & Jolkovski, 1987), counselor empathic ability (Peabody & Gelso, 1982), counselor anxiety management (Hayes & Gelso, 1991), counselor self-integration (McClure & Hodge, 1987), and counselor conceptualizing ability (Robbins & Jolkovski, 1987). The five factors were described, as was their role in countertransference management.

When we construct theory, as when we examine where research comes from, we not only rely centrally on research but also make use of our own personal or clinical experiences. This personal part is inevitable and forms a fundamental link in the theory-research-theory-research chain.

The Cycle of Scientific Work

Thus far I have examined how theory generates research and how research generates and refines theory. Further, theory has been defined, and the qualities of a good theory have been discussed. We can now explore what I would suggest is the heart of science: how theory and research *reciprocally relate* to one another. The relationship of theory and research in science is deeply synergistic. The two go hand in hand, working together to create an optimal product—namely, good science. This synergistic relationship was described nicely by Stanley Strong (1991) in his discussion of "the cycle of scientific work" (p. 208). Strong

(1991), like many before him (e.g., Meehl, 1954; Reichenbach, 1938), considered two contexts in which science occurs: the context of discovery and the context of testing. (Others call the latter the *context of justification*.) He suggested that scientific work cycles between these two contexts. Strong's comments are worth noting:

> In the context of discovery, the scientist invents and constructs concepts of the dynamics that underlie and are expressed in observed events. In this task, the scientist draws on all of the ideas, observations, hunches, and creativity he or she can muster. As concepts emerge, the scientist invents ways to tie them to observable events and specifies how symptoms of the dynamics are to be measured. Equipped with a theory, the scientist enters the context of testing. In this context, the scientist generates observations with which to test the assertions of the theory. Observations inevitably reveal inadequacies in constructs and measures. Armed with more observations, ideas, and hunches, the scientist returns to the context of discovery to alter the theory or invent a new one. (p. 208)

One might, of course, add that the cycle is unending, as theories become modified and eventually give way to other theories, which in turn guide research, are tested repeatedly, modified, and so on. (I should note that Strong's observations were directed at science from one particular philosophical position, what he calls the "Galilean mode." This accounts for his emphasis on theorizing about underlying dynamics. Strong's views, however, are applicable to science more generally.)

Some researchers, it should be added, do not appear to believe that an inevitable link and cycle exist between theory and research. For example, in a thoughtful analysis, Mahrer (1988) suggested that hypothesis-testing research (which derives from and tests theory) has not proven to be very fruitful in the area of psychotherapy research. Hypothesis-testing research has been predominant in psychology, according to Mahrer, and has impeded discovery. What is needed is a discovery-oriented approach in which the researcher approaches his or her data free from the biases and constraints caused by hypotheses. Mahrer believes that this will allow fresh understandings to emerge.

The scientist is, of course, free to do research that does not seek to test hypotheses. There is nothing about science that dictates the statement and testing of hypotheses derived from theory. In addition, discovery-oriented approaches may indeed be very fruitful at this point in the history of therapy research. At the same time, I would suggest that the researcher cannot be freed from theory. His or her theories, at times informal rather than formal, about the phenomena being studied will guide the researcher at each and every step in the research process. Discovery-oriented research is probably best at certain points in the scientific process. For example, when theory and hypothesis testing seem to bring us to a dead end and no fresh insights seem forthcoming in an area, discovery-oriented research may be just what is needed. Yet even in this situation, as the findings from discovery-oriented research accrue, they will inevitably be used to create and refine theories about the phenomena under investigation, and these theories will then serve to generate subsequent hypotheses to be tested. In this way, discovery-oriented research may be seen as part of the context of discovery: It discovers relationships that help form theory, which then becomes examined within the context of testing or justification.

Further Comments on Applying Theories in Research

In this chapter, I have focused mostly on the interplay of theory and research in science. Given scientific psychology's historical tendency to neglect the role of theory in science, I would like to make a few additional comments on how theory is applied in research.

Generally speaking, theories are used at each and every step in the research process. They come into play most centrally, however, at three points: (a) idea generation, (b) hypothesis generation, and (c) interpretation of results. The initial steps in an empirical study involve the first two, generating the idea to be studied and forming hypotheses, or at least research questions. An example of idea and hypothesis generation may be seen in two of the recent studies in our countertransference research program (Gelso, Fassinger, Gomez, & Latts, 1995; Hayes & Gelso, 1993). In these experiments, we examined the impact of the sexual orientation of filmed client-actors and actresses on countertransference reactions of therapists in training. On the basis of theory suggesting that people, including counselors, tend to react more negatively to gay and lesbian individuals than heterosexuals (which, in turn, may be seen as based on the broader theory that people react more negatively to those who are different from themselves), we hypothesized that there would be greater countertransference reactions at behavioral, affective, and cognitive levels to gays (Hayes & Gelso, 1993) and lesbians (Gelso et al., 1995) than to heterosexual clients. Theory also suggested the hypothesis that a theoretical construct called *homophobia*, defined as prejudicial attitudes and negative stereotypes toward gays and lesbians, would mediate counselors' countertransference reactions to gay and lesbian client-actors and actresses in the two studies. When counselors responded to the filmed clients at certain stopping points on the films, the results indicated no difference in counselor-trainees' countertransference reactions to filmed gay and lesbian clients than to heterosexual clients, but we did find a significant relationship between counselor homophobia and the behavioral indication of countertransference (i.e., avoidance of the client's feelings involving relationships and sexual problems). The higher the measured homophobia, the greater the counselor avoidance in both studies.

In the Gelso et al. (1995) study, we also hypothesized that female counselor-trainees would exhibit greater countertransference than male counselor-trainees in response to a filmed lesbian client-actress, whereas we did not hypothesize a difference between female and male counselors toward the heterosexual client-actress. (Male client-actors were not used in this study, but if they had been, we would have expected male counselors to have greater countertransference than female counselors to gay male client-actors.) This hypothesis was based on the theory that people will respond more negatively to homosexuality when it involves members of their own sex than when it involves members of the opposite sex, partly because same-sexed interactions are more likely stir up subconscious fears in counselors of same-sexed attractions. Our hypothesis was supported for the cognitive measure of countertransference: errors in recall of the number of sexual words used by the client actress. Female counselors made more recall errors than males with the lesbian client-actress, whereas males and females did not differ in response to the heterosexual client.

You can see that, as is most often the case in psychological research, some of our hypotheses were supported and others were not. The "failed" hypotheses required that we revise our minitheory of the relationship between client sexual orientation, counselor gender, counselor homophobia, and counselor countertransference. The revised theory will then stimulate hypotheses for our subsequent studies.

At this point, it might be useful to clarify how the terms *theory* and *theoretical proposition* may be distinguished from the term *hypothesis.* Although there are no absolute distinctions (in fact, in the earlier quote, Rychlak, 1968, appeared to use the terms synonymously), generally theories contain theoretical propositions, and hypotheses are derived from these propositions. Hypotheses tend to be more specific than the propositions, and, as can be seen in the above examples drawn from countertransference research, are the statements that are directly tested in empirical research.

As indicated at the beginning of this section, theory also comes into play most centrally when the experimenter seeks to interpret or explain his or her findings. Findings consistent with hypotheses that were in turn derived from a given theory are, of course, explained by that theory. When unexpected findings occur, however, the researcher tends to search for an existing theory to make sense out of them or can create a theory of his or her own to explain the results. This new theory may be embedded in a larger theoretical system. An example of creating a theory to explain unexpected findings occurred with two countertransference studies (Latts & Gelso, 1995; Robbins & Jolkovski, 1987). In both these studies, a classic criss-cross interaction was found between therapist-trainees' (a) awareness of countertransference feelings and (b) use of a counseling theory in their work in affecting a measure of countertransference behavior with filmed client-actresses and actors. Both teams of researchers found that countertransference behavior (avoidance of and withdrawal from the client's material) was least when therapists were high on awareness of countertransference feelings and high in the use of a theory in their counseling. This finding was expected and made theoretical sense to the researchers. If the therapist is sharply aware of his or her feelings and has a theoretical context into which those feelings may be placed, the therapist is less likely to act out countertransference behaviors with the client.

The surprising finding was that high use of theory combined with low awareness of countertransference feelings resulted in the greatest amount of countertransference behavior. In reflecting on these findings, the researchers theorized that when counselors are unaware of countertransference feelings, their use of counseling theory may serve a defensive function. They may intellectualize about the client and the relationship, but there is a lack of emotional understanding. The use of a counseling theory in the absence of emotional self-understanding is ineffective in deterring counselors from enacting countertransference behavior with clients. Although the researchers created this theory, you can see where it is, in turn, based on a broader theory—namely, psychodynamic theory.

As I have suggested earlier in this chapter, we should not forget the role of personal or clinical experience in guiding the theoretician and researcher. Our experiences in the world, and with clients if we are in practice fields (and/or, as clients ourselves, if we are theorizing about and studying therapeutic interventions), guide us in a profound way in our selection of theories to generate hypotheses and explain findings. Although these experiences must be guided by reason and managed (not unlike countertransference management!) if they are to most effectively lead us, they are an inevitable part of the process.

Summary

In this chapter, I claimed that there is an inevitable, profound, and synergistic link between theory and research in psychological science. The definition and elements of theory, as well as the characteristics of "good theory," were noted. The cycle of science was discussed to exemplify how theory and research interrelate. Finally, the use of theory in early and later stages of the research process was examined, and my research on therapist countertransference was used to exemplify the uses of theory.

Recommended Readings

If the student is interested in reading further examples of the theory-research cycle, three references might be most helpful. Strong (1991, pp. 208-209) presents a vivid personal example of his use of theory in research, demonstrating how his research findings required him to modify and at times even scrap his theories. Rotter (1990) clearly displays how a theoretical construct, in this case internal versus external locus of control, is most scientifically useful when embedded in a broader theoretical construct and programmatically studied. Finally, McClelland (1993) gives a fascinating summary of the interaction of research and theory in examining the construct of need for achievement and adding to that a second construct, need for power, in an attempt to explain certain behavior patterns.

References

Bordin, E. S. (1979). The generalizability of the psychoanalytic concept of the working alliance. *Psychotherapy: Theory, Research, and Practice, 16,* 252-260.

Gelso, C. J. (1991). Galileo, Aristotle, and science in counseling psychology: To theorize or not to theorize. *Journal of Counseling Psychology, 38,* 211-213.

Gelso, C. J., Fassinger, R. E., Gomez, M. J., & Latts, M. G. (1995). Countertransference reactions to lesbian clients: The role of homophobia, counselor gender, and countertransference management. *Journal of Counseling Psychology, 42,* 356-364.

Hayes, J. A., & Gelso, C. J. (1991). Effects of therapist-trainees' anxiety and empathy on countertransference behavior. *Journal of Clinical Psychology, 47,* 284-290.

Hayes, J. A., & Gelso, C. J. (1993). Male counselors' discomfort with gay and HIV-infected clients. *Journal of Counseling Psychology, 40,* 86-93.

Hayes, J. A., Gelso, C. J., VanWagoner, S., & Diemer, R. (1991). Managing countertransference: What the experts think. *Psychological Reports, 69,* 139-148.

Latts, M. G., & Gelso, C. J. (1995). Countertransference behavior and management with survivors of sexual assault. *Psychotherapy, 32,* 405-415.

Mahrer, A. R. (1988). Discovery-oriented psychotherapy research: Rationale, aims, and methods. *American Psychologist, 43,* 694-703.

McClelland, D. C. (1993). Motives and health. In G. G. Brannigan & M. R. Merrens (Eds.), *The undaunted psychologist* (pp. 129-141). New York: McGraw-Hill.

McClure, B. A., & Hodge, R. W. (1987). Measuring countertransference and attitude in therapeutic relationships. *Psychotherapy, 24,* 325-335.

Meehl, P. E. (1954). *Clinical versus statistical prediction.* Minneapolis: University of Minnesota Press.

Peabody, S. A., & Gelso, C. J. (1982). Countertransference and empathy: The complex relationship between two divergent concepts in counseling. *Journal of Counseling Psychology, 29,* 240-245.

Reichenbach, H. (1938). *Experience and prediction.* Chicago: University of Chicago Press.

Robbins, S. B., & Jolkovski, M. P. (1987). Managing countertransference: An interactional model using awareness of feeling and theoretical framework. *Journal of Counseling Psychology, 34,* 276-282.

Rotter, J. B. (1990). Internal versus external control of reinforcement: A case history of a variable. *American Psychologist, 45,* 489-493.

Rychlak, J. F. (1968). *A philosophy of science for personality theory.* Boston: Houghton Mifflin.

Strong, S. R. (1991). Theory-driven science and naive empiricism in counseling psychology. *Journal of Counseling Psychology, 38,* 204-210.

VanWagoner, S., Gelso, C. J., Hayes, J. A., & Diemer, R. (1991). Countertransference and the reputedly excellent therapist. *Psychotherapy, 28,* 411-421.

Index

About the Editors

Frederick T. L. Leong is an Associate Professor of Psychology at The Ohio State University. He obtained his Ph.D. from the University of Maryland in 1988 with a double specialty in counseling and industrial/organizational psychology. He has authored or coauthored over 50 articles in various counseling and psychology journals and 14 book chapters. He was the coeditor (with Uma Sekaran) of *Womanpower: Managing in Times of Demographic Turbulence* (1992, Sage) and (with James Whitfield) of the American Psychological Association (APA) bibliography entitled *Asians in the United States: Abstracts of the Psychological and Behavioral Literature, 1967-1991* (1992). His most recent book is the edited volume *Career Development and Vocational Behavior of Racial and Ethnic Minorities* (1995). He is a Fellow of the APA (Divisions 17 and 45). His major research interests are in vocational psychology (career development of ethnic minorities), cross-cultural psychology (particularly culture and mental health and cross-cultural psychotherapy), and organizational behavior.

James T. Austin is an Assistant Professor of Psychology at The Ohio State University, specializing in industrial/organizational psychology. He received his Ph.D. in 1987 from Virginia Polytechnic Institute and State University. His research on goal setting, criterion measurement, and structural equation modeling has appeared in industrial/organizational psychology and quantitative journals.

About the Contributors

Robert M. Arkin is Professor of Psychology (Social) and Undergraduate Dean for the Arts and Sciences at The Ohio State University. He just completed a term as associate editor for the *Personality Processes and Individual Differences* section of the *Journal of Personality and Social Psychology* and has served as associate editor for another major publication outlet for personality and social psychology, the *Personality and Social Psychology Bulletin*. He conducts research on the self, the role of the self in social interaction contexts, and individual differences in self- and other-perception processes in social interaction. In particular, he is interested in the topics of self-presentation, social identity, and competence appraisals (self and other).

Pam M. Baxter is Adjunct Lecturer in Information Science and Policy Studies at State University of New York at Albany and affiliated with Mann Library at Cornell University. Formerly, she was the head of the Psychological Sciences Library and Professor of Library Science at Purdue University.

Nancy E. Betz is Professor of Psychology at The Ohio State University. She received the Ph.D. in psychology from the University of Minnesota in 1976. Since joining the faculty at Ohio State in 1976, she has focused her research and writing on the career development of women, applications of self-efficacy theory to career development, the underrepresentation of women and minorities in the sciences and engineering, and psychological assessment. She served as editor of the *Journal of Vocational Behavior* from 1984 to 1990 and has also served on the editorial boards of the *Journal of Counseling Psychology, Journal of Vocational Behavior, Journal of Career Assessment,* and *Psychology of Women Quarterly*. She is a Fellow of the American Psychological Association and American Psychological Society and a recipient of the John Holland Award for Research Integrating Career and Personality Psychology.

John G. Borkowski, Andrew J. McKenna Family Professor of Psychology, has been at the University of Notre Dame for 28 years. He received his Ph.D. at the University of Iowa in 1965 and taught for 2 years at Oberlin College. His research interests include metacognitive development, educational interventions for at-risk children, and social-cognitive development in children of adolescent mothers. His research has been supported by the National Institutes of Health, the Public Health Service, and the Office of Education.

Elke Brenstein received her Ph.D. degree in applied experimental psychology from Southern Illinois University at Carbondale. Her area of specialization is individual differences in learning, cognition, and personality. As the coauthor of the Inventory of Learning Process—Revised (with R. R. Schmeck), she has done extensive research on individual differences in learning styles and strategies of college students. She has also examined the practical implications of differences in the way people perceive and use information in other areas such as career choice, organizational development, family dynamics, and interpersonal communication. She has published several articles on these topics in academic journals and has given a number of workshops to help people understand and value interpersonal diversity.

Robert F. Calderón is a graduate student in industrial/organizational psychology at The Ohio State University. He received his B.A. from Northwestern University. He is currently involved in research on goal-setting processes and quantitative techniques.

Peter Y. Chen obtained his Ph.D. degree in industrial/organizational psychology, with a psychometrics minor, from the University of South Florida in 1991. He is an Assistant Professor of Psychology at Ohio University. His research interests include job stress, work violence, training, and measurement. His works have been published in the *Journal of Applied Psychology, Journal of Occupational and Organizational Psychology, Journal of Organizational Behavior, Journal of Management,* and various books.

Harris Cooper received his Ph.D. in social psychology from the University of Connecticut in 1975. He spent a year as a Postdoctoral Fellow at Harvard University and a year teaching at Colgate University. Since 1977, he has taught at the University of Missouri, where he is currently the Frederick A. Middlebush Professor of Psychology and a Research Associate at the Center for Research in Social Behavior. His research interests follow two paths: research synthesis and the application of social psychology to educational policy issues.

David N. Dickter is a graduate student in industrial/organizational psychology at The Ohio State University. He received his B.A. from the University of Pennsylvania and is currently involved in research on individual differences in time urgency.

David L. DiLalla is Associate Professor of Psychology at Southern Illinois University. He earned his doctorate at the University of Virginia and completed a postdoctoral fellowship at the University of Colorado. His research interests include personality and psychopathology, as well as behavioral genetics.

Stephen J. Dollinger is Professor of Psychology and Director of Clinical Training at Southern Illinois University. He earned his doctorate at the University of Missouri—Columbia, and his research interests include various topics in personality and clinical child psychology.

Nancy Dorr is currently a graduate student in social psychology at the University of Missouri-Columbia. She is interested in research on intergroup relations.

Charles B. Fields is Professor and Chair of the Department of Criminal Justice at California State University at San Bernardino. He has a B.A. and M.A. in political science from Appalachian State University and received his Ph.D. in criminal justice from Sam Houston University in 1984. His most recent articles/reviews have appeared in the *Journal of Criminal Justice, Criminal Justice Policy Review, Quarterly Journal of Ideology,* and *Journal of Criminal Law and Criminology,* among others. He was formerly President of the Southern Criminal Justice Association and is Region Two Trustee on the Executive Board of the Academy of Criminal Justice Sciences.

Heather C. Finley is a fourth-year counseling psychology doctoral student at The Ohio State University. Throughout her graduate education, she has worked part time as an individual therapist, emergency services counselor, career counselor, and assistant residence hall director. She is currently working on a qualitative dissertation exploring the identity development of women with multiple minority status.

Charles J. Gelso received his Ph.D. in counseling psychology from The Ohio State University in 1970. He is a Professor of Psychology and Co-Director of Training, Counseling Psychology Doctoral Program, University of Maryland. His research and professional interests revolve around the client-therapist relationship in psychotherapy and what he terms the "research training environment" in graduate education.

Leslie A. Gill completed her doctoral studies in the Psychology Department at Southern Illinois University in Carbondale. She worked as a Research Assistant in Dr. Dennis Molfese's Developmental Neuropsychology Laboratory in the same department.

Robert D. Goddard III is Associate Professor of Management at Appalachian State University and founder and President of Organizational Development Associates (ODA), a firm providing a variety of management consulting and training services. ODA specializes in employee opinion survey design and administration as a basis of improving the quality of work life for organizations. He is a past editor of the Southeast Decision Sciences Institute (SE DSI) *Proceedings* and has been Vice President—Membership, and Vice President—Student Liaison for SE DSI. He has served two terms as Vice President for Educator Programs for Pi Sigma Epsilon (the national professional fraternity for marketing, sales management, and selling) and has also served as its National Secretary for two terms. He currently serves on the board of directors of Epsilon Chi Omicron, the international business honor society, and is a member of the editorial board of the *Journal of Global Business*.

Pamela S. Highlen received her Ph.D. in counseling psychology from Michigan State University. She is currently Associate Professor of Psychology at The Ohio State University. Her theoretical and research interests include transpersonal and multicultural psychology. Recent work includes development of the Self Identity Inventory (SII) based on the Optimal Theory Applied to Identity Development (OTAID) model, the application of transpersonal psychology to vocational assessment with racial/ethnic minorities, and a chapter on multicultural counseling and therapy and organizational development. She maintains a part-time private practice.

Theresa Kenny earned her B.A. from the University of Colorado at Denver in 1988, with an English major, psychology minor, and honors in humanities certificate. She then earned her M.S. in library and information science from the University of Illinois at Urbana-Champaign in 1989 and spent several years working in various units of the University of Illinois Library—Reference, Interlibrary Lending, Circulation—and as Extramural (Extension) Librarian. Since August of 1993, she has been Assistant Education and Psychology Librarian in Morris Library, Southern Illinois University at Carbondale.

Kwok Leung, Ph.D., teaches at the Department of Psychology at the Chinese University of Hong Kong. His research interests include cross-cultural psychology, justice, and conflict resolution. He is an associate editor of the *Journal of Cross-Cultural Psychology*. He recently co-authored, with Dr. van de Vijver, a chapter in the *Handbook of Cross-Cultural Psychology* and a book on research methodology.

Paul E. Levy received his Ph.D. in industrial/organizational psychology from Virginia Tech in 1989. He is currently an Associate Professor of Industrial and Organizational Psychology and Chair of the I/O program at the University of Akron. His research interests include performance appraisal, feedback processes, motivation, and job-related attitudes. His research in these areas has appeared in journals such as *Personnel Psychology, Journal of Personality and Social Psychology, Organizational Behavior and Human Decision Processes*, and *Applied Psychology: An International Review*.

Michelle Marks is a Ph.D. candidate in industrial/organizational psychology at George Mason University. She received her M.A. degree in 1993 from George Mason University with a specialization in industrial/organizational psychology. She has published articles on creativity and problem solving and on sexual harassment. Her research is in the areas of leadership and problem solving, leader and shared mental models, and team performance. She is currently working on a dissertation in the area of team adaptation in novel and stressful situations.

Tina B. Martin is a doctoral student in the Psychology Department at Southern Illinois University in Carbondale. She works as a Research Assistant in Dr. Dennis Molfese's Developmental Neuropsychology Laboratory in the same department.

William C. McCready is Director of the Public Opinion Laboratory and Associate Professor of Sociology at Northern Illinois University. Previously he was a Senior Research Associate at the Center for Urban Research and Policy Studies at the University of Chicago; Director of the Center for the Study of American Pluralism, National Opinion Research Center, University of Chicago; and member of the faculty of the School of Social Service Administration at the University of Chicago. He obtained his M.A. from the University of Chicago (1966) and his Ph.D. in sociology from the University of Illinois (1972). His research concentrations include survey design and analysis, sociology of the family, alcohol studies, religion and ethnic groups, urban sociology, and policy design and analysis. He has taught at Loyola University of Chicago, the University of Chicago, and Northern Illinois University. He has consulted with California State University at San Marcos on the establishment of their Social and Behavioral Research Center, is a member of the Survey Advisory Committee for the Metropolitan Chicago Information Center, and is a former member of the National Academy of Science's Committee for a National Urban Policy. He is on the Research Advisory Committee of the Chicago Urban League and has conducted survey design workshops for the American Medical Association as well as many universities. He recently directed a national survey for the Smithsonian Institution and has conducted more than 50 "customer satisfaction" studies for businesses, including McDonald's Corporation. He has directed over $5 million in research and is the author or coauthor of several books, book chapters, articles, and papers, including *Young Catholics in the United States* (1981, with Fee, Greeley, and Sullivan), *Ethnic Drinking Subcultures* (1983, with Greeley and Theisen), *Hispanics in the United States* (1985, with Cafferty), and a chapter in *Hispanics and the Nonprofit Sector* (O'Neill and Gallegos, 1991). He is also the former editor of the journal *Ethnicity*.

Naomi M. Meara, Professor of Psychology at the University of Notre Dame, received a doctorate in counseling psychology from The Ohio State University. With Lyle D. Schmidt and others, she has written in ethics and related areas on such topics as the ethics of researching the counseling process, ethics and psychoanalytic counseling, principle and virtue ethics, and self-regarding virtues. She coauthored *Psychoanalytic Counseling* with Michael J. Patton.

Dennis L. Molfese received his Ph.D. in 1972 from The Pennsylvania State University in experimental psychology, with a specialization in developmental psycholinguistics and neuropsychology. He is currently Professor of Psychology, Physiology, and Behavioral and Social Sciences and serves as Chair of the Department of Behavioral and Social Sciences in the School of Medicine at Southern Illinois University at Carbondale. In addition to teaching courses in child psychology, neuropsychology, and brain and language, he conducts and publishes research concerned with the relationship between brain function and language and cognition across the life span. He is editor-in-chief of the journal *Developmen-*

tal Neuropsychology and has edited several books on brain lateralization and the neuropsychology of individual differences.

Kristen L. Murray completed her doctoral studies in the Psychology Department at Southern Illinois University in Carbondale. She worked as a Research Assistant in Dr. Dennis Molfese's Developmental Neuropsychology Laboratory in the same department.

Donna K. Nagata is Associate Professor of Clinical Psychology at the University of Michigan, Ann Arbor. She received her doctorate from the University of Illinois, Urbana-Champaign. Her major research interests focus on the intergenerational impact of the Japanese American internment, Asian American mental health, and family interaction. Among her most recent publications are the book *Legacy of Injustice: Exploring the Cross-Generational Impact of the Japanese American Internment*, a chapter entitled "Coping With Internment: A Nisei Woman's Perspective," and an article "Assessing Asian American Acculturation and Ethnic Identity: The Need for a Multidimensional Framework."

Kathryn C. Oleson is Assistant Professor of Psychology at Reed College. She received her Ph.D. in social psychology from Princeton University in 1993 and was a National Institute of Mental Health Postdoctoral Fellow at The Ohio State University from 1993 to 1995. Her research focuses primarily on interpersonal perception. In particular, she is interested in competence appraisals (self and others), self-presentation, self-concept change, social identity, self-stereotyping, and stereotype change.

Samuel H. Osipow is Professor of Psychology at The Ohio State University. He has served as the editor of the *Journal of Vocational Behavior* and the *Journal of Counseling Psychology* and is currently serving as the editor of *Applied and Preventive Psychology*. He is also the author of *Theories of Career Development* and has coedited seven books. He is a Past-President of the Division of Counseling Psychology of the American Psychological Association, Past-Chair of the Department of Psychology of The Ohio State University, and Past-Chair of the Board of Directors of the Council for the Register of Health Providers in Psychology.

Cindy J. Peters completed her doctoral studies in the Psychology Department at Southern Illinois University in Carbondale. She worked as a Research Assistant in Dr. Dennis Molfese's Developmental Neuropsychology Laboratory in the same department.

Christopher Peterson is Professor of Psychology at the University of Michigan, associated with the Clinical Psychology and Personality programs. He received his Ph.D. in social and personality psychology from the University of Colorado and subsequently respecialized in clinical psychology and experimental psychopathology at the University of Pennsylvania. He is interested in the cognitive determinants of depression and physical illness and is the author of more than 100 articles, chapters, and books, including *Cognitive Structure* (with W. A. Scott and D. W. Osgood); *Health and Optimism* (with L. M. Bossio); *Learned Helplessness* (with S. F. Maier and M. E. P. Seligman); *Introduction to Psychology; Personality,* and *The Psychology of Abnormality*. He has served as consulting editor for *Journal of Abnormal*

Psychology, Journal of Personality and Social Psychology, and *Psychological Bulletin* and is currently a member of the American Psychological Association Media Referral Service.

Rhonda Pfaltzgraff is a doctoral student in industrial/organizational psychology at The Ohio State University. She graduated from Bethel College, North Newton, Kansas, in 1993 with bachelor's degrees in psychology and business administration. Her primary interests are organizational commitment and cross-cultural issues in organizations.

Joseph G. Ponterotto is Professor of Counseling Psychology in the Division of Psychological and Educational Services at Fordham University, Lincoln Center, New York. His primary research interests are in the area of multicultural counseling. His recent coauthored and coedited books include the *Handbook of Racial/Ethnic Minority Counseling Research; Affirmative Action on Campus; Preventing Prejudice: A Guide for Counselors and Educators;* and the *Handbook of Multicultural Counseling.*

Jeffrey G. Reed currently works for Xerox Corporation in the Document Production Systems Division as a Process and Planning manager whose responsibilities include development of plans and management of work processes for new products. Past positions have included work as a program manager, software design manager, user interface software developer, management trainer, assistant professor of industrial/organizational psychology, educational researcher, and college reference librarian. He is licensed as a psychologist in New York State and holds a Ph.D. (Kansas State) and M.S. (Towson State) in psychology, an M.L.S. (Maryland) in library and information science, a B.A. (Muskingum) in political science, and certificates in business (New York University) and program evaluation (Massachusetts).

Mary Roznowski is Associate Professor in the industrial/organizational psychology program at The Ohio State University. She received her Ph.D. from the University of Illinois in 1986 and has published her research in various industrial/organizational psychology journals, including the *Journal of Applied Psychology,* the *Journal of Vocational Behavior,* and *Organizational Behavior and Human Decision-Making Processes.* Her primary research interests are in individual differences and job attitudes.

Lyle D. Schmidt, a 1959 Ph.D. from Missouri, has taught an ethics seminar to graduate students in clinical, counseling, and school psychology at The Ohio State University for 25 years. He chaired the university's Behavioral and Social Sciences Human Subjects Review Committee from 1980 to 1983 and was a member of the Policy and Coordinating Committee for Human Subjects Review from 1980 to 1987. He served on the Ethics Committee of the Central Ohio Psychological Association from 1981 to 1983 (Chair in 1982), was Chair of the American Psychological Association Committee on Accreditation in 1989, and served two terms on the Council of Representatives.

Panagiotis A. Simos completed his doctoral studies in the Psychology Department at Southern Illinois University in Carbondale. He worked as a Research Assistant in Dr. Dennis Molfese's Developmental Neuropsychology Laboratory in the same department.

Lisa A. Steelman has completed her M.A. in industrial/organizational psychology and is pursuing her Ph.D. in the same field at the University of Akron. Her research interests include performance appraisal, feedback seeking, and motivation.

Margaret S. Stockdale received her Ph.D. from Kansas State University in industrial/organizational psychology in 1990. She is currently Assistant Professor of Psychology at Southern Illinois University at Carbondale. In addition to teaching courses in industrial/organizational psychology, organizational behavior, and applied research consulting, she conducts and publishes research on issues affecting women in the workplace. She is coeditor of *Independent Consulting for Evaluators* and the *Journal of Vocational Behavior's* special issue on sexual harassment. She is editor of the book, *Women and Work: Vol. 5. Sexual Harassment* and coauthor of *Women and Men in Organizations: Sex and Gender Issues at Work*, forthcoming.

Arlene A. Tan, M.A., is currently pursuing a doctoral degree in life span development within the experimental psychology program at Southern Illinois University, Carbondale. She assists Dr. Dennis Molfese in his electrophysiological research investigating neurolinguistic and developmental issues.

Steven J. Trierweiler is Associate Professor in the Department of Psychology and Associate Research Scientist in the Program for Research on Black Americans at the Institute for Social Research at the University of Michigan, Ann Arbor. He received his Ph.D. in clinical psychology at the University of Illinois at Urbana-Champaign. His research focuses on clinical judgment and decision making in psychodiagnostic interviewing in cross-racial/ethnic contexts, interpersonal event memory narratives, and interaction in couples and families. He has a long-standing interest in quantitative and qualitative research methods and in the development of scientific thinking in applied contexts. Recent publications include a chapter and article on research training for professional psychologists and an article dealing with the investigation of interpersonal memory narratives in psychotherapy.

Fons van de Vijver, Ph.D., teaches in the Department of Psychology at Tilburg University. His main area of research is cross-cultural studies of cognition. Recently, he co-authored, with Dr. Kwok Leung, a chapter in the *Handbook of Cross-Cultural Psychology* and a book on research methodology. He is an associate editor of the *Journal of Cross-Cultural Psychology.*

Alan Vaux, Ph.D., is Professor of Psychology at Southern Illinois University. He holds Ph.D. degrees in psychology from Trinity College (Dublin, Ireland) and in social ecology from the University of California at Irvine. He is a Fellow of the American Psychological Association and the American Psychological Society, an associate editor of the *Journal of Social and Personal Relationships,* and a member of the editorial board of the *American Journal of Community Psychology.* He is author of *Social Support: Theory, Research and Intervention,* coeditor of *Independent Consulting in Evaluation,* and author or coauthor of over 50 articles/chapters and 60 conference papers. He has served as Director of Applied Research Consultants, a graduate-student-staffed applied research consulting firm, and has supervised over

40 master's and doctoral research projects. His research interests include social support, community psychology, and applied methodology.

Peter Villanova completed his doctoral work in industrial/organizational psychology at Virginia Tech in 1987. His research interests include employee work attitudes, personnel selection, and performance appraisal. He has published his work in the *Journal of Applied Psychology, Academy of Management Journal, Personnel Psychology, Human Resource Management Review, Journal of Business and Psychology, Journal of Psychology, Journal of Abnormal Psychology, Educational and Psychological Measurement, Sex Roles,* and *Applied Psychology: An International Review.* He has served as a consultant to public and private organizations in the areas of employee satisfaction, turnover, selection, and performance appraisal.

Bruce E. Wampold received his Ph.D. degree in counseling psychology at the University of California, Santa Barbara, in 1981. Currently he is Professor and Chair of the Department of Counseling Psychology at the University of Wisconsin—Madison. He is a Fellow of the American Psychological Association and is a licensed psychologist in Wisconsin. He is the associate editor of the *Journal of Counseling Psychology* and past associate editor of *Behavioral Assessment.*

Robert Alan Yaffee currently holds two appointments. He is a Statistical Consultant at the Statistics and Social Science Group of the Academic Computing Facility, Courant Institute of Mathematical Science, New York University and also a Research Scientist at the Division of Geriatric Psychiatry of the State University of New York Health Science Center at Brooklyn. After earning his Ph.D. in political science at the New School for Social Research, he taught advanced statistics and empirical research in the Hunter College Department of Sociology Masters of Social Research Program (1988–1989), served as a statistician in the Memorial Sloan Kettering Cancer Center Department of Social Work Research (1988–1989) and a statistical consultant to the Maryland Task Force on Gambling Addiction, 1989–1990. From 1988 to 1989, he was an Associate Research Scientist in the Division of Sociomedical Sciences in the Columbia University School of Public Health, after which he became Director of Research at the Compulsive Gambling Center, Inc. in Baltimore, Maryland (1991–1994). He has lectured on, among other things, statistical packages, categorical data analysis, logit and logistic regression, structural equation systems, survival analysis, time series analysis, and forecasting. He has written on psychological problems of pathological gamblers and their spouses, gambling addiction severity, coaddiction among compulsive gamblers, economic and social costs of pathological gambling, and logistic regression analysis. His current research interests include statistical forecasting and immigration research.

Stephen J. Zaccaro is Associate Professor of Psychology and the Associate Director in the Center for Behavioral and Cognitive Studies at George Mason University. He was previously on the faculty at Virginia Polytechnic Institute and State University. From 1981 to 1982, he was an Assistant Professor at the College of the Holy Cross. He received his Ph.D. in 1981 and his M.A. in 1980 from the University of Connecticut, with a specialization in social psychology. He has published articles on group processes, organizational behavior and human decision processes, leadership, and work attitudes in such journals as *Journal of Organizational Behavior, Journal of Military Psychology, Group and Organizational Studies, Social Psychology Quarterly,* and *Personality and Social Psychology Bulletin.* He has also edited (with Anne Riley) a book entitled *Occupational Stress and Organizational Effectiveness* and has contributed chapters on work stress and work group processes. He was coeditor (with Edwin Fleischman and Michael Mumford) of three special issues of *Leadership Quarterly* on individual differences and leadership. He is currently a member of the American Psychological Association, the Society for Industrial/Organizational Psychology, and the American Psychological Society. He has directed projects in the areas of team performance and shared mental models, leadership training, cognitive and metacognitive leadership capacities, and executive leadership.

Barbara H. Zaitzow is Assistant Professor in the Department of Political Science and Criminal Justice at Appalachian State University. She has a B.A. in sociology from San Diego State University and an M.S. and a Ph.D. in sociology from Virginia Polytechnic Institute and State University. Currently, she is assisting local and state officials seeking the increased use of intermediate sanctions as an alternative to imprisonment. A member of several national and regional sociological and criminal justice organizations, her primary research areas of interest include female criminality, corrections, and alternatives to incarceration.